HORIZONS IN COMPUTER SCIENCE RESEARCH

VOLUME 4

HORIZONS IN COMPUTER SCIENCE

Additional books in this series can be found on Nova's website
under the Series tab.

Additional E-books in this series can be found on Nova's website
under the E-books tab.

HORIZONS IN COMPUTER SCIENCE RESEARCH

VOLUME 4

THOMAS S. CLARY
EDITOR

Nova Science Publishers, Inc.
New York

Library of Congress Cataloging-in-Publication Data

ISBN 978-1-61324-262-9
ISSN: 2159-2012

Published by Nova Science Publishers, Inc. † New York

CONTENTS

PREFACE

This book presents original results on the leading edge of computer science research. Each article has been carefully selected in an attempt to present substantial research results across a broad spectrum. Topics discussed in this compilation include multi-path routing protocols for ad hoc networks; development of software to characterize particulate matter in air pollution; web-based software infrastructure for service-oriented science; clinical applications of wearable monitoring systems; distributed computing; encryption software and computer science firewalls.

Chapter 1 - This chapter starts with an introduction to Artificial Intelligence (AI) including some historical background of the technology. Artificial Intelligence may be defined as a collection of several analytic tools that collectively attempt to imitate life (1). In the last twenty years Artificial Intelligence has matured to a sct of analytic tools that facilitate solving problems which were previously difficult or impossible to solve. The trend now is the integration of these tools, as well as with conventional technologies such as statistical analysis, to build sophisticated systems capable of solving challenging problems. Artificial Intelligence is used in areas such as medical diagnosis, credit card fraud detection, bank loan approval, smart household appliances, subway systems, automatic transmissions, financial portfolio management, robot navigation systems, and many more. In the oil and gas industry these tools have been used to solve problems related to pressure transient analysis, well log interpretation, reservoir characterization, and candidate well selection for stimulation, among others. Artificial neural networks, evolutionary programming and fuzzy logic are among the paradigms that are classified as Artificial Intelligence. These technologies exhibit an ability to learn and deal with new situations by possessing one or more attributes of "reason", such as generalization, discovery, association and abstraction (2). This chapter is organized in four sections. First three sections are focused on the definition of some of the AI tools which are most commonly practiced and show some of their applications in the upstream oil and gas industry. In the first section artificial neural networks, are introduced as information processing systems that have certain performance characteristics in common with biological neural networks. This section will conclude with detail presentation of an application of neural networks in the upstream oil and gas industry. Second section is intended to provide an overview of evolutionary computing, its potential combination with neural networks to produce powerful intelligent applications, and its applications in the oil and gas industry. The most successful intelligent applications incorporate several artificial intelligence tools in a hybrid manner. These tools complement each other and amplify each other's effectiveness.

An overview of evolutionary computation and its background is presented, followed by a more detailed look at genetic algorithms as the primary evolutionary computing. The article will continue and conclude by exploring the application of a hybrid neural network/genetic algorithm system to a petroleum engineering related problem. Fuzzy logic is the focus of the third section. An overview of the subject is provided followed by its potential application in petroleum engineering related problems. In this section, application of fuzzy logic for re-stimulation candidate selection in a tight gas formation in the Rocky Mountains will be reviewed. This particular application was chosen because it uses fuzzy logic in a hybrid manner integrated with neural networks and genetic algorithms. In the fourth and final section, some other applications of these tools in reservoir characterization, production modeling and performance prediction are presented.

Chapter 2 - Within an ad hoc wireless network, multi-path routing can result in reduced end-to-end delay, increased path reliability, an increase in aggregate bandwidth, load-balancing to equalize energy consumption, and congestion avoidance, as well as acting as a security mechanism. This Chapter reviews multi-path routing in ad hoc networks. The operation of selected single-path ad hoc routing is described, as well-known protocols such as AODV and DSR are the starting points for their multi-path enhancements. An analysis of the operation of existing multi-path protocols is included. The Chapter contains a study of the design principles behind multi-path routing. As an application case study, multi-description coding of video streaming over multi-paths is illustrated for a vehicular ad hoc network.

Chapter 3 - This chapter presents the Scanning Electron Microscope (SEM) integrated with image processing technique as a tool for physical characterization of particulate matter. The characterization process involves steps of image reading, preprocessing, segmentation, feature extraction, and representation. In these steps, selection of optimal image segmentation algorithm is the key for analyzing the captured images of fine particulate matter. A review of popular image analyzing software available for analyzing SEM images is presented. A new software employing Image processing and Support Vector Machines (SVM) for particle characterization is presented. SVM use gray level histograms as an image feature to select the best segmentation algorithm for the particle images.

Chapter 4 - The paper presents a Web-based software infrastructure for service-oriented scientific environments. The concept of Service-Oriented Science introduced by Ian Foster in 2005 refers to scientific research enabled by distributed networks of interoperating services. The service-oriented architecture opens up new opportunities for science by enabling wide-scale sharing, publication and reuse of scientific applications, as well as automation of scientific tasks and composition of applications into new services. The authors argue that existing service-oriented grid middleware, though providing a mature software infrastructure for federation of computing resources, is too complex and don't provide adequate tools for building service-oriented scientific environments. Therefore the authors propose a novel software infrastructure aimed on radical simplification of service development, deployment and use. In contrast to grid middleware based on Web Services specifications the proposed infrastructure embraces a more lightweight approach by using the REST architectural style, Web technologies and Web 2.0 application models. According to the proposed approach each service represents a RESTful web service with a unified API enabling service introspection, request submission and retrieval of request results. The RESTful API supports asynchronous request processing and passing large data files as links. The core component of proposed software infrastructure is a service container which implements the RESTful API and provides a hosting environment for services. The service container simplifies service development and deployment by providing ready-to-use adaptors for command-line, Java and grid applications. The service composition is a crucial aspect of service-oriented systems enabling various application scenarios. Therefore we implemented a workflow management system with a Web-based graphical user interface. The user interface is inspired by Yahoo! Pipes and provides easy-to-use tools for building workflows by connecting services with each other. The created workflow can be published as a new service thus contributing back to the environment.

Chapter 5 - The future of healthcare is based on new devices for a more accurate and personalized diagnosis and treatment anywhere. Shorter hospital stays and distribute assistance (Home Care) already represents the trend in the development and management of national healthcare services. The consolidation of such a scenario andits diffusion can be achieved only through the specific development of new technologies oriented to support distributed monitoring of patients for disease prevention, follow-up and rehabilitation. Such technologies can be integrated with the different mobile communication networks that permeated our society. In a monitoring network context, creating nodes with wearable monitoring systems and sensors probably represent a key winning factor in order to provide easy-to-use, affordable and personalized solutions. This chapter shows representative case studies to demonstrate the key role of the wearable technologies in the provision of different health processes and services. We will show the experiences in pre-term newborn monitoring, the quantitative approach to support diagnosis in a rare but severe neurological pathology (Tourette Syndrome) and in a Parkinson's Disease, and the multi-factorial analysis to optimize assistive technology.

Chapter 6 - The paper presents a hierarchical software infrastructure for solving large scale optimization problems on the Grid. The proposed toolset support exact and heuristic search strategies and runs on distributed systems consisting of different nodes ranging from PCs to large publicly available supercomputers. It efficiently copes with difficulties arising in such systems: the software diversity, unreliability of nodes and different ways of job submission. The distinctive feature of our approach is the use of different communication packages on different levels: on the top level we use ICE middleware coupled with TCP/IP sockets and within a single computing element either MPI or POSIX Threads libraries are used. Such approach imposes minimal requirements on the computing element software and efficiently utilizes the communication facilities of each node by using native communication mechanism. Developed infrastructure has been applied to molecular conformation problem that plays an important role in computational chemistry. New results were obtained demonstrating that general purposed optimization algorithm can efficiently cope with hard optimization problems providing the sufficient computational resources are employed.

Chapter 7 - Configuration platforms based on function blocks and links such as Function Block Diagram (FBD) are used widely in designing and implementing distributed intelligent control network (DICN). Traditionally, FBD and Ladder Diagram (LD) are two completely different programming languages with different data models and compilation algorithms to generate different data and instructions for field intelligent nodes. Essential difference exists between implementation methods of control strategies with the two programming languages for data exchange within and between different nodes, which make it difficult for unification of programming languages in configuration platform, hybrid programming and improvement of control systems' openness and compliancy. Besides, products and systems developed based on WorldFIP technology are all above control level. No fully distributed intelligent control system based on field intelligent nodes is implemented. In the first part of this chapter, a kind of generalized FBD model for distributed intelligent control network is described. Scheme for implementing such model in field intelligent node is presented in detail. Transformation models for language elements in LD are presented based on the described model. The model is flexible and widely applicable. Application of the proposed model in design and development of configuration platform software for distributed intelligent system show the effectiveness of the model. In the second part of this chapter, a practical and general-purposed FBA model is presented. Data storage segmentation model for field intelligent nodes are expounded in detail. Concept of user layer in WorldFIP communication model is described and data model for user layer is defined. The schedule algorithms for the proposed FBA model are presented in detail. Guided by the FBA model, design and implementation of distributed intelligent system based on Function Block and FBA is achieved.

Chapter 8 - The Italian Nosocomial Infections Surveillance in Intensive Care Units (ICUs) (SPIN-UTI) project of the Italian Study Group of Hospital Hygiene (GISIO – SItI), was implemented to ensure standardisation of definitions, data collection and reporting procedures coherently with the HELICS-ICU benchmark. Before starting surveillance, participant ICUs were gathered in order to involve the key stakeholders in the project through participated planning. Four electronic data forms for web-based data collection, were designed. The six-months patient-based prospective survey was performed from November 2006 to May 2007. The SPIN-UTI network included 49 ICUs, 3,053 patients with length of stay longer than two days and 35,498 patient-days. Furthermore, since validity is one of the most critical factors concerning surveillance of nosocomial infections (NIs). A validation study was performed after the end of the surveillance survey. For each selected ICU, all medical records including all clinical and laboratory data were retrospective reviewed by the trained physicians of the validation team and a positive predictive value, a negative predictive value, sensitivity and specificity were computed. The results of this study are useful to identify methodological problems within the surveillance program and they have been used to plan and perform training for surveillance personnel and to design and implement the second edition of the SPIN-UTI project. The SPIN-UTI project showed that introduction of ongoing surveillance does seem to be possible in many Italian hospitals. The study provided the opportunity to participate in the HELICS project using benchmark data for comparison and for better understanding of factors that impact on associated risks.

Chapter 9 - Wearable Biomedical Systems (WBS) integrate a complexity of components and technologies which are all crucial even though, sometimes, extremely simple: sensors, actuators, materials, data communication, power control units, user interfaces, new algorithms for signal processing, mechanical components, washability, characteristics and stability of the sensors and their placement on the body. Moreover those factors could change according to the activities or actions monitored and anthropometric characteristics of subjects. It's worth noting that is a very high number of features but each essential for the proper functioning of the entire system (without discussing the ethical and legal aspects of measuring and process sensitive personal data). From here we can identify many strategic areas for the development of WBS. In order to correctly address the research, especially the industrial one and its potential exploitation, it is fundamental a rigorous analysis of the state of the art both scientific and especially about the Intellectual Property Rights (IPR) and related issues. In this context, in recent years the result of innovations supported by the international research has primarily focused on IPR issues about textile sensors and electronic systems. This chapter offers an overview of this knowledge.

Chapter 10 - The present article examines the infrastructure of the Lithuanian Internet network and the possibilities to develop an Internet monitoring system, which would provide the environment for the regulatory authorities to monitor the state of the network and disruptions of communication. Assessment of Lithuanian Internet network infrastructure identified that are significantly important for the functioning of the entire country Internet network. It is proposed to perform monitoring of the network at the critical nodes level, which would help to collect data on the node status and errors, communication interruptions or register specific packet flows, generated by cyber attacks.

Chapter 11 - Encryption is a necessary mechanism for secure data storage and transmission. Chaos-based encryption is an important encryption mechanism that is used for audio, image, video, electroencephalograms (EEG), and electrocardiographs (ECG) multimedia signals. Chaos sequences are popular because they increase unpredictability more than other types of random sequences. The authors have developed a two-dimensional (2D) chaos-based encryption scheme that can be applied to signals with transmission bit errors in clinical electroencephalography (ECG) and mobile telemedicine. The authors used a 2D chaotic scrambler and a 2D permutation scheme to achieve ECG visual encryption. The visual encryption mechanism was realized by first scrambling the input ECG signal values, then multiplying a chaotic 2D address scanning order encryption to randomize reference values. Simulation results show that when the correct deciphering parameters are entered, ECG signal with a transmission bit error rate of 10^{-7} are completely recovered; furthermore, the percent root-mean-square difference values for clinical ECG signals is 0.2496%. However, when there is an input parameter error, for example, an initial point error of 0.00000001%, these clinical ECG signals become unrecoverable. The proposed chaos-based 2D encryption is well suited for applications to clinical ECG signals.

Chapter 12 - Packet classification has become one of the most important application techniques in network security since the last decade. The technique involves a traffic descriptor or user-defined criteria to categorize packets to a specific forwarding class which will be accessible for future security handling.

In this chapter, the authors present two new schemes, Hierarchical Cross-Producting and Controlled Cross-producting, to achieve fast packet classification. The first scheme simplifies the classification procedure and decreases the distinct combinations of fields by hierarchically decomposing the multi-dimensional space based on the concept of telescopic search. Analogous to the use of telescopes with different powers, which is defined as the degree to which a telescope multiplies the apparent diameter of an object in optical terms, a multiple-step process is used to search for targets. In this scheme, the multi-dimensional space is endowed with a hierarchical property which self-divides into several smaller subspaces, whereas the procedure of packet classification is translated into recursive searching for matching subspaces. The required storage of our scheme could be significantly reduced since the distinct field specifications of subspaces are manageable. Next, the authors combine the technique of cross-producting with linear search to make packet classification both fast and scalable. The new algorithm, Controlled Cross-producting, could improve the scalability of cross-producting significantly with respect to storage, while maintaining the search latency. In addition, we introduce several refinements and procedures for incremental update. The performance of both algorithms is evaluated based on both real and synthetic filter databases. The experimental results demonstrate the effectiveness and scalability of both schemes.

Chapter 13 - The notion of distributed model-based diagnosis (DMBD) of a class of discreteevent systems, namely active systems, is introduced with the support of six requirements. First, the active system properties relevant to DMBD are established. Second, a variety of observers are allowed, each observer watching the system under a different view. Third, uncertain observations are considered. Fourth, the diagnostic process is expected to be performed in a distributed, virtually parallel, way. Fifth, the diagnostic process is required to be supported by some computational optimization criteria. Finally, candidate diagnoses are supposed to be given incrementally, at different run-time points. Emphasis is put on the last two requirements. In particular, an algebra is introduced and equivalence rules for algebraic expressions are defined to substantiate the optimization of the diagnostic process. Then, a method for producing an increasingly refined complete set of candidate diagnoses is envisaged.

Chapter 14 - In this chapter, the authors present techniques to defeat Denial of Service (DoS) and Distributed Denial of Service (DDoS) attacks. In the first part, the authors describe client puzzle techniques that are based on the idea of computationally exhausting a malicious user when he attempts to launch an attack. In the second part the authors are introducing some basic principles of game theory and we discuss how game theoretical frameworks can protect computer networks. Finally, we show techniques that combine client puzzles with game theory in order to provide DoS and DDoS resilience.

Chapter 15 - Signcryption is a cryptographic primitive that fulfills both the functions of digital signature and public key encryption simultaneously, at a cost significantly lower than that required by the traditional signature-then-encryption approach. In this chapter, the authors present a new identity-based signcryption scheme that is fully secure without random oracles. The authors prove its semantic security under the decisional bilinear Diffie-Hellman assumption and its unforgeability under the computational Diffie-Hellman assumption in the standard model. Our construction is based on Paterson and Schuldt's recently proposed identity-based signature scheme.

Chapter 16 - In the last decade, chaos has emerged as a new promising candidate for cryptography because many chaos fundamental characteristics such as a broadband spectrum, ergodicity, and high sensitivity to initial conditions are directly connected with two basic properties of good ciphers: confusion and diffusion. In this chapter we recount some of the saga undergone by this field; the authors review the main achievements in the field of chaotic cryptography, starting with the definition of chaotic systems and their properties and the difficulties it has to outwit. According to their intrinsic dynamics, chaotic cryptosystems are classified depending on whether the system is discrete or continuous. Due to their simplicity and rapidity the discrete chaotic systems based on iterative maps have received a lot of attention. In spite of the significant achievements accomplished in this field, there are still many problems, basically speed, that restrict the application of existing encoding/decoding algorithms to real systems. The major advantages and drawbacks of the most popular chaotic map ciphers in terms of security and computational cost are analyzed. The most significant cryptanalytic techniques are considered and applied for testing the security of some chaotic algorithms. Finally, future trends in the development of this topic are discussed.

In: Horizons in Computer Science Research, Volume 4   ISBN: 978-1-61324-262-9
Editor: Thomas S. Clary   © 2011 Nova Science Publishers, Inc.

Chapter 1

APPLICATION OF ARTIFICIAL INTELLIGENCE IN THE UPSTREAM OIL AND GAS INDUSTRY

Shahab D. Mohaghegh[1,2] and Yasaman Khazaeni[2]
[1]Intelligent Solutions, Inc.
[2]West Virginia University,
Morgantown, West Virginia, US

ABSTRACT

This chapter starts with an introduction to Artificial Intelligence (AI) including some historical background of the technology. Artificial Intelligence may be defined as a collection of several analytic tools that collectively attempt to imitate life (1). In the last twenty years Artificial Intelligence has matured to a set of analytic tools that facilitate solving problems which were previously difficult or impossible to solve. The trend now is the integration of these tools, as well as with conventional technologies such as statistical analysis, to build sophisticated systems capable of solving challenging problems.

Artificial Intelligence is used in areas such as medical diagnosis, credit card fraud detection, bank loan approval, smart household appliances, subway systems, automatic transmissions, financial portfolio management, robot navigation systems, and many more. In the oil and gas industry these tools have been used to solve problems related to pressure transient analysis, well log interpretation, reservoir characterization, and candidate well selection for stimulation, among others.

Artificial neural networks, evolutionary programming and fuzzy logic are among the paradigms that are classified as Artificial Intelligence. These technologies exhibit an ability to learn and deal with new situations by possessing one or more attributes of "reason", such as generalization, discovery, association and abstraction (2).

This chapter is organized in four sections. First three sections are focused on the definition of some of the AI tools which are most commonly practiced and show some of their applications in the upstream oil and gas industry. In the first section artificial neural networks, are introduced as information processing systems that have certain performance characteristics in common with biological neural networks. This section will conclude with detail presentation of an application of neural networks in the upstream oil and gas industry.

Second section is intended to provide an overview of evolutionary computing, its potential combination with neural networks to produce powerful intelligent applications, and its applications in the oil and gas industry. The most successful intelligent applications incorporate several artificial intelligence tools in a hybrid manner. These tools complement each other and amplify each other's effectiveness. An overview of evolutionary computation and its background is presented, followed by a more detailed look at genetic algorithms as the primary evolutionary computing. The article will continue and conclude by exploring the application of a hybrid neural network/genetic algorithm system to a petroleum engineering related problem.

Fuzzy logic is the focus of the third section. An overview of the subject is provided followed by its potential application in petroleum engineering related problems. In this section, application of fuzzy logic for re-stimulation candidate selection in a tight gas formation in the Rocky Mountains will be reviewed. This particular application was chosen because it uses fuzzy logic in a hybrid manner integrated with neural networks and genetic algorithms.

In the fourth and final section, some other applications of these tools in reservoir characterization, production modeling and performance prediction are presented.

1. Neural Networks and Their Background

In this section some historical background of the technology will be mentioned followed by definitions of artificial intelligence and artificial neural networks. After the definitions, more general information on the nature and mechanism of the artificial neural network and its relevance to biological neural networks will be offered.

1.1. A Short History of Neural Networks

Neural network research can be traced back to a paper by McCulloch and Pitts(3) in 1943. In 1957 Frank Rosenblatt invented the Perceptron(4). Rosenblatt proved that given linearly separable classes, a perceptron would, in a finite number of training trials, develop a weight vector that will separate the classes (a pattern classification task). He also showed that his proof holds independent of the starting value of the weights. Around the same time Widrow and Hoff (5) developed a similar network called Adeline. Minskey and Papert (6) in a book called "Perceptrons" pointed out that the theorem obviously applies to those problems that the structure is capable of computing. They showed that elementary calculation such as simple "exclusive or" (XOR) problems cannot be solved by single layer perceptrons.

Rosenblatt(4) had also studied structures with more layers and believed that they could overcome the limitations of simple perceptrons. However, there was no learning algorithm known which could determine the weights necessary to implement a given calculation. Minskey and Papert doubted that one could be found and recommended that other approaches to artificial intelligence should be pursued. Following this discussion, most of the computer science community left the neural network paradigm for twenty years (7). In early 1980s Hopfield was able to revive the neural network research. Hopfield's efforts coincided with development of new learning algorithms such as backpropagation. The growth of neural network research and applications has been phenomenal since this revival.

1.2. Structure of a Neural Network

An artificial neural network is an information processing system that has certain performance characteristics in common with biological neural networks. Therefore it is appropriate to describe briefly a biological neural network before offering a detail definition of artificial neural networks. All living organisms are made up of cells. The basic building blocks of the nervous system are nerve cells, called neurons. Figure 1 shows a schematic diagram of two bipolar neurons.

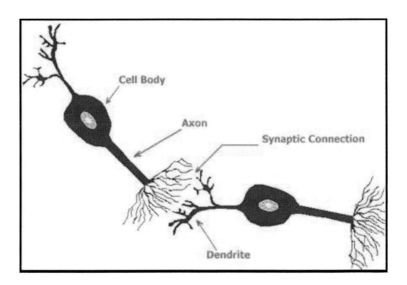

Figure 1. Schematic diagram of two bipolar neurons.

A typical neuron contains a cell body where the nucleus is located, dendrites and an axon. Information in the form of a train of electro-chemical pulses (signals) enters the cell body from the dendrites. Based on the nature of this input the neuron will activate in an excitatory or inhibitory fashion and provides an output that will travel through the axon and connects to other neurons where it becomes the input to the receiving neuron. The point between two neurons in a neural pathway, where the termination of the axon of one neuron comes into close proximity with the cell body or dendrites of another, is called a *synapse*. The signals traveling from the first neuron initiate a train of electro-chemical pulse (signals) in the second neuron.

It is estimated that the human brain contains on the order of 10 to 500 billion neurons (8). These neurons are divided into modules and each module contains about 500 neural networks(9). Each network may contain about 100,000 neurons in which each neuron is connected to hundreds to thousands of other neurons. This architecture is the main driving force behind the complex behavior that comes so natural to us. Simple tasks such as catching a ball, drinking a glass of water or walking in a crowded market require so many complex and coordinated calculations that sophisticated computers are unable to undertake the task, and yet is done routinely by humans without a moment of thought. This becomes even more interesting when one realizes that neurons in the human brain have cycle time of about 10 to 100 milliseconds while the cycle time of a typical desktop computer chip is measured in nanoseconds. The human brain, although million times slower than common desktop PCs, can perform many tasks orders of magnitude faster than computers because of it massively parallel architecture.

Artificial neural networks are a rough approximation and simplified simulation of the process explained above. An artificial neural network can be defined as an information processing system that has certain performance characteristics similar to biological neural networks. They have been developed as generalization of mathematical models of human cognition or neural biology, based on the assumptions that:

- Information processing occurs in many simple elements that are called neurons (processing elements).
- Signals are passed between neurons over connection links.
- Each connection link has an associated weight, which, in a typical neural network, multiplies the signal being transmitted.
- Each neuron applies an activation function (usually non-linear) to its net input to determine its output signal (10).

Figure 2 is a schematic diagram of a typical neuron (processing element) in an artificial neural network. Output from other neurons is multiplied by the weight of the connection and enters the neuron as input. Therefore an artificial neuron has many inputs and only one output. The inputs are summed and subsequently applied to the activation function and the result is the output of the neuron.

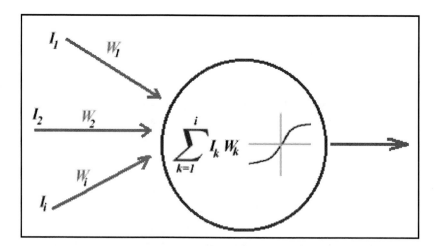

Figure 2. Schematic diagram of an artificial neuron or a processing element.

1.3. Mechanics of Neural Networks Operation

An artificial neural network is a collection of neurons that are arranged in specific formations. Neurons are grouped into layers. In a multi-layer network there are usually an input layer, one or more hidden layers and an output layer. The number of neurons in the input layer corresponds to the number of parameters that are being presented to the network as input. The same is true for the output layer. It should be noted that neural network analysis is not limited to a single output and that neural nets can be trained to build neuro-models with multiple outputs. The neurons in the hidden layer or layers are mainly responsible for feature extraction. They provide increased dimensionality and accommodate tasks such as classification and pattern recognition. Figure 3 is a schematic diagram of a fully connected three layered neural network.

There are many kinds of neural networks. Neural network scientists and practitioners have provided different classifications for neural networks. One of the most popular classifications is based on the training methods. Neural nets can be divided into two major categories based on the training methods, namely supervised and unsupervised neural networks. Unsupervised neural networks, also known as self-organizing maps, are mainly clustering and classification algorithms. They have been used in oil and gas industry to interpret well logs and to identify lithology. They are called unsupervised simply because no feedback is provided to the network. The network is asked to classify the input vectors into groups and clusters. This requires a certain degree of redundancy in the input data and hence the notion that redundancy is knowledge(11).

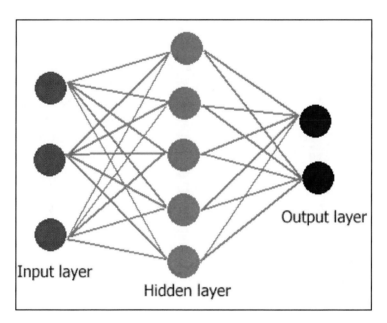

Figure 3. Schematic diagram of a three-layer neuron network.

Most of the neural network applications in the oil and gas industry are based on supervised training algorithms. During a supervised training process both input and output are presented to the network to permit learning on a feedback basis. A specific architecture, topology and training algorithm is selected and the network is trained until it converges. During the training process neural network tries to converge to an internal representation of the system behavior. Although by definition neural nets are model-free function approximators, some people choose to call the trained network a neuro-model.

The connections correspond roughly to the axons and synapses in a biological system, and they provide a signal transmission pathway between the nodes. Several layers can be interconnected. The layer that receives the inputs is called the input layer. It typically performs no function other than the buffering of the input signal. The network outputs are generated from the output layer. Any other layers are called hidden layers because they are internal to the network and have no direct contact with the external environment. Sometimes they are likened to a "black box" within the network system. However, just because they are not immediately visible does not mean that one cannot examine the function of those layers. There may be zero to several hidden layers. In a fully connected network every output from one layer is passed along to every node in the next layer.

In a typical neural data processing procedure, the database is divided into three separate portions called training, calibration and verification sets. The training set is used to develop the desired network. In this process (depending on the paradigm that is being used), the desired output in the training set is used to help the network adjust the weights between its neurons or processing elements. During the training process the question arises as when to stop the training. How many times should the network go through the data in the training set in order to learn the system behavior? When should the training stop? These are legitimate questions, since a network can be over trained. In the neural network related literature over-training is also referred to as memorization. Once the network memorizes a data set, it would be incapable of generalization. It will fit the training data set quite accurately, but suffers in generalization. Performance of an over-trained neural network is similar to a complex non-linear regression analysis.

Over-training does not apply to some neural network paradigms simply because they are not trained using an iterative process. Memorization and over-training is applicable to those networks that are historically among the most popular ones for engineering problem solving. These include back-propagation networks that use an iterative process during the training.

In order to avoid over training or memorization, it is a common practice to stop the training process every so often and apply the network to the calibration data set. Since the output of the calibration data set is not presented to the network, one can evaluate network's generalization capabilities by how well it predicts the calibration set's output. Once the training process is completed successfully, the network is applied to the verification data set.

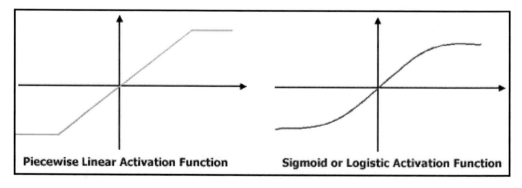

Figure 4. Commonly used activation functions in artificial neurons.

During the training process each artificial neuron (processing element) handles several basic functions. First, it evaluates input signals and determines the strength of each one. Second, it calculates a total for the combined input signals and compares that total to some threshold level. Finally, it determines what the output should be. The transformation of the input to output - within a neuron - takes place using an activation function. Figure 4 shows two of the commonly used activation (transfer) functions.

All the inputs come into a processing element simultaneously. In response, neuron either "fires" or "doesn't fire"; depending on some threshold level. The neuron will be allowed a single output signal, just as in a biological neuron - many inputs, one output. In addition, just as things other than inputs affect real neurons, some networks provide a mechanism for other influences. Sometimes this extra input is called a bias term, or a forcing term. It could also be a forgetting term, when a system needs to unlearn something (12).

Initially each input is assigned a random relative weight (in some advanced applications – based on the experience of the practitioner- the relative weight assigned initially may not be random). During the training process the weight of the inputs is adjusted. The weight of the input represents the strength of its connection to the neuron in the next layer. The weight of the connection will affect the impact and the influence of that input. This is similar to the varying synaptic strengths of biological neurons. Some inputs are more important than others in the way they combine to produce an impulse. Weights are adaptive coefficients within the network that determine the intensity of the input signal. The initial weight for a processing element could be modified in response to various inputs and according to the network's own rules for modification.

Mathematically, we could look at the inputs and the weights on the inputs as vectors, such as $I_1, I_2 \ldots I_n$ for inputs and $W_1, W_2 \ldots W_n$ for weights. The total input signal is the dot, or inner, product of the two vectors. Geometrically, the inner product of two vectors can be considered a measure of their similarity. The inner product is at its maximum if the vectors point in the same direction. If the vectors point in opposite directions (180 degrees), their inner product is at its minimum. Signals coming into a neuron can be positive (excitatory) or negative (inhibitory). A positive input promotes the firing of the processing element, whereas a negative input tends to keep the processing element from firing. During the training process some local memory can be attached to the processing element to store the results (weights) of previous computations. Training is accomplished by modification of the weights on a continuous basis until convergence is reached. The ability to change the weights allows the network to modify its behavior in response to its inputs, or to learn. For example, suppose a network identifies a production well as "an injection well." On successive iterations (training), connection weights that respond correctly to a production well are strengthened and those that respond to others, such as an injection well, is weakened until they fall below the threshold level and the correct recognition of the well is achieved.

In the back propagation algorithm (one of the most commonly used supervised training algorithms) the network output is compared with the desired output - which is part of the training data set, and the difference (error) is propagated backward through the network. During this back propagation of error the weights of the connections between neurons are adjusted. This process is continued in an iterative manner. The network converges when its output is within acceptable proximity of the desired output.

2. EVOLUTIONARY COMPUTING

Evolutionary computing, like other virtual intelligence tools, has its roots in nature. It is an attempt to mimic the evolutionary process using computer algorithms and instructions. However, why would we want to mimic the evolution process? The answer will become obvious once we realize what type of problems the evolution process solves and whether we would like to solve similar problems. Evolution is an optimization process (13). One of the major principles of evolution is heredity. Each generation inherits the evolutionary characteristics of the previous generation and passes those same characteristics to the next generation. These characteristics include those of progress, growth and development. This passing of the characteristics from generation to generation is facilitated through genes.

Since the mid 1960s, a set of new analytical tools for intelligent optimization have surfaced that are inspired by the Darwinian evolution theory. The term "evolutionary computing" has been used as an umbrella for many of these tools. Evolutionary computing comprises of evolutionary programming, genetic algorithms, evolution strategies, and evolution programs, among others. For many people, these tools (and names) look similar and their names are associated with the same meaning. However, these names carry quite distinct meanings to the scientists deeply involved in this area of research. Evolutionary programming, introduced by John Koza (14), is mainly concerned with solving complex problems by evolving sophisticated computer programs from simple, task-specific computer programs. Genetic algorithms are the subject of this article and will be discussed in detail in the next section. In evolution strategies (15), the components of a trial solution are viewed as behavioral traits of an individual, not as genes along a chromosome, as implemented in genetic algorithms. Evolution programs (16) combine genetic algorithms with specific data structures to achieve its goals.

2.1. Genetic Algorithms

Darwin's theory of survival of the fittest (presented in his 1859 paper titled *On the Origin of Species by Means of Natural Selection*), coupled with the selectionism of Weismann and the genetics of Mendel, have formed the universally accepted set of arguments known as the evolution theory (15).

In nature, the evolutionary process occurs when the following four conditions are satisfied (14):

- An entity has the ability to reproduce.
- There is a population of such self-reproducing entities.
- There is some variety among the self-reproducing entities.
- This variety is associated with some difference in ability to survive in the environment.

In nature, organisms evolve as they adapt to dynamic environments. The "fitness" of an organism is defined by the degree of its adaptation to its environment. The organism's fitness determines how long it will live and how much of a chance it has to pass on its genes to the next generation. In biological evolution, only the winners survive to continue the evolutionary process. It is assumed that if the organism lives by adapting to its environment, it must be doing something right. The characteristics of the organisms are coded in their genes, and they pass their genes to their offspring through the process of heredity. The fitter an individual, the higher is its chance to survive and hence reproduce.

Intelligence and evolution are intimately connected. Intelligence has been defined as the capability of a system to adapt its behavior to meet goals in a range of environments (15). By imitating the evolution process using computer instructions and algorithms, researchers try to mimic the intelligence associated with the problem solving capabilities of the evolution process. As in real life, this type of continuous adaptation creates very robust organisms. The whole process continues through many "generations", with the best genes being handed down to future generations. The result is typically a very good solution to the problem. In computer simulation of the evolution process, genetic operators achieve the passing on of the genes from generation to generation. These operators (crossover, inversion, and mutation) are the primary tools for spawning a new generation of individuals from the fit individuals of the current population. By continually cycling these operators, we have a surprisingly powerful search engine. This inherently preserves the critical balance needed with an intelligent search: the balance between exploitation (taking advantage of information already obtained) and exploration (searching new areas). Although simplistic from a biologist's viewpoint, these algorithms are sufficiently complex to provide robust and powerful search mechanisms.

2.2. Mechanism of a Genetic Algorithm

The process of genetic optimization can be divided into the following steps:

1. Generation of the initial population.
2. Evaluation of the fitness of each individual in the population.
3. Ranking of individuals based on their fitness.
4. Selecting those individuals to produce the next generation based on their fitness.
5. Using genetic operations, such as crossover, inversion and mutation, to generate a new population.
6. Continue the process by going back to step 2 until the problem's objectives are satisfied.

The initial population is usually generated using a random process covering the entire problem space. This will ensure a wide variety in the gene pool. Each problem is encoded in the form of a chromosome. Each chromosome is collection of a set of genes. Each gene represents a parameter in the problem. In classical genetic algorithms, a string of 0s and 1s or a bit string represents each gene (parameter). Therefore, a chromosome is a long bit string that includes all the genes (parameters) for an individual. Figure 5 shows a typical chromosome as an individual in a population that has five genes. Obviously, this chromosome is for a problem that has been coded to find the optimum solution using five parameters.

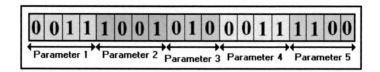

Figure 5. A chromosome with five genes.

The fitness of each individual is determined using a fitness function. The goal of optimization is usually to find a minimum or a maximum. Examples of this include the minimization of error for a problem that must converge to a target value or the maximization of the profit in a financial portfolio. Once the fitness of each individual in the population is evaluated, all the individuals will be ranked. After the ranking, it is time for selection of the parents that will produce the next generation of individuals. The selection process assigns a higher probability of reproduction to the highest-ranking individual, and the reproduction probability is reduced with a reduction in ranking.

After the selection process is complete, genetic operators such as crossover, inversion and mutation are incorporated to generate a new population. The evolutionary process of survival of the fittest takes place in the selection and reproduction stage. The higher the ranking of an individual is, the higher the chance for it to reproduce and pass on its gene to the next generation.

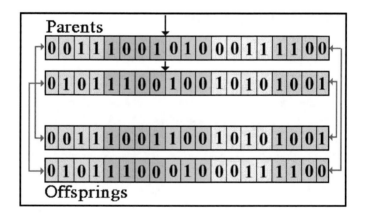

Figure 6. Simple crossover operator.

In crossover, the two parent individuals are first selected and then a break location in the chromosome is randomly identified. Both parents will break at that location and the halves switch places. This process produces two new individuals from the parents. One pair of parents may break in more than one location at different times to produce more than one pair of offspring. Figure 6 demonstrates the simple crossover.

There are other crossover schemes besides simple crossover, such as double crossover and random crossover. In double crossover, each parent breaks in two locations, and the sections are swapped. During a random crossover, parents may break in several locations. Figure 7 demonstrates a double crossover process.

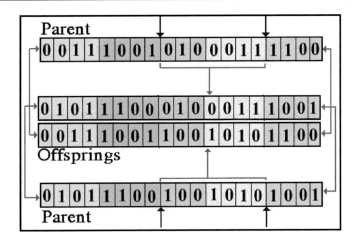

Figure 7. Double crossover operator.

As was mentioned earlier, there are two other genetic operators in addition to crossover. These are inversion and mutation. In both of these operators the offspring is reproduced from one parent rather than a pair of parents. The inversion operator changes all the 0s to 1s and all the 1s to 0s from the parent to make the offspring. The mutation operator chooses a random location in the bit string and changes that particular bit. The probability for inversion and mutation is usually lower than the probability for crossover. Figure 8 and Figure 9 demonstrate inversion and mutation.

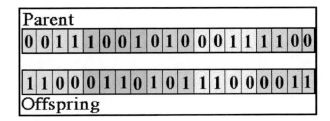

Figure 8. Inversion operator.

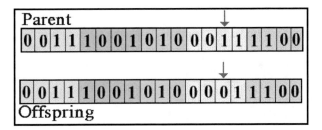

Figure 9. Mutation operator.

Once the new generation has been completed, the evaluation process using the fitness function is repeated and the steps in the aforementioned outline are followed. During each generation, the top ranking individual is saved as the optimum solution to the problem. Each time a new and better individual is evolved, it becomes the optimum solution. The convergence of the process can be evaluated using several criteria. If the objective is to minimize an error, then the convergence criteria can be the amount of error that the problem can tolerate. As another criterion, convergence can take place when a new and better individual is not evolved within four to five generations. Total fitness of each generation has also been used as a convergence criterion. Total fitness of each generation can be calculated (as a sum) and the operation can stop if that value does not improve in several generations. Many applications simply use a certain number of generations as the convergence criterion.

As you may have noticed, the above procedure is called the classic genetic algorithms. Many variations of this algorithm exist. For example, there are classes of problems that would respond better to genetic optimization if a data structure other than bit strings were used. Once the data structure that best fits the problem is identified, it is important to modify the genetic operators such that they accommodate the data structure. The genetic operators serve specific purposes – making sure that the offspring is a combination of parents in order to satisfy the principles of heredity – which should not be undermined when the data structure is altered.

Another important issue is introduction of constraints to the algorithm. In most cases, certain constraints must be encoded in the process so that the generated individuals are "legal". Legality of an individual is defined as its compliance with the problem constraints. For example in a genetic algorithm that was developed for the design of new cars, basic criteria, including the fact that all four tires must be on the ground, had to be met in order for the design to be considered legal. Although this seems to be quite trivial, it is the kind of knowledge that needs to be coded into the algorithm as constraints in order for the process to function as expected.

3. FUZZY LOGIC

The science of today is based on Aristotle's crisp logic formed more than two thousand years ago. The Aristotelian logic looks at the world in a bivalent manner, such as black and white, yes and no, and 0 and 1. Development of the set theory in the late 19th century by German mathematician George Cantor that was based on the Aristotle's bivalent logic made this logic accessible to modern science. Then, the subsequent superimposition of probability theory made the bivalent logic reasonable and workable. Cantor's theory defines sets as a collection of definite, distinguishable objects. Figure 10 is a simple example of Cantor's set theory and its most common operations such as complement, intersection and union.

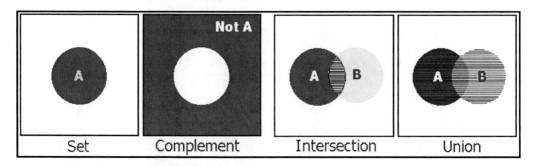

Figure 10. Operations of conventional crisp sets.

First work on vagueness dates back to the first decade of 1900, when American philosopher Charles Sanders Peirce noted that "vagueness is no more to be done away with in the world of logic than friction in mechanics (17)." In the early 1920s, Polish mathematician and logician Jan Lukasiewicz came up with three-valued logic and talked about many-valued or multi-valued logic (18). In 1937, quantum philosopher Max Black published a paper on vague sets (19). These scientists built the foundation upon which fuzzy logic was later developed.

Lotfi A. Zadeh is known to be the father of fuzzy logic. In 1965, while he was the chair of the electrical engineering department at UC Berkeley, he published his landmark paper "Fuzzy Sets" (20). Zadeh developed many key concepts including the membership values and provided a comprehensive framework to apply the theory to many engineering and scientific problems. This framework included the classical operations for fuzzy sets, which comprises all the mathematical tools necessary to apply the fuzzy set theory to real world problems. Zadeh used the term "fuzzy" for the first time, and with that he provoked much opposition. He became a tireless spokesperson for the field. He was often harshly criticized. For example, Professor R. E. Kalman said in a 1972 conference in Bordeaux, "Fuzzification is a kind of scientific permissiveness; it tends to result in socially appealing slogans unaccompanied by the discipline of hard scientific work (2)." (It should be noted that Kalman is a former student of Zadeh's and the inventor of famous Kalman filter, a major statistical tool in electrical engineering. Kalman filter is the technology behind the Patriot missiles used in the Gulf War to shoot down Iraqi SCUD missiles. There have been claims that it has been proven that use of fuzzy logic can increase the accuracy of the Patriot missiles considerably.(21; 22) Despite all the adversities fuzzy logic continued to flourish and has become a major force behind many advances in intelligent systems.

The term "fuzzy" carries a negative connotation in the western culture. The term "fuzzy logic" seems to both misdirect the attention and to celebrate mental fog (23). On the other hand, eastern culture embraces the concept of coexistence of contradictions as it appears in the Yin-Yang symbol. While Aristotelian logic preaches A or Not-A, Buddhism is all about A and Not-A.

Figure 11. The Yin-Yang symbol.

Many believe that the tolerance of eastern culture for such ideas was the main reason behind the success of fuzzy logic in Japan. While fuzzy logic was being attacked in the United States, Japanese industries were busy building a multi-billion dollar industry around it. Today, Japanese hold more than 2000 fuzzy related patents. They have used the fuzzy technology to build intelligent household appliances such as washing machines and vacuum cleaners (Matsushita and Hitachi), rice cookers (Matsushita and Sanyo), air conditioners (Mitsubishi), and microwave ovens (Sharp, Sanyo, and Toshiba), to name a few. Matsushita used fuzzy technology to develop its digital image stabilizer for camcorders. Adaptive fuzzy systems (a hybrid with neural networks) can be found in many Japanese cars. Nissan has patented a fuzzy automatic transmission that is now very popular with many other cars such as Mitsubishi and Honda (23).

3.1. Fuzzy Set Theory

The human thought, reasoning, and decision-making process is not crisp. We use vague and imprecise words to explain our thoughts or communicate with one another. There is a contradiction between the imprecise and vague process of human reasoning, thinking, and decision-making and the crisp, scientific reasoning of black and white computer algorithms and approaches. This contradiction has given rise to an impractical approach of using computers to assist humans in the decision-making process, which has been the main reason behind the lack of success for traditional artificial intelligence or conventional rule-based systems, also known as expert systems. Expert systems as a technology started in early 1950s and remained in the research laboratories and never broke through to consumer market.

In essence, fuzzy logic provides the means to compute with words. Using fuzzy logic, experts no longer are forced to summarize their knowledge to a language that machines or computers can understand. What traditional expert systems failed to achieve finally became reality (as mentioned above) with the use of fuzzy expert systems. Fuzzy logic comprises of fuzzy sets, which are a way of representing non-statistical uncertainty and approximate reasoning, which includes the operations used to make inferences (2).

Fuzzy set theory provides a means for representing uncertainty. Uncertainty is usually either due to the random nature of events or due to imprecision and ambiguity of information we have about the problem we are trying to solve. In a random process, the outcome of an event from among several possibilities is strictly the result of chance. When the uncertainty is a product of randomness of events, probability theory is the proper tool to use. Observations and measurements can be used to resolve statistical or random uncertainty. For example, once a coin is tossed, no more random or statistical uncertainty remains.

Most uncertainties, especially when dealing with complex systems, are the result of a lack of information. The kind of uncertainty that is the outcome of the complexity of a system is the type of uncertainty that rises from imprecision, from our inability to perform adequate measurements, from a lack of knowledge, or from vagueness (like the fuzziness inherent in natural language). Fuzzy set theory is a marvelous tool for modeling the kind of uncertainty associated with vagueness, with imprecision, and/or with a lack of information regarding a particular element of the problem at hand(24). Fuzzy logic achieves this important task through fuzzy sets. In crisp sets, an object either belongs to a set or it does not. In fuzzy sets, everything is a matter of degrees. Therefore, an object belongs to a set to a certain degree. For example, the price of oil today is $24.30 per barrel. Given the price of oil in the past few years, this price seems to be high. But what is a high price for oil? A few months ago, the price of oil was about $10.00 per barrel. Everybody agrees that $10.00 per barrel is low. Given how much it costs to produce a barrel of oil in the United States, one can say that the cut-off between low and high for oil price is $15.00 per barrel. If we use crisp sets, then $14.99 is low, and $15.01 is high. However, imagine if this was the criterion that was used by oil company executives to make a decision. The fact is, while $15.01 is a good price that many people will be happy with, $16.00 is better, and $20.00 is even better. Categorizing all these prices as high can be quite misleading. Fuzzy logic proposes the following fuzzy sets for the price of oil.

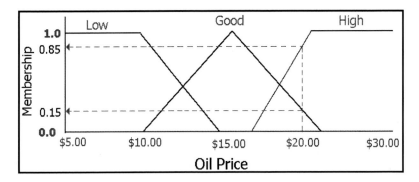

Figure 12. Fuzzy sets representing the price of oil.

The most popular (although not yet standard) form of representing fuzzy set and membership information is as follows:

$$\mu_A(x) = m$$

This representation provides the following information: the membership μ of x in fuzzy set *A* is *m*. According to the Figure 12, when the price of oil is $20.00 per barrel, it has a membership of 0.15 in the fuzzy set "Good" and a membership of 0.85 in the fuzzy set "High". Using the above notation to represent the oil price membership values,

3.2. Approximate Reasoning

When decisions are made based on fuzzy linguistic variables (low, good, high) using fuzzy set operators (And, Or), the process is called the approximate reasoning. This process mimics the human expert's reasoning process much more realistically than the conventional expert systems. For example, if the objective is to build a fuzzy expert system to help us make a recommendation on enhanced recovery operations, then we can use the oil price and the company's proven reserves to make such a recommendation. Using the fuzzy sets in Figure 12 for the oil price and the fuzzy sets in Figure 13 for the company's total proven reserves, we try to build a fuzzy system that can help us in making a recommendation on engaging in enhanced recovery operations as shown in Figure 14.

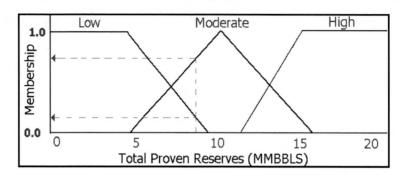

Figure 13. Fuzzy sets representing the total proven reserves.

The approximate reasoning is implemented through fuzzy rules. A fuzzy rule for the system being explained here can have the following form:

Rule #1: If the Price of Oil is High *and* the Total Proven Reserves of the company is Low then Engaging in Enhanced Recovery practices is Highly Recommended.

Since this fuzzy system is comprised of two variables and each of the variables consists of three fuzzy sets, the system will include nine fuzzy rules. These rules can be set up in a matrix as shown in Figure 15.

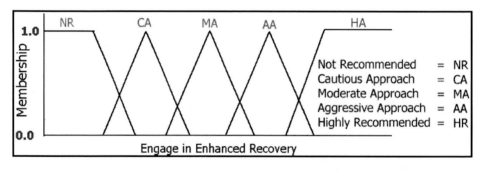

Figure 14. Fuzzy sets representing the decision to engage in enhanced recovery.

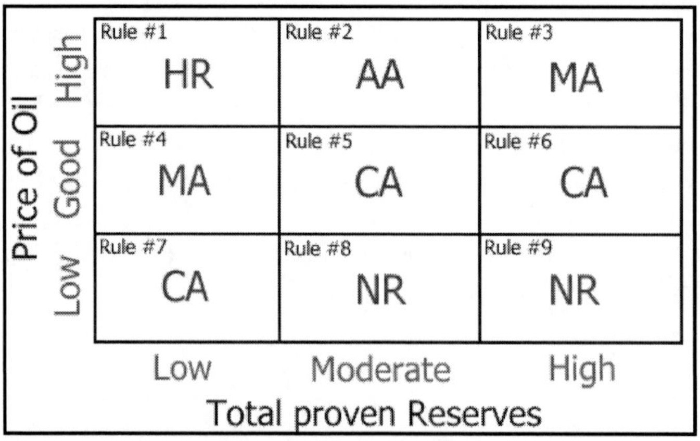

	Rule #1 HR	Rule #2 AA	Rule #3 MA
	Rule #4 MA	Rule #5 CA	Rule #6 CA
	Rule #7 CA	Rule #8 NR	Rule #9 NR

Price of Oil: High / Good / Low
Total proven Reserves: Low / Moderate / High

Figure 15. Fuzzy rules for approximate reasoning.

The abbreviations that appear in the matrix above correspond to the fuzzy sets defined in Figure 15. As one can conclude from the above example, the number of rules in a fuzzy system increases dramatically with addition of new variables. Adding one more variable consisting of three fuzzy sets to the above example, increases the number of rules from 9 to 27. This is known as the "curse of dimensionality."

3.3. Fuzzy Inference

A complete fuzzy system includes a fuzzy inference engine. The fuzzy inference helps us build fuzzy relations based on the fuzzy rules that have been defined. During a fuzzy inference process, several fuzzy rules will be fired in parallel. The parallel rule firing, unlike the sequential evaluation of the rules in the conventional expert system, is much closer to the human reasoning process. Unlike in the sequential process that some information contained in the variables may be overlooked due to the step-wise approach, the parallel firing of the rules allows consideration of all the information content simultaneously. There are many different fuzzy inference methods. We will look at a popular method called the Mamdani's inference method (25). This inference method is demonstrated graphically in Figure 16. In this figure, a case is considered when the price of oil is $20.00 per barrel and the company has approximately 9 MMBBLs of proven reserves. The oil price is represented by its membership in fuzzy sets "Good" and "High", while the total proven reserves is represented in fuzzy sets "Low" and "Moderate". As shown in Figure 16, this causes four rules to be fired simultaneously. According to Figure 15 these are rules #1, #2, #4, and #5. In each rule, the fuzzy set operation "And", the intersection between the two input (antecedents) variables, is evaluated as the minimum and consequently is mapped on the corresponding output (consequent). The result of the inference is the collection of the different fuzzy sets of the output variable as shown on the bottom of the figure.

A crisp value may be extracted from the result as mapped on the output fuzzy sets by defuzzifying the output. One of the most popular defuzzification procedures is to find the center of the mass of the shaded area in the output fuzzy sets.

4. APPLICATIONS IN THE OIL AND GAS INDUSTRY

4.1. Neural Networks Applications

Common sense indicates that if a problem can be solved using conventional methods, one should not use neural networks or any other artificial intelligence technique to solve them. For example, balancing your checkbook using a neural network is not recommended. Although there is academic value to solving simple problems, such as polynomials and differential equations, using neural networks to show its capabilities, they should be used mainly in solving problems that otherwise are very time consuming or simply impossible to solve by conventional methods.

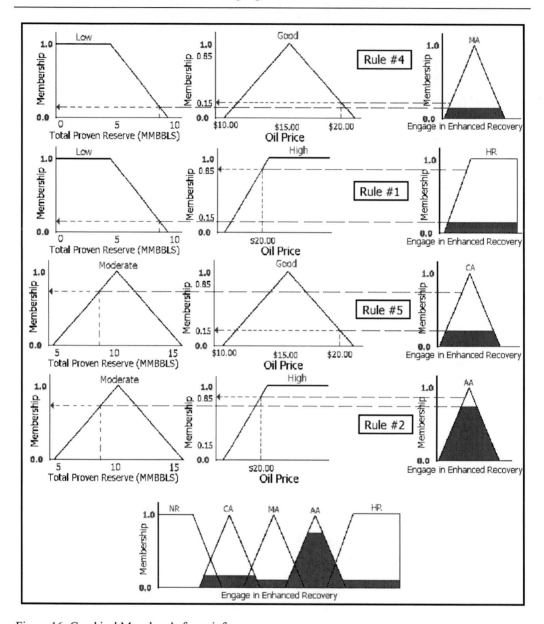

Figure 16. Graphical Mamdany's fuzzy inference.

Neural networks have shown great potential for generating accurate analysis and results from large historical databases. The kind of data that engineers may not consider valuable or relevant in conventional modeling and analysis processes. Neural networks should be used in cases where mathematical modeling is not a practical option. This may be due to the fact that all the parameters involved in a particular process are not known and/or the inter-relation of the parameters is too complicated for mathematical modeling of the system. In such cases a neural network can be constructed to observe the system behavior (what types of output is produced as a result of certain set of inputs) and try to mimic its functionality and behavior. In this section few examples of applying artificial neural networks to petroleum engineering related problems is presented.

4.1.1. Reservoir Characterization

Neural networks have been utilized to predict or virtually measure formation characteristics such as porosity, permeability and fluid saturation from conventional well logs (26; 27; 28). Using well logs as input data coupled with core analysis of the corresponding depth, these reservoir characteristics were successfully predicted for a heterogeneous formation in West Virginia. There have been many attempts to correlate permeability with core porosity and/or well logs using mathematical or statistical functions since the early 1960s (29). It was shown that a carefully orchestrated neural network analysis is capable of providing more accurate and repeatable results when compared to methods used previously (30).

Figure 17 is a cross-plot of porosity versus permeability for the "Big Injun" formation in West Virginia. It is obvious that there are no apparent correlation between porosity and permeability in this formation. The scatter of this plot is mainly due to the complex and heterogeneous nature of this reservoir.

Well logs provide a wealth of information about the rock, but they fall short in measurement and calculation of its permeability. Dependencies of rock permeability on parameters that can be measured by well logs have remained one of the fundamental research areas in petroleum engineering. Using the conventional computing tools available, scientists have not been able to prove that a certain functional relationship exists that can explain the relationships in a rigorous and universal manner. Authors suggest that if such dependency or functional relation exists, an artificial neural network is the tool to find it.

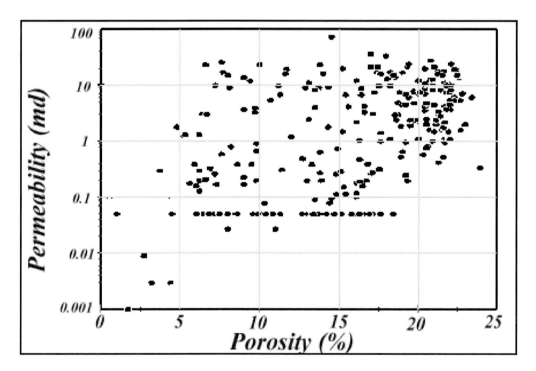

Figure 17. Porosity and permeability cross-plot for Big Injune formation.

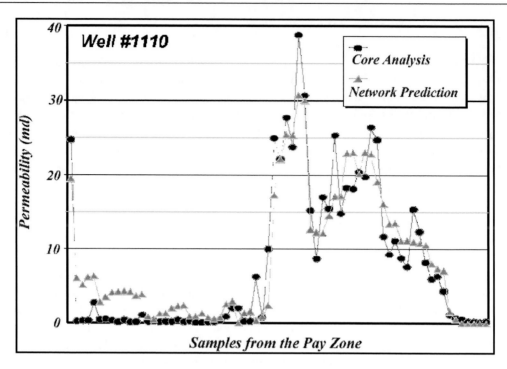

Figure 18. Core and network permeability for well 1110 in Big Injun formation.

Using geophysical well log data as input (bulk density, gamma ray, and induction logs), a neural network was trained to predict formation permeability measured from laboratory core analyses. Log and core permeability data were available from four wells. The network was trained with the data from three wells and attempted to predict the measurements from the fourth well. This practice was repeated twice each time using a different well as the verification well. Figure 18 and Figure 19 show the result of neural network's prediction compared to the actual laboratory measurements. Please note that the well logs and core measurements from these test wells were not used during the training process. In a similar process well logs were used to predict (virtually measure) effective porosity and fluid saturation in this formation. The results of this study are shown in Figure 20 through Figure 22. In these figures solid lines show the neural network's predictions. The core measurements are shown using two different symbols. The circles are those core measurements that were used during the training process and the triangles are the core measurements that were never seen by the network.

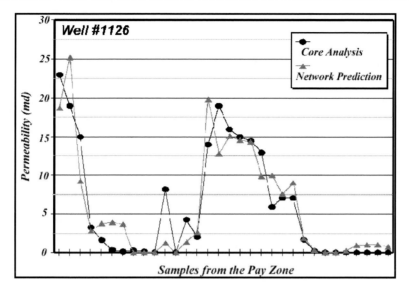

Figure 19. Core and network permeability for well 1126 in Big Injun formation.

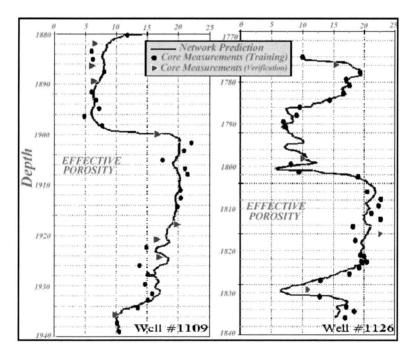

Figure 20. Core and network effective porosity for well 1109 and 1126 in Big Injun formation.

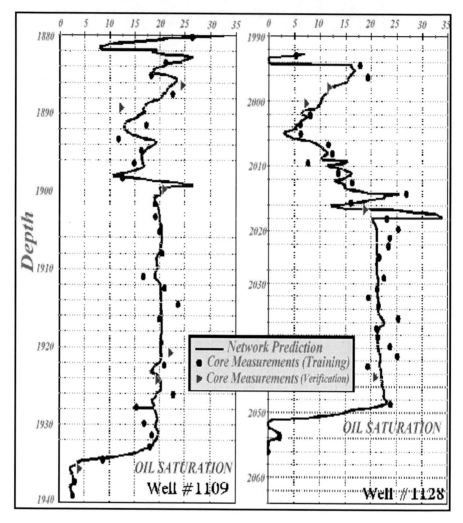

Figure 21. Core and network oil saturation for well 1109 and 1128 in Big Injun formation.

4.1.2. Virtual Magnetic Resonance Imaging Logs

Magnetic Resonance Imaging logs are well logs that use nuclear magnetic resonance to measure free fluid, irreducible water (MBVI), and effective porosity (MPHI) accurately. Permeability is then calculated using a mathematical function that incorporates these measured properties. MRI logs can provide information that result in an increase in the recoverable reserve. This takes place simply by including the portions of the pay zone into the recoverable reserve calculations that were excluded during the analysis using only the conventional well logs. MRI logs accomplishes this task by estimating the economically recoverable hydrocarbon (identification of a combination of water and hydrocarbon saturation as well as the reservoir permeability) that has been overlooked. In a recent paper it was shown that neural networks have the potential to be used as an analytical tool for generation of synthetic magnetic resonance imaging logs from conventional geophysical well logs (31). In this study four wells from different locations in the United States were used to show the potential of this proposed approach. These wells were from Utah, Gulf of Mexico, East Texas and New Mexico. In each case part of the well data is used to train a neural network and the rest of the rest of the well data are used as verification. As it is mentioned in the paper this method is most useful for fields with many wells from which only a handful need to be logged using magnetic resonance imaging tools. These wells can be strategically placed to capture as much reservoir variation as possible. Then a virtual MRI application can be developed based on these wells and applied to the rest of the wells in the field. Figure 23 is an example for such a strategy.

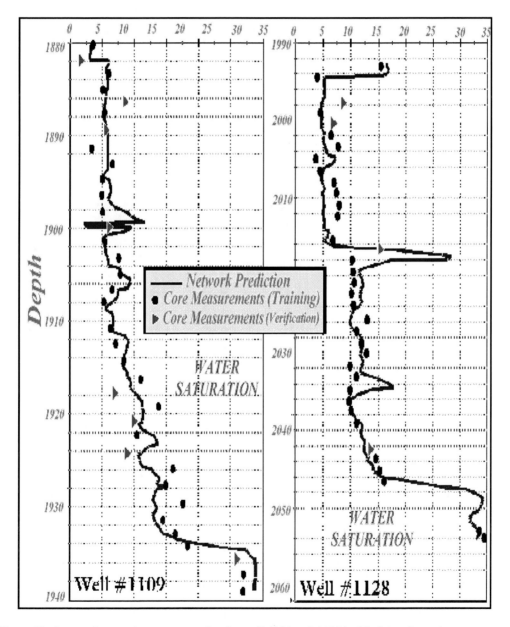

Figure 22. Core and network water saturation for well 1109 and 1128 in Big Injun formation.

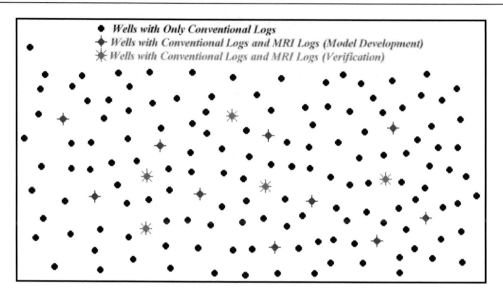

Figure 23. Using virtual MRI log methodology in a typical field.

Table 1. Results of virtual MRI logs for four wells in the United States

Well Location	MRI Log	Data Set	Correlation Coefficient
East Texas	MPHI	Verification Data set	0.941
		Entire Well	0.967
	MBVI	Verification Data set	0.853
		Entire Well	0.894
	MPERM	Verification Data set	0.966
		Entire Well	0.967
Utah	MPHI	Verification Data set	0.800
		Entire Well	0.831
	MBVI	Verification Data set	0.887
		Entire Well	0.914
	MPERM	Verification Data set	0.952
		Entire Well	0.963
Gulf of Mexico	MPHI	Verification Data set	0.853
		Entire Well	0.893
	MBVI	Verification Data set	0.930
		Entire Well	0.940
	MPERM	Verification Data set	0.945
		Entire Well	0.947
New Mexico	MPHI	Verification Data set	0.957
		Entire Well	0.960
	MBVI	Verification Data set	0.884
		Entire Well	0.926

Table 1 shows the accuracy of this methodology when applied to the four wells being studied. For each well the methodology was applied to three different MRI logs namely MPHI (effective porosity), MBVI (irreducible water saturation), and MPERM (permeability). For each log the table shows the correlation coefficient both for the entire well data set (training data and verification data) and for only the verification data set. The verification data set includes data that had not been seen previously by the network. The correlation coefficient of this methodology ranges from 0.80 to 0.97. As expected, the correlation coefficient for the entire well data set is better than that of the verification data set. This is due to the fact that the training data set is included in the entire well data set and that correlation coefficient for the training data is usually higher than the verification data set.

MRI logs are also used to provide a more realistic estimate of recoverable reserve as compared to conventional well logs. Table 2 shows the recoverable reserve calculated using actual and virtual MRI logs. Recoverable reserve calculations based on virtual MRI logs are quite close to those of actual MRI logs since during the reserve calculation a certain degree of averaging takes place that compensates for some of the inaccuracies that are associated with virtual MRI logs. As shown in Table 2 in all four cases the recoverable reserve calculated using Virtual MRI logs are within 2% of those calculated using actual MRI logs. In the case of the well in the Gulf of Mexico the percent difference is about 0.3%. Although there is not enough evidence to make definitive conclusions at this point, but it seems that recoverable reserve calculated using virtual MRI logs are mostly on the conservative sides.

Table 2. Recoverable reserve calculations using actual and virtual MRI logs

Well Location	MRI Type	Reserve (MMSCF/Acre)	Percent Difference
Texas	Actual	414.58	-1.57
Texas	Virtual	407.95	-1.57
New Mexico	Actual	192.73	-1.91
New Mexico	Virtual	189.05	-1.91
Gulf of Mexico	Actual	1,904.93	+0.30
Gulf of Mexico	Virtual	1,910.70	+0.30
Utah	Actual	1,364.07	-1.81
Utah	Virtual	1,339.56	-1.81

Figure 24 Figure 24. Virtual MRI log results for the well in East Texas, for verification data set and the entire well data set. And Figure 25 show the comparison between actual and virtual MRI logs for the well located in East Texas.

There are many more applications of neural networks in the oil and gas industry. They include application to field development (32), two-phase flow in pipes (33)(34), identification of well test interpretation models (35)(36)(37), completion analysis (38)(39), formation damage prediction (40), permeability prediction (41)(42), and fractured reservoirs (43)(44).

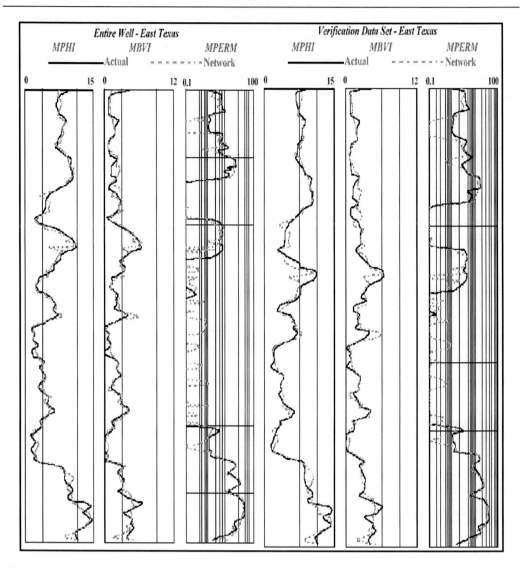

Figure 24. Virtual MRI log results for the well in East Texas, for verification data set and the entire well data set.

4.2. Genetic Algorithms Applications

There have been several applications of genetic algorithms in the petroleum and natural gas industry. The first application in the literature goes back to one of Holland's students named David Goldberg. He applied a genetic algorithm to find the optimum design for gas transmission lines(45). Since then, genetic algorithms have been used in several other petroleum applications. These include reservoir characterization(46) and modeling(47), distribution of gas-lift injection(48), petrophysics(49) and petroleum geology(50), well test analysis(51), and hydraulic fracturing design(52; 53; 54).

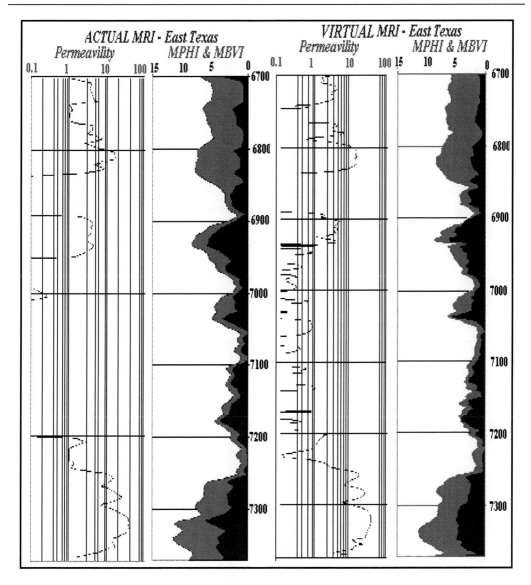

Figure 25. Actual and Virtual MRI log results for the well in East Texas.

As it was mentioned earlier, virtual intelligence techniques perform best when used to complement each other. The first hybrid neural network/genetic algorithm application in the oil and gas industry was used to design optimum hydraulic fractures in a gas storage field(53; 54). A brief review of the hybrid neural network/genetic algorithm is presented here.

Virtual intelligence techniques were utilized to design optimum hydraulic fractures for the Clinton Sand in Northeast Ohio. In order to maintain and/or enhance deliverability of gas storage wells in the Clinton Sand, an annual restimulation program has been in place since the late sixties. The program calls for as many as twenty hydraulic fractures and refractures per year. Several wells have been refractured three to four times, while there are wells that have only been fractured once in the past thirty years. Although the formation lacks detailed reservoir engineering data, there is wealth of relevant information that can be found in the well files. Lack of engineering data for hydraulic fracture design and evaluation had, therefore, made use of 2D or 3D hydraulic fracture simulators impractical. As a result, prior designs of hydraulic fractures had been reduced to guesswork. In some cases, the designs were dependent on engineers' intuition about the formation and its potential response to different treatments – knowledge gained only through many years of experience with this particular field. The data set used in this study was collected using well files that included the design of the hydraulic fractures. The following parameters were extracted from the well files for each hydraulic fracture treatment: the year the well was drilled, total number of fractures performed on the well, number of years since the last fracture, fracture fluid, amount of fluid, amount of sand used as proppant, sand concentration, acid volume, nitrogen volume, average pumping rate, and the service company performing the job. The matchup between hydraulic fracture design parameters and the available post fracture deliverability data produces a data set with approximately 560 records.

The first step in this study was to develop a set of neural network models of the hydraulic fracturing process in the Clinton Sand. These models were capable of predicting post fracture deliverability given the input data mentioned above. Figure 26 shows the neural model's predictions compared to actual field results for three years. Data from these years were not used in the training process.

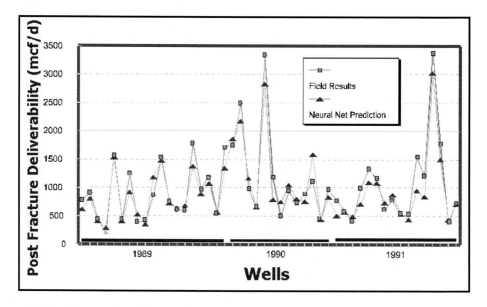

Figure 26. Neural network model's predictive capability in the Clinton Sand.

Once the neural network model's accuracy was established, it was used as the fitness function for the genetic algorithm process to form the hybrid intelligent system. The input data to the neural network can be divided into three categories:

- Basic well information
- Well production history
- Hydraulic fracture design parameters such as sand concentration, rate of injection, sand mesh size, fluid type, etc.

From the above categories, only the third (hydraulic fracture design parameters) are among the controllable parameters. In other words, these are the parameters that can be modified for each well to achieve a better hydraulic fracture design. A two-stage process was developed to produce the optimum hydraulic fracture design for each well in the Clinton Sand. The optimum hydraulic fracture design is defined as the design that results in the highest possible post fracture deliverability. Figure 27 is a schematic diagram of the hybrid neuro-genetic procedure.

The neural network for the first stage (neural module #1) is designed and trained to perform a rapid screening of the wells. This network is designed to identify the so-called "dog wells" that would not be enhanced considerably even after a frac job. This way the genetic optimization can be concentrated on the wells that have a realistic chance of deliverability enhancement. The second stage of the process is the genetic optimization routine. This stage is performed on one well at a time. The objective of this stage is to search among all the possible combinations of design parameters and identify the combination of the hydraulic fracture parameters for a specific well that results in the highest incremental post fracture deliverability.

This second stage process (the genetic optimization routine) starts by generating 100 random solutions. Each solution is defined as a combination of hydraulic fracture design parameters. These solutions are then combined with other information available from the well and presented to the fitness function (neural network). The result from this process is the post fracture deliverability for each solution. The solutions are then ranked based on the highest incremental enhancement of the post fracture deliverability. The highest-ranking individuals are identified, and the selection for reproduction of the next generation is made. Genetic operations such as crossover, inversion and mutations are performed, and a new generation of solutions is generated. This process is continued until a convergence criterion is reached.

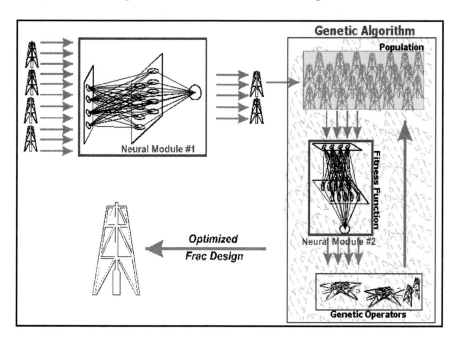

Figure 27. Hybrid neuro-genetic procedure for optimum hydraulic fracture design in the Clinton Sand.

This process is repeated for all the wells. The wells with highest potential for post fracture deliverability enhancement are selected as the candidate wells. The combination of the design parameters identified for each well is also provided to the operator to be used as the guideline for achieving the well's potential. This process was performed for the wells in Figure 6. The result of the genetic optimization is presented in Figure 28 through Figure 30. Since the same neural networks have generated all the post fracture deliverabilities, it is expected that the post fracture deliverabilities achieved after genetic optimization have the same degree of accuracy as those that were predicted for each well's field result. In these figures, the green bars show the actual PFD of the wells achieved in the field. The red bars show the accuracy of the neural network used as the fitness function in the genetic optimization routine when it is predicting the PDF, given the design parameters used in the field. The blue bars show the PDF resulting from the same neural network that produced the red bars, but with the input design parameters the genetic algorithms proposed.

Please note that the process indicates that some wells cannot be enhanced, regardless of the modification in the fracture design, while other wells can be enhanced significantly. This finding can have important financial impact on the operation and can help the management make better decisions in allocation of investment.

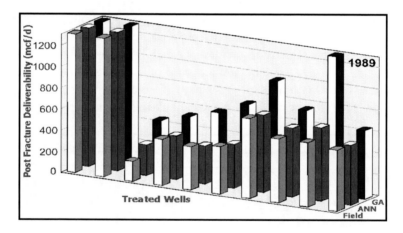

Figure 28. Enhancement in PFD if this methodology had been used in 1989.

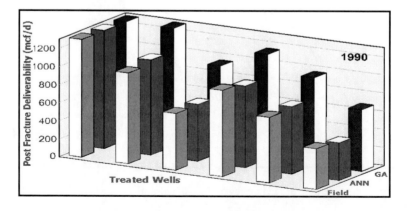

Figure 29. Enhancement in PFD if this methodology had been used in 1990.

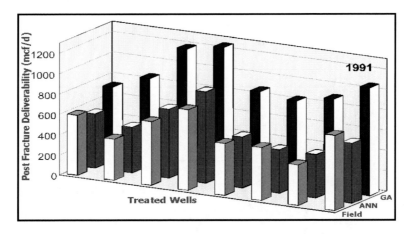

Figure 30. Enhancement in PFD if this methodology had been used in 1991.

In another application, genetic algorithms were used in combination with neural networks to develop an expert hydraulic fracture designer(54). The intelligent system developed for this purpose is capable of designing hydraulic fractures in detail, providing the pumping schedule in several stages (or in a ramp scheme), and identifying the fluid type and amount, proppant type and concentration, and the pumping rate. It was shown that fracture designs proposed by this intelligent system are comparable to those designed by expert engineers with several years of experience.

4.3. Fuzzy Logic Applications

Fuzzy logic has been used in several petroleum engineering related applications. These applications include petrophysics(55; 56), reservoir characterization(57), enhanced recovery(58; 59), infill drilling(60), decision making analysis(61), and well stimulation(62; 63; 64). In this section we review an application that incorporates fuzzy logic in a hybrid manner in concert with neural networks and genetic algorithms. In this example of use of the intelligent systems in petroleum engineering, neural networks, genetic algorithms, and fuzzy logic are used to select candidates for restimulation in the Frontier formation in the Green River Basin(64). As the first step of the methodology, neural networks are used to build a representative model of the well performance in the Frontier formation. Table 3 is a list of input parameters used in the neural network model building process.

Once the training, testing, and validation of the neural networks were completed, the training data set had a correlation coefficient of 0.96, and the verification data set had a correlation coefficient of 0.72. As a by-product of the neural network analysis and by using a methodology called "backward elimination," an attempt was made to identify the most influential parameters in this data set. The results of neural network backward elimination analysis are demonstrated in Figure 31.

In this figure, all four categories of the input data are shown. The most influential category has the lowest R squared. This figure shows that reservoir quality is the most important category, followed by the completion and stimulation categories that seem to be equally important. The location-related input parameters seem to be the least important parameters when compared to others. Note that among all the parameters involved in this analysis only the last three stimulation related parameters (see Table 3) are considered as being controllable.

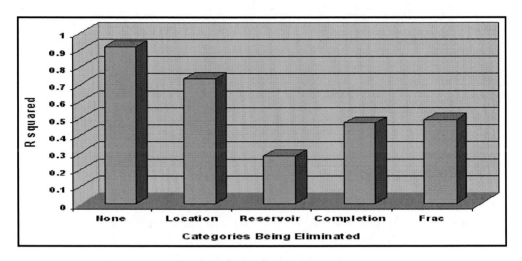

Figure 31. Influence of parameters in the stimulation process in Frontier formation.

Table 3. Input parameters for the neural network analysis

Category	Input Parameter	Comments
Location	X	X coordinates of the well (east-west)
	Y	Y coordinates of the well (north-south)
	KB Elevation	Kelly Bushing Elevation
Reservoir	Permeability	From Type Curve matching analysis
	Drainage Area	From Type Curve matching analysis
	Total Gas-Ft	Sum(Porosity * gas saturation * net pay) (all zones)
Completion	Total H Completed	Total completed thickness (all zones)
	Total No. of Holes	Total number of perforation holes
	Completion Date	Date of well completion
	Number of Zones	Total number of zones completed
Frac	Frac Number	A well may have up to 7 frac jobs
	Fluid type	Gelled oil, ungelled oil, linear gel, cross-linked gel
	Fluid Volume	Total amount of fluid pumped in all fracs
	Proppant Amount	Total amount of proppant pumped in all fracs

This brings us to the second step of the analysis that involves the genetic optimization of the stimulation parameters. In this step, the last three input parameters shown in Table 3 (namely fluid type, total fluid volume, and total proppant amount) are used in the optimization process. Using the neural network model developed in the first step of the analysis as the "fitness" function of the evolution process, the algorithm searches through all possible combinations of the aforementioned three stimulation parameters and tries to find the combination that results in the highest five-year cumulative production (5YCum). This process is repeated for every well individually. The difference between the optimized 5YCum and the actual 5YCum is considered to be the potentially missed production that may be recovered by restimulation. The outcome of this process is called the potential 5YCum and is used as one of the three inputs into step three which is the fuzzy decision support system using approximate reasoning.

		Pressure Low			Pressure Medium			Pressure High		
Fracs/Zone	High Med. Low — Low	NO T	Maybe FT	Maybe FT	Maybe T	Yes FT	Yes FT	Yes T	Yes VT	Yes VT
	Med.	NO VT	NO T	Maybe FT	NO FT	Maybe T	Yes FT	Maybe VT	Yes T	Yes VT
	High	NO VT	NO VT	NO T	Maybe FT	NO FT	Maybe T	Maybe VT	Maybe VT	Yes T
		Low	Med.	High	Low	Med.	High	Low	Med.	High
		Potential Five Year Cum.			Potential Five Year Cum.			Potential Five Year Cum.		

Figure 32. Rules used in the fuzzy decision support system.

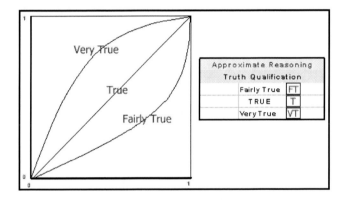

Figure 33. Truth qualification for the fuzzy rules.

Step three is a three-input, one-output, fuzzy system. The inputs include the above-mentioned potential 5YCum, a calculated parameter called Fracs per Zone (FPZ), and pressure. The engineers in the field brought this parameter to our attention. They mentioned that there are wells that have been completed in all zones (there can be as many as 7 zones present) but only one hydraulic fracture has been performed. In other words, the ratio of the number of treatments performed to the total number zones completed is an important factor. We also found that long-term pressure surveys had been performed in 1995 on many wells. The issue with the pressure surveys is that the shut-in time and the depth where the pressure readings were taken were not consistent throughout the field. This introduces serious imprecision in the pressure values as a comparative value from well to well. Therefore, all the three input parameters were subjected to fuzzy sets using low, moderate, and high fuzzy sets. The output of the fuzzy system is the degree of which a well is a candidate for restimulation. The output fuzzy sets include: 1) the well is a candidate, 2) the well may be a candidate, and 3) the well is not a candidate. The system includes 27 fuzzy rules that are qualified using a set of three truth functions. Figure 32 shows the 27 rules with truth qualification for the fuzzy systems. Figure 33 shows the truth qualification functions used for the approximate reasoning implementation in the fuzzy system. As demonstrated in this figure, each rule can be true, fairly true, or very true.

Using this three-step process, all the wells (belonging to a particular operator) in the Frontier formation was processed. A list of restimulation candidates was identified.

4.3.1. Results

It should be noted that the intelligent systems approach for this application was modified as a result of its application to three different formations, two in the Rocky Mountains and one in East Texas. The fuzzy decision support system was the most recent addition to the process. The new and improved intelligent systems approach, that included the fuzzy logic component, picked well GRB 45-12 as candidate #20, while this well was missed as a candidate prior to the addition of fuzzy logic to this procedure. An engineer with several years of experience in this field also had suggested this well as a candidate. The fuzzy decision support system was able to capture the engineer's knowledge and use it in an automatic process for all the wells in the study. Figure 34 shows the result of restimulation on Well GRB 45-12.

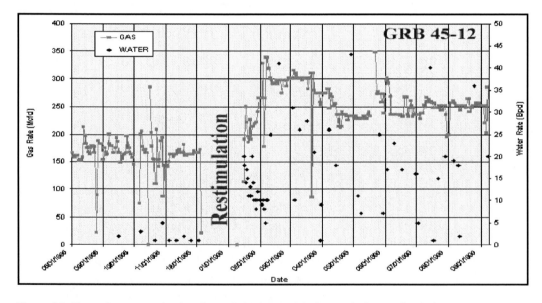

Figure 34. Gas and water production for well GRB-45-12 before and after restimulation.

REFERENCES

[1]   Zaruda, J. M., Marks, R. J. and Robinson, C. J. *Computational Intelligencem Imitating Life,*. Poscataway, NJ: IEEE Press, 1994.

[2]   Eberhart, R., Simpson, P. and Dobbins, R. *Computational Intelligence PC Tools.* Orlando, FL: Academic Press, 1996.

[3] McCulloch, W. S. and Pitts, W. *A Logical Calculus of Ideas Immanent in Nercous Activity.* 1943. pp. 115-133. Vol. 5.

[4] Rosenblatt, F. *The Perceptron: Probabilistic Model for Information Storage and Organization in the Brain.* 1958. pp. 386-408. Vol. 65.

[5] Widrow, B. Generalization and Information Storage in Networks if Adeline Neurons. [book auth.] M. C. Yovits, G. T. Jacobi and G. D. Goldstein. *Self-Organizing Systems.* Chicago: s.n., 1962, pp. 435-461.

[6] Minsky, M. L. and Papert, S. A. P. *Perceptrons.* Cambridge, MA: MIT Press, 1969.

[7] Hertz, J., Krogh, A. and Palmer, R.G. *Introduction to the Theory of Neural Computation.* Redwood City, CA: Addison-Wesley Publishing Company, 1991.

[8] Rumelhart, D. E. and McCelland, J. L. *Parallel Distributed Processing, Exploration in the microstructure of Cognition,.* Cambridge, MA: MIT Press, 1986. Vol. 1: Foundations.

[9] Stubbs, D. *Neurocomputers.* 1988. Vol. 5.

[10] Fausett, L. *Fundamentals of Neural Networks, Archintectures, algorithms, and applications.* Englewood Cliffs, NJ: Prentice Hall, 1994.

[11] Barlow, H. B. *Unsupervised Learning.* 1988. pp. 295-311. Vol. 1.

[12] McCord-Nelson, M. and Illingworth, W. T. *A Practical Guide to Neural Nets.* Reading, MA: Addison-Wesley Publishing, 1990.

[13] Mayr, E. *Toward a new Philosophy of Biology: Observations of an Evolutionist.* Cambridge, MA: Belknap Press, 1988.

[14] Koza, J. R. *Genetic Programming, On the Programing of Computers by Means of Natural Selection.* Cambridge, MA: MIT Press, 1992.

[15] Fogel, D. B. *Evolutionary Computation, toward a New Philosophy of Machine Intelligence.* Picataway, NJ: IEEE Press, 1995.

[16] Michalewicz, Z. *Genetic Algorithms + Data Structure = Evolution Programs.* New York, NY : Springer-verlag, 1992.

[17] Freeman, E. *The Relevance of Charles Pierce.* La Shall, IL: Moinst Library of Philosophy, 1983. pp. 157-158.

[18] Lukasiewicz, J. *Elements of Mathematical Logic.* New York, NY: The MacMillan Company, 1963.

[19] Black, M. Vagueness: An Exercise in Logicak Analysis. *Philosophy of Science.* 1937, Vol. 4, pp. 437-455.

[20] Zadeh, L. A. Fuzzy Sets. *Information and Control.* 1965, Vol. 8, pp. 338-353.

[21] Kosko, B. *Fuzzy Thinking.* New York, NY: Hyperion, 1991.

[22] Kosko. *Neural Networks and Fuzzy Systems.* Englewood Cliffs, NJ : Prentice Hall, 1992.

[23] McNeill, D. and Freiberger, P. *Fuzzy Logic.* New York, NY: Simon & Schuster, 1993.

[24] Ross, T. *Fuzzy Logic with Engineering Applications.* New York, NY: McGraw-Hill Inc, 1995.

[25] Jamshidi, M. and et.al. *Fuzzy Logic and Controls: Software and Hardware Applications.* Englewood Cliffs, NJ: Prentice Hall, 1993.

[26] Mohaghegh, S., et al. Design and Development of an Artificial Neural Network for Estimation of Formation Permeability. *SPE Computer Applications.* December 1995, pp. 151-154.

[27] Mohaghegh, S., Arefi, R. and Ameri, S. Petroleum Reservoir Characterization with the Aid of Artificial Neural Networks. *Journal of Petroleum Science and Engineeing.* 1996, Vol. 16, pp. 263-274.

[28] Mohaghegh, S., Ameri, S. and Arefi, R. Virtual Measurement of Heterogeneous Formation Permeability Using Geophysical Well Log Responses. *The Log Analysi.* March/April 1996, pp. 32-39.

[29] Balan, B., Mohaghegh, S. and Ameri, S. State-of-the-art in Permeability Determination from Well Log Data, Part 1: A Comparative Study, Model Development. *SPE Eastern Regional Conference, SPE 30978.* September 1995.

[30] Mohaghegh, S., Balan, B. and Ameri, S. State-of-the-art in Permeability Determination from Well Log Data: Part 2: Verifiable, Accurate Permeability Prediction, the Touch-Stone of All Models. *SPE Eastern Regional Conference, SPE 30979.* September 17-21, 1995.

[31] Mohaghegh, S., Richardson, M. and Ameri, M. Virtual Magnetic Resonance Imaging Logs: Genration of Synthetic MRI Logs From Conventional Well Logs. *SPE Eastern Regional Conference, SPE 51075.* November 9-11, 1998.

[32] Doraisamy, H., Ertekin, T. and Grader, A. Key Parameters Controlling the Performance of Neuro Simulation Applications in Field Development. *SPE Eastern Regional Conference, SPE 51079.* November 9-11, 1998.

[33] Ternyik, J., Bilgesu, I. and Mohaghegh, S. Virtual Measurement in Pipes, Part 2: Liquid Holdup and Flow Pattern Correlation. *SPE Eastern Regional Conference and Exhibition, SPE 30976.* September 19-21, 1995.

[34] Ternyik, J., et al. Virtual Measurement in Pipes, Part 1: Flowing Bottomhole Pressure Under Multi-phase Flow and Inclined Wellbore Conditions. *SPE Eastern Regional Conference and Exhibition, SPE 30975.* September 19-21, 1995.

[35] Sung, W., Hanyang, U. and Yoo, I. Development of HT-BP Neural Network System for the Identification of Well Test Interpretation Model. *SPE Eastern Regional Conference and Exhibition, SPE 30974.* September 19-21, 1995.

[36] Al-Kaabi, A. and Lee, W. J. Using Artificial Neural Nets to Identify the Well Test Interpretation Model. *SPE Formation Evaluation.* September 1993, pp. 233-240.

[37] Juniradi, I. J. and Ershaghi, I. Complexities of Using Neural Networks In Well Test Analysis of Faulted Reservoir. *SPE Western Regional Conference and Exhibition.* March 26-28, 1993.

[38] Shelly, R., et al. Granite Wash Completion Optimazation with the Aid of Artificial Neural Networks. *Gas Technology Symposium, SPE 39814.* March 15-18, 1998.

[39] Shelly, R., et al. Red Fork Analysis with the Aid of Artificial Neural Networks. *Rocky Mountain Regional Meeting / Low Permeabiloity Reservoir Symposium.* April 5-8, 1998.

[40] Nikravesh, M., et al. Prediction of Formation Damage During the Fluid Injection into Fractured Low Permeability Reservoirs via Neural Networks. *Formation Damage Symposium, SPE 31103.* February 16-18, 1996.

[41] Wong, P. M., Henderson, D. J. and Brooks, L. J. Permeability Determination using Neural Networks in the Ravva Field, Offshore India. *SPE Reservoir Evaluation and Engineering.* 1998, Vol. 2, pp. 99-104.

[42] Wong, P. M., Taggart, I. J. and Jian, F. X. A Critical Comparison of Neural Networks and Discriminant Analysis in Lithofacies, Porosity and Permeability Predictions. *Journal of Petroleum Geology.* 1995, Vol. 2, pp. 191-206.

[43] Ouense, A., et al. Use of Neural Networks in Tight Gas Fractured Reservoirs: Application to San Juan Basin. *Rocky Mountain Regional Meeting / Low Permeability Reservoir Symposium.* April 1998, pp. 5-8.

[44] Zellou, A., Ouense, A. and Banik, A. Improved Naturally Fractured Reservoir Characterization Using Neural Networks, Geomechanics and 3-D Seismic. *SPE Annual Technical Conference and Exhibition.* October 22-25, 1995.

[45] Goldberg, D. E. *Computer Aided Gas Pipeline Operartion Using Genetic Algorithms and Rule Learning,.* University of Michigan, Ann Arbor, MI: PhD Dissertation, 1983.

[46] Guerreiro, J.N.C and et.al. Identification of Reservoir Heterogeneties Using Tracer Breakthrough Profiles and Genetic Algorithms. *Latin American and Caribean Petroleum Engineering Conference and Exhibition, SPE 39066.* August 1997.

[47] Sen, M.K. and et.al. Stochastic Reservoir Modeling Using Simulated Annealing and Genetic Algorithm. *SPE Annual Technical Conference and Exhibition, SPE 24754.* October 4-7, 1992.

[48] Martinez, E. R. and et.al. Application of Genetic Algorithm on the Distribution of Gas-Lift Injection. *SPE Annual Technical Conference and Exhibition.* September 25-28, 1994.

[49] Fang, J. H. and et.al. Genetic Algorithm and Its Application to Petrophisics. *Unsolicited, SPE 26208.* 1992.

[50] Hu, L. Y. and et.al. Random Genetic Simulation of the Internal Geometry of Deltaic Sandstone Bodies. *SPE Annual Technical Conference and Exhibition , SPE 24714.* October 4-7, 1992.

[51] Yin, et al. An Optimum Method of Early-Time Well Test Analysis - Genetic Algorithm. *International Oil and Gas Conference and Exhibition, SPE 50905.* November 2-6, 1998.

[52] Mohaghegh, S., et al. A Hybrid, Neuro-Genetic Approach to Hydraulic Fracture Treatment Design and Optimization. *SPE Annual Technical Conference and Exhibition, SPE 36602.* October 6-9, 1996.

[53] Mohaghegh, S., Platon, V. and Ameri, S. Candidate Selection for Stimulation of Gas Storage Wells Using Available Data with Neural Networks and Genetic Algorithms. *SPE Eastern Regional Meeting, SPE 51080.* November 9-11, 1998.

[54] Mohaghegh, S., Popa, A. S. and Ameri, S. Intelligent Systems Can Design Optimum Fracturing Jobs. *SPE Eastern Regional Conferene and Exhibition, SPE 57433.* October 21-22, 1999.

[55] Zhanggui and et.al. Integration of Fuzzy Methods into Geostatistics for Petrophysical Property Distribution. *SPE Asia Pacific Oil and Gas Conference and Exhibition.* October 12-14, 1998.

[56] Chen, H. C., et al. Novel Approaches to the Determination of Archie Parameters II: Fuzzy Regression Analysis. *Unsolicited, SPE 26288.* 1993.

[57] Zhou, et al. Determining Reservoir Properties in Reservoir Studies Using a Fuzzy Neural Network. *SPE Annual Technical Conference and Exhibition.* October 3-6, 1993.

[58] Chung, T., Carrol, H. B. and Lindsey, R. Application of Fuzzy Expert Systems for EOR Project Risk Analysis. *SPE Annual Technical Conference and Exhibition, SPE 30741.* October 22-25, 1995.

[59] Nikravesh, M., et al. Field-wise Waterflood Management in Low Permeability, Fractured Oil Reservoirs: Neuro-Fuzzy Approach. *SPE International Thermal Operations and Heavy Oil Symposium.* February 10-12, 1997.

[60] Wu, C. H., Lu, G. F. and Yen, J. Statistical and Fuzzy Infill Drilling Recovery Models for Carbonate Reservoirs. *Middle East Oil Conference and Exhibition.* March 17-22, 1997.

[61] Yong, et al. Fuzzy-Grey-Element Relational Decision- Making Analysis and Its Application. *SPE India Oil and Gas Conference and Exhibition, SPE 39579.* February 17-19, 1998.

[62] Xiong and Hongjie. An Investigation into the Application of Fuzzy Logic to Well Stimulation Treatment Design. *SPE Permian Basin Oil and Gas Recovery Conference.* March 16-18, 1994.

[63] Rivera, V. P. Fuzzy Logic Controls Pressure in Fracturing Fluid Characterization Facility. *SPE Petroleum Computer Conference, SPE 28239.* 1994.

[64] Mohaghegh, S., Reeves, S. and Hill, D. Development of an Intelligent Systems Approach to Restimulation Candidate Selection. *SPE Gas Technology Symposium, SPE 59767.* April 2000.

In: Horizons in Computer Science Research, Volume 4   ISBN: 978-1-61324-262-9
Editor: Thomas S. Clary   © 2011 Nova Science Publishers, Inc.

Chapter 2

MULTI-PATH ROUTING PROTOCOLS
FOR AD HOC NETWORKS

B. Rahimzadeh Rofoee[1], N. Qadri[2], M. Fleury[3] and M. Ghanbari[4]

University of Essex, School of Computer Science and Electronic Eng,
Colchester, Essex, CO4 3SQ, United Kingdom

ABSTRACT

Within an ad hoc wireless network, multi-path routing can result in reduced end-to-end delay, increased path reliability, an increase in aggregate bandwidth, load-balancing to equalize energy consumption, and congestion avoidance, as well as acting as a security mechanism. This Chapter reviews multi-path routing in ad hoc networks. The operation of selected single-path ad hoc routing is described, as well-known protocols such as AODV and DSR are the starting points for their multi-path enhancements. An analysis of the operation of existing multi-path protocols is included. The Chapter contains a study of the design principles behind multi-path routing. As an application case study, multi-description coding of video streaming over multi-paths is illustrated for a vehicular ad hoc network.

1. INTRODUCTION

An ad hoc network [1] is a decentralized one in which the nodes self-configure the network. Nodes are normally mobile, communicating through wireless links. In the IEEE 802.11 (or WiFi) family of wireless networks, an ad hoc network is one that does not require an access point to a wired network or infrastructure. There are two main types: Mobile Ad Hoc Networks (MANETs) (see Section 2) and Vehicular Ad Hoc Networks (VANETs) (see Section 4). VANETs have more restrictive mobility patterns because of the presence of roads, while MANETs have lower speeds as normally the transceivers are assumed to be carried by people at

---

[1] E-mail address: brahim@essex.ac.uk.
[2] E-mail address: nnawaz@essex.ac.uk.
[3] E-mail address: fleum@essex.ac.uk.
[4] E-mail address: ghan@essex.ac.uk.

walking pace. However, the main focus of this paper is the routing protocols and, in particular, multi-path routing protocols. There has been an intense academic examination [2] of ad hoc network routing protocols from the time when this type of network became of interest (see Section 2). Consequently, this Chapter can only hope to introduce some aspects of this topic.

Due to the volatility of wireless channels and the changing wireless environment, as people or vehicles move through an area, multi-path communication is intuitively more attractive than attempting to select an optimal single path through an ad hoc network. Multi-path routing is the selection of different paths of transmission instead of a single-path, in order to achieve greater performance of the network. Simultaneous communication across the multiple paths may occur, but it is also possible to alternate communication across the multi-paths, or indeed to select from a set of multi-paths, choosing another path when a prior one becomes unusable. In a mobile network, the most likely cause of that eventuality is when nodes on a network path move out of range or cease to participate in the network. Figure 1 illustrates single-path and multi-path routings. In this example, packets are transmitted on alternate paths in Figure 1b from the buffer, whereas in Figure 1a only one route is available. Multi-path algorithms are more reliable in communication in ad hoc networks in contrast to single path, especially when communicating over highly loaded networks with a higher density of nodes per unit area. In addition to that, multipath communication achieves greater utilization of network resources. After this basic introduction, we now consider the background to routing protocols on MANETs.

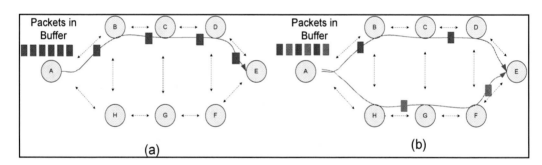

Figure 1. (a) Single path communication (b) Multi-path Communication.

2. ROUTING IN A MANET

Since the first appearance of wireless ad-hoc networks in the DARPA packet radio networks in the 1970s [3], they have become an interesting research object in the computer industry. In the 1990s, the concept of commercial ad-hoc networks arrived with notebook computers and other viable wireless communications equipment. At the same time, the idea of a collection of mobile nodes was proposed at several research conferences. The IEEE 802.11 subcommittee (Internet Engineering Task Force MANET working Group) had adopted the term 'ad-hoc networks' and the research community had started to look into the possibility of deploying ad-hoc networks in various areas of application, whenever a network infrastructure is missing or has been destroyed (such as in disaster-affected areas, during urban crises, in military operations, for remotely deployed sensor networks, within homes between Bluetooth devices). During the last decade, tremendous improvements have been made in research into ad hoc networks. Due to their ability to create and organize a network without any central management, MANETs are characterized as the art of networking without a network [4].

A MANET can be defined as a self-organizing and autonomous system of mobile nodes that communicate over wireless links. Since the nodes are mobile, the network topology may change rapidly and unpredictably over time. The network is decentralized, whereby all network activity including discovering the topology, routing functionality and message delivery is executed by the nodes themselves [5]. MANETs introduce a new communication paradigm, which does not require a fixed infrastructure —they rely on wireless terminals for routing and transport services. Therefore, a MANET can be flexibly and rapidly deployed. The special features of a MANET bring about great opportunities together with severe challenges. Due to their highly dynamic topology, the absence of an established infrastructure for centralized administration, bandwidth constrained wireless links, and limited resources, MANETs are hard to design in terms of an efficient and reliable network [6].

A robust and flexible routing approach is required to efficiently use the limited resources available in such networks, while at the same time being adaptable to the changing network conditions such as network size (scalability), traffic density, and mobility. The routing protocol should be able to provide efficient route establishment with minimum overhead, delay, and bandwidth consumption, along with a stable throughput. Furthermore, the possibility of asymmetric links, caused by different power levels among mobile hosts and other factors such as terrain variability, make routing protocols more complicated than in other networks.

For this purpose, various protocols has been introduced and authors of each proposed protocol claim that the algorithm proposed by them brings enhancements and improvements over a number of different strategies, under different scenarios and network conditions. However, only a few protocols have actually been implemented (beyond the simulation stage) and not all of these have been assessed in depth. Many articles such as [7-13] have provided a protocol assessment that is specific and often does not allow general conclusions to be drawn. Therefore, it is difficult to determine which protocols may perform better under different network scenarios.

To achieve the required efficiency, routing protocols for MANETs must satisfy special characteristics. Important characteristics are identified by the IETF (Internet Engineering Task Force) MANET Charter in Request for Comment (RFC) 2501. The fundamental characteristics required by ideal mobile ad hoc routing protocol are expanded below:

- *Distributed routing:* Routing protocols must be fully distributed, as this approach is more fault tolerant than centralized routing.
- *Adaptive to topology changes:* Routing must adapt to frequent topological and traffic changes that result from node mobility and link failure.
- *Proactive/Reactive operation:* The routing algorithm may intelligently discover the routes on demand. This approach will be useful to efficiently utilize the bandwidth and energy resources but comes at the cost of additional delay. However, in certain conditions the delay incurred by on-demand operation could be unacceptable.
- *Loop-free routing:* Routes free from loops and stale paths are desirable. Perhaps to increase robustness, multiple routes should be available between each pair of nodes.

- *Robust route computation and maintenance:* The smallest possible number of nodes must be involved in the route computation and maintenance process, so as to achieve minimum overhead and bandwidth consumption.
- *Localized state maintenance:* To avoid propagation of overheads, localized state maintenance is desirable.
- *Optimal usage of resources:* The efficient utilization and conservation of resources such as battery power, bandwidth, computing power and memory is required.
- *Sleep mode operations:* To reduce energy consumption, the routing protocol should be able to employ some form of sleep mode operation. Nodes that are inactive should switch to sleep mode for arbitrary periods.
- *Quality of Service:* Routing algorithms are required to provide certain levels of Quality of Service (QoS) in order to meet specific application requirements.
- *Security:* Some form of security protection is desirable to prevent disruption due to malicious modifications of protocol operations.

Mobile ad hoc routing protocols can be classified in many ways depending upon their route construction and maintenance mechanisms, route selection strategy, topology formation, update mechanism, utilization of specific resources, type of cast (unicast, broadcast ...) and so on [14]. Here they are classified by several characteristics the basis of the classification is discussed below. Figure 2 is a taxonomy for routing protocols.

2.1. Approaches Based on Route Construction, Maintenance and Update Mechanisms

These protocols can be described as the way the route is constructed, updated, and maintained, and route information is obtained at each node and exchanged between the nodes. Based upon these characteristics, routing protocols can be divided broadly into three categories.

a. Proactive (Table-driven) Routing

The first category is proactive or table-driven routing protocols each node consistently maintains up-to-date routing information for all known destinations. This type of protocol keeps routing information in one or more tables and maintains routes at each node by periodically distributing routing tables throughout the network or when the topology changes. Each node keeps information on all the routes, regardless of whether or not these routes are needed. Therefore, control overhead in these protocols could be high, especially for large networks or in a network where nodes are highly mobile. However, the main advantage of these protocols is that the routes are readily available when required and end-to-end delay is reduced during data transmission. In comparison, routes which are determined reactively introduce latency from the need to discover a route to the destination. The most popular proactive protocols are Destination Sequenced Distance Vector (DSDV) [15], Optimized Link State Routing (OLSR) [16], Wireless Routing Protocol (WRP) [17], Fisheye State Routing (FSR) [18], and Distance Routing Effect Algorithm (DREAM) [19].

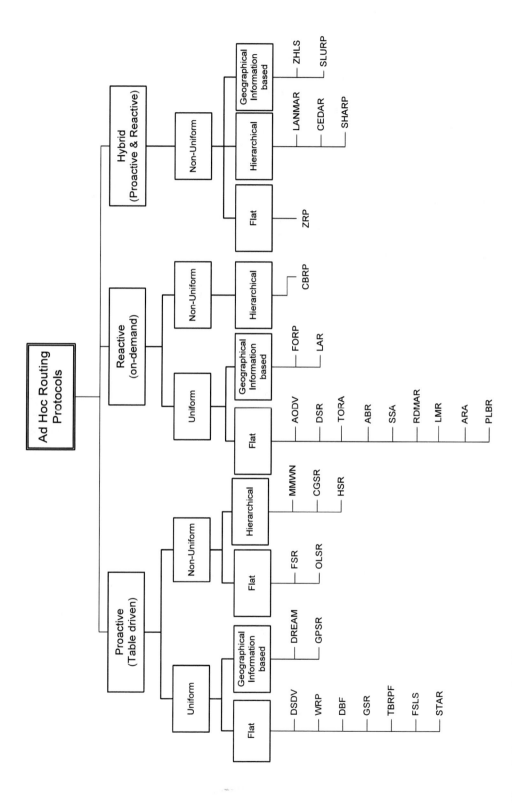

Figure 2. Taxonomy of mobile ad hoc routing protocols.

b. Reactive (On-demand) Routing

The second category is reactive or on-demand routing protocols in which the routes are discovered only when they are actually needed. These protocols consist of route discovery and route maintenance processes. The route discovery process is initiated when a node wants to send data to a particular destination. Route discovery usually continues by flooding the network with route-request packets. When a destination node or node holding a route to a destination is reached, a route-reply is sent back to the source node by instantiating routing information at the appropriate intermediate nodes. Once the route reply reaches the source, data can be sent to the destination. The route maintenance process deletes failed routes and re-initiates route discovery in the event of topology change. The advantage of this approach is that the overall overhead is likely to be reduced compared to proactive approaches. However, as the number of sessions increases the overhead generated by route discovery becomes high and may exceed that of proactive protocols. Some example reactive routing protocols are Ad-hoc On-demand Distance Vector (AODV) [20], Dynamic Source Routing (DSR) [21], Location Aided Routing (LAR) [22], and Temporally Ordered Routing Algorithm (TORA) [23].

c. Hybrid Routing

The third category is hybrid routing protocols which combine the advantages of both proactive and reactive routing. These protocols usually divide the network into zones such that each node sees the network as a number of zones. The routes to nodes close to each other or within a particular zone are proactively maintained and the routes to far-away nodes are determined reactively by a route-discovery strategy. The well-known hybrid routing protocols are Zone Routing Protocol (ZRP) [24], Sharp Hybrid Adaptive Routing Protocol (SHARP) [25], and Zone-based Hierarchical Link State (ZHLS) [26].

2.2. Approaches Based on Logical Organization, Network Configuration and Utilization of Specific Resources

These protocols are based on the way nodes organize themselves logically, the way nodes participate in route computations and the way nodes' location or routes are obtained based on geographical information. Based on these characteristics routing protocols are divided into two main categories: a) Uniform routing; and b) Non-uniform routing.

a. Uniform Routing

In uniform routing, all nodes are equal and each node participates in route computations. Each node generates routing control messages and replies to routing control requests in the same way. Thus, every node supports exactly the same functionality as the other. Uniform protocols can be sub-divided into flat and Geographical Information (GI) based routing protocols. The GI-based protocols proposed to date are mostly uniform except for ZHLS and the Scalable Location Update Routing Protocol (SLURP) [27], which are non-uniform routing protocols.

Flat Uniform Routing

In flat-routing, nodes do not form a specific structure or hierarchy. Each node has similar roles. Nodes that are within the transmission range of each other form a connection, where the only limitations are determined by connectivity conditions or security constraints. The major advantage of this routing structure is that there are multiple paths between source and destination, which reduces traffic congestion and traffic bottlenecks in the network. Single points of failure in the case of a hierarchical routing protocol with a cluster head (a special node within each cluster that coordinates the traffic in and out of the cluster) could lead to larger control overheads arising from network reconfiguration. Nodes in flat routing require significantly lower power for transmission in comparison to cluster heads [28].

Geographical Information Based Uniform Routing

In this type of protocol the location of the nodes can be obtained by utilizing the Global Positioning System (GPS); alternatively, the relative coordinates of nodes can be obtained by calculating the distance between the nodes and exchanging this information with neighboring nodes. The distance between nodes can be estimated on the basis of incoming signal or time delays in direct communications [29]. The main advantage of this approach is that the protocols can improve routing performance and reduce control overheads by effectively utilizing location information. All the protocols in this category assume that all nodes know their positions and the network topology of nodes corresponds well with the geographical distance between them. The drawback of this approach is that its above mentioned assumptions are often not acceptable and location information may not be accurate at all times [8].

b. Non-uniform Routing

In non-uniform routing, the way of generating and/or replying to routing control messages may be different for different groups of nodes. In these protocols, only a few nodes are involved in route computation. For instance, some nodes broadcast received routing requests, while others do not. Non-uniform protocols attempt to reduce routing overhead by reducing the number of nodes involved in route computation. Moreover, they have a cost introduced for maintaining a high-level structure and the need for complex algorithms. Non-uniform protocols can be logically sub-divided into flat (based on neighbor selection) and hierarchical routing.

Flat Non-uniform Routing

In this routing approach, each node selects some subset of its neighbors to take a distinguished role in route computation and/or traffic forwarding. Each node makes its selection independently and there is no negotiation between nodes to attain node consensus. A node's selection is also not affected by non-local topology changes [30].

Hierarchical Non-uniform Routing

In hierarchical routing protocols, the nodes organize themselves into groups, called clusters. Within each cluster a cluster head or gateway node is selected which coordinates all the traffic in and out of their clusters. Routing between two nodes from different clusters is usually performed by their cluster heads. The depth of the network can vary from single to multiple levels depending upon the number of hierarchies. The advantage of this approach is that each node maintains route to its cluster head only, which means that routing overheads are much lower compared to flooding routing information through the network. However, these protocols require complex algorithms for the creation and reconfiguration of clusters when cluster heads fails. Along with this there are significant overheads associated with maintaining clusters [28], such as the possible instability in the system due to a high rate of change of cluster heads at high mobility. Additional interfaces are also required to avoid cluster head conflicts. Power consumption at the cluster head is higher than at a normal node, resulting in frequent changes of cluster heads. The latter may lead to frequent multiple path breaks and overhead involved in exchanging packets for the sake of the cluster head selection process [31].

2.3. Overview of Well-Known Routing Protocols

Dynamic Source Routing (DSR)

DSR is an on-demand routing protocol based on the concept of source routing [21]. Mobile nodes are required to maintain route caches that contain the source routes of which the mobile is aware. The route cache entries are continually updated as new routes are learned. The protocol consists of two main phases: 1) route discovery and 2) route maintenance. When a node wants to send a packet to a destination it first checks its route cache to determine whether it already has a valid route to the destination. If it has a valid route to the destination, it will use that route to send the packet. Otherwise, it initiates a route discovery process by broadcasting a route request packet.

Maintaining a route cache is very beneficial for networks with low mobility, as in this way routes will be valid for a longer period. In addition, the route cache information can also be utilized by intermediate nodes to efficiently reduce control overheads. However, the broken links are not locally repaired by a route maintenance mechanism. Therefore, this is a disadvantage of this protocol. Along with that, stale route cache information could also result in variations during the route reconstruction phase. The connection setup delay is higher than in table-driven protocols. The protocol performs better with static nodes and slow-moving nodes but its performance degrades with an increase in mobility [32].

Ad hoc On-demand Distance Vector (AODV)

The AODV routing protocol is a type of on-demand (reactive) protocol [20]. AODV shares the same on-demand characteristics of DSR and uses the same discovery process to find routes when required. There are two major differences between AODV and DSR. AODV employs a traditional routing table with one entry per destination, whereas DSR maintains multiple route cache entries for each destination. Another difference is that AODV relies on routing table entries to propagate route replies back to the source and subsequently to route data packets to their destination. AODV employs the destination sequence numbers procedure to identify the recent route. All routing packets are tagged with sequence number assigned by the destination in order to indicate the freshness of route and avoid the formation of routing loops. Sequence numbers are incremented each time a node sends an update. A route is considered to be more favorable if its sequence number is higher. A node updates its route only if the sequence number of the last stored packet is greater than the sequence number of the current packet received. AODV uses periodic beaconing (periodic broadcast of routing path updates) and the sequence numbering procedure of DSDV but minimizes the number of required broadcasts by creating routes on demand, as opposed to maintaining a complete list of routes as in DSDV.

One of the disadvantages of AODV is that the presence of intermediate nodes can lead to inconsistent routes if the source's sequence number is very old and the intermediate nodes have a higher (but not the latest) destination sequence number, thereby resulting in stale entries. Also multiple *RouteReply* packets in response to a single *RouteRequest* packet can lead to heavy control overheads, thereby introducing extra delays as the size of network increases. Another shortcoming is that periodic beaconing leads to unnecessary bandwidth consumption [31].

Fisheye State Routing (FSR)

FSR is a proactive, non-uniform routing protocol, employing a link-state routing algorithm [18]. To reduce the overhead incurred by periodic link-state packets, FSR modifies link-state routing in the following three ways:

1. Link-state packets are no longer flooded; instead, only neighboring nodes exchange the topology table information;
2. The link-state exchange is solely time-triggered and not event-triggered;
3. Instead of periodically transmitting the entire link-state information, FSR uses different exchange intervals for different types of entries in the topology table.

Link-state entries corresponding to nodes within a predefined distance (scope) are propagated to neighbors more frequently (intra updates) than entries of nodes outside the scope (inter updates). FSR is suitable for large and highly mobile network environments, as it triggers no control messages on link failures. Broken links will not be included in the next link state message exchange. This means that a change on a far away link does not necessarily cause a change in the routing table. However, scalability comes with a price of reduced accuracy, because as mobility increases the route to remote destinations becomes less accurate [31].

There are four configuration parameters for FSR, the value of which depends on factors such as mobility, node density and transmission range:

1) Size of the scope: This parameter specifies the scope radius of a node as a number of hops.

2) Time-out for the neighboring nodes: If a node does not hear from a neighbor specified by this value, the neighboring node will be deleted from the neighbor list.

3) Intra scope update interval: Update interval of sending the updates of the nodes within the scope radius.

4) Inter scope update interval: Update interval of sending the updates of the nodes outside the scope radius.

Location-Aided Routing (LAR)

LAR is analogous to on-demand routing protocols such as DSR but it uses location information to reduce routing overheads [22]. LAR assumes that each node knows its physical location by using the GPS. GPS information is used to restrict the flooded area of route request packets. Two different schemes are proposed by the authors [22]. In scheme 1, the source defines a circular area in which the destination may expected to be present is the *ExpectedZone*. The position and size of the *ExpectedZone* is decided based on the past location and speed information of the destination. In the event of the non-availability of past information about the destination, the entire network area is considered to be the *ExpectedZone*. The smallest rectangular area that includes this circle and the source is the *RequestZone* and is determined by the source. This information is attached to a route request by the source and only nodes inside the *RequestZone* propagate the packet. In scheme 2, the source calculates the distance between the destination and itself. The source includes the distance and location of destination in a route request and sends it to neighbors. When neighboring nodes receive this packet, they compute their distance to the destination, and relay the packet only if their distance to the destination is less than or equal to the distance indicated by the packet. When forwarding the packet, the node updates the distance field with its distance to the destination. In both schemes, if no *RouteReply* is received within the timeout period, the source retransmits a route request via pure flooding. The major advantages of LAR are: an efficient use of geographical position information; reduced control overhead; and increased utilization of bandwidth. The disadvantage is that each node must support GPS.

3. Ad Hoc Multi-path Routing Protocols

Compared to single-path routing protocols, with a multi-path protocol there may be no need to initiate route discovery again if a link in the path is broken, as suitable alternatives may already exist, though there is no guarantee of this. Because multiple paths are sought it is also possible that amongst these routes of better quality can be selected. The ability to counteract congestion through a selection of routes is also an attractive prospect. Various general benefits may arise such as reduced end-to-end delay [32], increased path reliability [33], an increase in aggregate bandwidth [34], load-balancing to equalize energy consumption [35], and congestion avoidance [36]. Multipath routing can also act as a security mechanism [37].

There are many multi-path routing algorithms [38, 39, 40], even when their scope is limited to ad hoc networks.

3.1. Example Multi-path Routing Protocols

Split Multipath Routing (SMR) [41] was based on DSR and it introduces the notion of maximally disjoint paths based on finding the number of similar nodes that two paths have in common. The main motivation of SMR appears to have been to demonstrate the advantage of multi-path routing, whereas, given the experience of SMR, it is possible to draw lessons from its example and make some adaptations for different test scenarios. SMR prevents intermediate nodes replying in order to ensure enough route requests reach the destination. In that way, the destination can select maximally disjoint routes. SMR also alters the *Route Request (RREQ)* forwarding mechanism of DSR by forwarding duplicate *RREQ*s, provided they originate on different input links. The intention of this modification is to allow the arrival of more disjoint routes at the destination. However, it imposes a burden on the network, because of the number of circulating *RREQ*s. In fact, in the performance analysis of [40], SMR's performance was found to degrade with increasing node density because of excessive control overhead.

In multi-path DSR (MP-DSR) [42], each node maintains an estimate of the reliability of links by monitoring the signal strength of beacon packets that all nodes periodically broadcast. The product of link availabilities along a path is a measure of link reliability. Link availability is also the basis of the decision by intermediate nodes to relay *RREQs*, which takes place even when duplicate RREQs arrive up to a preset limit to accept duplicate *RREQs*. The destination node accumulates reliable but disjoint paths up to a pre-determined number of such paths. The path selection is subject to a time-out to prevent waiting for too long for a set of paths.

As an alternative to DSR-based protocols, the Ad hoc On demand Multipath Distance Vector (AOMDV) [43] was also designed with reliability in mind in networks with frequent topology changes. Because of hop-by-hop routing, it is possible to have routing loops unless destination sequence numbers increase monotonically (as the AODV protocol [20]) along the path. However, unlike single-path AODV, it is also possible to have different hop counts associated with any destination if multiple paths are propagated. Therefore, to avoid this possibility, AOMDV chooses the maximum hop count to a particular destination as the destination's advertised hop count. In AOMDV, link disjointness is established by a distributed mechanism in which only the first RREQ to arrive from the same source over different links is relayed.

In [40], AOMDV was found to perform well in high-mobility scenarios but another AODV variant, AOMDV_Multipath [44] was preferable if the node mobility was low and node density was high. In AODV_Multipath, duplicate *RREQ*s are forwarded by nodes in order to maximize the number of routes found. However, as *Route Replies (RREPs)* return and nodes overhear *RREP* transmissions, nodes remove duplicate *RREQ*s from their *RREQ* tables. Thus, disjoint routes are established at *RREP* time.

3.2. Multi-path Performance Evaluation

A drawback of multi-path routing is that a higher number of out-of-order packets may arrive at the destination, because different packets take different routes to travel. An increasing number of available paths may create re-ordering problems. Out-of-order arrival necessitates the implementation of reordering buffers in the nodes. This creates another issue of how much buffer space is needed for specific applications considering energy consumption and storage memory constraints. Therefore, the degree to which the multipath routing protocol is optimized in delivering data in their original order can be an evaluation factor of the routing protocol performance for specific scenarios.

Another disadvantage of multi-path routing is the increased complexity due to the implementation of routing buffers and the need for extra computations for different multi-path mechanisms. The increase in control overhead can be another issue in using multi-path techniques due to the necessary modification and functions. Multi-path routing protocols such as SMR) [41] and AOMDV [43], unlike many single-path protocols, do not allow nodes other than destination node to reply to route-request packets even if they have routes to the requested destination, because the routes which are not initiated originally by the destination for the source node may not be the optimum disjoint routes for the use of source node. Thus, many route-request packets are re-flooded into network and get re-propagated until they reach the destination node.

4. DESIGN PRINCIPLES OF MULTI-PATH PROTOCOLS

An overview of single-path DSR protocol [21] appeared in Section 2.1. This protocol is convenient for the design of multi-path routing algorithms for the following reasons:

- It is more efficient to select an on-demand routing protocol for irregular communication sessions between random nodes. However, unlike AODV [20], and many other on-demand protocols, DSR does not route on a hop-by-hop basis, which reduces the overhead from sending beacon or 'HELLO' messages.
- Under the DSR protocol, each node holds a route cache in which it keeps track of any (multiple) routes to particular destinations. The route cache in DSR has the benefit of storing a number of routes for a set of destinations. Storing sets of available routes allows more control over what routes can be chosen for data transmission. Besides faster transmission normally occurs, as there is no need for renewed route discovery. DSR ordinarily accumulates these routes during route request operations. In promiscuous mode, a node can also listen-in to messages that are not sent to it and do not pass through it, thus building-up its cache. The route-cache facility of DSR makes it appropriate for adaptation to multiple path data delivery.
- The DSR protocol is a source-initiating protocol in which the source node determines which path the data packet should take to get to the destination. Unlike the hop-by-hop structure of AODV, DSR allows selection of routes by knowing which nodes are present on each route. DSR is a routing protocol which has two main phases in its functioning structure: 1) route discovery; 2) route maintenance; with the addition of route caching.

Route discovery: is based on two main functions, route request and route reply. As in all on-demand protocols, a source floods route-request messages via its nearest neighbors. As mentioned previously, unlike some other on-demand protocols, DSR does not employ beacon or 'hello' messages. There are also various pruning methods to reduce the number of circulating request messages. If an intermediate node already has a route to the destination it replies with a route-reply message. On receiving a route-request, the destination also replies through the reverse path that the route-request message has taken.

Route maintenance: in the DSR protocol is based on the acknowledgment from a receiving node that a sending node receives after each transmission over a link. When a receiving node on the path realizes an error has probably occurred because of an acknowledgment time-out, an error packet is generated and sent back to the originator of the lost packet in order to inform that node about an error in a link on the path. Henceforth, the source node and all the listening nodes will truncate paths which transmit over that link. The source route must re-start route discovery.

Route caching: each node employs a route cache in order to store all the routes, whether it has received them in the route-reply packets from the destination node or by extracting the route from the header of overheard packets. This helps DSR to be time efficient by taking advantage of the routes already obtained and stored in the route cache. In doing so, control overhead traffic is also reduced.

In the first example considered, the destination node returns more than one route back to the source on the basis of maximally node-disjointness, the property adopted from SMR [41]. However, unlike SMR, intermediate nodes are allowed to also return route replies that contain routes that are not necessarily disjoint. At packet transmission time, the source node selects the shortest path on the basis of the least number of hops, as this is expected on average to increase the reliability of the path. In that sense, though this protocol selects from multiple paths it is not strictly a multi-path transmission system as it does not transmit simultaneously over different routes. Instead, it exploits multiple paths to select a path at any one time. Like SMR it provides a more efficient way compared to DSR [21] of selecting higher quality routes. DSR itself is more indiscriminate in its selection of routes, as in DSR every route request is responded to even if a node has already responded. A number of factors are balanced in this protocol. For example, allowing intermediate nodes to reply reduces overhead even though there is a risk that these replies are based on stale route caches. The net effect of this protocol is a reduction in end-to-end delay compared to DSR.

The second example protocol is based on the first but is assumed to provide still more reliable conditions for data transmission. Consequently, in this variant, intermediate nodes no longer supply route replies. The destination also delays its choice until several route request packets have arrived. It is expected that compared to DSR, the packet loss ratio will be reduced, though no gain in end-to-end delay will occur.

The first example protocol is now considered in more detail. For route discovery, the broadcast of route-request packets is similar to that of DSR. A node broadcasts route-request packets (RREQs) whenever it has packets in the buffer for a specific route, provided it has no existing route to the destination node in its route cache. Aspects of this protocol are captured in the pseudo-code of Figure 3.

Another route cache named *RREQ*-route-cache is implemented in the two protocols other than the originally route cache employed by DSR This cache is used to store the routes obtained from *RREQ* packets at the destination node for the purpose of selecting *RREPs*. The fastest route is sent in a route-reply (*RREP*) from the destination node. This route is simply the reverse route to that in the first *RREQ* header to be received in this communication session. The destination node also performs a check to ensure that an *RREQ* is from the current communication session and not a prior session. At the same time as receiving the first

RREQ, a timer is set, after which further *RREQs* are received. After the time-out, the destination node searches among its cached routes to find the route which is the maximally node-disjoint route to the first route-reply path. If there are multiple routes meeting this condition, the route with the shortest hop count is taken for the second *RREP* and sent back to the source with this route. This process can extend beyond two routes by finding the next candidate node-disjoint path.

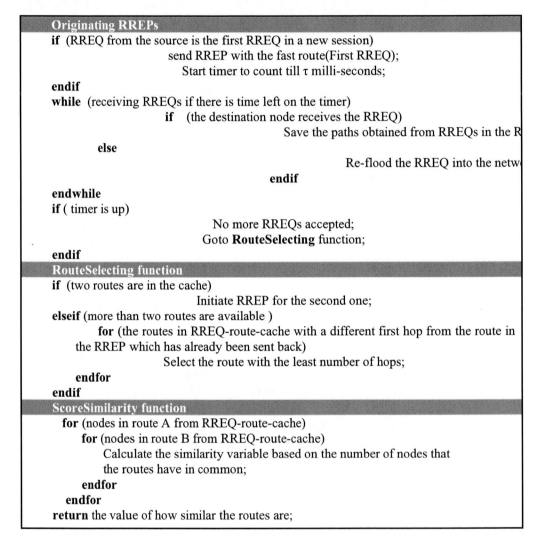

Figure 3. Pseudo-code for aspects of the first example protocol.

The intermediate nodes are also allowed to send *RREPs* back to the originator of the route requests. This is permitted despite the fact that routes sent back by intermediate nodes are not particularly reliable as they can come from stale route caches in DSR [21] or MP-DSR [42]. Letting intermediate nodes reply has the advantage of limiting the number of control packets flooded into the network for finding new routes, which leads to less control packets and faster data transmission. Therefore, we see that the main motivation of this example protocol is to reducing control overhead. To implement this, intermediate nodes also set a timer after receiving their first *RREQ*.

Each node may generate gratuitous route replies. A gratuitous route-reply is generated by a node which overhears a sent packet. If that node is on the route of the packet, the node makes an *RREP* to the source if the route reduces the hop count of the path. Gratuitous route-replies are a feature originally appearing in DSR [21]. They are not specifically mentioned as a feature of SMR [41] or MPDSR [42].

When the source node receives the first *RREP* it starts transmitting its buffered data to the destination immediately. For each new packet the node rechecks its route cache to use the route with minimal hop count to achieve fast delivery of the packet. Therefore, though there are multiple routes available, the source node selects the route with the shortest number of hops at each transmission time. This is similar to DSR, with no aim of selecting disjoint routes.

If a route fails, route recovery to find new routes to the destination is not employed unless no routes are found in the route cache of the source node. As in DSR, route error (*RERR*) packets are generated by nodes that realize the misbehavior of their neighboring nodes. The error packets inform other nodes about a failed link and affected paths are torn down.

The major effect of the applied modifications in this algorithm compared to the original DSR protocol is a reduction in end-to-end delay, thanks to an efficient selection of routes and use of *RREPs*. Besides, a reduction in packet drops is expected as more reliable routes (routes with shorter hop counts) are selected by the source. However, while using routes from intermediate nodes helps the speedy functioning of the protocol, it also leads to more packet drops, which counteracts the gain from utilizing more reliable routes at the source.

In the route discovery phase of the second example protocol, similarly to the first, each node broadcasts *RREQs* whenever it has packets in its buffer for a specific route but has no routes to the destination node. Upon receiving the first *RREQ* packet a timer is triggered at the destination. The destination acquires the routes of all the incoming *RREQs* during the time allowance of the timer and saves them in order of hop count. Therefore, unlike the first protocol, the second example protocol does not send the fastest route back to the source node. Aspects of this protocol are captured in the pseudo-code of Figure 4.

Paths are sent back to the originator of the *RREQ* packets. Clearly, the fewer the paths selected the more likely it is that the paths will have no nodes in common.

In this protocol, unlike the first, intermediate nodes do not send *RREPs* to increase route availability. That is more routes arrive from the destination but the replies are less reliable than if they came from intermediate nodes. When the originator of the *RREQs* receives the first *RREP* from the destination, it starts a timer and waits for a pre-set amount of time to receive subsequent *RREP* packets. After receiving a pre-set number of routes or after a time-out, whichever is earlier, the node starts to send its buffered packets to the desired destination. The routes are used in turn to spread the load on the different paths. In the case of no route notification before time-out, the route discovery mechanism is employed to find a fresh disjoint set of routes. Increasing the time to gather routes using the timer, introduced in this protocol, results in a small delay but potentially results in finding more reliable routes.

Starting to transmit data by the source node
Upon receiving the first route reply packet start a timer;
if (a second RREP is received from the destination)
Choose a t route different from the previous route (using the **ScoreSimilarity** function) used at this node to transmit the data;
Start sending buffered packets;
endif
if (timer is up)
Start sending data packets;
endif
Originating RREPs
if (RREQ from the source X is the first RREQ received)
Start timer to count till τ milli-seconds;
endif
while (receiving RREQs if there is time left on the timer)
if (the destination node receives a RREQ)
Save the paths obtained from the RREQ in the
else
Re-flood the RREQ in to the netwo
endif
endwhile
if (timer is up)
Go to **RouteSelecting** function;
endif
RouteSelecting function
if (one route is in the cache)
Initiate RREP for that;
elseif (at least two routes exist for the source)
for (A certain number of routes in cache)
Give appropriate values to each pair of routes based on the **ScoreSimilarity** function;
endfor
Select two routes which have the smallest value of
(**ScoreSimilarity** + X*hopcount of route A + X*hopcount of route B);
Initiate RREPs for the selected routes;
endif
ScoreSimilarity function (used by both dest and src nodes)
for (nodes in route A)
for (nodes in route B)
Calculate the similarity variable based on the number of nodes each routes have in common;
endfor
endfor
return the value of how similar routes are;

Figure 4. Pseudo-code for aspects of the second example protocol.

The implemented modifications are expected to lead to a greater packet delivery ratio, though there are an increased number of control packets. No significant change is made to the average end-to-end delivery of the protocol compared to DSR.

5. MULTI-PATH CASE STUDY OF VIDEO STREAMING ON A VEHICULAR AD HOC NETWORK

In this study, multi-path video streaming is used. In addition, the first example multi-path routing protocol is utilized. As described in Section 3, the latter locates multi-path routes but only exploits one of these paths at any one time. Therefore, each of the example protocol is applied to each of the multi-path video streaming routes. This Section now introduces essential background information, which is required to understand the results.

5.1. Multiple Description Coding

The IEEE 802.11p standard [45] operating in ad hoc mode facilitates Vehicular Ad Hoc Network (VANET) development, taking advantage of 75 MHz of spectrum (separated into seven 10 MHz channels) widely available in the 5.9 GHz range. As a result, increased safety and traffic efficiency [46] is expected to arise from in-vehicle WLAN provision. Additionally, value-added services such as 'infotainment' and business applications [45] are contemplated. Roadside sources of multimedia content [47], possibly linked in a backbone network, can disseminate pre-encoded video or serve to notify a passing vehicle of available video sequences in circulation within the VANET.

Because passing vehicles may not linger sufficiently for a full video sequence to be transferred from a roadside unit, partial storage in any one vehicle may occur. Vehicles with partial video sequences may also later stop or leave the vicinity. Video can still be delivered from distributed senders if vehicles form a Peer-to-Peer (P2P) network, because the video can be progressively downloaded from multiple vehicles that have at some time passed a roadside source. (Progressive download is a hybrid form of streaming that has one of the characteristics of simple file download, in that data *may* be buffered on a disc rather than a small RAM buffer prior to playout but also has one of the characteristics of streaming in that playout starts when the first chunk in sequence arrives and is continuous thereafter.) The vehicles act as peers in the P2P overlay network. The encoded video sequence is divided into chunks and streamed from multiple peers to a single destination that lacks some or all of the sequence. Progressive download implies that display is overlapped with delivery, implying that packets within chunks cannot be resent as this would cause time gaps in the display. Therefore, it is important to minimize packet loss. This is also because in motion compensated predictive coding loss of a packet will cause error propagation, resulting in video quality degradation that, unless corrected, spreads out from a lost packet.

Multiple path communication is common in this type of network because single paths are frequently broken or those paths may experience poor channel conditions. Moreover, Multiple Description Coding (MDC) of the video [48] enables the path diversity of the underlying VANET to be exploited by sending alternative descriptions of the video from different peers. Temporal decomposition of the video into multiple descriptions is common but has two problems: 1) though the bandwidth over any one path is reduced the efficiency decreases because of the need to include additional intra-coded frames [49]; 2) if error drift between the descriptions is to be avoided specialist codecs are required [50].

Spatial decomposition of a video frames into slices, through checkerboard Flexible Macroblock Ordering (FMO) [51] in the H.264/Advanced Video Codec (AVC), allows lost chunks from one description to be reconstructed from chunks in another description. As the same frame structure is preserved, no extra frames are required and error drift is actively prevented by the decomposition.

Figure 5 is an example of the P2P slice compensation scheme for MDC with FMO, assuming the receiver lacks all of the video sequence. Within a stream before decomposition into two descriptions, an initial intra-coded I-frame is followed by predictive-coded P-frames, supported by gradual decoder refresh (a way of preventing temporal error drift without using period I-frames). Notice that Bi-predictive (B)-frames do not occur in the less complex Baseline profile of H.264/AVC. The *same* video stream transported in MDC form is available from two sets of peers (MDC 1 and 2). That is the MDC 1 and 2 streams are duplicates of each other that are transported using MDC and are NOT two descriptions of the same video. Each frame within a video stream (MDC 1 or 2) is further split into two slices (slices 0 and 1) to form two descriptions.

The associated slice numbers in Figure 5 do not refer to a decoding sequence but to the original display frame order, as output by the encoder. Suppose P_{4S1} and P_{6S1} from MDC 1 and P_{2S1}, P_{4S1}, P_{6S0} and P_{6S1} from MDC 2 are lost. P_{2S1} of MDC 2 can be directly replaced by P_{2S1} of MDC 1. P_{4S1} of MDC 2 can be reconstructed from P_{4S0} from MDC 2. (There are other possibilities.) Similarly, a lost P_{6S1} can be decoded from P_{6S0} of MDC 1. To reconstruct P_{4S1} and P_{6S1} the properties of checkerboard FMO are used.

Both VANETs and P2P networks are decentralized, autonomous and highly dynamic in a fairly similar way. In both cases, network nodes contribute to the overall system performance in an intermittent and unpredictably manner but nonetheless exhibit a high level of resilience and availability. Prior work has explored the possibility of file download [52]. Figure 6 illustrates a P2P application overlay over a VANET, in which an overlay network is placed over the network layer. The overlay node placement is logically different to that of the physical placement of the nodes.

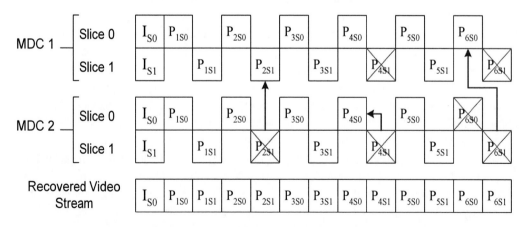

Figure 5. An example of the proposed slice compensation scheme with MDC and FMO, with arrows indicating the relationship 'can be reconstructed from'.

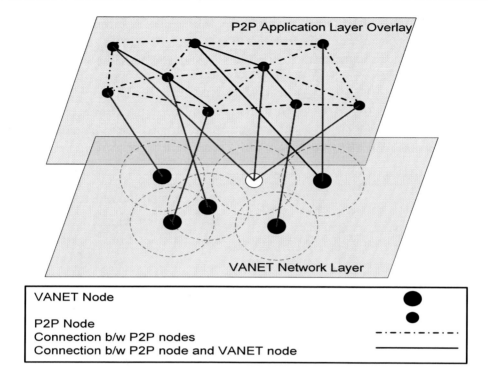

Figure 6. An example of a P2P application overlay over an ad hoc network, after [51].

5.2. Applying Multi-path Routing to VANET Video Streaming

The slice compensation scheme was compared to a simple form of MDC. In the simplified MDC, there were just two senders and chunks formed by slicing without FMO. In this scheme, slice 0 is taken from the top half of a frame and slice 1 is taken from the bottom part of a frame. The slice 0s formed one description and slice 1s formed the other description. Obviously, if packets from one chunk are lost then these can be replaced by those from the other but if the same packet is lost from both senders then reconstruction is no longer possible and previous frame replacement is required. Handover of senders also occurs periodically.

In the case of the slice compensation scheme, the chunk size was set to 30 Real-Time Protocol (RTP) packets, each bearing one H.264/AVC Network Adaptation Layer (NAL) unit, implying 15 frames per chunk or 1 s of video at 15 fps. The FMO NAL unit size was approximately half that of the size before slicing, i.e. RTP packet size was around 260 B (Constant BitRate (CBR) video is never exactly CBR because of coding issues). The need to accommodate FMO mapping information [7] in the NAL unit generally results in larger FMO slicing packets compared to simple slicing.

In terms of network performance, Figure 7 shows that, for both variants of MDC, as the density of the network increases then the packet loss ratio (number of lost packets to total sent) decreases. The bars reflect average (arithmetic means). Because of path diversity the number of packets lost is much reduced compared to what one would normally expect. Moreover, the packet loss ratios for the slice compensation scheme (labeled MDC with E.

Res) are consistently below those of the simplified MDC scheme. Therefore, there is a gain from increasing the number of paths from two to four. In fact, the ratios are also stable when the number of vehicles is increased from 60 to 100, implying an efficient solution once a certain network density has been reached. However, a problem now arises at the sparse density of 20 vehicles. This is because in some of the fifty test runs it was likely that the vehicles were widely separated and road obstacles reduced the chance of the vehicles approaching close enough to facilitate chunk exchange. In these runs, the packet loss ratio was as high as 40%, which explains the large 95% confidence intervals.

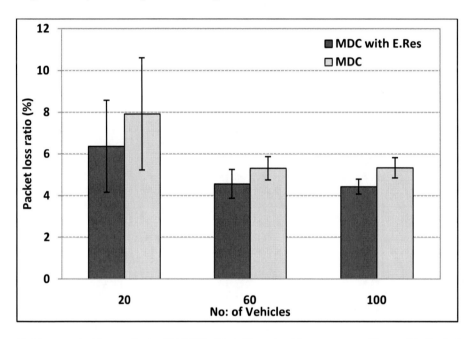

Figure 7. Mean packet loss ratio by VANET size with and withour error resilience (R. Res) showing 95% confidence intervals.

Mean per packet overhead (measured in terms of additional packets required to route each packet) increases with the number of vehicles in the network, Figure 8, reflecting the extra hops traversed. This effect is a consequence of the extra congestion and interference introduced by more dense networks in an urban VANET. As a result the routing protocol has to 'work harder' to maintain the low packet loss routes. From Figure 8, the multi-path routing protocol when used with more senders (four rather than two) becomes progressively better than the simple scheme, presumably because it has a better chance to find some of its routes more efficiently than others, increasing the overall efficiency.

Figure 9 shows the resulting video quality for one of the fifty simulation runs. The run was selected so that the indicators were within the confidence intervals of Figures 7 and 8. Also included in Figure 8 is the Peak Signal-to-Noise Ratio (PSNR) for zero packet loss. This shows that there is a considerable penalty from using FMO because the extra bits taken up in macroblock mapping, for a given fixed target CBR, are no longer available to improve the video quality. Nevertheless H.264/AVC has achieved good Quarter Common Intermediate Format (QCIF) quality for both schemes. However, when the packet loss ratio increases due to FMO with error concealment the slice compensation scheme is able to almost completely maintain video quality, while the simple MDC scheme results in deteriorating quality. Below 25 dB quality is unacceptable.

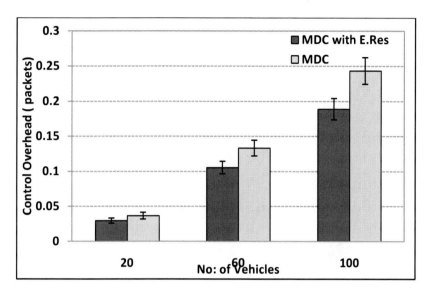

Figure 8. MDC per packet overhead by VANET size with and without error resilience (E. Res) showing 95% confidence intervals.

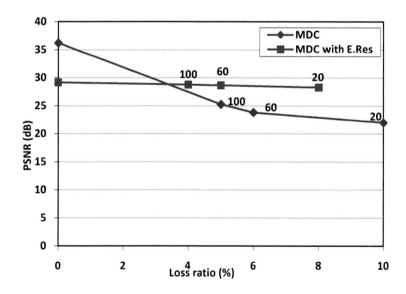

Figure 9. Example MDC video quality with and without error resilience, annotated with network size.

CONCLUSION

There is probably no one ideal routing protocol exploiting multiple paths. This is because the variety of possible applications and network configurations does not allow there to be an all-purpose protocol. By selecting from the techniques that have been applied in multi-path protocol research it is possible to construct an appropriate routing protocol. As an illustration of this viewpoint, consider the selection of maximally disjoint routes, which the multi-path SMR protocol introduced. Using maximally-disjoint routes with a high number of hops has at least one disadvantage: as the channel capacity is limited, if a packet remains longer within the network available resources are utilized inefficiently. Additionally, as a packet travels over a path with a greater number of hops, it is more exposed to the high levels of uncertainty within the physical medium. Consequently, packet delivery failure becomes more probable. These conditions necessitate delivering the packets over routes which have fewer hops and are more reliable. Therefore, in addition to a reliability factor for the routes, the number of hops in each route should be taken into account during route selection to reduce the risks from disjoint paths taking too long a path (one with many hops). Some applications of ad hoc networks, such as the provision of emergency networks in disaster areas, are not general-purpose but dedicated to a specific purpose such as providing video coverage of the scene. Application-specific multi-path routing protocols can then be adapted for these purposes.

REFERENCES

[1] Toh, C. K. *Ad hoc mobile wireless networks*; Prentice Hall: Upper Saddle River, NJ, 2001.

[2] Siva Ram Murthy, C.; Manoj, B.S. Ad hoc wireless networks: *Architectures and protocols*; Prentice Hall, Upper Saddle River, NJ, 2004.

[3] Jubin, J.; Tornow, J. D. The DARPA packet radio network protocols; *Proc. of the IEEE* 1987, Vol. 71(1), 21-32.

[4] Jiang, S.; Liu, Y.; Jiang, Y.; Yin, Q. Provisioning of adaptability to variable topologies for routing schemes in MANETs; *IEEE J. on Selected Areas in Communications* 2004, Vol. 22(7), 1347-1356.

[5] Giordano, S. Mobile ad-hoc networks; In *Handbook of Wireless Network and Mobile Computing*, Stojmenovic, I.; Ed.; John Wiley & Sons: Chichester, U.K., 2001.

[6] Goldsmith, J.; Wicker, S. Design challenges for energy-constrained ad hoc wireless networks; *IEEE Wireless Commun. Mag.* 2002, Vol. 9, 8-27.

[7] Broch, J.; Maltz, D.A.; Johnson, D.-B.; Hu, Y.-C.; Jetcheva, J. A performance comparison of multi-hop wireless ad hoc network routing protocols; *Proc. of the 4th Annual ACM/IEEE Int'l Conf. on Mobile Computing and Networking* 1998, 85-97.

[8] Jiang, H.; Garcia-Luna-Aceves, J.J. Performance comparison of three routing protocols for ad hoc networks; *Proc. of IEEE Int. Conf. on Computer Communications and Networks* 2001, 547 -554.

[9] Das, S.R.; Perkins, C.E.; Royer, E.M. Performance comparison of two on-demand routing protocols for ad hoc networks; *Proc. of IEEE INFOCOM* 2000, 3-12.

[10] Boukerche, A.; Performance evaluation of routing protocols for ad hoc wireless networks; *Mobile Networks and Applications*, 2004, Vol. 9(4), 333-342.

[11] Johansson, P.; Larsson, T.; Hedman, N. Scenario-based performance analysis of routing protocols for mobile ad-hoc networks; *Proc. of the 5th ACM/IEEE Int. Conf. on Mobile Computing and Networking,* 1999, 195-206.

[12] Trung, H.D.; Benjapolakul, W.; Duc, P.M. Performance evaluation and comparison of different ad hoc routing protocols; *Computer Communications* 2007, Vol. 30(11-12), 2478-2496.

[13] Lee, S.J.; Hsu, J.; Hayashida, R.; Gerla, M.; Bagrodia, R. Selecting a routing strategy for your ad hoc network; Computer Communications 2003, Vol. 26(7), 723-733.

[14] Feeney, L.M. *A taxonomy for routing protocols in mobile ad hoc networks*; Swedish Institute of Computer Science Tech. Report, 1999.

[15] Perkins, C.E.; Bhagwat, P. Highly dynamic destination-sequenced distance-vector routing (DSDV) for mobile computers; Proc. of ACM SIGCOMM's Conf. on Communications Architectures, *Protocols and Applications* 1994, 234-244.

[16] Clausen, T.; Jacquet, P. *Optimized Link State Routing Protocol* (OLSR), RFC 3626; IETF Network Working Group 2003.

[17] Murthy, S.; Garcia-Luna-Aceves, J.J. An efficient routing protocol for wireless networks; *Mobile Networks and Applications* 1996, Vol. 1(2) 183-197.

[18] Pei, G.; Gerla, M.; Chen, T.-W. Fisheye state routing: A routing scheme for ad hoc wireless networks; *Proc. of the IEEE Int. Conf. on Communications* 2000, 70-74.

[19] Basagni, S.; Chlamtac, I.; Syrotiuk, V.R.; Woodward, B.A. A distance routing effect algorithm for mobility (DREAM); Proc. *of the ACM/IEEE Int. Conf. on Mobile Computing and Networking* 1998, 76-84.

[20] Perkins, C.E.; Royer, E.M. Ad hoc on-demand distance vector routing(AODV); *Proc. of the 2nd IEEE Workshop on Mobile Computing Systems and Applications* 1999, 90-100.

[21] Johnson, D.N.; Maltz, D.A.; Broch, J. DSR The Dynamic Source Routing protocol for multihop wireless ad hoc networks; In *Ad Hoc Networking; Perkins*, C.E.; Ed.; Addison-Wesley: Boston, MA, 2001.

[22] Ko, Y.B.; Vaidya, N.H. Location Aided Routing (LAR) in mobile ad hoc networks; *Wireless Networks* 2000, Vol. 6(4), 307-321.

[23] Park, V.D.; Corson, M.S. A highly adaptive distributed routing algorithm for mobile wireless networks; *Proc. of IEEE INFOCOM* 1997, 1405-1413.

[24] Zygmunt, J.H.; Marc, R.P. ZRP: a hybrid framework for routing in ad hoc networks; In *Ad Hoc Networking; Perkins*, C.E.; Ed.; Addison-Wesley: Boston, MA, 2001, 221-253.

[25] Venugopalan, R.; Zygmunt, J.H.; Emin, G.S. SHARP: a hybrid adaptive routing protocol for mobile ad hoc networks; *Proc. of the 4th ACM Int. Symposium on Mobile Ad Hoc Networking & Computing* 2003, 303-314.

[26] Joa-Ng, M.; Lu, I. A peer-to-peer zone-based two-level link state routing for mobile ad hoc networks; *IEEE J. on Selected Areas in Communications* 1999, Vol. 17(8), 1415-1425.

[27] Woo, S.-C.M.; Singh, S. Scalable routing protocol for ad hoc networks; Wireless Networks 2001, Vol. 7(5), 513-529.

[28] Haas, Z.J.; Tabrizi, S. On some challenges and design choices in ad-hoc communications; Proc. of IEEE Military Communications Conf. 1998, 187-192.

[29] Stojmenovic, I. Position-based routing in ad hoc networks; *IEEE Commun. Mag.* 2002, Vol. 40 (7), 128-134.

[30] Chiang, C.C.; Wu, H.K.; Liu, W.; Gerla, M. Routing in clustered multi-hop, mobile wireless networks with fading channel; *Proc. of IEEE Singapore Int. Conf. on Communications* 1997.

[31] Abolhasan, M.; Wysocki, T.; Dutkiewicz, E. A review of routing protocols for mobile ad hoc networks; *Ad Hoc Networks* 2003, Vol. 2(1), 1-22.

[32] Javan, N.T.; Deghan, M. Reducing end-to-end delay in multi-path routing algorithms for mobile ad hoc networks; *Mobile Ad-Hoc and Sensor Networks*, LNCS 4864 2007, 715-724.

[33] Leung, R.; Liu, J.; Poon, E.; Chan, A.-L.C.; Li, B. MP-DSR: A QoS-aware multipath dynamic source routing protocol for wireless ad-hoc networks; *Proc. of 26th IEEE Ann. Conf. on Local Computer Networks* 2001, 132-141.

[34] Liao, W.-H.; Tseng, Y.-C.; Wang, S.-L.; Sheu, J.-P. A multi-path QoS routing protocol in a wireless mobile ad hoc network; *Proc. of IEEE Int. Conf. on Networking* 2001, 158-167.

[35] Ganesan, D.; Govindan, R.; Shenker, R.S.; Estrin, D. Highly resilient energy efficient multipath routing in wireless sensor networks. *Proc. Of 2nd ACM Int. Symp. on Mobile Ad Hoc Networking & Computing* 2002, 11 - 25.

[36] Hashim, R.; Nasir, Q.; Harous, S. Congestion aware multi-path Dynamic Source Routing protocol (CAWMP-DSR) for mobile ad-hoc network; *Proc. of Int. Conf. on Advances in Mobile Multimedia* 2007, 199-206.

[37] Lee, C.L.-K.; Lin, X.-H.; Kwok, Y.-K. A multipath ad hoc routing approach to combat wireless link insecurity; *Proc. of IEEE Int. Conf. on Communications* 2003, 448–452.

[38] Mueller, S.; Tsang, R.P.; Ghosal, D. Multipath routing in mobile ad hoc networks: Issues and challenges; *Performance Tools and Applications to Networked Systems*, LNCS 2965 2004, pp. 209-234.

[39] Toussaint, M.T. *Multipath routing in mobile ad hoc networks*; Tech. Report, Technical University of Delft, Netherlands, Aug. 2003.

[40] Parissidis, G. Lenders, V.; May, M.; Plattner, B. Multi-path routing protocols in wireless mobile ad hoc networks: A quantitative comparison; *Proc. of 6th Int. Conf. on Next Generation Teletraffic and Wired/Wireless Advanced Networking* 2006, 313-326.

[41] Lee, S.-J.; Gerla, M. Split multipath routing with maximally disjoint paths in ad hoc networks; *Proc. of IEEE Int. Conf. on Comunnications* 2001, 3201-3205.

[42] Leung, R.; Liu, J.; Poon, E.; Chan, A.-L.C.; Li, B. MP-DSR: A QoS-aware multipath dynamic source routing protocol for wireless ad-hoc networks; *Proc. of 26th IEEE Ann. Conf. on Local Computer Networks* 2001, 132-141.

[43] Marina, M.K.; Das, S. On-demand multi-path distance vector routing in ad hoc networks; *Proc. of IEEE Int. Conf. on Network Protocols* 2001, 14–23.

[44] Ye, Z.; Krishnamurthy, S.V.; Tripathi, S.K. A framework for reliable routing in mobile ad hoc networks; *Proc. of IEEE INFOCOM* 2003, 270-280.

[45] Jiang, D.; Delgrossi, L. IEEE 802.11p: Towards an international standard for wireless access in vehicular environments; *Proc. of IEEE Vehicular Technol. Conf.* 2008, 2036-2040.

[46] Biswas, S.; Tatchiko, R.; Dion, F. Vehicle-to-vehicle wireless communication protocols for enhancing highway traffic safety; IEEE Comms. Mag.2007, Vol. 44(1), 74-82.

[47] Lochert, C.; Scheuerrmann, B.; Wewetzer, C.; Luebke, A.; Mauve, M. Data aggregation and roadside unit placement for a traffic information system; *5th ACM Workshop on VehiculAr Inter-NETworking* 2008, 58-65.

[48] Frossard, P.; de Martin, J.C.; Civanlar, M.R. Media streaming with network diversity; *Proc. of IEEE* 2008, Vol. 96(1), 39-53.

[49] Apostolopoulos, J. Reliable video communication over lossy packet networks using multiple state encoding and path diversity; *Visual Communs.: Image Processing* 2001, 392-409.

[50] Wang, Y.; Reibman, A.R.; Lin, S. Multiple description coding for video delivery; Proc. of the IEEE 2005, Vol. 93(1), 57-70.

[51] Lambert, P.; de Neve, W.; Dhondt, Van de Walle, R. Flexible macroblock ordering in H.264/AVC; J. of Visual Commun. and Representation 2004, Vol. 17 (2), 358-378.

[52] Oliveira, L.B.; Siqueira, I.G.; Loureiro, A.F. On the performance of ad hoc routing protocols under a peer-to-peer application; *J. of Parallel and Distributed Computing* 2005, Vol. 65(11), 1337 - 1347.

In: Horizons in Computer Science Research, Volume 4   ISBN: 978-1-61324-262-9
Editor: Thomas S. Clary   © 2011 Nova Science Publishers, Inc.

Chapter 3

DEVELOPMENT OF SOFTWARE TO CHARACTERIZE PARTICULATE MATTER IN AIR POLLUTION

K. Mogireddy[1], V. Devabhaktuni[1], A. Kumar[2], P. Aggarwal[1] and P. Bhattacharya[3]

[1]EECS Department, Univ. of Toledo, MS 308,
2801 W. Bancroft Street, Toledo, OH, 43606, US
[2]Department of Civil Engineering, Univ. of Toledo, MS 307,
2801 W. Bancroft Street, Toledo, OH, 43606, US
[3]School of Computing Sciences& Informatics, Univ. of Cincinnati,
814B Rhodes Hall, Cincinnati, OH 45221, US

ABSTRACT

This chapter presents the Scanning Electron Microscope (SEM) integrated with image processing technique as a tool for physical characterization of particulate matter. The characterization process involves steps of image reading, preprocessing, segmentation, feature extraction, and representation. In these steps, selection of optimal image segmentation algorithm is the key for analyzing the captured images of fine particulate matter. A review of popular image analyzing software available for analyzing SEM images is presented. A new software employing Image processing and Support Vector Machines (SVM) for particle characterization is presented. SVM use gray level histograms as an image feature to select the best segmentation algorithm for the particle images.

1. INTRODUCTION

Particulate Matter (PM) is a complex mixture of minute solid particles and liquid droplets found in the air [1]. It consists of a number of components such as acids (nitrates and sulfates), organic chemicals, metals, and soil or dust particles. These particles can arise both from natural sources (*e.g.*, volcanoes, dust storms, forest fires, etc.) as well as human activities (*e.g.*, burning of fossil fuels in vehicles, power plants, and various industrial processes). Particles are mainly categorized based on physical (shape and size) and chemical properties [2]. As particles are irregular in shape, aerodynamic diameter is used for classification. Particles having aerodynamic diameter less than 0.1 μm are called ultrafine particles ($PM_{0.1}$). Similarly, $PM_{2.5}$ and PM_{10} are the particles have aerodynamic diameter less than 2.5 μm and 10 μm respectively. $PM_{2.5}$ are called fine particles and PM_{10} are the inhalable particles as these particles can enter into human lung when inhaled. Understanding the size and shape of PM is every important to study its effects on human health and environment.

The size of the particle determines where in the respiratory tract it will be deposited when inhaled. Particles having aerodynamic diameter greater than 10 μm are generally filtered in the nose and throat and do not cause problems, but PM_{10} can enter into the lungs causing health problems. $PM_{2.5}$ can penetrate deep into the lungs [3]-[5], causing damage to the alveolar tissues. Further, this creates various health problems like irritation of the lung tissues, which further results in a cough and other severe respiratory problems for individuals with asthma or heart diseases. Similarly, extremely small particles with diameter less than 100 nm may even pass through the lungs and affect other vital organs such as brain. The size of PM also determines its effect on environment [6]. For example, $PM_{2.5}$ are the major cause of reduced visibility in parts of the United States.

Shape is another major physical property of PM, which determines the effect on human health [7]. For example, geometrically angular shapes have more surface area than round shapes which increases the PM binding capacity to other potentially more dangerous substances thus causing more health problems. Particle shape analysis and its effect on human health is a relatively new field of investigation. The morphology of atmospheric particles received significant attention in recent years due to the particle shape affecting their chemical properties. Shandilya and Kumar [8] studied the morphology of particles present in a bio-diesel bus and characterized the particles into 14 different shapes. Further, this study showed the relationship between particle shape and its chemical properties. For example, smooth square particles were found to contain the elements Na, Mo, Cl, Ca, Al, Si, S, K, Pd, Mg, Ag, Ti, V and Fe. The semi-coarse square particles contained Na, Mo, Pd, Cl, Al, Si, S, K, and Ca while the coarse square particles had Al, Mo, Cl, Pd, Na, Mg and Ca [8].

In Section 2, a review of various techniques for PM characterization is presented. Section 3 describes the basic image processing steps involved in the characterization of PM from captured images. In Section 4, a comparison of commercially available software for analyzing particle images obtained from a Scanning Electron Microscope (SEM) is presented. Section 5 presents an automated selection of optimal image segmentation algorithm by SVMs and Section 6 concludes the Chapter.

2. CURRENT PARTICLE CHARACTERIZATION TECHNIQUES

The physical and chemical characteristics of PM will determine the effect on the environment and public health. This development stimulated interest in investing various analytical techniques. These techniques are capable of determining particle size and shape distribution along with the analysis of chemical composition of individual aerosol particles. Some of these techniques are discussed below.

2.1. Gravimetric Approach

The gravimetric approach is a method for quantitative determination of chemical substances based on the mass of a substance [9]. If the procedure is followed carefully, this technique provides precise quantitative analysis of chemical compounds present in the sample. The main disadvantage of this method is that it usually provides the chemical analysis of a single element, or a limited group of elements, at a time.

2.2. Atomic Absorption Spectroscopy

Atomic absorption spectroscopy is the technique that measures the absorption of radiation, as function of frequency or wavelength, due to its interaction with a sample [10]. This technique is used to determine the chemical substance of a sample and also to quantify its amount. Atomic absorption can identify most of the metals in the periodic table but cannot determine size or shape of the particles [11].

2.3. High Performance Liquid Chromatography

High Performance Liquid Chromatography (HPLC) extracts the chemical compound from mixture of compounds on the basis of polarity [12]-[14]. It is an automated process that takes only a few minutes to produce results. However, it requires costly equipment and trained technicians to operate the machinery. Moreover, it can only be used for chemical characterization.

2.4. Gas Chromatography-mass Spectrometry

Gas Chromatography-Mass Spectrometry (GC-MS) is a method that combines the features of GC and MS for identifying chemical substances present in a test sample [15], [16]. The GC works on the principle that a mixture separates into individual substances upon heating. Then MS identifies the separated chemical substances by measuring their mass. However, this technique can only be used for chemical characterization.

2.5. SEM AND ENERGY DISPERSIVE X-RAY

Scanning Electron Microscope with Energy Dispersive X-Ray (EDX) is ideally suited for the chemical and physical characterization of particulate matter [17], [18]. SEM technique uses electrons to provide magnified images, better feature resolution, wider range of magnification, and a greater depth-of-field in comparison to the conventional light microscope [19]-[21]. The spatial resolving power of the SEM technique is in the submicron level, which makes it well-suited for PM_{10} analysis. The EDX analysis system works as an integrated feature of SEM. The EDX plots the X-ray frequency for each energy level. These peaks depict highest frequencies of X-rays at corresponding energy levels. Each of these peaks is unique to an atom, and therefore corresponds to a single element. The higher a peak in a spectrum, the more concentrated the element is in the specimen. SEM/EDX method can be performed in three different ways which are discussed below.

2.5.1. Manual SEM

In this SEM technique [22], the filter paper is scanned manually and whenever the particle is observed, the particle's shape and size are measured by drawing grids across the filter paper. For chemical characterization, EDX analysis is used. The main drawback of the manual method is the high computational time for analyzing a single sample and the continuous human intervention is necessary.

2.5.2. Computer Controlled SEM

Computer Controlled SEM (CCSEM) is the process of automating the SEM technique for particle analysis [23]. If the particles have a good spatial distribution, an automated analysis can be performed using the CCSEM technique. Computer controlled SEM allows numerous simultaneous measurements of the individual particle size, shape (aspect ratio), and elemental composition in an efficient manner. In CCSEM mode, the filter paper is divided into smaller grids and each grid is scanned automatically. Computer controlled SEM analysis is generally conducted by operating a SEM in Back Scattered Electron (BSE) mode as this mode yields a much more uniform and stable video signal from the filter background. This thereby enables the user to precisely set the detection threshold [24], [25]. Particle brightness in the BSE mode is governed by the effective atomic number of the particle. Particles with high atomic number (*e.g.*, iron-rich) have a high BSE yield and appear brighter on the SEM image, while particles with low atomic number (*e.g.*, carbon, sulfates, organics, and biological) appear dim. To identify a particle, the computer compares the BSE signal collected at each point in a grid to the preset detection threshold. Once a signal above the threshold is detected the particle is identified and the measurement mode is enabled. In measurement mode, the distance between grid points is much smaller than in the detection mode, and the preset measurement threshold has a lower gray-scale value than the detection threshold. The computer draws chords through the particle's center of mass within the confines of the measurement threshold so as to determine the particle's size, aspect ratio and area. Each sample may take up to eight hours for the complete analysis of the filter paper. CCSEM analysis may under report data on small, low atomic number particles such as sulfates and carbonaceous particles. This problem is particularly troublesome for $PM_{2.5}$ samples that are typically dominated by such particles.

2.5.3. SEM Integrated with Image Analyzing Techniques

The latest technology for identifying and analyzing the size of PM are computer vision-based image processing methods [26]. The first attempt to use image processing for PM began in the mid 80s, when custom systems were designed using components including a microscope, camera, frame-grabber card, and software written by the end-user [27]. Development accelerated in the mid 90s, with rapidly enhanced computational power and improved microscopes. This use of modern image analysis systems for particle characterization has the capability of analyzing thousands of particles with size less than 1 μm in a matter of minutes.

PM characterization can be done using image processing methods integrated with SEM. The procedure is a highly efficient and automatic technique [28]. The method involves image acquisition and image analysis.

- *Image acquisition*: The process of creating a digital image from the physical scene. A SEM is used to capture the images of the filter paper by dividing the filter paper into smaller grids. The whole process can be automated by using commercially available SEM automation software such as Smart Particle Investigator (SmartPI) [29].
- *Image analysis*: The process of extracting meaningful information from images. Image analyzing software/techniques are used to analyze the particle images obtained from the SEM to find size, shape, area, etc., of individual particle present in filter images. Generally five steps are involved in analyzing an image and are given in Section 3.

The literature review of particle characterization using SEM is summarized in Table 1.

Table 1. Literature review of Particle characterization using SEM

Author	Year	Name of the Publication	Purpose	Method
P. Fruhstorfer and R. Niessner [30]	1994	Identification and classification of airborne soot particles using an automated SEM/EDX	Chemical classification and size determination of airborne PM	CCSEM coupled with EDX
A. M. Nazar *et al.* [28]	1996	Image processing for particle characterization	To implement image processing method for statistical determination of various morphologic parameters including area, diameter, eccentricity, and form factor of the particles.	Image processing methods such as watershed and SKIZ used for segmentation and shape factor is used for shape determination
A. K. H. Kwan *et al.* [31]	1999	Particle shape analysis of coarse aggregate using digital image processing	To compare manual and digital image processing techniques for particle characterization	Image processing techniques are used to analyze the particle shape characteristics

Table 1. Continued

Author	Year	Name of the Publication	Purpose	Method
Y. Mamane *et al.* [32]	2001	Evaluation of CCSEM applied to an ambient urban aerosol sample	To examine several issues related to the quality and validity of CCSEM data for PM characterization	CCSEM with EDX
N. H. M. Caldwell *et al.* [33]	2003	Particle analysis using neural networks and image processing in the SEM	To develop neural networks, which can themselves determine particle present in particles images properties based on image properties	Neural networks and image processing with SEM
A. Iordanidis *et al.* [34]	2008	ESEM-EDX characterization of airborne particles from an industrialized area of northern Greece	Characterize individual airborne particles collected from industrialized area	Environmental SEM coupled with EDX
T. Martinez *et al.* [35]	2008	Characterization of PM from the metropolitan zone of the valley of Mexico by SEM and EDX analysis	Characterize the chemical and structural behavior of PM_{10}, classify them in groups, and correlate them with sources, atmospheric behavior and effects on human health	SEM coupled with EDX
C. Igathinathane *et al.* [36]	2008	Shape identification and particles size distribution from basic shape parameters using ImageJ	To develop ImageJ plugin that extracts the dimensions, shape and particle size distribution from a digital image	ImageJ software for analyzing particle images
L. Zamengo *et al.* [37]	2009	Combined SEM and image analysis to investigate airborne submicron particles: A comparison between personal samplers	To compare commonly used personal samplers and verify their collection efficiency with regards to submicron particles	ImageJ software with SEM

3. PRINCIPLE OF PM CHARACTERIZATION BY SEM INTEGRATED WITH IMAGE ANALYZING TECHNIQUES

Analyzing the SEM images (after the images have been acquired) for particle characterization consists of five steps: image reading, preprocessing, segmentation, feature extraction, and representation as shown in Figure 1 [28].

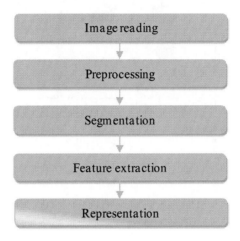

Figure 1. Image processing steps for PM characterization.

3.1. Image Reading

Image reading is the first step for PM characterization using the SEM integrated with image processing technique. It converts the particle image into formatted numerical values, which are then processed by a computer. Images are represented as two-dimensional (2-D) array of points called pixels. Each pixel represents the irradiance at the corresponding grid position. The position of the pixel is specified by $M \times N$ matrices, where M and N denotes the position of the pixel in M^{th} row and N^{th} column. Figure 2 shows pixel representation of a binary image. Every rectangular grid in this image represents a pixel, where each pixel has an associated intensity value. For a binary image these values will be 0 or 1 (0 represents black and 1 represents white) and for a gray image these value ranges from 0 to 255.

3.2. Preprocessing

This step improves the quality of the captured image before further analysis can be performed. The preprocessing step may include noise reduction, contrast enhancement, etc. Noise reduction is the process of removing/reducing imperfections such as unwanted dots, lines, smudges etc., from the images while contrast enhancement increases the contrast between object (particle) and background (filter paper).

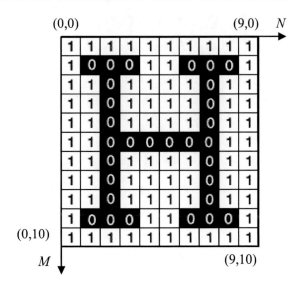

Figure 2. Representation of an image as pixels.

3.3. Segmentation

Segmentation is the most vital step in analyzing images for PM characterization. Segmentation refers to the process of partitioning a digital image into multiple segments (sets of pixels) [38]. The goal of segmentation is to simplify and/or change the representation of an image into a more meaningful and easier to analyze format. Typically, segmentation locates objects and boundaries (lines, curves, etc.) in images so as to identify particles in the image. In other words, segmentation is the process of assigning a label to every pixel in an image such that the pixels with the same labels share similar visual characteristics (*e.g.*, pixel intensity value) [39].

For particle images, segmentation methods should accurately separate particle pixels from background pixels. Currently, there are many segmentation techniques but most of these do not yield satisfactory results for all types of images, *i.e.*, one segmentation algorithm may not give the best result for all kind of images. For example, images with bimodal histogram, Otsu method shows best result and for images having sharp edges, edge-based segmentation algorithm shows best result [40]. So selection of optimal segmentation algorithm for each image is important for achieving good segmentation result.

One of the main challenges during segmentation is separating the connected particles present in the images as it will readily change the estimate of its physical characteristics such as count, size, shape etc. Techniques like Watershed [28], Skeltonization by Influence Zone (SKIZ) [28], Fuzzy C-Mean (FCM) [41], etc., can be used to separate the connected particles.

3.4. Feature Extraction

After separating the particles from the background in an image (using segmentation), particle features such as area, perimeter, size, shape, etc., have to be extracted. First, the connected component labeling algorithm [42]-[44] is used to uniquely label each particle present in image and then size, area, and other features of particles are determined. As particles are irregular in shape, the size of particle is defined as the longest distance between two edges of the particle. Finding the shape of the particle is a difficult problem and is separately discussed in Section 3.4.1.

3.4.1. Shape of PM

Particle shape analysis is a very complex problem in PM characterization. The shape factor or form factor (ff) can be used to characterize the shape of an object [45]. It compares the object's area (A) to its perimeter (P) and is defined by:

$$ff = \frac{4\pi A}{P^2}.$$

(1)

Smooth and round objects have a form factor close to unity while elongated objects have a smaller form factor ($0 < ff < 1$). Table 2 shows shape factor for different shapes shown in Figure 3.

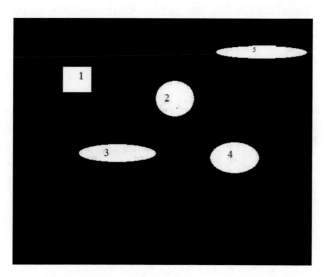

Figure 3. Synthetic image showing various shapes.

Table 2. Shape factors for different shapes shown in Figure 3

Shape	Shape factor
1	0.816
2	0.913
3	0.462
4	0.837
5	0.1721

The area is evaluated by enumerating the number of pixels inside the object. The perimeter (the length of object's border) is difficult to be estimated on digital images, and several methods have been proposed [46]. Figure 4 illustrates the simplest method for determining the perimeter of object. The steps followed are as follows:

- A new image, Figure 4 (b), is created by an erosion (morphologic operator to erode boundaries of the object) of the segmented image, Figure 4 (a), by a square (3 × 3) structural element. This operation removes the boundary pixels of particles in image as shown in Figure 4 (b).
- To only keep the borders, an Exclusive-Or operation is performed between the images shown in Figure 4 (a) and Figure 4 (b). Resultant image is shown in Figure 4 (c). The object's border is extracted as 1-pixel wide curve.
- The perimeter of particle is determined by counting the number of pixels along the border.

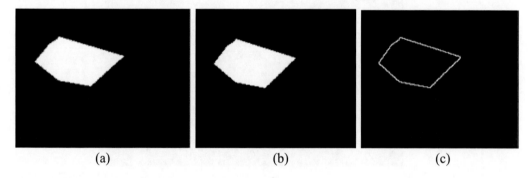

      (a)   (b)   (c)

Figure 4. Method to determine the perimeter of an object: (a) synthetic image showing irregular object, (b) image obtained by erosion, (c) boundary of obtained object.

3.5. REPRESENTATION

Data such as the size and shape of particles present in filter paper is processed by conventional statistical methods, and the results can be represented by various types of graphs, histograms, and tables. This data can be used by environmental engineers to study the effect of PM on human health, the environment, etc.

To demonstrate the use of image processing algorithm for physical characterization of PM, a case study is presented in Section 3.6. Various commercially available image analyzing software for PM characterization are discussed in Section 4.

3.6. CASE STUDY I: USE OF EXTENDED SOBEL EDGE DETECTION METHOD FOR STUDYING THE PM EMISSION DURING AGRICULTURAL ACTIVITIES

For the case study, the Extended Sobel Edge Detection (ESED) [47] method is used to characterize and compare the airborne particles present in an agricultural field during pre-application and post-application of fertilizer to the field. Particles are collected on two different filter papers; one is before applying fertilizers to land and second is after applying fertilizers to agricultural field. The images of the filter paper is captured using FEI Quanta 3D SEM by dividing the filter paper into small grids. The settings of the SEM are shown in Table 3. Particles present on the filter paper appear as bright spots in the images. Particles are collected on the filter papers using GRIMM 1.108 aerosols counter during the application of biosolids on farm fields of Ohio.

Table 3. SEM setting used for capturing images

Acceleration voltage (KeV)	30
Magnification	201
Working distance (mm)	8.8
Detector	BSE

The captured images of particles are analyzed using ESED method and results are compared for two filter paper. The results show that there is a sharp increase in number of particles when fertilizers are applied to the field. Size distribution of PM in an agricultural field before and after applying fertilizer is shown in Figure 5.

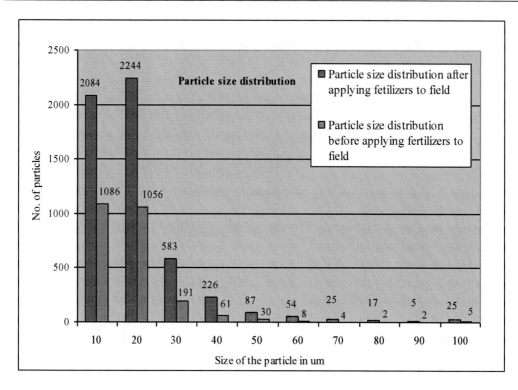

Figure 5. Particle size distribution during pre-application and post-application of fertilizers to the agricultural field.

4. COMMERCIAL SOFTWARE FOR INTEGRATING SEM AND IMAGE ANALYZING TECHNIQUES FOR PM CHARACTERIZATION

Various commercial software are available for analyzing the particle images obtained from SEM. The software can identify the particles present in the image and also determine size, shape, and other features of the particle. ImageJ [48] and Scanning Probe Image Processor (SPIP) [49] are the most popular software used for analyzing the SEM images. The list of frequently used image analysis software and their features are provided in Table 4. Features of these specific commercially available software packages are discussed in Table 5. Software such as PAX-it [50], Clemex Vision PE [51], SmartPI, and a software package developed by Evans Analytical Group (EAG) and Image Pro [52] can automate the SEM controls for capturing images and also automate image analysis.

Table 4. Popular image analysis software tools

Software	Features
ImageJ	Read, edit and analyze the images ImageJ is written in Java, which allows it to run on Linux, Mac OS X and Windows, in both 32-bit and 64-bit modes
SPIP	Read, edit and analyze the images SPIP is the preferred software package for nano and micro scale image processing at high-tech companies and leading research institutes
ImageSXM	Read, edit, display and analyze the images It is developed as an extension to ImageJ to handle scanning microscope images
PAX-it	The PAX-it image analysis software provides the most commonly sought measurement tools
Clemex Vision PE	Clemex Vision is an intuitive software program created to easily develop custom image analysis macros without writing a single line of code
Image Pro	Image-Pro includes the tools needed to easily acquire, enhance, process, measure, and share your images It can be used for atomizing the microscope control
SmartPI	Incorporates all aspects of SEM control, image processing, and EDS analysis for particle detection and characterization within a single application

Two main drawbacks are observed in presently available commercial image software for PM analysis. These drawbacks are discussed in detail in Sections 4.1 and 4.2.

Table 5. Features of image analysis software tools

Features	ImageJ	Spip	ImageSXM	Pax-it	Clemex Vision	Image Pro	SmartPI
Microscopic image file format supported	✓	✓	✓	✓	✓	✓	✓
Morphological filters	✓	✓	✓	✓	✓	✓	✓
Enhancement filters	✓	✓	✓	✓	✓	✓	✓
Manual measurement	✓	✓	✓	✓	✓	✓	✓
Automatic count and size tools	✓	✓	✓	✓	✓	✓	✓
Display measurement as histogram	✓	✓	✓	✓	✓	✓	✓
Microscope automation	×	×	×	✓	✓	✓	✓
Macro programming tools	✓	×	✓	×	✓	✓	✓
Morphological measurements on the detected objects	✓	✓	✓	✓	✓	✓	✓
Automatic particle characterization	×	×	×	✓	✓	✓	✓

4.1. Overlapped or Connected Particles in Images

One of the main drawbacks of existing software for particle characterization is the failure to identify the overlapped or connected particles. When overlapped particles appear in particle images, the existing software or techniques treat it as a single particle. This may lead to an error during physical characterization of PM such as size and shape distribution. The occurrence of connected particles in particle images is very common. The algorithms used for separating overlapped particles are discussed in Section 4.1.1 and 4.1.2. The region in the image where the particles touch will have lower intensity than the particle body, since less light is captured [41]. Although this region has less intensity than non-overlapped particles body, the intensity is still higher than that of the background. This means that when one transforms the image into binary format, *i.e.*, black-white format, these regions are viewed as a single object. Two existing algorithms for separating connected particles are discussed below.

4.1.1. FCM Algorithm for Separating Connected Particles

Data clustering is the process of dividing data elements into classes or clusters so that items in the same class are similar, and items in different classes are dissimilar. The FCM algorithm is a type of data clustering algorithm that attempts to partition a finite collection of n elements $X=\{x_1, x_2, ..., x_n\}$ into a collection of c ($c \leq n$) fuzzy clusters with respect to a given criterion. Given a finite set of data, the algorithm returns a list of c cluster center $C=\{c_1, c_2, ..., c_c\}$ and partition matrix $U= u_{i,j} \in [0,1]$, $i = 1, 2,..., n, j =1, 2,..., c$, where each element ($u_{i,j}$) is called membership value that represents the degree by which element x_i belongs to the cluster c_j. M. Korath, A. Abbas (2008) [41] used FCM clustering method for the separation of overlapped particles in particle images. FCM algorithm for separating connected particle is shown in Figure 6.

For the separation of connected particles, a given criteria can be intensity range of the gray scale image. For each pixel, the features intensity range is calculated in a small neighborhood of size say [3×3]. These features are then subjected to the FCM clustering for two clusters *i.e.*, pixels are divided into two clusters/classes based on intensity range. The implementation of algorithm depicted that there is high membership value of the connected and boundary regions in one class and a very low value in other class. When thresholding is applied to clustered image (image formed by replacing input image's pixel intensity values with membership values), binary image is obtained by highlighting the connected regions. This image is then subtracted from the original binary image (*i.e.*, thresholding the input image) to obtain image with overlapped particles separated.

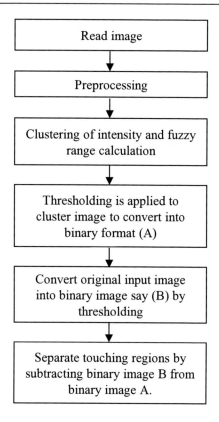

Figure 6. FCM algorithm for separating connected particles.

4.1.2. SKeletonization by Influence Zone (SKIZ)

To separate the objects by SKIZ [28], [53], particle regions in an image are first selected by thresholding as illustrated in Figure 7. Then, the selected regions are eroded by appropriate structural (square, diamond, line, etc.) elements until most of the connected particles get separated. The number of erosions is limited to prevent small particles from being erased. At this point, the background is skeletonized resulting in a network of thin lines between each residual particle. The skeleton is finally subtracted from the original image, drawing thin boundaries between each connected particle. SKIZ is highly powerful when particle size is homogeneous.

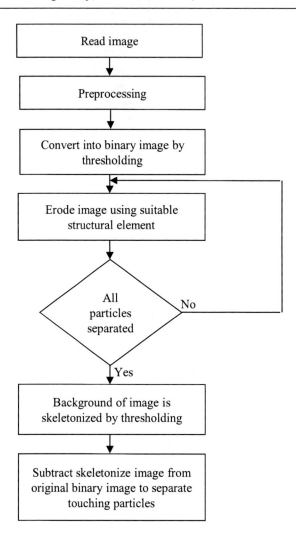

Figure 7. SKIZ algorithm.

4.2. Selection of Optimal Image Segmentation Algorithm

Another drawback that is observed in image analyzing software such as ImageJ, SPIP, etc. is the inability to automatically determine the best segmentation method for a given image. For each image, the segmentation algorithm is manually selected from a stack of available algorithms based on the user's experience and knowledge. As previously discussed, each image segmentation algorithm gives satisfactory results for a particular type of image. For PM characterization using SEM integrated with image processing method, automatic selection of suitable segmentation algorithm is required for each image captured by the SEM to achieve efficiency and robustness. Mogireddy *et al.* (2010) [47] presented a Support Vector Machine (SVM) technique for selecting the best segmentation algorithm for particle images based on image features. This technique is described in detail in Section 5.

5. SELECTION OF OPTIMAL IMAGE SEGMENTATION ALGORITHM BY SUPPORT VECTOR MACHINES

SVMs are a set of related supervised learning methods developed by Vapnik and his colleagues [54]. The SVM constructs a hyperplane or set of hyperplanes in a high or infinite dimensional space, which can be used for classification, regression and other tasks. Basic linear separating hyperplane for a two class problem is shown in Figure 8. Given a set of training examples belonging to two different categories, class one and class two, an SVM training algorithm builds a model that predicts which class a new image falls into.

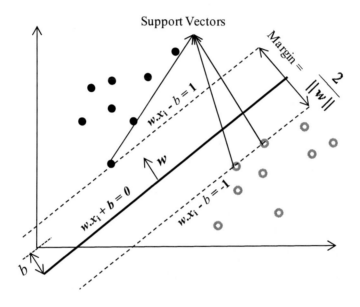

Figure 8. Basic linear separating hyperplane for two class problems.

Mogireddy *et al.* (2010) presented a SVM method to automatically predict the optimal segmentation algorithm for each image captured by SEM and then analyze these images for PM characterization. In this method, SVM is used as learning based technique for predicting the suitable segmentation algorithm for an image based on its features like a gray level histogram. Selection of the optimal image segmentation algorithm using an SVM has two stages, training and validating. In the training stage, a database is created using random images along with the optimal segmentation algorithm for those images and is fed to SVM. The SVM then classifies the training images into different classes by constructing hyperplanes such that images having similar features belong to a class, thereby learning the relationship between image features and segmentation algorithms. It is assumed that the application of a segmentation algorithm to all images belonging to a class will show comparable performance. In the validation stage, the SVM evaluates a particular class based on its previous training and thus predicts the suitable segmentation algorithm.

5.1. Designed Software

Mogireddy *et al.* (2010) [47] developed a graphical user interface (GUI) using image processing techniques and a SVM for analyzing particles images. A snapshot of the GUI is shown in Figure 9. Like other image processing software, this GUI is provided with basic image processing tools such as reading, editing, preprocessing, etc. In addition, it has the unique capability of selecting the best image segmentation method based on image features using SVM.

Figure 9. GUI for PM characterization.

The main features of this GUI are discussed below:

o   GUI can be used for reading, editing, and analyzing particle images.
o   It includes preprocessing methods for noise reduction and contrast enhancement.
o   The number of segmentation methods such as Otsu thresholding [55], Kapur thresholding [56], Rosin thresholding [57], edge-based segmentation, etc. are available for selection.
o   GUI has the capability for both manual and automatic selection of the segmentation algorithm for an image. If auto-selection is executed, the best segmentation algorithm from the above mentioned list is selected using SVM technique.
o   Particle features such as size, shape, area, etc. can be determined from the image.

5.2. Case Study II: Examples of Selecting Optimal Image Segmentation Algorithm Using SVM

The efficiency of a SVM in predicting the optimal image segmentation algorithm from a set of algorithms is presented here. Different cases considered to study the efficiency of SVM are presented in Sections 5.2.1, 5.2.2 and 5.2.3. Each case presents the accuracy of SVM in predicting the best algorithm from a set of two, three and five algorithms respectively. Kapur thresholding [56], Rosin thresholding [57], Otsu thresholding [55], Minimum error thresholding [58] and ESED algorithms are used in this study. Kapur thresholding method iteratively determines the threshold such that entropy between the two halves of the created histogram is minimized. The Rosin thresholding method is based on the assumption that there is one dominant population of pixels in the image that produces one dominant peak located at the lower end of the histogram. The Rosin method finds the largest peak in the histogram and draws a straight line from the top of the peak to first zero-valued bin and then threshold value is given by the index of the histogram bin that provides the minimum perpendicular distance to this line. The Otsu method is based on the assumption that the image to be threshold contains two classes of pixels and then calculates the optimum threshold separating those two classes so that their combined intra-class variance is minimal.

5.2.1. Case 1

This case presents the efficiency of the SVM in predicting the optimal image segmentation algorithm from a set of two (Kapur thresholding and Otsu thresholding) algorithms. Table 6 shows the SVM efficiency in predicting best segmentation algorithm from a set of two algorithms. Figure 10 shows a comparison of SVM selected algorithm with other algorithm present in the set. Figure 11 shows a comparison of SVM predicted algorithm with another algorithm present in a set in estimating the number of particles present in the image shown in Figure 10 (a).

Table 6. Results showing efficiency of SVM in predicting the best algorithm from two algorithms

No. of training images	No. of validating images	No. of images with correct prediction	No. of images with incorrect prediction	Efficiency (%)
10	25	18	7	72
20	40	30	10	75
25	25	20	5	80
35	30	24	6	80
45	25	21	4	84

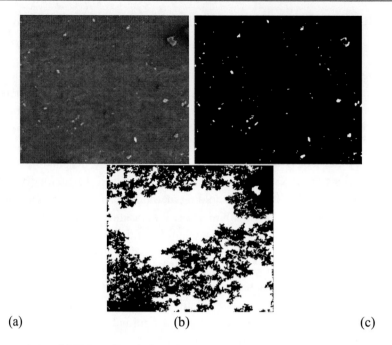

(a)   (b)   (c)

Figure 10. Comparison of SVM predicted algorithm with other algorithms: (a) SEM image of particles, (b) SVM predicted method (Kapur thresholding) output, (c) Otsu thresholding output.

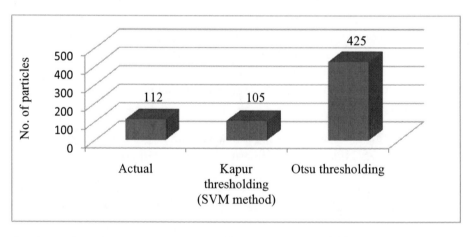

Figure 11. Comparison showing estimated number of particles by two different algorithms.

5.2.2. Case 2

This case presents the efficiency of SVM in predicting the optimal image segmentation algorithm from a set of three (Kapur thresholding, Rosin thresholding and Otsu thresholding) algorithms as illustrated by Table 7. Figure 12 shows a comparison of SVM selected algorithm with other two algorithms. SVM predicted method (*i.e.*, Kapur thresholding) is able to better estimate the number of particles than other methods as illustrated in Figure 13.

**Table 7. Results showing efficiency of SVM in predicting
the best algorithm from three algorithms**

No. of training images	No. of validating images	No. of images with correct prediction	No. of images with incorrect prediction	Efficiency (%)
10	25	16	9	64
20	40	27	13	67
25	25	18	7	72
35	30	22	8	73
45	25	20	5	80

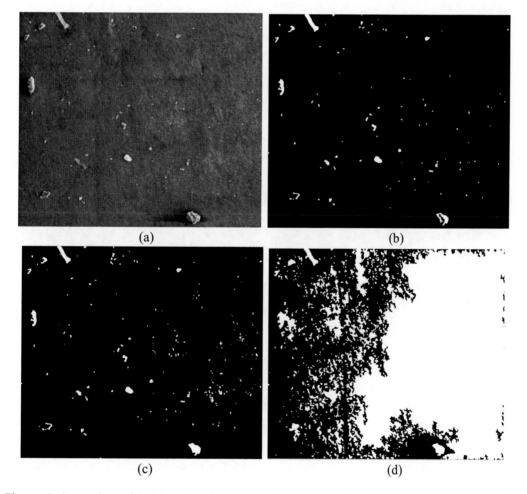

Figure 12. Comparison of SVM predicted methods with other methods: (a) SEM image of particles, (b) SVM predicted method (Kapur thresholding output), (c) Rosin thresholding method output, (d) Otsu thresholding output.

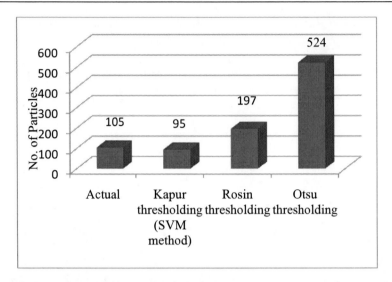

Figure 13. Comparison showing estimated number of particles by three different algorithms.

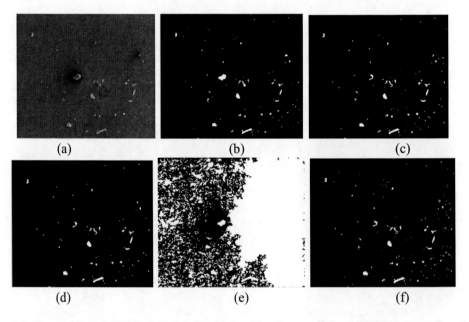

Figure 14. Comparison of SVM predicted algorithm with other methods: (a) SEM image of particles, (b) SVM predicted method (ESED method) output, (c) Kapur thresholding output, (d) Otsu thresholding output, (e) Rosin thresholding output, (f) Minimum error thresholding output.

5.2.3. Case 3

This case presents the efficiency of SVM in predicting the optimal image segmentation algorithm from a set of five (ESED method, Kapur thresholding, Rosin thresholding, Otsu thresholding, and Minimum error thresholding) algorithms as shown in Table 8. Figure 14 shows a comparison of SVM predicted algorithm output with outputs of other algorithms present in a set. SVM predicted algorithm (*i.e.*, Extended Sobel edge detection method) is able to better estimate the number of particles than other methods as illustrated in Figure 15.

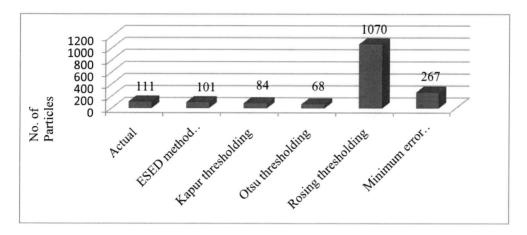

Figure 15. Comparison showing estimated number of particles by five different algorithms.

Table 8. Results showing efficiency of SVM in predicting the best algorithm from five algorithms

No. of training images	No. of validating images	No. of images with correct prediction	No. of images with incorrect prediction	Efficiency (%)
10	25	15	10	60
20	40	24	16	60
25	25	16	9	64
35	30	20	10	66
45	25	17	8	68

CONCLUSION

This chapter presented a review of SEM techniques for particulate matter characterization. It is essential to determine physical and chemical properties of these particles as human health depends on it. This chapter also presented a new software for particulate matter characterization which is based on SVM and image analyzing techniques. The SVM method showed encouraging results in automating the selection of the best segmentation algorithm and thus automates the process of particle identification and characterization of particulate matter.

ACKNOWLEDGMENTS

The authors would like to thank Dr. F. Akbar and Dr. K. Czajkowski of the University of Toledo for incorporating particulate data collection into their field study, without which, the data used in this chapter would be difficult to obtain. Financial support from the EECS Department and the U.S. Department of Agriculture is gratefully acknowledged. Filter images considered in the various examples were provided by Mr. A. Bhat, PhD candidate, working on characterization of particulate matter emitted during land application of biosolids. Dr. Devabhaktuni acknowledges the critical reviews provided by Dr. M. Deo of the University of Michigan (Ann Arbor, USA).

REFERENCES

[1]   "Particulate Matter," [Online document], 2010 Sept. 30, Available: http://www.epa.gov/pm/

[2]   D. J. Jasminka, "Physical and chemical characterization of PM suspended in aerosols from the urban area of Belgrade," *Journal of the Serbian Chemical Society,* vol. 74, no. 11, pp. 1319-1333, 2009.

[3]   N. Englert, "Fine particles and human health-a review of epidemiological studies," *Toxicology Letters,* vol. 149, pp. 235-242, 2004.

[4]   R. D. Peng, H. H. Chang, M. L. Bell, A. McDermott, S. L. Zeger, J. M. Samet, and F. Dominici, "Coarse PM air pollution and hospital admissions for cardiovascular and respiratory diseases among medicare patients," *Journal of American Medical Association*, vol. 299, no. 18, pp. 2172-2179, 2008.

[5]   M. J. Vallius, J. Ruuskanen, A. Mirme, and J. Pekkanen, "Concentrations and estimated soot content of PM_1, $PM_{2.5}$ and PM_{10} in sub-arctic urban atmosphere," *Environmental Science and Technology,* vol. 34, pp. 1919-1925, 2000.

[6]   P. Kothai, P. Prathibha, I. V. Saradhi, G. G. Pandit, and V. D. Puranik, "Characterization of atmospheric particulate matter using PIXE technique," *International Journal of Environmental Science and Engineering,* vol. 1, no. 1, pp. 27-30, 2009.

[7]   C. Davidson, P. Robert, and S. Paul, "Airborne particulate matter and human health: a review," *Aerosol Science and Technology*, vol. 39, no.8, pp. 737-749, 2005.

[8]   K. Shandilya and A. Kumar, "Morphology of single inhalable particle inside public transit biodiesel fueled bus," *Journal of Environmental Sciences*, vol. 22, no. 2, pp. 263-270, 2010.

[9]   E. Andrews, P. Saxena, S. Musarra, L. M. Hildemann, P. Koutrakis, P. H. McMurray, I. Olmez, and W. H. White, "Concentration and composition of atmospheric aerosols from the 1995 SEAVS experiment and a review of the closure between chemical and gravimetric measurements," *Journal of the Air and Waste Management Association*, vol. 50, pp. 648-664, 2000.

[10]   L. E. Ranweiler and J. L. Moyers, "Atomic absorption procedure for analysis of metals in atmospheric particulate matter," *Environmental Science and Technology*, vol. 8, pp. 152-156, 1974.

[11]   H. G. Seiler, A. Sigel, and H. Sigel, "*Handbook on metals in clinical and analytical chemistry,*" New York, U.S.A. CRC Press, 1994.

[12] M. N. Kayali, S. Rubio-Barroso, and L. M. Polo-Diez, "Rapid PAH determination in urban particulate air samples by HPLC with fluorometric detection and programmed excitation and emission wavelength pairs," *Journal of Chromatographic Science,* vol. 33, no. 4, pp. 139-142, 1995.

[13] B. S. Das and G. H. Thomas, "Fluorescence detection in high performance liquid chromatographic determination of polycyclic aromatic hydrocarbons," *Analytical Chemistry*, vol. 50, no. 7, pp. 967-973, 1978.

[14] T. I. Sikalos, E. K. Paleologos, and M. I. Karayannis, "Monitoring of time variation and effect of some meteorological parameters in polynuclear aromatic hydrocarbons in Ioannina, Greece with the aid of HPLC-fluorescence analysis," *Talanta*, vol. 58, no. 3, pp. 497-510, 2002.

[15] J. O. Allen, N. M. Dookeran, K. A. Smith, and A. F. Sarofim, "Measurement of PAHs associated with size-segregated atmospheric aerosols in Massachusetts," *Environmental Science & Technology*, vol. 30, no. 3, pp. 1023-1031, 1996.

[16] H. H. Yang, S. O. Lai, L. T. Hsieh, H. J. Hsueh, and T. W. Chi, "Profiles of PAH emission from steel and iron industries," *Chemosphere*, vol. 48, no. 10, pp. 1061-1074, 2002.

[17] H. V. Malderen, R. V. Grieken, N. V. Bufetov, and K. P. Koutzenogii, "Chemical characterization of individual aerosol particles in central Siberia," *Environmental Science and Technology*, vol. 30, pp. 312-321, 1996.

[18] T. Armstrong and R. Buseck, "Quantitative chemical analysis of individual micro particles using the electron microprobe theoretical," *Analytical Chemistry*, vol. 47, issue 13, pp. 2178-2192, 1975.

[19] G. S. Casuccio, S. F. Schlaegle, T. L. Lersch, G. P. Huffman, Y. Chen, and N. Shah, "Measurement of fine particulate matter using electron microscopy techniques," *Fuel Processing Technology*, vol. 85, pp. 763– 779, 2004.

[20] T. G. Dzubay and Y. Mamane, "Use of electron microscopy data in receptor models for PM$_{10}$," *Atmospheric Environment*, vol. 23, no. 2, pp. 467-476, 1989.

[21] Laskin, J. P. Cowin, and M. J. Iedema, "Analysis of individual environmental particles using modern methods of electron microscopy and X-ray microanalysis," *Journal of Electron Spectroscopy and Related Phenomena*, vol. 150, pp. 260-274, 2006.

[22] L. Heasman and J. Watt, "Particulate pollution case studies which illustrate uses of individual particle analysis by scanning electron microscope," *Environmental Geochemistry and Health*, vol. 11, pp. 157-162, 1989.

[23] Y. Mamane, R. Willis, and T. Conner, "Evaluation of CCSEM applied to an ambient urban aerosol sample," *Aerosol Science and Technology,* vol. 34, pp. 97-107, 2001.

[24] J. Lee and J. F. Kelly, "Back-scattered electron imaging for automated particle analysis," in: *Microbeam Analysis*, San Francisco Press, 1979.

[25] R. J. Lee and J. F. Kelly, "Overview of SEM-based automated image analysis," *Scanning Electron Microscopy,* vol. 1, pp. 303, 1980.

[26] J. P. Zingerman, S. C. Mehta, J. M. Salter, and G. W. Radebaugh, "Validation of a computerized image analysis for particle size determination Pharmaceutical applications," *International Journal of Pharmaceutics*, vol. 88, pp. 303-312, 1998.

[27] D. Johnson, J. Watt, and E. Culbard, "Automated image analysis in scanning electron microscopy as an aid in tracing the source of lead in household and other dusts," *Heavy Metals in the Environment,* vol. 2, pp. 404-406, 1985.

[28] M. Nazar, F. A. Silva, and J. J. Ammann, "Image processing for particle characterization," *Materials characterization,* vol. 30, pp. 165-173, 1996.

[29] SmartPI, Carl Zeiss, [Online document], Available: http://www.smt.zeiss.com/maximum-particleanalysis.

[30] P. Fruhstorfer and R. Niessner, "Identification and classification of airborne soot particles using an automated SEM/EDX," *Mikrochimica Acta,* vol.113, pp. 239-250, 1994.

[31] K. H. Kwan, C. F. Mora, and J. J. Ammann, "Particle shape analysis of coarse aggregate using digital image processing," *Cement and Concrete Research,* vol. 29, pp. 1403-1410, 1999.

[32] Y. Mamane, R. Willis, and T. Conner, "Evaluation of CCSEM applied to an ambient urban aerosol sample," *Aerosol Science and Technology,* vol. 34, pp. 97-107, 2001.

[33] N. H. M. Caldwell, B. C. Breton, D. M. Holburn, and T. C. W. Young, "Particle analysis using neural networks and image processing in the SEM," *Microscopy and Microanalysis,* vol. 9, pp. 738-739, 2003.

[34] Iordanidis, J. Buckman, A. G. Triantafyllou, and A. Asvesta, "ESEM-EDX characterisation of airborne particles from an industrialised area of northern Greece," *Environ Geochem Health,* vol. 30, pp. 391-405, 2008.

[35] T. Martinez, J. Lartigue, P. Avila-Perez, L. Carapio-Morales, G. Zarazua, M. Navarrete, S. Tejeda, and L. Cabrera, "Characterization of particulate matter from the metropolitan zone of the valley of Mexico by SEM and energy dispersive X-ray analysis," *Journal of Radio analytical and Nuclear Chemistry,* vol. 276, pp. 799-806, 2008.

[36] C. Igathinathane, L. O. Pordesimo, E. P. Columbus, W. D. Batchelor, and S. R. Methuku, "Shape identification and particles size distribution from basic shape parameters using ImageJ," *Computers and electronics in agriculture,* vol. 63, pp. 168-182, 2008.

[37] L. Zamengo, N. Barbiero, and M. Gregio, "Combined scanning electron microscopy and image analysis to investigate airborne submicron particles: a comparison between personal samplers," *Chemosphere,* vol. 76, pp. 313-323, 2009.

[38] Y. J. Zhang, "A survey on evaluation methods for image segmentation," *Pattern Recognition,* vol. 29, no. 8, pp. 1335-1346, 1996.

[39] K. S. Fu and J. K. Mui, "A survey on image segmentation," *Pattern Recognition,* vol. 13, pp. 3-16, 1981.

[40] Spirkovska, L. "A summary of image segmentation techniques," *Ames research center,* Moffett field, California, NASA Technical Memorandum 104022, June 1993.

[41] J. M. Korath, A. Abbas, and J. A. Romagnoli, "A clustering approach for the separation of touching edges in particle images", *Particle & Particle Systems Characterization,* vol. 25, no. 2, pp. 143-152, 2008.

[42] R. Strandh and J. O. Lapeyre, "An efficient union-find algorithm for extracting the connected components of a large-sized image," Citeseerx, [Online document] 2004. Available http://citeseerx.ist.psu.edu/viewdoc/summary?doi=10.1.1.2.5996

[43] Bieniek and A. Moga, "An efficient watershed algorithm based on connected components," *Pattern Recognition,* vol. 33, pp. 907-916, 2000.

[44] R. C. Gonzalez and R. E. Woods, Digital image processing, U.S.A.: Addision-Weseley Publication Company, 3rd Edition, 2008.

[45] F. Podczeck, "A shape factor to assess the shape of particles, using image analysis," *Powder technology*, vol. 93, pp. 47-53, 1997.

[46] J.C. Russ, Computer assisted microscopy: The Measurement and Analysis of Images, New York, Plenum Press, 1992.

[47] K. Mogireddy, V. Devabhaktuni, A. kumar, P. Aggarwal, and P. Bhattacharya, "A new approach to simulate characterization of particulate matter employing support vector machines," Submitted: *Journal of Hazardous Materials*.

[48] ImageJ, US National Institutes of Health, Bethesda, MD, U.S.A., [Online document], Available: http://rsb.info.nih.gov/nih-imageJ

[49] Scanning Probe Image Processor, Image Metrology, Horsolm, Denmark, [Online document], Available: http://www.imagemet.com/

[50] Pax-it image analysis software, Pax-it, Villa Park, IL, U.S.A., [Online document], Available: http://www.paxit.com/paxit/particle_size_analysis.asp

[51] Clemex Vision PE, Clemex intelligent microscopy, Quebec, Canada, [Online document], Available: http://www.clemex.com/Products/ImageAnalysis/Software/VisionPE.aspx.

[52] Image Pro, MediaCybernetics, Bethesda, MD, U.S.A., [Online document], Available: http://www.mediacy.com/index.aspx?page=IPP

[53] E. Preteux, "Watershed and skeleton by influence zones: A distance-based approach," *Journal of Mathematical Imaging and Vision*, vol. 1, pp. 239-255, 1992.

[54] C. Cortes and V. Vapnik, "Support vector networks," *Machine Learning*, vol. 20, pp. 273-297, 1995.

[55] N. Otsu, "A threshold selection method from gray-level histogram," *IEEE Transactions on Systems, Man, and Cybernetics*, vol. 9, pp. 62-66, 1979.

[56] J. N. Kapur, P. K. Sahoo, and A. K. C. Wong, "A new method for gray-level picture thresholding using the entropy of the histogram," *Computer Vision, Graphics, and Image Processing*, vol. 29, no. 3, pp. 273-285, 1985.

[57] P. L. Rosin, "Unimodal thresholding," *Pattern Recognition*, vol. 34, no. 11, pp. 2083-2096, 2001.

[58] J. Kittler and J. Illingworth, "Minimum error thresholding," *Pattern Recognition*, vol. 19, pp. 41-47, 1986.

In: Horizons in Computer Science Research, Volume 4   ISBN: 978-1-61324-262-9
Editor: Thomas S. Clary   © 2011 Nova Science Publishers, Inc.

Chapter 4

WEB-BASED SOFTWARE INFRASTRUCTURE FOR SERVICE-ORIENTED SCIENCE

Alexander Afanasiev and Oleg Sukhoroslov

Centre for Grid Technologies and Distributed Computing, ISA, RAS

ABSTRACT

The paper presents a Web-based software infrastructure for service-oriented scientific environments. The concept of Service-Oriented Science introduced by Ian Foster in 2005 refers to scientific research enabled by distributed networks of interoperating services. The service-oriented architecture opens up new opportunities for science by enabling wide-scale sharing, publication and reuse of scientific applications, as well as automation of scientific tasks and composition of applications into new services. We argue that existing service-oriented grid middleware, though providing a mature software infrastructure for federation of computing resources, is too complex and don't provide adequate tools for building service-oriented scientific environments. Therefore we propose a novel software infrastructure aimed on radical simplification of service development, deployment and use. In contrast to grid middleware based on Web Services specifications the proposed infrastructure embraces a more lightweight approach by using the REST architectural style, Web technologies and Web 2.0 application models. According to the proposed approach each service represents a RESTful web service with a unified API enabling service introspection, request submission and retrieval of request results. The RESTful API supports asynchronous request processing and passing large data files as links. The core component of proposed software infrastructure is a service container which implements the RESTful API and provides a hosting environment for services. The service container simplifies service development and deployment by providing ready-to-use adaptors for command-line, Java and grid applications. The service composition is a crucial aspect of service-oriented systems enabling various application scenarios. Therefore we implemented a workflow management system with a Web-based graphical user interface. The user interface is inspired by Yahoo! Pipes and provides easy-to-use tools for building workflows by connecting services with each other. The created workflow can be published as a new service thus contributing back to the environment.

1. INTRODUCTION

In solving scientific problems, a modern researcher is often faced with the lack of resources on her computer, whether information resources, processing power or software applications. However, the required resources can be found on remote servers, computing facilities or colleagues' desktops, distributed administratively and geographically. Modern networks and distributed computing technologies make it possible to provide remote access to such resources and enable integration of distributed resources in the context of scientific applications.

The first milestone on the path to widespread integration of resources of the scientific community was the emergence of the World Wide Web in the early 90's. Now the Web is the largest distributed system that provides access to a vast collection of information resources. The success of the Web stems from a number of important features of its architecture. Client-server model of Web retains control over the resource in the hands of its owner, allowing one to quickly update resource and control access to it. At the same time, the use of unidirectional hyperlinks makes it easy to refer to Web resources without requiring the participation of their respective owners. The Web is based on open standards that allow the use of independent implementations of web servers and clients.

Simultaneously with the advent of Web, the first steps to integrate distributed computing resources have been taken. The concept of metacomputing was proposed to use geographically distributed supercomputers as an integrated computing environment for solving complex scientific problems. This vision has been evolved into global grid infrastructures, focused on the integration of high-performance computing and data storage resources to support international scientific communities. Voluntary computing projects using the power of idle desktop computers have also been emerged.

Despite the impressive amount of aggregated resources, the range of today's grid users and applications is relatively narrow. This is caused mainly by the lack of high-level services, allowing the user to formulate the problem to solve via familiar, "problem-oriented" interface and transforming the problem into the computational tasks that run in grid. The complexity of existing grid middleware makes it difficult to develop such services. Thus there is a technological barrier between researchers and grid computing infrastructures.

The modern grid systems are focused on integration of high-performance computing resources for solving problems with extremely high demands on such resources, as well as problems allowing decomposition into many similar independent tasks. We argue that the concept of grid computing can be employed for a wider class of problems whose distinctive feature is the possibility of their decomposition into a set of, probably different and dependent, coarse-grained subproblems. This class actually covers a wide range of computational problems in mathematics, physics, chemistry, biology, etc. For solving such problems, a researcher can use a set of services for solving typical computational or mathematical problems composed in accordance with the scheme of solving the original problem. The emergence of systems enabling researchers to solve complex problems by composition of distributed application services can bring distributed computing environments to a new level.

At present, scientific projects relying on collaboration between geographically distributed, often – international, teams of researchers are gathering pace. We are now facing the acute problem of using the best practices and resources of all parties involved in such distributed scientific projects. More often than not, the issue involves not only computing facilities, but computational packages, applications, models, archives or data bases. This problem may be solved by transforming theses resources into remotely accessible services. Publication and share of scientific research findings, application and commercialization of such findings, and the creation of educational resources are other examples when a necessity to create such services may occur.

Service Oriented Architecture (SOA) constitutes the underlying concept of the proposed vision. As an approach for organizing a computing infrastructure, SOA develops such infrastructure starting from problems to be solved rather than technologies. It focuses on shared reuse of standard functionality implemented as remotely accessible services. New applications may be developed by means of finding and composing existing services. Service functionality may be used in several applications simultaneously. Thus, the service may be unaware of any context it is being used in. Moreover, a service may use functionality of other services during request processing. Thereby, SOA enables the transition from monolithic distributed applications to applications comprising a set of loosely coupled, dynamically discovered distributed services.

The relevance of proposed vision is confirmed by a concept of Service-Oriented Science [1], announced by Ian Foster, one of the originators of grid computing, in 2005. This concept refers to scientific research enabled by distributed networks of interoperating services. So-called service-oriented architectures define standard interfaces and protocols that allow developers to encapsulate information tools as services that clients can access without knowledge of, or control over, their internal workings. Thus, tools formerly accessible only to the specialist can be made available to all; previously manual data-processing and analysis tasks can be automated by having services access services, thus opening up new opportunities for science on the whole. In 1999, John Taylor introduced a concept of e-Science, which is closely related to the Service-Oriented Science, but has a much broader meaning.

This vision also conforms to the recently popular Software-as-a-Service (SaaS) model, where the application is provided to users as a remotely accessible service. This model offers a number of advantages over the traditional distribution model. Application vendors maintain total control over the application and run-time environment, thus simplifying application maintenance and update, and its commercialization. At the same time, application users do not need to acquire specific equipment, or perform regular application installation, configuration and maintenance. User's expenses can be reduced to service fees for commercial services, calculated on the basis of the actual resource usage.

The proposed vision, which embraces almost all stages of scientific research, consists in developing next generation distributed computing environments providing access to problem solving services and forming an infrastructure for scientific cooperation. Such infrastructure shall rely on a service-oriented approach: users transform their applications into remotely accessible services which can be found and employed by other users to solve specific problems. It should be noted that service-oriented scientific environments do not negate current grid systems. Instead such environments should rely on grid computing infrastructures in order to perform complex computations and store large amounts of data. Thus, we are facing a natural evolution of the grid concept and the implementation of new system layers above the existing infrastructure. The novelty of this approach consists in shifting away from aggregation of computing resources to focus on problems which can be solved by using aggregated resources. If grid systems developed from the bottom upwards, starting from raw computing resources, then service-oriented environments are focused on mapping applied problems to available grid resources by means of creating problem solving services.

At present, no elaborated approaches to implementing service-oriented scientific environments are available. This is due to the relative recency of this direction, and to a number of complex problems hindering the implementation of such environments, in particular as follows:

- Standardization and interoperability of services on the levels of protocols, interfaces, formats and data semantics;
- Secure access to services, including data protection, user authentication and authorization, resource usage accounting, etc.;
- Lowering technological barriers for potential service developers by means of simplifying service development and deployment procedures;
- Flexible service scalability, including on demand use of external computing resources;
- Lowering technological barriers for potential service users by means of problem solving environments (workspaces) hiding the technical details of service implementation and the complexity of an underlying computing infrastructure;
- Mechanisms for service publication, annotation and quality evaluation allowing the user to easily find the relevant service;
- Simple mechanisms for creation of user communities (virtual organizations), which would provide the contexts for resource sharing.

Despite the expertise gained in solving similar problems in the context of grid systems, present solutions are generally difficult to use and have to be reviewed. Next generation service-oriented environments should enable operation of small and middle-sized virtual communities due to expanding the range of services and resources. Therefore, drastic simplification of software deployment, management of user communities, and service development procedures is required. The available grid service development tools, such as Globus Toolkit, are primarily focused on developers of low-level grid services, difficult to use and based on controversial Web service specifications.

Besides the technological challenges to implementing service-oriented scientific environments, there are issues of organizational and methodological nature. For example, there are no generally accepted practices and mechanisms to involve researchers in the process of creating services, which potentially might become a new way of publication and validation of scientific results in the future.

To overcome the described problems, we propose to use the experience of developing a new generation of web-based applications, termed Web 2.0. The essence of Web 2.0 is in breaking the model of passive information consumer and transforming the Web into a platform for creating applications. Web 2.0 also focuses on formation of virtual communities of users for collaborative creation, editing and processing of information. An important aspect of Web 2.0 is the proliferation of web services that provide remote programmatic access to applications via the HTTP protocol. Many popular web applications (e.g., Google Maps), have not only a web-based user interface, but also an application programming interface (Web API) making it possible to integrate this service into any external application. Web service composition tools, such as Yahoo! Pipes, enable users to literally build a new application (aka mashup) from existing services and then make it available for everyone as a new service. This aspect is extremely important, because it triggers the self-development and growth of the service ecosystem. The focus on the end user convenience and ease of service development has led to the avoidance of complicated technologies and standards (such as SOAP, WSDL and UDDI) in favor of lightweight approaches based on the REST architectural style.

The paper presents a MathCloud environment which implements a web-based software infrastructure for service-oriented scientific environments. The main goals of the proposed infrastructure is to provide a unified access to problem solving computing services and to enable integration of these services in the context of scientific applications. The proposed approach assigns primary importance to the simplification of service development, ease of access to services and use of open technologies. For this purpose, the REST architectural style, modern Web technologies and Web 2.0 application models are used. Service-oriented approach allows the user of MathCloud to abstract away from the specific resources required to solve the problem and to formulate a request in terms of its research domain, thereby increasing the ease of use of the environment. The proposed approach is also well suited for integration of scientific applications, such as numerical libraries and solvers. If the processing of service request requires substantial computing resources, the request can be, transparently for the user, transformed into computational tasks that run on a cluster or grid. Thus the proposed approach helps to eliminate the existing barriers between researchers and grid computing infrastructures.

2. ARCHITECTURE

The architecture of MathCloud consists of several layers, shown in Fig. 1.

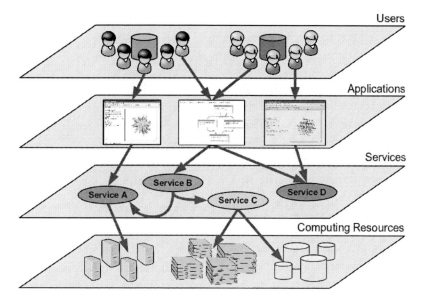

Figure 1. MathCloud architecture.

2.1. Computing Resources Layer

The lower layer of MathCloud architecture comprises various computing resources used for operating services (e.g., computing and data storage facilities). Such computing infrastructure, including unified mechanisms for accessing computing resources, has already been developed within modern grid systems. However, it should be noted that existing grid infrastructures are designed for time-limited computing jobs and do not support deployment of services. A new model enabling lease of virtualized computing resources (cloud computing) is being actively developed within commercial systems, such as Amazon EC2, thus allowing for the long-term operation of services on such resources.

The layer of computing resources does not actually refer to the service-oriented environment but emerges from resources available to service developers and users. Such resources may be accessed via respective computing infrastructure interfaces. However, due to inherent complexity of such interfaces and grid middleware, MathCloud provides ready-to-use adapters which enable automatic translation of service requests into jobs submitted to computing resources. Such adapters also considerably simplify transformation of existing grid applications into services.

2.2. Services Layer

The Services layer implements remote programmatic access to specific functionality required by users. Application services, which represent core components of MathCloud environment, focus on solving applied problems of a specific class and provide the basis for application development. System services provide such universal functionality as service publication and discovery. Additional services (e.g., data processing of transformation services) are allowed. As mentioned above, services depend on underlying computing resources used for complex computations and data storage.

Let us consider the model of application service in MathCloud.

The application service (hereinafter referred to as 'the service') represents a program component which is remotely accessible through a network, and supports a solution for a certain class of problems using appropriate computing algorithms. In accordance with the client-server model, the service processes incoming client's requests to solve specific problems. A client's request includes a parameterized description of the problem, which is formulated as a finite set of input parameters. Having processed the request successfully, the service returns the result to client as a finite set of output parameters.

To interact with a service a client needs to know the list of input and output parameters of the service. This information is part of the service description published somewhere or provided by the service upon the client's request. The description of service parameters defines the contract to be followed by the client and service. This description should support machine interpretation in order to enable message validation, generation of client code or implementation of dynamic calls.

The described service model is quite general and can be applied to a large class of services which may or may not provide access to computing algorithms. In particular, these include services providing access to databases, or services performing data processing or conversion. Nevertheless, in the context of MathCloud we consider mostly algorithmic services focused on solving computational problems. Let us describe some distinctive features of such services.

First of all, each service request is processed independently from other requests. In other words, request results depend only on values of input parameters provided by the client regardless of the results of other requests. This feature can be formulated as a restriction requiring a client to store all application state. While leaving behind some interactive client-server applications relying on a client session stored on the server side, this restriction makes it possible to simplify the service interface and implementation, and to increase scalability and fault-tolerance of the environment. It should be mentioned that this restriction is often imposed to services within the service-oriented architecture.

The second important feature of algorithmic services concerns the processing of client's request (problem solving), which often involves performing time-consuming computations and may be accompanied by running jobs on computing facilities or in grids. In this case the service cannot return the result immediately after receiving the request. The processing of such requests should be performed in an asynchronous mode, by converting incoming requests into asynchronous jobs. The job identifier is returned in response to the client's request so that the client may check the status of his job (pull mode) and receive the result. The client may also receive notifications on any job state change from the service (push mode).

Third, there are increasingly many algorithmic services receiving large volumes of data at input and/or generating them as results. Effective transfers of large-volume parameters should be provided for such services using appropriate data transfer mechanisms across the network. In this case, a service request or a request result may not contain the actual parameter values, but only links to appropriate data files.

Besides that, the service description should include information not only about service parameters, but also about the class of problems solved by the service, used algorithms and numerical methods, accuracy of results, etc. It is rather difficult to make a formal description of such information in a machine-interpretable form due to specific requirements of certain application domains. In general, such information may be provided in any form suitable for the user's review.

In order to simplify reuse and composition of services within different applications, it is essential to unify remote access to services. For these purposes, MathCloud uses REST architectural style and JSON format. The unified interface to be implemented by all MathCloud application services is described in Chapter 3.

The MathCloud environment is an open distributed system, where in order to participate a service should only comply with the unified service interface. The choice of service implementation technologies and programming languages is left to the developer. Nevertheless, ready-to-use tools which simplify service development are required, especially for unskilled developers. Such tools are very important in order to quickly transform to services existing applications (e.g., solvers with command line interface). Therefore a general-purpose service runtime or container called Everest was developed (see Chapter 4).

2.3. Applications Layer

The Applications layer implements remote access to MathCloud services via application interfaces. A web browser is recommended for use as a standard application run-time environment giving a number of advantages: the application is immediately ready for use without being installed on the user's computer, while the application developer retains total control over the application, making it possible to update application and track its usage. Just as for services, the architecture should not impose any significant constraints on technologies and programming languages used for application development.

It should be noted that some services may already have an end-user interface. However, one should distinguish between service and application concepts in general. While a service provides a programming interface for applications, an application provides an interface for users. So, one service may be simultaneously used in several applications. And vice versa: a number of services may be simultaneously involved in one application. Let us discuss the last option in a greater detail.

The key function of proposed service-oriented environment is to provide support for service composition, which enables the user to create new applications from available services and then publish these applications as new services, thus contributing to the environment. In general, services may be composed by using any programming tools (e.g., scripting languages). However, similar to the case of service development, ready-to-use tools are to be provided in order to simplify service composition and be readily available to unskilled users. Therefore we implemented a workflow management system with a Web-based graphical user interface (see Chapter 5). The user interface is inspired by Yahoo! Pipes and provides easy-to-use tools for building workflows by connecting services with each other.

2.4. Users Layer

The social aspects of the environment are concentrated on the Users layer. These include issues related to the creation and management of user communities. Such communities, similar to virtual organizations in grids, can be formed within certain research areas or projects to provide contexts for sharing services and resources. First, publication, annotation and accounting of services may be performed within such a community. Second, just as for the grid, access to services may be regulated depending on the user's membership in a specific community. Third, application interfaces may be integrated into community portals, thus providing convenient access to community-related services. This layer of MathCloud architecture is currently the least well-developed one since current efforts are focused on the lower technological layers.

3. SERVICE INTERFACE

The described architecture is fairly general and can be implemented by using various distributed programming technologies. The choice of technology depends on a number of factors, such as popularity, ease of development and use of an open source license. The availability of open standards and a set of independent implementations of underlying technology are crucial within scientific service-oriented environments in order to allow for the participation of different entities and parties. For MathCloud it is also important that the used technology conforms as closely as possible to the described model of algorithmic service.

Currently, the dominant technology for building service-oriented systems are web services based on SOAP protocol and numerous WS-* specifications (hereinafter referred to as 'big web services'). The specifications of big web services are open standards focused on implementation of various aspects of service-oriented architecture on top of the Web. These specifications are actively supported by major vendors, which led to the widespread use of big web services and the appearance of many implementations, including open source ones.

A common criticism of big web services is their excessive complexity and incorrect use of the core principles of Web architecture, which casts doubt on the prefix "web" in their title. The advantages of using big web services only apply to certain classes of applications supporting complex business processes that occur in corporate and government systems, while rarely present in Web 2.0 or scientific applications. This led to the emergence of alternative, more lightweight approaches to implementation of web services based on direct use of HTTP protocol.

In 2000, Roy Fielding, one of the principal authors of the HTTP specification, published doctoral dissertation [2] describing the key architectural principles of the Web. These architectural principles defined in the form of restrictions imposed on the architecture of distributed system are known as Representational State Transfer (REST) architectural style. The central concepts of REST are resource, its' identifier and representation. REST introduces the following constraints on the system architecture: client-server separation, stateless client-server protocol (application state is held on the client side), caching of server responses, uniform resource interface, layered architecture with intermediaries. These restrictions enable such properties of the Web architecture as scalability, extensibility and openness. REST style is generic and can be applied to architecture of web-based applications and other distributed systems.

Thanks to the uniform interface for accessing resources, the use of open standards (HTTP, URI) and the presence of multiple proven implementations (web servers, HTTP libraries for all modern programming languages), REST provides maximum freedom for independent development of web services and related client applications. Another important factor is the ease of service development compared to big web services that makes it possible to maximize both the number of potential developers and users of services, while ensuring the compatibility of different implementations and extensive reuse of services. This led to a proliferation of the so-called RESTful Web-services [3], especially within Web 2.0 applications.

Thus, in contrast to modern grid middleware based mostly on big web services, MathCloud embraces a more lightweight approach by using the REST architectural style, Web technologies and Web 2.0 application models. According to the proposed approach each MathCloud service represents a RESTful web service with a unified interface accessible via HTTP. The service interface takes into account features of algorithmic services by supporting asynchronous request processing and passing large data parameters as links. Also, in accordance with service-oriented approach, the designed interface supports introspection, i.e. obtaining information about the service. The proposed interface allows independent implementations in various programming languages.

In accordance with the principles of REST, the interface of MathCloud service is formed by a set of resources identified by URIs and accessible via standard HTTP methods (Table 1). These resources are:

- Service, identified by SERVICE_URI;
- Job, identified by JOB_URI;
- File, identified by FILE_URI;
- Server, identified by SERVER_URI (optional resource).

Table 1. Resources and methods of service interface

Resource	GET	POST	DELETE
Service SERVICE_URI	Get service description	Submit request to service	---
Job JOB_URI	Get job status and results	---	Cancel job, delete job results
File FILE_URI	Get file contents	---	---
Server SERVER_URI	Get list of services located on the server	---	---

The service resource supports two HTTP methods. GET method returns to the client the service description. POST method allows client to submit a request to server. The request body contains values of input parameters describing a problem to solve. Some of these values may contain identifiers of file resources. In response to the request, the service creates a new subordinate job resource and returns to the client identifier and current representation of the job resource.

The job resource supports GET and DELETE methods. GET method returns job representation with information about current job status. This information includes job state which may take the following values:

- WAITING — the job is not started yet;
- RUNNING — the job is running;
- DONE — the job is completed successfully;
- FAILED — the job is failed.

If the job is completed successfully (DONE state), then the job representation also contains job results in the form of values of output parameters. Some of these values may contain identifiers of file resources. If some of output values have became available during the job execution, these values can be included in the job representation without waiting for the job to finish.

The DELETE method of job resource allows client to cancel job execution or, if the job is already executed, delete job results. This method destroys the job resource and its subordinate file resources.

The file resource represents a part of client request or job result provided as a remote file. The file contents can be downloaded via the GET method.

The optional server resource is designed for cases in which a single HTTP server hosts several services. In these cases it may be useful to get a list of services located on the server. For these purposes, GET method is reserved. The service resource is subordinate to corresponding server resource.

Note that the described interface does not prescribe specific templates for resource URIs, which may vary between implementations. Nevertheless, it is recommended to respect the described hierarchical relationships between resources while constructing these URIs.

The described interface supports job processing in both synchronous and asynchronous modes. Indeed, if the job result can be immediately returned to the client, then it is transmitted inside the returned job resource representation along with the indication of DONE state. If, however, the processing of request will take a time, it is stated in the returned job resource representation by specifying the appropriate job state (WAITING or RUNNING). In this case, the client uses the passed JOB_URI for further checking of job state and obtaining its results.

Such a scheme, on the one hand, provides a maximum freedom of services in selecting a strategy for processing each individual request. On the other hand, the client implementation is required to support both scenarios. Why some requests can be processed quickly, while others do not? This may be due to the dependence of the algorithm execution time on the values of input parameters, or due to the high rate of incoming requests and their possible prioritization. Thus, in general, it is difficult a priori to predict the mode of processing the request. These considerations led to the described interface.

Consider data representation formats to be used during communication between client and service. The most widely used data representation formats on the Web are HTML, XML and JSON. The first one is used mainly to display information to the user via web browser. Two other formats are used for implementing web services. XML, designed as an universal format for data exchange between software systems, is widely used by big web services. JSON (JavaScript Object Notation) format has gained popularity in the past few years as a lightweight alternative to XML used by many web applications and RESTful web services.

As a primary data representation format for MathCloud service interface JSON has been chosen for the following reasons:

- More compact representation of data structures, while XML is focused on representation of arbitrary documents;
- The libraries for reading and writing JSON data are available for all major programming languages;
- Tight integration with JavaScript language simplifying creation of Ajax-based web interfaces.

A known disadvantage of JSON is the lack of standard tools for description and validation of the JSON data structure, comparable to XML Schema. However, there is an active ongoing work on such format called JSON Schema [4], which is currently used in MathCloud for describing service parameters.

The HTTP protocol supports specification of request format via the Content-Type header, as well as dynamic negotiation of response format via the Accept header. The values of these headers represent identifiers of MIME types registered with IANA. These features of HTTP allow the service to support, within the described interface, multiple representation formats used depending on the type of client or other circumstances.

For example, the service implementation can support HTML as an additional representation format in order to make the service accessible to users via Web browser. Also, a standard "multipart/form-data" format can be used in order to submit a request to service via a Web form. However, the specific representations of requests and responses for such additional formats are not prescribed in the service interface specification.

Table 2 lists possible representation formats of requests and responses for each resource-method pair within the interface of MathCloud service. The described interface can be easily extended in the future by adding new formats.

Table 2. Possible data representation formats within the service interface

Resource	GET	POST	DELETE
Service SERVICE_URI	Accept: aplication/json text/html	Content-Type: application/json multipart/form-data Accept: aplication/json text/html	---
Job JOB_URI	Accept: aplication/json text/html	---	---
File FILE_URI	Content-Type: determined by the file type	---	---
Server SERVER_URI	Accept: aplication/json text/html	---	---

4. SERVICE CONTAINER

The availability of ready and easy to use tools for creating services is very important for expanding the range of potential service developers. To simplify the process of service development in MathCloud a service container called Everest was implemented. The container represents a universal service runtime which implements the above service interface.

The universality of Everest means that it makes it easy, in many cases without writing a code, to transform into MathCloud services a wide range of existing applications. Besides that, the support for pluggable adapters allows one to attach arbitrary service implementations and computing resources. For example, such adapter can implement access to grid infrastructure by transforming service requests to jobs submitted to grid.

Everest is based on Jersey library, a reference implementation of JAX-RS (Java API for RESTful Web Services) specification. Fig. 2 shows the architecture of Everest. The container uses built-in Jetty Web server for interaction with service clients. Incoming HTTP requests are forwarded to Jersey and then to Everest. The communication between Jersey and Everest is implemented by means of Java classes that correspond to resources from the described service interface (ServerResource, ServiceResource, JobResource, FileResource).

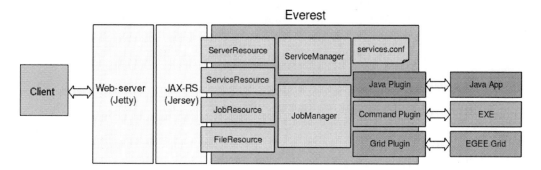

Figure 2. Everest architecture.

Everest is processing client requests in accordance with configuration information. The ServiceManager component maintains a list of services deployed in the container and their configuration. This information is read at startup from configuration files. The configuration of each service consists of two parts:

- external service description, transmitted to clients (service annotation, descriptions of input and output parameters);
- internal service configuration, which contains information on the service implementation (adapter and its configuration settings).

The JobManager component manages the processing of incoming requests. The requests are converted into jobs and placed in a queue served by a configurable pool of handler threads. During job processing, handler thread invokes adapter specified in the service configuration.

The components that implement processing of service requests (jobs) are provided in the form of pluggable adapters. Each adapter implements a standard interface through which the container passes request parameters, monitors the job state and receives results. The adapter implementation usually converts a service request to an execution of external application. After successful application execution the adapter collects results and changes the job state to DONE.

Currently the following universal adapters are implemented:

- Command adapter for integration of command-line applications;
- Java adapter for integration of Java applications;
- gLite adapter for integration of grid applications based on gLite middleware.

The Command adapter converts service request to an execution of specified command in a separate process. The internal service configuration contains the command to execute and information about mappings between service parameters and command arguments or external files.

The Java adapter performs invocation of a specified Java class inside the current Java virtual machine, passing request parameters inside the call. The specified class must implement standard Java interface. The internal service configuration includes the name of the corresponding class.

The gLite adapter performs translation of service request into a grid job submitted to the EGEE grid infrastructure, which is based on gLite middleware. This adapter can be used both to convert to service existing grid application and to port existing service implementation to the grid. The internal service configuration contains the name of grid virtual organization, the path to the grid job description file and information about mappings between service parameters and job arguments or files.

Note that the Command and gLite adapters enable one to convert existing applications into services without developing additional software components. This feature makes it possible for unskilled users to quickly publish as services a wide range of existing applications.

Each service deployed in Everest is published via described service interface. In addition to standard JSON format, Everest supports complementary HTML version of this interface allowing users to access the service via a web browser.

5. SERVICE COMPOSITION

In order to simplify composition of MathCloud services for problem solving a workflow management system is developed. The system supports description, storage, publication and execution of workflows composed of multiple services. Workflows are represented as directed acyclic graphs and described by means of a visual editor. The described workflow can be published as a new composite service and then executed by sending request to this service. The system hides from users the low-level details of service calls and data transfer between services, leaving only the need for correct connection of services with each other. This enables rapid development of new applications and services by users without distributed programming skills. The graphical representation of workflow allows to visualize relationships between services. Such representation also allows one to quickly make changes to existing workflows by adding or replacing actions, thus creating new workflows and services.

The workflow management system has client-server architecture (Fig. 3). The client part of the system is represented by workflow editor, while the server part contains workflow management service (WMS) and workflow runtime.

The workflow editor implements a graphical user interface of the system. The editor is a client of WMS, and can run on any machine on the network. The main functions of the editor are viewing and editing of workflows. The created workflow can be saved and executed on the server side. In this case the editor can display the state of a running workflow instance.

The WMS implements a remote interface for storing workflows created with the editor. In accordance with the service-oriented approach, the WMS also performs the deployment of each saved workflow as a new MathCloud service. The subsequent workflow execution is performed by sending a request to the new composite service through the standard interface described in Chapter 3.

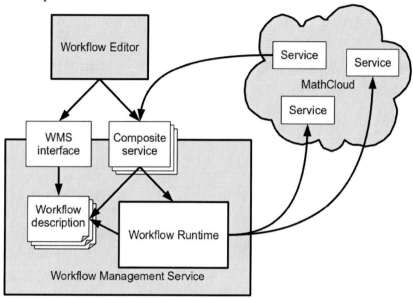

Figure 3. The architecture of workflow management system.

The workflow runtime is processing requests to composite services. Each request triggers creation and execution of the new instance of corresponding workflow. In order to do this the workflow runtime receives description of the workflow and the values of its input parameters. The runtime performs interpretation of the workflow description by executing specified actions (including invocation of external services), updates the status of workflow and collects the results of workflow execution.

5.1. Workflow Editor

The workflow editor is implemented as a Web application in JavaScript language. Thus the editor can be used without installation on any computer running a modern Web browser. The editor is created with extensive use of Ajax techniques and is based on a number of JavaScript libraries, such as WireIt, YUI and InputEx. This allowed us to make the editor interface lightweight, intuitive and user friendly.

Fig. 4 shows the interface of the workflow editor. The right side of the editor contains a list of available services and other basic blocks from which the user can compose a workflow. The upper part is a main menu that provides access to basic operations with workflows, such as opening, saving, running, etc. The main area of the editor contains a graphical representation of workflow.

The workflow is represented in the form of a directed acyclic graph whose vertices correspond to workflow blocks and edges define data flow between the blocks. Each block has a set of inputs and outputs displayed in the form of round ports at the top and at the bottom of the block respectively. Each block implements certain logic of processing of the input data. Data transfer between blocks is realized by connecting the output of one block to the input of another block. Each input or output has associated data type. The compatibility of data types is checked during connecting the ports.

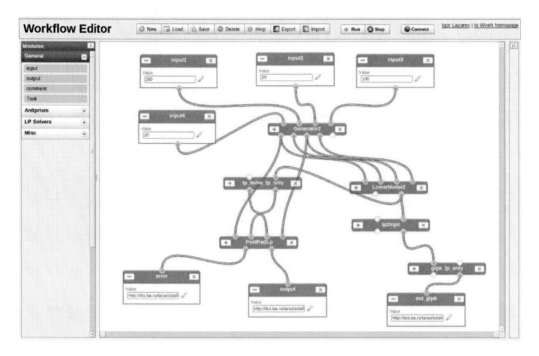

Figure 4. The interface of the workflow editor.

The following types of workflow blocks are implemented at the moment:

- Input — used to define and set the input parameter of the workflow;
- Output — used to define and display the output parameter of the workflow;
- Service — invokes the specified MathCloud service;
- JavaScript — performs execution of the specified code in JavaScript;
- Python — performs execution of the specified code in Python;
- Comment — contains arbitrary comments.

The introduction of MathCloud service in a workflow is realized by creating a new Service block and specifying the service URI. The editor retrieves service description and extracts information about the number, types and names of input and output parameters of the service. This information is used to dynamically generate the corresponding inputs and outputs of the block. The block title is set to the name of the service. If the service is unreachable the block is painted red.

To simplify the creation of Input and Output blocks, the editor supports automatic generation of such blocks by clicking on input or output of any existing block.

The JavaScript and Python blocks help to increase the flexibility of workflows by introducing the code snippets (scripts). A script is specified as a function whose signature is used to dynamically generate inputs and title of the corresponding block. The block output corresponds to the return value of the function. The execution of script is performed on the server side, inside the workflow runtime.

The editor allows a user to save created workflow in the WMS. The user can also browse a list of saved workflows, open or delete a workflow, and import or export workflow description in JSON format.

An important feature of the editor is ability to run a workflow and display its state during the execution. Before the workflow can be run it is necessary to set the values of all input parameters of the workflow via the appropriate Input blocks. After the user clicks on the Run button, the editor makes a call with the specified input parameters to the composite service representing the workfow. Then the editor performs a periodic check of the status of running job, which includes information about states of individual blocks of the workflow. This information is displayed to the user by painting each workflow block in the color corresponding to its current state (Fig. 5). After successful completion of the workflow, the values of workflow output parameters are displayed in the Output blocks. Each workflow instance has a unique URI (same as the job resource in the service interface) which can be used to open the current state of the instance in the editor at any time. This feature is especially important in cases where the workflow runs for a long time.

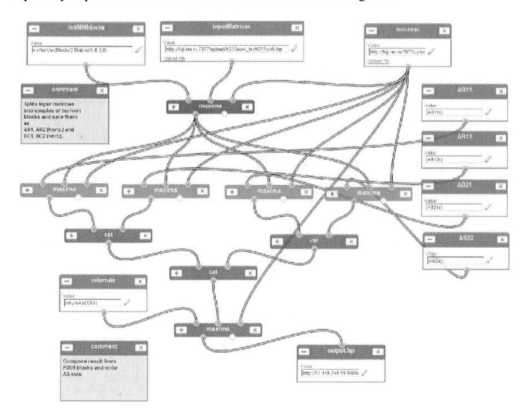

Figure 5. The visualization of running workflow instance (executed blocks are painted green, running blocks are turquoise, waiting blocks are blue).

5.2. Workflow Management Service

The WMS implements remote interface for storage of workflows created with the editor, and performs deployment of saved workflows as new MathCloud services. The remote interface of WMS is based on HTTP protocol and REST style. This provides a most convenient way to interact with the service from the workflow editor. In accordance with the REST principles, the interface of WMS is formed by a set of resources identified by URIs and accessible via standard HTTP methods (Table 3). These resources are:

- WMS itself, identified by WMS_URI;
- Workflow, identified by WORKFLOW_URI;
- Composite service, identified by SERVICE_URI;
- Proxy, identified by PROXY_URI.

Table 3. Resources and methods of WMS interface

Resource	GET	POST	PUT	DELETE
Workflow management service WMS_URI	Get list of stored workflows	Create new workflow	—	—
Workflow WORKFLOW_URI	Get workflow description	—	Update workflow	Delete workflow
Composite service SERVICE_URI	Get service description	Run workflow	—	—
Proxy PROXY_URI	Get description of service with specified URI	—	—	—

The WMS resource supports the following HTTP methods:

- GET – returns the list of stored workflows in JSON format; each list item contains workflow URI, name and short description;
- POST – creates new workflow. The request contains workflow description in JSON format. The WMS saves the description and deploys a new composite service. The response contains URIs of created workflow and service resources.

The workflow resource supports the following HTTP methods:

- GET – returns current workflow representation in JSON format, containing workflow description and URI of composite service;
- PUT – updates workflow description. The request contains new workflow description. The WMS updates the description and redeploys the composite service;

- DELETE – deletes workflow. The WMS deletes stored workflow description and undeploys the composite service. The method destroys corresponding workflow and service resources.

The composite service implements standard RESTful interface described in Chapter 3. The execution of workflow is initiated by sending a request to its composite service. Thus, from the client's point of view, the composite service is no different from ordinary MathCloud services. This enables, for example, the use of existing workflow as a block in a new workflow. The only extension of the standard service interface is that the representation of job resource contains additional information on the status of individual blocks of the workflow. This information is used by the workflow editor to visualize the state of a running workflow.

The auxiliary proxy is used by the workflow editor in order to obtain a description of service added to workflow. Due to web browser security policy, the editor can not send GET request directly to the service which is located on a different web server. Therefore, the editor sends a GET request to a proxy resource running on a web server of the editor, specifying the service URI in a query parameter. The proxy retrieves description of the service and returns it to the editor.

CONCLUSION

The paper presented a MathCloud environment which implements a web-based software infrastructure for service-oriented scientific environments aimed on radical simplification of service development, deployment and use. In contrast to grid middleware based on Web Services specifications the proposed infrastructure embraces a more lightweight approach by using the REST architectural style, Web technologies and Web 2.0 application models.

An important aspect of MathCloud architecture not discussed in this paper is security. It is obvious that in some cases it is desirable to restrict access to the service, and that the viability of the proposed environment will depend on the availability of robust security mechanism. This includes authentication of users and services, access policy description, authorization, data protection, and delegation of credentials. A prototype of such security mechanism for MathCloud based on HTTPS and X.509 certificates is developed. Current implementation also supports an alternative way to authenticate users using public identity providers and OpenID protocol.

Another important component of MathCloud currently under development is service catalogue supporting publication, discovery and monitoring of services.

These issues will be discussed in detail in further papers.

REFERENCES

[1]   I. Foster. Service-Oriented Science // *Science.* – 2005. – V. 308, N. 5723. - P. 814-817.

[2]   Fielding, R.T. Architectural styles and the design of network-based software architectures. *PhD Dissertation.* Dept. of Information and Computer Science, University of California, Irvine, 2000.

[3]   L. Richardson, S. Ruby. *RESTful Web Services.* O'Reilly, 2007.

[4]   *JSON Schema.* http://www.json-schema.org/

In: Horizons in Computer Science Research, Volume 4   ISBN: 978-1-61324-262-9
Editor: Thomas S. Clary   © 2011 Nova Science Publishers, Inc.

Chapter 5

EXAMPLE OF CLINICAL APPLICATIONS
OF WEARABLE MONITORING SYSTEMS

G. Andreoni[1], M. Bernabei, P. Perego, A. Barichello and L. Piccini
Politecnico di Milano, INDACO Dept., via Durando 38/A, 20158 Milan, Italy

ABSTRACT

The future of healthcare is based on new devices for a more accurate and personalized diagnosis and treatment anywhere.

Shorter hospital stays and distribute assistance (Home Care) already represents the trend in the development and management of national healthcare services. The consolidation of such a scenario andits diffusion can be achieved only through the specific development of new technologies oriented to support distributed monitoring of patients for disease prevention, follow-up and rehabilitation. Such technologies can be integrated with the different mobile communication networks that permeated our society. In a monitoring network context, creating nodes with wearable monitoring systems and sensors probably represent a key winning factor in order to provide easy-to-use, affordable and personalized solutions.

This chapter shows representative case studies to demonstrate the key role of the wearable technologies in the provision of different health processes and services. We will show the experiences in pre-term newborn monitoring, the quantitative approach to support diagnosis in a rare but severe neurological pathology (Tourette Syndrome) and in a Parkinson's Disease, and the multi-factorial analysis to optimize assistive technology.

INTRODUCTION

The future of healthcare is based on new technologies and systems for a more accurate, personalized and widespread diagnosis and treatment of pathologies aimed at improving the quality of care. To achieve this goal, the management and coordination of the whole range of health services, from primary to tertiary care, must undergo radical structural changes. Welfare and education of citizens have become primary elements which also lead to the

---

[1] E-mail address: giuseppe.andreoni@polimi.it (Corresponding author)

increase prevention and early diagnosis, with the need to offer care services outside hospitals, in the sphere of everyday life. The ambitious objective is to enable reliable, efficient, economic and interactive health services in any place at any time to anyone (Lymberis and Gatzoulis, 2006).

The introduction of these new ways of delivering care services needs also that citizen / patient should have a more central role. Self-responsibility is fundamental, but it is strictly related to easy-to-use- biomedical technologies implementing these services.

Telemedicine should be no more an eternal promise but an effective framework: the ongoing experiments to develop and validate new services and / or processes should become reality. Only in this way we can meet the main macroeconomic challenges regarding the expectation of citizens to receive high quality services, demographic changes with the aging population, increasing the prevalence of chronic diseases and increasing health expenditure (Doughty et al., 1996). In this context, the role of technological innovation is strategic and fundamental. Among the most relevant innovations, Personal Health Systems (PHS) are a recent concept (late 1990s) introduced to support these trends and the development of health services by the exploitation of the innovation in science and technology such as the biomedical, micro-and nano-technologies, and the innovation in the Information and Communication Technologies (ICT).

PHS are about placing the individual citizen/patient in the center of the healthcare delivery process. They allow citizens/patients to have more responsibility in managing their own health and interacting, whenever is necessary, with care providers. In doing so, PHS aim to bring benefits to citizens and health authorities alike: first, by improving the quality of care for the individuals themselves and second, by containing the rising healthcare costs through proper and efficient use of technological capabilities (Lymberis and Gatzoulis, 2006).Wearable Biomedical Systems (WBS) are a specific category of PHS: in particular, they can be defined as integrated systems on a wearable platform (in the sense of clothing or devices attachable to the body) and can offer solutions for continuous monitoring by measuring non-invasive biomedical, biochemical and physical parameters. Thus WBS are an ideal platform for multi-parametric non-intrusive monitoring of health status which provide a remote primary and secondary prevention. This way is possible to obtain the early diagnosis and management of several diseases (in particular cardiovascular and / or respiratory, but also metabolic pathologies and physical rehabilitation), but also to support elderly and disabled people.

In this scenario, characterized by an increasing demand for continuity of care, the WBS would allow monitoring of patients over extended periods of time, allowing them to continue their normal daily activities and enjoy their social life. Furthermore they could help in developing a multi-factorial user's health profile for a more detailed and comprehensive view of the subject's condition that could become very important –even not always strictly necessary - in the processes of prevention, early diagnosis and management of the disease. This latter is fundamental for elderly people and covers a substantial proportion of health expenditure (De Rossi and Lymberis, 2004). This also will implement the concept of *personalized care.* Prevention and early detection of diseases would have a direct impact on the cost of healthcare, when some treatment or hospitalization or improper access to health facilities/institutions could be avoided. In many cases, patients have chronic recurrent costs of hospitalization, with inefficiencies for acute events. Demographic changes indicate that the proportion of elderly in the population increased and will increase even more significantly in coming decades. Consequently, the trend is evolving to the increasing incidence of chronic diseases.

Remote monitoring and home care represent the current clinical needs and expectations in the near future and WBS are ideal platforms to address these needs.

Wearable physiological monitoring systems are intelligent medical monitoring devices, which provide real-time feedback to the wearer or remote monitoring station. The wearable physiological monitoring by means of embedded sensors and wires integrated into the fabric of the wearer has a number of drawbacks. Each physiological sensor is integrated with its processing electronics and a wireless transceiver to form a network of sensors. A wearable network of physiological sensors integrated into a vest of the individual acquires the data and transmits them to a remote monitoring station continuously, where the health status of the individuals is remotely monitored. The applications of the WBS are numerous. Many clinical and research programs can benefit from an affordable, accurate, and wearable method of monitoring a patient or subject's lifestyle outside the confines of the laboratory or physician's office. These systems are capable of monitoring the health status of individuals who perform very high risk jobs like soldiers in a battle field, fire fighters, mine workers, etc. Furthermore these systems will be useful for monitoring the health status of the elderly people at home. The wearable physiological monitoring systems must give reliable and protected (e.g. encrypted) recordings of medical data compared to the conventional physiological monitoring systems. They are supposed to function as long as 48-72 hours for continuous monitoring, without any failure. Continuous monitoring with early detection of anomalies has likely potential to provide patients with an increased level of confidence, which in turn may improve quality of life. In addition, ambulatory monitoring will allow patients to engage in normal activities of daily life, rather than staying at home or close to specialized medical services.

In this chapter we present three applications of wearable monitoring systems that from research are going to be exploited in the clinical practice. The first case-study is related to wearable solutions supporting diagnosis, and in particular the quantification of the clinical severity of motor disorders through motor holter systems applied in the Tourette Syndrome. The second example refers to the application of wearable solutions in extensive biosignal monitoring: a textile electrodes system for measuring cardiac activity in pre-term newborns in Neonatal Intensive Care Unit is presented in this chapter. Finally we present a wearable solution supporting the Rehabilitation process, and specifically we introduce a multimodal quantitative approach in orthoses and prostheses selection/customization.

APPLICATION OF WEARABLE SYSTEMS IN CLINICS

Wearable Solutions Supporting Diagnosis: Quantifying Motor Disorders through Motor Holter Systems – Case Studies in Parkinson's Disease and Tourette Syndrome

Movement disorders may be often due to neurologic diseases associated with an abnormal activity of central and peripheral nervous systems. Common manifestations of well-known pathologies like Dystonia, Parkinson's Disease (PD) and Tourette Syndrome (TS) are represented by tremors, freezing of gait and tics. Despite the neurologic origin of these disorders, they burden the motor function and jeopardize the movement efficiency of the people who are afflicted in such a way that interferes with daily activities and significantly impairs quality of life.

The standard clinical evaluation for diagnosis and rehabilitation is currently carried out through routine examinations and videotape analysis in the strictly controlled ambulatory environment. The severity of motor symptoms are assessed through several standard rating scales (Unified Parkinson's Disease Rating Scale, UPDRS, Yale Global Tic Severity Scale, YGTSS) largely based on patient self-reports and brief observations of simple motor tasks. The diagnosis protocol is therefore related to the physician subjective evaluation and to the unreliable patient self-report, whereas motor symptoms may vary unpredictably in an inter/intra individual way and are strongly related to the contextual environment of the trial. Moreover, many pathological manifestations are difficult to elicit in a routine clinical examination and no objective methods are currently used to identify the disease severity outside of the clinic and in a long-term continuous way.

The need for a quantitative assessment of motor deficit is a strong requirement in order to plan an effective care strategy and rehabilitation pathway for two major reasons. First of all, the involved neuroleptic pharmacological treatments (neuroleptic medications, α2-adrenergic agonists, and dopamine agonists as well as local injections of botulinum toxin) suffer from "on/off" individual phases and progressive refractoriness due to drug tolerance. Moreover, the optimal pharmacological dosage lacks for an objective correlation with the symptomatic course as it cannot be assessed in a straightforward and univocal manner. The same issue occurs in respect to a recently adopted surgical approach that use a Deep Brain Stimulation (DBS) implant, which requires to set several parameters (current intensity and frequency, monopolar/bipolar electrodes activation) to meet different symptomatic evidence. The second reason is primarily related to the inter-rater reliability that is strongly compromised by the subjectivity of the examiner and by the lack of a only rating system which may fulfills the patient expectations and improve the compliance between users and care givers.

In recent years several studies have been carried out to investigate the chance of exploiting wearable devices (WD) in order to bridge the gap between symptoms evaluation and clinical treatments through a quantitative measure of the motor deficit. WD seemed to be the preferable solution due to their cost-effective, non-intrusive characteristic and to the possibility for a long-term monitoring in the daily life environment. Despite the potentiality of gathering extraordinary amount of data through such sensors/systems, techniques and protocols that could take full advantage of a continuous wireless monitoring are currently lacking for a specific and exhaustive assessment in the field of neuromotor diseases.

Moore et Al. (2006) have developed a new system for long-term monitoring of gait in PD. The characteristics of every stride taken over 10-h epochs were acquired using a lightweight ankle-mounted sensor array that transmitted data wirelessly to a small pocket PC at a rate of 100 Hz. Stride was calculated from the vertical linear acceleration and pitch angular velocity of the leg with an accuracy of 5 cm. Results from 5 PD patients demonstrate the effectiveness of long-term monitoring of gait in a natural environment. The small, variable stride length characteristic of Parkinsonian gait, and fluctuations of efficacy associated with levodopa therapy, such as delayed onset, wearing off, and the 'off/on' effect, could reliably be detected from long-term changes in stride length. As a further development, Moore et Al. (2007) have specifically designed a new method to evaluate the Freezing of Gate (FOG) in PD, with the assessment of clinically reliable severity indexes. In this study an ambulatory FOG monitor was validated in 11 PD patients. The vertical linear acceleration of the left shank was acquired using an ankle-mounted sensor array that transmitted data wirelessly to a pocket PC at a rate of 100 Hz. Power analysis showed high-frequency components of leg movement during FOG in the 3–8 Hz band that were not apparent during volitional standing, and power in this 'freeze' band was higher ($p > 0.0001$) during FOG preceded by walking (turning or obstacles) than FOG preceded by rest (gait initiation). A freeze index (FI) was defined as the power in the 'freeze' band divided by the power in the 'locomotor' band (0.5–3 Hz) and a threshold chosen such that FI values above this limit were designated as FOG. A global threshold detected 78% of FOG events and 20% of stand events were incorrectly labeled as FOG. Individual calibration of the freeze threshold showed evidence of improved accuracy and sensitivity of the device to 89% for detection of FOG with 10% false positives.

Acceleration measurements carried out through wearable devices have shown a strong reliability in respect to videotape examination if the aim is to detect and identify normal motor activity. A more complex and troubling challenge is required in order to apply this kind of technology to pathological conditions since symptomatic events are masked by normal movements and in this context they represent an unwished noise. Therefore, starting from the quantitative inertial measurements provided by the wearable device, two major issues seemed to be the core problems to design an effective and reliable system able to manage movement disorders. The former is a monitoring protocol which could fit the body distribution of the highly variable motor symptoms and that may be able to catch and maximize the most useful inertial parameter in respect to the pathological features to be characterized. The latter is a post-processing analysis which could involve an identification and classification step that aims to highlight and assess the severity of motor abnormalities hided within the physiological activities.

In 2004, Bonato et Al. proposed a first attempt to detect motor fluctuations in PD using non-linear data mining techniques like fractal estimates, approximate entropy values, and correlation dimension estimates which appeared to meet the non-linear pattern of interesting pathological events like tremor. Accelerometer (ACC) and surface electromyographic (EMG) signals were recorded during the execution of a standardized set of motor assessment tasks (sitting, finger-to-nose, tapping, sit-to-stand, walking, and stand-to-sit). ACCs were placed on the right and left upper arm, right and left forearm, right and left thigh, right shin, and sternum. EMG sensors were placed on the following muscles: right and left right biceps brachii, right erector spinae, right vastuslateralis, and right tibialis anterior. The EMG and ACC sensors were connected to an ambulatory system (Vitaport 3, Temec BV, The Netherlands) equipped with data acquisition hardware and software to collect and store the bioelectrical signals. The preliminary results reported by Bonato et Al. (2004) indicate that wearable device measurements associated with data mining techniques have a large potential. It is expected that these tools will allow identifying motor patterns of primary and secondary movement disorders in PD, such as tremor, rigidity, dyskinesia, akinesia, and dystonia in a manner that is both objective and automatic.

Patel et Al. (2007) focused only on acceleration measurement and developed software for a novel wireless sensor platform for home monitoring of persons with PD. They analyzed the sensor data collected using wired wearable sensors to evaluate two important factors: (1) optimal window length to extract features from data and (2) ranking of features based on their ability to form tight distinct clusters. Finally, they tested the ranked features with a simple linear classifier to assess the impact on accuracy in predicting clinical scores of bradykinesia and dyskinesia. The WD was the SHIMMER sensor platform (Intel Digital Health Group's Sensing Health with Intelligence, Modularity, Mobility, and Experimental Reusability) which combines on-line computation, radio communication, triaxial sensors, and a large flash memory into a wearable rugged plastic enclosure that measures 1.75" x 0.8" x 0.5" and weighs 10 g. Examining twelve PD individuals, they found evidence of a significant correlation between the clinical ranking of bradykinesia and dyskinesia in respect to the features ranking provided by the system on the base of their ability to form well-defined clusters.

Though a WD with an embedded inertial sensor and a data storage memory may be able to provide the quantitative measurements required for a long-term monitoring of movement disorders, the ability to catch motor abnormalities is strongly dependent on the huge amount of the different manifestations occurred. The Tourette Syndrome (TS) case is an evident example of how a quantitative decision support system could be jeopardized by the high variability of motor symptoms. TS is a chronic neurologic disorder characterized by multiple motor and phonic tics that wax and wane over time. The wide range of visible and audible signs may induce subjectivity in the evaluation process, in spite of the rules set by literature for defining TS scores (YGTSS). Moreover, (i) symptoms vary unpredictably over time; (ii) patients are able to suppress in part or totally their symptoms for minutes to hours; (iii) situational stimuli can change tic expression. Multiple variables such as frequency, number of tic-types, intensity, complexity, body distribution, suppressibility, and interference with normal activities are commonly considered to assess the severity of TS.

The chance to overcome such a complexity has been studied in 2009 (Bernabei et Al.) analyzing a sample of twelve subjects affected by TS. They used a wearable actigraph based on a commercial system (PROTHEO I, SXT – Sistemi per Telemedicina) composed by a 3D acceleration sensor (LIS3L06AL, STMicroelectronics), a Bluetooth[©] transmission module (PAN1540, Panasonic), and a rechargeable LiIon battery contained in a plastic case of 92 x 58 x 25 mm (Figure 1).

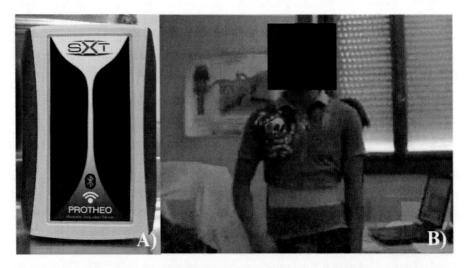

Figure 1. A) PROTHEO I monitoring system (SXT – Sistemi per Telemedicina). B) A moment of the ambulatory protocol with a TS subject wearing the device on the back (position L3-L4) through an elastic belt. While sending the inertial data to the PC, the subject carries out the required task sequence.

The signal post-processing was specifically designed to analyze acceleration data by: eliminating noise; detecting peaks connected to pathological events; and classifying intensity and frequency of motor tics into quantitative scores. A nonlinear median filtering and an adaptive thresholding were used to discriminate spikes due to tic events from the ones determined by normal movements. A specific frequency and intensity scale was defined on the base of the ambulatory scoring system to meet the current evaluation process and suit the detection ability of the inertial sensor. An expert physician, blinded for inertial data, provided a scoring index through videotape analysis on the base of the standard clinical scale (YGTSS) for tic intensity and frequency. The automatic quantitative assessment and the operator qualitative evaluation, the latter taken as the gold standard, were compared in order to define sensitivity, specificity and accuracy of the WD system in respect to the classification of tic events. Major findings from this study showed that a specific recognition and classification system based on a WD has the potentiality to manage the high variability of a neurologic motor disorder with an overall sensitivity, specificity and accuracy of (mean ± SD) 75±10%, 70±15%, 74±14%, respectively. As reported by Moore et Al. (2007) about the FOG in PD, a subject-specific calibration has shown to be a proper approach to improve the reliability of the system even in the TS case. In fact, an individual modulation of the adaptive thresholding resulted in a better performance for tic-recognition, with a sensitivity, specificity and accuracy increase up to 80.8% ± 8.5%, 75.8% ± 17.3%, and 80.5% ± 12.2%, respectively.

The proposed methodologies gave promising performances in terms of automatic motor abnormalities detection and classification in a standard clinical context. These WD-based systems may emerge as conventional tools for both clinical investigations and home-environment/long-term monitoring of motor disorders. To reach this goal and to create the bases for the definition of new standards, efforts should be spent to design both monitoring and calibration protocols able to take into account the body distribution of pathological events and the complete range of the motor tasks usually occurring during daily life. The expression of a neurologic motor disorder requires a non-invasive approach and a long-term monitoring to maximize the pathological manifestations that are often misunderstood during a brief examination in an ambulatory environment. WDs may offer a significant support to the care decision system through the chance to continuously record abnormal motor events and objectively quantifying the correlation between pharmacological/ surgical treatments and the actual disease course during post-operative and rehabilitation periods.

Wearable Solutions Supporting Monitoring: Textile Electrodes System for Pre-term Newborns in Neonatal Intensive Care Unit

Recent studies and investigations regarding the care of premature infants introduced, during the normal clinical practice, new care methods which aim to stabilize posture and environmental relationships of the child, minimizing external troubles and favouring a beneficial contact with parents (Kangaroo mother care) (Westrup B, 2007).

The critical clinical condition of preterm infants mainly resides in the fact that the organs of the fetus continue to grow until the thirty-seventh gestational week that is the limit beyond which the birth is considered completed and below which we can define them premature infants.

Pre-term infants and those with serious diseases or born at term weighing less than 2500gr are accommodated in the Neonatal Intensive Care Unit or NICU, that through the work of neonatologists and experienced staff, has as primary purpose to provide medical and appropriate care to the new-born at risk by integrating information coming from different devices connected to the child and performing diagnostic and personalized treatment plans.

NICU is a complex and fragile environment where the introduction of innovative technologies becomes a crucial aim because it can introduce important changes to standard monitoring methods improving the existing ones, make them the less invasive and intrusive as possible, promoting the effective development of new "care" action lines (Piccini L. et al., 2008).

The preterm and ill neonates are placed in incubator where they are continuously monitored and treated, but at the same time, they need the interaction with their parents. This interaction is problematic because of the monitoring system devices. Usually in NICU the monitored signs include body temperature, electro-cardiogram (ECG), respiration and the degree of blood oxygen saturation (SpO2). In most cases the vital parameters are obtained with adhesive electrodes (e.g. 3M™ Red dot 2269T) or invasive deices in the case of respiration (e.g. C-PAP) those cause two main problems:

- the adhesive sensors on fragile skin can cause open wounds and their removal can generates injuries that often allow the introduction of bacteria or irritating particles into the body, as well as increased suffering to the new-born;
- the detachment of the parents from their baby due to the impediment of all medical equipment, wires and patches (Figure 2);

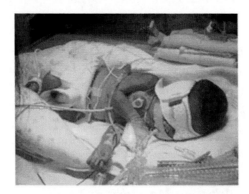

Figure 2. Example of neonate monitored in Neonatal Intensive Care Unit.

Therefore, the design and develop of new non-intrusive methods for monitoring vital signs in neonatal intensive care unit is necessary.

Recent progresses in electronic sensor and communication technology allow the development of new health monitoring system using wearable electronic devices, smart textiles electrodes and wireless transmission (Di Rienzo et al, 2010).

In neonatal area, some efforts have been done towards noninvasive new-born monitoring like the sensor belt (Ciani et al, 2008) for monitoring heart-rate, respiratory rate, body temperature and movements in NICU, but we are still far from a true newborn noninvasive monitoring system that solves the two main problems show above.

This chapter discusses and analyzes the performance of a garment properly designed for premature infants that can monitor the heart rate through a particular configuration of electrodes and thereby provide comfort to the baby and certainty in measure.

The garment we refer to, will be a suitably designed pyjama on which we have applied wearable sensors that connected to a measure system and a first processing station transmits wireless data collected to a receiving station.

This way is possible to minimize the discomfort of the child and at the same time to provide results that are comparable or even better than those provided by standard ECG devices that use the Ag-AgCl adhesive electrodes.

The system is composed by wearable sensors that are applied to a little pyjamas realized for preterm new-borns. A major study was conducted on the choice of yarn applied to sensitive pyjamas that is composed of different proportions of silver which strongly influences the conductivity of the signal. Even the application mode of the sensors to the pyjamas and the place of application have been analyzed and gradually improved.

The best pajama is composed by:

- conductive yarn to the arms;
- adjustable sleeves;
- clamps connected at the conductive yarn outgoing from baby's pelvis.

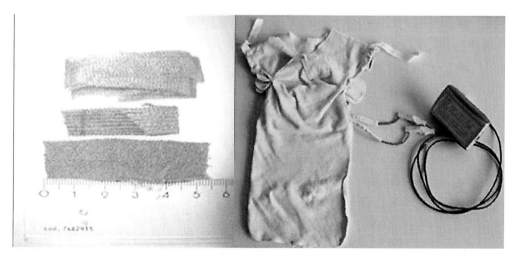

Figure 3. a) three different types of conductive yarn which differ each other from the silver used for their composition. b) the "pigiamino" system.

Two similar pajamas are discussed in this chapter:

- the first one is elasticated, so automatically adjustable;
- the second one is elasticated and coated with an elastic band supplied with different buttonholes and a button which permits the correct width of the sleeves around the arms of each acquired new-born.

We called the first one C-Elastico and the second one C-Bottoncini. Both gave us good results even if C-Bottoncini reached the best.

The signals detected by sensorized tissues are transmitted through the connector to a device placed outside the incubator composed by an acquiring sheet for temperature, one for acceleration and two acquiring sheets for cardiac signal sensors which are all properly connected to the electronics module that acts as interface between sensors and part of the digital data processing. The electronic unit can be conveniently placed outside the incubator to avoid obstruction at the baby and it communicates with a receiving station set to the data processing which usually is a laptop pc via the Bluetooth module inside.

Tests were carried out at the Neonatal Intensive Care Unit of the Hospital "A. Manzoni" of Lecco that gave us the opportunity to acquire 26 subjects (12 male and 14 female, only 1 baby born at the correct term) born prematurely from December 2008 through to June 2010 weighting from 0.8 kg and 3.64 kg and without serious pathologies during our tests. The protocol used is composed by 2 tests lasting 5 minutes each one with the new-born wearing the sensorized garment and 4 standard electrodes applied on the thorax during the first test (2 electrodes) and on the arms (2 electrodes on each arm) near our conductive tissue, during the second one.

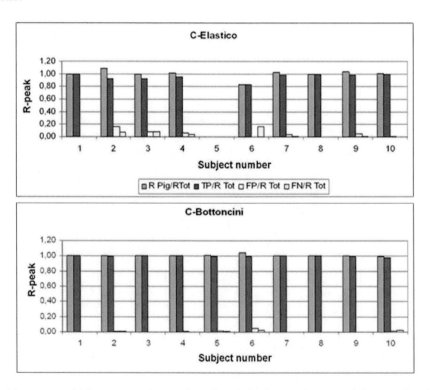

Figure 4. histograms which represent the number of R-peak, the TP, the FP and the FN of each pajama normalized with the total number of R-peak detected on the signal coming from standard electr odes.

The useful signal is defined as the acquired signal where the signal allows to get the cardiac frequency of each new-born. The duration of the useful signal compared to the total length of the test expressed in percentage is 67% for the C-Elastico and 78.4% for the C-

Bottoncini. Other results are reported in the histograms below, where there are the total number of peaks detected by the algorithm, the TP (true positives), the FP (false positives) and the FN(false negatives) of both the useful signals of the pajamas normalized with the total number of peaks detected by the same algorithm and in the same hardware conditions at the same times of the signal coming from Ag-AgCl electrodes put on the chest of the baby.

The obtained sensitivity (S)for the C-Elasticois 98.0% and its positive predictivity (PP) is 97.1%, while for the C-Bottoncini are S=99.6% and PP=99.0%. The number of FP and FN is bigger in C-elastico than in C-bottoncini like we can see in figure 4, but Sensitivity and Positive Predictivity are high in both the pajamas.

Moreover the signal detected with the wearable sensors shown the same amplitude of the same one acquired with standard electrodes (figure 5).

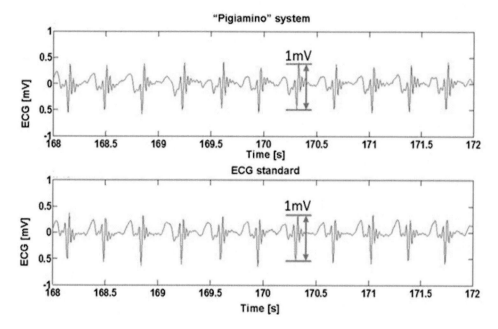

Figure 5. ECG amplitude in mV coming from our "pigiamino" system compared with the coming from standard electrodes one.

The developed system composed by the pajamas and the device, shows good results about the quality of measure and it is comparable with the normal monitoring methods.

Wearable Solution Supporting Rehabilitation: A Multimodal Quantitative Approach in Ortheses and Prostheses Selection/customization

A physiological motor activity requires muscular strength, joint mobility and coordination of the central nervous system. This constraint is strongly compromised in patients with neuromuscular diseases like Post-Polio Syndrome (PPS) or Cerebral Palsy (CP) and extremely altered in case of disabling conditions such as an upper/lower limb amputation. Functional recovery for these subjects should take into account a complete and systematic assessment of the orthotic/prosthetic devices after surgical treatments and during the rehabilitation period.

Knee-Ankle-Foot (KAFO) or Ankle-Foot (AFO) orthoses are often recommended to support and improve motor efficiency in polio-survivors and children affected by CP with lower limb disability. However, a badly designed orthosis may be less attractive, may fail prematurely and may be detrimental for the patient. The ability of orthoses to lessen the patient symptoms varies with the anatomical location of the impairment and with its severity. For instance, KAFO users must adopt abnormal gait patterns to compensate for the knee motion constraints imposed by the brace. These abnormal compensatory patterns may lead to soft tissue injury and joint dysfunction at the hip and at the lower back, which, in turn, may cause pain and reduction in the range of motion. Walking with an immobilized knee also reduces walking efficiency by 24%, thereby leading to premature fatigue and limiting the distance a user can walk. Surveys have shown that increased energy demand from using KAFO is one of the major reasons for which KAFO rejection rates range from 60% to nearly 100%. The alteration of both energetic consumption and movement ability is an issue even more troubling for prosthesis users and the functional assessment of such devices should require a careful multifactorial analysis based on subjective (patient self-report) and objective parameters.

The effectiveness of patients' orthosis/prosthesis is commonly evaluated either by static joint-flexion of the orthosis or by visual observation of the brace on the patient during gait. A number of commercially available goniometers and electrogoniometers may be used to measure the range of motion of a joint. However, electromechanical systems used to quantify motion at various joints during gait are i) not portable enough, with hardware that may be obtrusive; ii) not application specific, i.e. a clinician has to modify his/her clinical protocol to make adequate use of the device; and, iii) expensive (e.g., camera-based optical measurement systems). In particular, instrumental gait analysis has become a valuable tool in clinical practice to evaluate functional abilities of subject with motor deficits. Nevertheless, its use is still limited to very few medical centers, and its ability to monitor a patient's spontaneous and typical walking capacity, opposed to best performance, is still limited by a number of setbacks primarily due to the measurement system. In particular, optoelectronic systems are costly, hardly portable and have a restricted field of view. These features limit their use to dedicated laboratories and restrict the acquisition of a subject's gait to few strides per trial, in conditions which can be far from steady state. In addition, the acquisition of gait in an unfamiliar and artificial environment, such as that of a laboratory, can psychologically condition the subject, who will over-perform with respect to his/her everyday life ability.

Wearable Devices (WD) are likely the optimal tool to overcome the measurement restrictions imposed by the present clinical standard and provide a reliable evaluation system within the selection/customization process for orthoses and prostheses.

A protocol named "Outwalk" was recently developed by Cutti et Al. (2009) to easily measure the thorax–pelvis and lower-limb 3D kinematics on children with cerebral palsy (CP) and amputees during gait in free-living conditions, by means of an Inertial and Magnetic Measurement System (IMMS). An IMMS consists of sensing units (SUs) which integrates one 3D accelerometer, gyroscope and magnetometer. Outwalk was originally conceived on the Xsens motion tracking system (Xsens Technologies, NL), consisting of up to 10 SUs (called MTx) connected by wire to a data-logger (Xbus Master), usually worn on the belt. The data-logger is connected via Bluetooth to a laptop which processes and stores the data collected. Each SU is hosted in a small box, weights 38 g, and is 39 x 54 x 28 mm. The data supplied by these sensors are combined to measure the 3D orientation (but not the position) of the SU's coordinate system (CS) with respect to a global, earth-based Coordinate System

(CS). Given this 3D orientation, an IMMS has the potential to estimate joint kinematics when: (1) an SU is attached to each body segment of interest; (2) at least one anatomical CS is defined for each body segment and (3) the orientation of the anatomical CS is expressed in the CS of the SU. Points of kinematics can then be obtained from the relative orientation of contiguous anatomical CSs (Denavit-Hartenberg convention). Moreover, Cutti et Al. (2009) compared both the Outwalk protocol and IMMS devices on four healthy subjects in respect to a reference protocol (CAST, Cappozzo 1995, Benedetti 1998) and measurement system (optoelectronic system; Vicon, Oxford Metrics Group, UK), providing results that suggest the commencement of clinical trials of Outwalk and WD instrumentation on populations of lower-limb amputees.

The critical part of the methods involving WD to infer the lower-limb joint kinematics is the definition of the anatomical CSs. In fact, the lack of information regarding the position of the sensors implies that the anatomical CSs cannot be defined through the calibration of single anatomical landmarks. Several pre-calibration techniques have been proposed by Cappozzo et Al. (1995) and Kontaxis et Al. (2009) to overcome this problem. Following their solutions, the initial CS for each segment may be evaluated through i) the rotation about the longitudinal axis of the whole body and a knee extension with minimal movement of the ankle, ii) the orientation of a minimum of two non-parallel lines for each body segment or iii) the knee mean flexion-extension axis. These protocols still require tasks that may not be easily performed by certain populations of subjects or are based on multiple calibration tasks, involving multiple specialized devices at the expense of simplicity and experiment duration.

A comparison with a physiological walking activity may be a reliable test in order to choose and fit an orthotic device on the base of the individual kinematic of an impaired subject. However, a kinematic analysis may be not sufficient to meet the actual needs of recovering the patient daily activities because of the energetic shift due to the distortion of the normal motor patterns. As a matter of fact, energy expenditure measurements, such as the physiological cost index (PCI), the total hearth beat index (THBI) and the oxygen cost/rate have proven to be a reliable index for quantifying penalties imposed by gait disability.

An assistive technology project proposed by Manzoni et Al. (2010) is currently dealing with a hybrid motor/energetic assessment of the functional efficiency of lower-limb ortheses. Gait basographic parameters and energetic expenditures during a Six-Minute Walking Test (6-MWT) were analyzed through a cost-effective, non-invasive polygraph, with a multichannel wireless transmission, that carried out: electrocardiogram (ECG); impedancecardiography (ICG); and lower-limb accelerations detection. The monitoring device was composed by an analogical circuit for the acquisition of ECG and ICG signal, and a digital board that provided data digitalization and transmission (figure 6). The data-logger also contained a 3D acceleration sensor (*MicroElectroMechanical System* (MEMS), LIS3L06AL, STMicroelectronics, range: $\pm 6g$, sensitivity: 1.6 g/V) and was fixed on the patient trunk through an elastic belt. The data-logger was powered by a rechargeable LiIon battery and provided 6-channels data to a remote processing unit through Bluetooth® class II transmission module (PAN1540, Panasonic).

The monitoring process was tested over a series of clinical trials in a population of four subjects affected by Post-Polio Syndrome (PPS). Each individual was tested twice fixing the wearable polygraph at the lumbar area (L2-L3): at the beginning of the rehabilitative period (t_0), before wearing the orthosis; and at the end of the rehabilitative training (t_1), while using the orthosis.

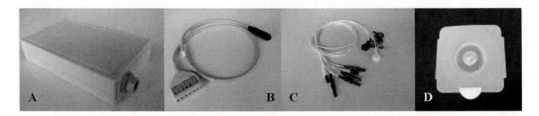

Figure 6. Wearable components of the ECG/ICG/acceleration cardiographic system by Manzoni et Al. (2010). A) Data-logger (117x70x23 mm). B) Holter main cable. C-D) Cable set and Cleartrace™ adhesive electrodes (ConMed Corporation).

Despite the overall inaccuracy intrinsically relying on indirect measurements and non-specific indexes, the multivariable methodology proposed by Manzoni et Al. spreads an improvement in the movement analysis field for motor impaired subjects by the means of a large spectrum of objective data provided by a WD in a non-invasive, easy-to-use fashion. The system provided less information in respect to the standard gait analysis, but they were referred to a continuous deambulation and were closer to everyday life conditions than a laboratory environment.

Though the current lack of an optimized reference for a clinical measurement protocol and the non-specific correlation between quantitative measures and pathological state, the potentialities of WDs in this field seem to be exceptionally appealing. They may be able to provide a reliable and handy evaluation tool which may avoid the resource waste due to an incorrect and user-unsuitable definition of an orthotic/prosthetic device, supporting the rehabilitation pathway with a more detailed and contextual information.

CONCLUSION

A recent market report was designed as a marketing tool for companies who currently manufacture or resell wearable computing or communications products, components, or accessories, or for companies who are considering entering these markets.

This study focuses on wearable computing/communication solutions for health care applications. The report contains actual 2006 wearable system shipments and evidenced that in the US alone, 76 million baby boomers will reach retirement age within the next decade. This massive shift in demographic has the potential to overwhelm today's health care system with a major crisis looming. One of the most critical issues is that in the current system infrequent and expensive visits to physicians' offices and the ER for preventive care is common. Moreover, 75-85% of today's health care spending is on chronic disease management. The report stressed about lack of more frequent and regular health monitoring. This is an especially acute issue with the elderly who have rapidly changing health states.

Wearable solutions being developed today to support monitoring of biophysical conditions can address many of these emerging issues across a broad cross-section of user groups. In addition to elderly care, disease management and general health and wellness represent significant segments that can benefit from more continuous, remote and personal monitoring solutions.

According to a new research report by Frost & Sullivan, the "Biosensors market" is categorized as a growth market which is expected to grow from $6.72 billion in 2009 to $14.42 billion in 2016. Biosensor adoption is increasing every year and the number of biosensor applications is continuously growing. Research analysts expect considerable growth to start emerging from the biodefense and home diagnostic market sectors in the near future considering the "development of newer biosensors is likely to change with newer application research."

The WBS are among this technologies and the research studies herein reported are specific but real cases of systems with a great potential impact for the future of health services. They face problems both for elderly people and newborns and could be an interesting paradigm of the new application scenarios.

REFERENCES

De Rossi D., Lymberis A. (eds), *Wearable Health Sysyems for Personalised Health Management*, IOS Press, Amsterdam, 2004.

De Rossi D., Lymberis A., Guest Editorial, IEEE Trans Inf Tech Biomed, Special Section on *New Generation of Smart Wearable Health Systems and Applications*, Guest Editors D. De Rossi, A. Lymberis, vol. 9(3): 293-294, 2005.

Doughty K., Cameron K., Garner P., Three generations of telecare of the elderly, *Journal of Telemedicine and Telecare*, Vol 2: 71-80, 1996.

Lymberis A., Gatzoulis L., Wearable Health Systems: from smart technologies to real applications. *Conf Proc IEEE Eng. Med. Biol. Soc.*: 6789-92, 2006.

VDC Research Group (Main analyst: Krebs David), Wearable Electronics Systems Global Market Demand Analysis*: Health Care Solutions*, Research Report # VDC6520, 2007.

Erik Grönvall, Luca Piccini, Alessandro Pollini, Alessia Rullo, Giuseppe Andreoni: Assemblies of Heterogeneous Technologies at the Neonatal Intensive Care Unit. In : B. Schiele et al. (Eds.): AmI 2007, *Lecture Notes in Computer Science* 4794, pp. 340–357, 2007. Springer-Verlag Berlin Heidelberg 2007, ISBN 978-3-540-76651-3.

A. Bonfiglio, S. Cerutti, D. De Rossi, G. Magenes (eds), *Sistemi indossabili intelligenti per la Salute e la Protezionedell'Uomo*, ed. Patron, 2008, pp. 357-384. ISBN 978-88-555-2994-5.

Ciani O, Piccini L, Parini S, Rullo A, Bagnoli F, Marti P, Andreoni G, Pervasive technology in Neonatal Intensive Care Unit: a prototype for newborns unobtrusive monitoring. *Proceeding at Annual International Conference of the IEEE Engineering in Medicine and Biology Society*. Vancouver (Canada), 2008.

Di Rienzo M, Meriggi P, Rizzo F, Castiglioni P, Lombardi C, Ferratini M, Parati G, Textile technology for the vital signs monitoring in telemedicine and extreme environments. IEEE transactions on information technology in biomedicine: a publication of the *IEEE engineering in Medicine and Biology Society*. May 2010. Volume 14, pp:711-717, 2010.

Piccini L, Ciani O, Grönvall E, Marti P, and Andreoni G, New monitoring approach for Neonatal Intensive Care Unit, in *5th International Workshop on Wearable Micro and Nanosystems for Personalized Health*, 2008.

Westrup B, "Newborn Individualized Developmental Care and Assessment Program (NIDCAP) — *Family-centered developmentally supportive care*" *Early Human Development* volume 83 pp 443–449, 2007.

Cutti AG, Ferrari A , Garofalo P, Raggi M, Cappello A, Ferrari A, 'Outwalk': a protocol for clinical gait analysis based on inertial and magnetic sensors, *Med Biol Eng Comput* (2010) 48:17–25.

Ferrari A, Cutti AG, Garofalo P, Raggi M, Heijboer M, Cappello A, Davalli A, *First in vivo assessment of ''Outwalk'': a novel protocol for clinical gait analysis based on inertial and magnetic sensors*, *Med Biol Eng Comput* (2010) 48:1–15.

Cappozzo A, Catani F, Croce UD et al (1995) Position and orientation in space of bones during movement: anatomical frame definition and determination. *Clin Biomech* **10**(4):171–178.

Benedetti MG, Catani F, Leardini A et al (1998) Data management in gait analysis for clinical applications. ClinBiomech 13(3):204–215.

Kontaxis A, Cutti AG, Johnson G et al (2009).A framework for the definition of standardized protocols for measuring upperextremity kinematics. *Clin Biomech* 24(3):246–253.

Gilsoo Cho, Yonsei University, Seoul, South Korea, *Smart Clothing: Technology and Applications*, CRC Press, December 23, 2009, ISBN: 9781420088526.

Paolo Bonato P, Sherrill DM, Standaert DG, Salles SS, Akay, Data Mining Techniques to Detect Motor Fluctuations in Parkinson's Disease, *Proceedings of the 26th Annual International Conference of the IEEE EMBS*, San Francisco, CA, USA, September 1-5, 2004.

Moore ST, MacDougall HG, Ondo WG, Ambulatory monitoring of freezing of gait in Parkinson's disease, *Journal of Neuroscience Methods* 167 (2008) 340–348.

Moore ST, MacDougall HG, Gracies JM, Cohen HS, Ondo WG, Long-term monitoring of gait in Parkinson's disease, *Gait & Posture* 26 (2007) 200–207.

Patel S, Lorincz K, Hughes R, Huggins N, Growdon JH, Welsh M, Bonato P, Analysis of Feature Space for Monitoring Persons with Parkinson's Disease With Application to a Wireless Wearable Sensor System, *Proceedings of the 29th Annual International Conference of the IEEE EMBS Cité Internationale*, Lyon, France August 23-26, 2007.

Bernabei M, Preatoni E, Mendez M, Piccini L, Porta M, Andreoni G, A Novel Automatic Method for Monitoring Tourette Motor Tics Through a Wearable Device, *Movement Disorders (in press)*.

Analytical Review of World Biosensors Market, Frost & Sullivan market report, 2010, pp.83.

In: Horizons in Computer Science Research, Volume 4   ISBN: 978-1-61324-262-9
Editor: Thomas S. Clary   © 2011 Nova Science Publishers, Inc.

Chapter 6

THE LAYERED SOFTWARE INFRASTRUCTURE FOR SOLVING LARGE-SCALE OPTIMIZATION PROBLEMS ON THE GRID

A. Afanasiev[1], Yu. Evtushenko[2] and M. Posypkin[1]

[1]Institution of Russian Academy of Sciences Institute for Systems Analysis of RAS
[2]Institution of Russian Academy of Sciences Dorodnicyn Computing Centre of RAS

ABSTRACT

The paper presents a hierarchical software infrastructure for solving large scale optimization problems on the Grid. The proposed toolset support exact and heuristic search strategies and runs on distributed systems consisting of different nodes ranging from PCs to large publicly available supercomputers. It efficiently copes with difficulties arising in such systems: the software diversity, unreliability of nodes and different ways of job submission. The distinctive feature of our approach is the use of different communication packages on different levels: on the top level we use ICE middleware coupled with TCP/IP sockets and within a single computing element either MPI or POSIX Threads libraries are used. Such approach imposes minimal requirements on the computing element software and efficiently utilizes the communication facilities of each node by using native communication mechanism. Developed infrastructure has been applied to molecular conformation problem that plays an important role in computational chemistry. New results were obtained demonstrating that general purposed optimization algorithm can efficiently cope with hard optimization problems providing the sufficient computational resources are employed.

1. INTRODUCTION

The objective of global optimization (GO) is to find an extreme value of a given function in a certain feasible region. GO problems frequently arise in practice. Application examples include potential energy minimization, financial and economical forecasting, robot design and manipulating, VLSI layout design and many others[1]. Unfortunately a significant fraction of such problems cannot be solved by existing methods on a single workstation. This makes the use of parallel and distributed computing inevitable.

At present researchers and practitioners in the GO field have different computational resources at their disposal. These resources can be roughly classified as follows:

- Personal computers and workstations;
- Small or mid-size clusters and shared memory multiprocessors;
- Publicly available large supercomputers accessed via batch system;
- Grid resources.

The choice of a particular hardware platform depends on a problem size. While simple optimization problems can be solved on a single workstation larger problems require parallel computers. However even computational resources of a single supercomputer are often insufficient for solving the most hard problem instances. For such complex problems the cumulative power of several supercomputers is demanded. These observations lead to a conclusion that today optimization software should provide a support for a variety of hardware platforms ranging from personal computers to large-scale distributed systems.

This paper describes a layered software infrastructure for global optimization (Fig.1). Its bottom layer is formed by BNB-Solver tool for solving GO problems on single-CPU workstations, shared memory machines and computational clusters. BNB-Solver provides C++ class templates for branch-and-bound, heuristic and hybrid algorithms. The upper layer is formed by BNB-Grid: a meta-computing environment aimed at harnessing computational resources of several geographically distributed supercomputers. BNB-Grid submits BNB-Solver applications to different computers. Submitted applications coordinated by BNB-Grid supervisor process cooperatively solve an optimization problem. The resolution process is interactively controlled by the user via GUI. BNB-Solver can be used as a standalone application as well as a BNB-Grid component.

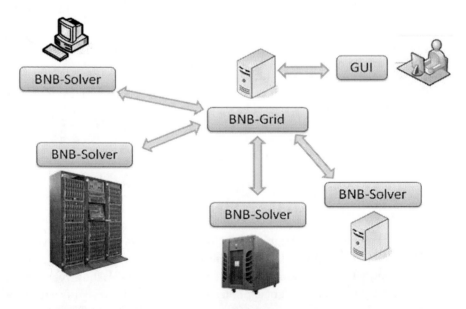

Figure 1. The general scheme of BNB-Grid and BNB-Solver tools interaction.

The paper is organized as follows. Section 2 describes target problems and resolution methods. In Section 3 BNB-Solver tool is considered. Section 4 gives a detailed explanation of other BNB-Grid components. In Section 5 experimental results for are presented. Section 6 provides a comparison with related work.

2. OVERVIEW OF OPTIMIZATION PROBLEMS AND RESOLUTION METHODS

The goal of global optimization is to find an extreme (minimal or maximal) value $f^* = f(x^*)$ of an objective function $f(x)$ on a *feasible domain* $X \subseteq R^n$. The value f^* and feasible point $x^* \in X$ are called *optimum* and *optimal solution* respectively. Without loss of generality one can consider only minimization problems: $f(x) \rightarrow \min, x \in X$.

Resolution methods for GO problems can be roughly classified according to the degree of rigor with which they approach the goal: *complete* (exact) methods find the optimum and prove its optimality, *incomplete* methods or *heuristics* find a feasible solution based on reasonable assumptions but do not guarantee optimality. Heuristic methods are applied when complete methods fail to solve the problem due to the lack of computational resources or time.

The Branch-and-Bound (B&B) is a general name for methods to split an initial problem into subproblems which are sooner or later eliminated by *bounding rules*. Bounding rules determine whether a subproblem can yield a solution better than the best solution found so far. The latter is called *incumbent solution*. Bounding is often done by comparing lower and upper bounds: a subproblem can be pruned if the lower bound for its objective is larger or equal to the current upper bound, i.e. incumbent solution. Thus quality upper bound significantly reduces the search space and in some cases leads to a dramatic performance improvements. *Hybrid* algorithms uses heuristics for improving incumbent solutions in B&B algorithms.

Numerous Branch-and-Bound algorithms were developed for different global optimization problems. Some of them were very successful for particular problem kinds, e.g. Travelling Salesman or Knapsack problems. However for many problems Branch-and-Bound methods require the amount of computing resources beyond the power of a single-CPU workstation. Fortunately Branch-and-Bound is highly suitable for parallel and distributed computing: after splitting the parts of the solution space can be processed simultaneously.

Another great advantage of B&B methods is that the general scheme does not significantly vary from one problem to another. The splitting and bounding rules may differ while keeping the general scheme almost intact. The direct consequence of this is the possibility to separate problem-independent and problem-specific parts. Such separation saves a lot of efforts when implementing a new problem or a new method. This is especially true for tools targeted at parallel and distributed environments because all support for parallel execution is reused for different optimization problems. We follow this approach in our tools: the computing space management, the work-distribution and communication among application processes is problem-independent.

Unfortunately for some problems (e.g. molecular conformation, protein folding) exact methods require an amount of resources far beyond the capabilities of existing computing systems. In such cases the problem is solved by heuristic procedures. Though the optimality is not proved heuristics usually find solutions close to optimum. We included the support for heuristic search in our tools. Similar to B&B the problem-specific and problem-independent parts allow separate implementation.

3. THE BNB-SOLVER FRAMEWORK

As already mentioned the BNB-Solver is a library for solving GO problems on serial machines, shared memory and distributed memory parallel computers. In BNB-Solver library we follow the standard approach taken in software frameworks for global optimization [2-5]: the problem-specific and problem-independent (core) parts are separated and implemented independently. Coupling of problem-specific and problem-independent parts is done via C++ template mechanism. Problem-specific branching operations, bounding rules and type definitions for subproblems and feasible points are encapsulated by a *problem factory* class. This class is substituted as a template argument within specializations of core classes. Below we consider core components for serial, shared and distributed memory implementations.

3.1. Serial Implementation

The core serial B&B component Traverse class template implements basic interface for branching: method branch splits a subproblem into a set of new subproblems by performing a given number of B&B steps. The certain implementation of the branch method is taken from the problem factory class substituted as a template argument.

3.2. Shared Memory Implementation

The core class PTraverse implements the multithreaded version of standard B&B scheme. Its branch method starts several threads that share a common pool of subproblems and maintain their own pools. Each thread performs a given threshold number of B&B steps storing resulting subproblems locally. After that the thread copies a chunk of subproblems from its local pool to the shared pool. Then the thread continues solution process with a subproblem taken from the local pool. If the local subproblem pool is exhausted the thread takes a new subproblem from the shared pool. If the shared pool is empty the requesting thread blocks until another thread fills it with subproblems.

In B&B methods every branching operation results in dynamic memory allocation for newly created subproblems. Memory allocation requires threads synchronization because the system memory is shared among multiple threads. In [6] it is observed that dynamic memory allocation causes severe performance losses of multithreaded B&B implementation. In BNB-Solver this problem is solved by a special memory manager that maintains local memory pools for every thread. Like Traverse class template PTraverse takes problem specific information from its template argument.

3.3. Distributed Memory Implementation

The general scheme of parallel implementation for distributed memory machines is depicted at the Fig. 2. In accordance with distributed memory programming paradigm the application consists of a set of MPI processes interacting via message-passing. At run-time processes are normally mapped onto different processors or cores.

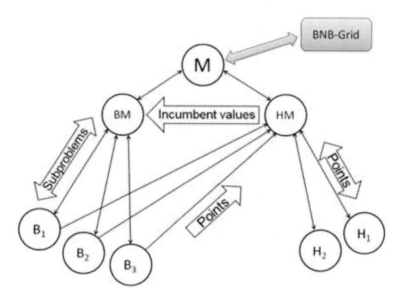

Figure 2. Distributed memory implementation in BNB-Solver.

The set of all processes is divided among B&B (BM and $\{B_i\}$) and heuristic (HM and $\{H_i\}$) parts. Master processes BM and HM manage B&B and heuristic slave processes respectively. Processes $\{H_i\}$ perform heuristic search by improving the collection of points maintained on process HM. New points are either generated by $\{H_i\}$ or borrowed from processes $\{B_i\}$ involved in B&B. New incumbent values produced by heuristics are transmitted through processes HM and BM to processes $\{B_i\}$ in order to facilitate bounding. The distributed memory solver is implemented by `MSSolver` class template with two template parameters – a class implementing tree traversal, i.e. implementing `branch` method and a class implementing the heuristic.

The supervisor process M provides an external interface to BNB-Solver. This interface is used by BNB-Grid to control computations and to exchange data with running application. If BNB-Solver runs as a standalone application this interface is used to read initial problem data from a file and to output the results.

3.4. Problem-specific Components

Core classes considered above provide general skeletons for different hardware platforms. To implement a solver for a concrete optimization problem one need to implement problem-specific classes and construct a solver for that problem substituting them as core classes' template parameters. BNB-Solver has been used to implement the following optimization algorithms:

- B&B and hybrid algorithms for boolean uni-dimensional knapsack;
- B&B algorithms for constraint continuous optimization;
- Stochastic algorithms for global optimization solver;
- B&B algorithms for traveling salesman problem.

4. THE SOFTWARE ARCHITECTURE OF BNB-GRID META-COMPUTING ENVIRONMENT

The BNB-Grid environment is aimed at solving optimization problems on a distributed system comprising geographically distributed heterogeneous computers. Computers called *computing elements* may range from personal computers to large publicly available clusters accessible via batch systems or Grid middleware. The tool is implemented entirely in Java on the top of object-oriented Internet Communication Engine (ICE) middleware [7]. ICE is a relatively new free framework for distributed computing. It provides nearly the same functionality as CORBA or DCOM but implemented in a more efficient and portable way. The four types of ICE objects in BNB-Grid are described in the Table 1.

Table 1. ICE-objects and their roles and interaction in the BNB-Grid environment

Name	Role	Multiplicity	Interaction
GUI	Graphical User Interface for interactive control over execution.	1	
CS-Manager	BNB-Grid's "brains" — a central component for managing workflow and work distribution.	1	
CE-Manager	Represents a single computing element. Responsible for starting and stopping BNB-Solver applications.	1..*	
App-Manager	Represents an instance of BNB-Solver application. Responsible for establishing connection and communication with the remote application.	1..*	

Below we consider different BNB-Grid components and their roles in detail.

4.1. Computing Element Management

Starting new BNB-Solver application instance is done by the following sequence of steps:

1. CE-Manager receives a request to start new application from CS-Manager;
2. CE-Manager t creates a new ICE-object instance of App-Manager;
3. App-Manager connects to a dedicated *proxy machine* via SSH and launches BNB-Proxy process;
4. App-Manager establishes a connection to BNB-Proxy;
5. BNB-Proxy process submits new instance of BNB-Solver application to the computing element;
6. The supervisor process of BNB-Solver application connects to BNB-Proxy.

The 6th step establishes a channel between App-Manager and BNB-Solver application. This channel is used to send work units and control data to and receive results from the running application. The proxy machine is a computer from which it is possible to submit jobs to the computing element. For a publicly available computational cluster the proxy machine is normally a cluster front-end node that is used by users to login and submit jobs to the batch system. For Grid site the proxy machine is any computer from which it is possible to submit jobs to that site. The job submission request is proceeded by a special shell script that encapsulates details of a particular batch system or Grid middleware and user credentials. BNB-Proxy selects a script suitable for a particular system. For the moment plain mpirun, PBS, Torque and Unicore Grid middleware are supported.

If the direct connection from the App-Manager to the proxy machine is prevented by firewall settings then App-Manager uses SSH for tunneling TCP/IP connection to BNB-Proxy. Our experience shows that for absolute majority of publicly accessible clusters the connection from computing nodes to the cluster front-end node is possible though the connection from computing nodes to the outside is blocked. Therefore we almost always use the cluster front-end node as a proxy machine.

For Grid sites the situation is more complex. If the TCP/IP connection from Grid computing element nodes to the proxy machine is allowed than there the standard communication scheme described above is used. Otherwise App-Manager communicates with BNB-Solver via files. The input and output data is transferred through the standard way provided by the Grid middleware. BNB-Solver application reads the initial data from the uploaded input file and BNB-Proxy reads the results from the downloaded output file. File-based communication introduces significant overheads that may prevent efficient implementation of algorithms with intensive data exchange. However many coarse grain methods like stochastic search or genetic algorithms can be efficiently implemented on systems consisting of such nodes.

4.2. Computing Space Management and Work Distribution

The CS-Manager is a Java program that performs two main tasks: computational space allocation and work distribution. Computational space allocation (or workflow construction) is a necessary first step before starting a computational process. It consists in submitting

BNB-Solver applications to available computing elements. The application is restarted after each occasional fault or termination forced by a batch system. Experiments show that in the presence of batch systems it is often more efficient to submit several applications with relatively small amount of requested CPUs rather than submitting a single big application because the latter usually stays in a queue unacceptably long.

Due to the irregular and highly unpredictable nature of optimization methods it is usually not possible to divide work among computing elements statically. The dynamically changing structure of computational space increases complexity. Therefore the only efficient approach is to distribute work dynamically along computations. In literature this approach is called *load balancing*. There were numerous studies of this subject. See [8, 9] for good surveys.

The BNB-Grid environment uses hierarchical two-level work distribution scheme. The top-level distribution is done by CS-Manager: it sends or requests work chunks from running BNB-Solver applications. The work chunk consists of several work units where the notion of unit depends on the running optimization method. For Branch-and-Bound methods the unit is a subset of a feasible solution set (a vertex in a search tree) while for heuristic algorithms it is a feasible solution.

The details of load-balancing algorithm are encapsulated by an implementation of a special `LoadBalancer` interface. By substituting different class definitions it is possible to select a suitable load-balancing strategy. We implemented two load-balancing schemes. In the first the relatively large number of units is generated before the resolution process begins. The load balancing consists in sending a unit of work to an available BNB-Solver application. This scheme was used for solving molecular conformation problem (Section 5). The second more sophisticated hierarchical scheme has been proposed in [10]. This scheme relies on a heuristics that redistributes work among computers in order to align the current workload. Our experiments showed that it can perform quite well for a knapsack problem.

Inside BNB-Solver application the load balancing is done by *centralized work pushing* mechanism. The master process acts like a sophisticated router or hub: it receives work units from CS-Manager and distributes them among working MPI processes running on cluster nodes. The detailed explanation of load balancing in BNB-Solver library is beyond the scope of this paper and can be found in [11, 12].

4.3. Reliable Computations

The Grid offers a huge amount of computational power. However that power comes for the price of reliability. The computing space formed by application sessions is changing dynamically: its elements can enter or leave at virtually arbitrary moments. Indeed BNB-Solver application can be forced to terminate by a batch system on a publicly available supercomputer or by network, hardware fault or reboot on a personal computer. Clearly a system for solving problems in such an environment should have means to cope with reliability issues.

BNB-Grid has a strictly defined notion of a state. The state contains a collection of feasible unexplored solutions for stochastic algorithms, collection of subsets of the feasible solution space for Branch-and-Bound algorithms and the best solution found so far called *incumbent solution*. A copy of a work portion submitted to a BNB-Solver instance (e.g. a collection of unexplored feasible solutions) is kept by CS-Manager. If BNB-Solver has processed the assigned work the saved copy is discarded. If the fault occurred the saved copy is merged with the state for processing later by some other instance of BNB-Solver. Thus no information is lost even in the case of an unexpected fault of some node.

The techniques described above do not help in the case of CS-Manager fault. To recover from such situations CS-Manager periodically saves its state including stored copies of assigned work to a file. In the case of fault the computations can be restarted from the latest saved state. In addition a user can save an intermediate state in the case the computations have to be temporally interrupted.

4.4. User Interface

BNB-Grid user interface is implemented as a separate ICE object with a strictly defined interface. Such separation allows implementing different user interfaces and building problem oriented environments on the top of BNB-Grid. At the moment we have implemented a general purposed GUI (Fig. 3) and a specialized GUI targeted at molecular conformation problem (Fig. 4).

The window of a general purposed GUI is divided into three panels. The first panel implements problem related activity: the user can load a problem definition, solver definition and load and save a problem state. The second panel lists available computing elements and their states. The last "Computing Space" panel lists established and terminated application sessions. Each session title is a name of respective computing element followed a session number enclosed in braces.

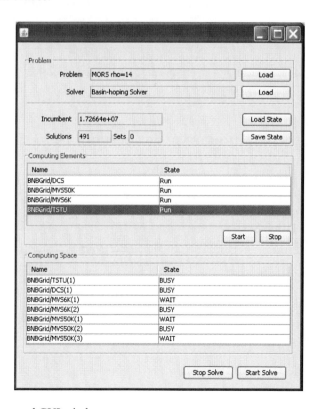

Figure 3. General purposed GUI window.

MC-CAD [13] is a problem-oriented environment supporting loading, storing, viewing and editing molecular conformations. It provides a convenient GUI (Fig. 4) based on the Avogadro editor [14]. This GUI connects to CS-Manager via the same interface as a general purposed GUI. BNB-Grid is used as a computational resource for minimizing the interaction energy of a given conformation.

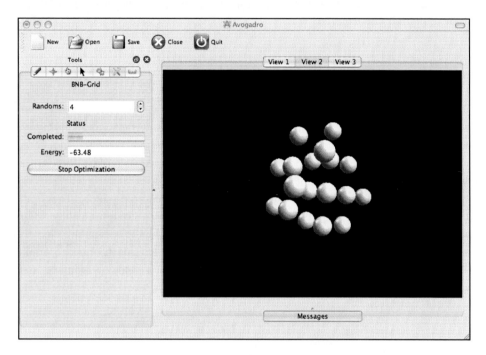

Figure 4. The main window of MC-CAD environment for molecular conformation problem.

5. EXPERIMENTAL RESULTS

We applied BNB-Grid to two problems. The first one is a knapsack problem [15]. Results for sample problem instances were earlier published in our paper [16]. For the space limitations we don not reproduce them here. The second problem is a famous and very challenging atomic cluster conformation problem [17]. The problem is stated as follows. Given positions $x = \{x^{(1)},...,x^{(n)}\}$ of n atoms a potential energy of a cluster is defined as a function

$$F(x) = \sum_{i=1}^{n} \sum_{j=i+1}^{n} v\left(\left\|x^{(i)} - x^{(j)}\right\|\right), \text{ where } \left\|x^{(i)} - x^{(j)}\right\| = \sqrt{\left(x_1^{(i)} - x_1^{(j)}\right)^2 + \left(x_2^{(i)} - x_2^{(j)}\right)^2 + \left(x_3^{(i)} - x_3^{(j)}\right)^2} \text{ is an}$$

Euclidian distance between atoms i and j and $v(r)$ is a pair potential function. We considered three pair potentials presented in the Table 2.

The potential energy minimization (PEM) is commonly recognized as one of the most hard global optimization problems. In spite of numerous studies (see [18] for a good survey) the search for globally minimal solutions is still an active field. New results are immediately available in the public database [19].

Table 2. Different pair potentials

Name	Formula
Lennard-Jones	$v_{LJ}(r) = r^{-12} - 2r^{-6}$
Morse	$v_M(r) = e^{\rho(1-r)}\left(e^{\rho(1-r)} - 2\right)$
Dzugutov	$v_D(r) = A\left(r^{-m} - B\right)e^{c/(r-a)}\Theta(a-r) + Be^{d/(r-b)}\Theta(b-r)$, where $\Theta(x) = \begin{cases} 0, \, x < 0, \\ 1, \, x \geq 0. \end{cases}$, $A = 5.82, B = 1.28, c = 1.10, m = 16, a = 1.87, b = 1.94, d = 0.27.$

Table 3. Computing elements used for experiments

Name	CPU Type	Number of Cores	Location
MVS50K	Intel Xeon E5450 3 GHz	7920	Joint Supercomputer Center (Moscow)
RNC	Intel Xeon 5365 3 GHz	3456	Russian Research Centre "Kurchatov Institute" (Moscow)
SKIF-URAL	Intel Xeon E5472 3 GHz	1328	South Ural State University, Chelyabinsk
MVS 6K	Intel Itanium 2, 2.2 GHz	256	Joint Supercomputer Center (Moscow)
OMEGA	Intel Xeon 5355 2 GHz	88	Institute for System Programming (Moscow)
MIET	Intel Xeon 5130 2 GHz	56	Moscow Institute of Electronic Technology (Zelenograd)

Attempts to solve the PEM problem with a proof of optimality for a given precision failed to cope with problems of more than 10 atoms [20]. Therefore the best known minima at the moment are putative optima in the sense there is no 100% guarantee that better solutions don't exist. All known minima were found by heuristic algorithms. The most successful algorithms combine geometry information and local search. Some general purpose algorithms can also perform quite well for this problem. In [21] Leary proposed a monotonic basin-hoping (MBH) algorithm which improved some previously known global minima for Lennard-Jones potential. MBH consists in a small perturbation followed by descending to a local minimum. This step is repeated until a given *max-no-improve* number of iterations are performed. After that the search is restarted from a different random point. Grosso et al. [22] reported that MBH requires too many restarts to be feasible for a Morse potential with $\rho = 14$ for more than 40 atoms. At present algorithms relying on geometric structure of the optimal cluster conformation outperforms general purpose ones. Nevertheless applying the latter makes a lot of sense because they serve as an additional check for the geometrically inspired heuristics because the latter may rely on wrong assumptions about the cluster structure. Moreover general purposed algorithms are very useful for conformational analysis when finding all local minima is required. Therefore solving PEM problem with by a general purpose algorithm is still an open and important problem.

We implemented a parallel version of monotonic basin hoping in BNB-Solver. Unlike original version parallel MBH simultaneously performs several perturbations of the current feasible solution and selects the best one. Computing equipment used in experiments is listed in Table 3 in the order of descending power. Clusters 1-6 were accessible via the batch system. The last node (OMEGA) was available in exclusive mode. Number of cores simultaneously harnessed in computations varied in a range 200-2400 with an average number of approximately 1200 cores. One instance of BNB-Solver occupied 8 cores. The number of simultaneously running BNB-Solver applications ranged from 50 to 600.

We selected most hard molecular conformation instances those were not solved by general purposed algorithms before. Best known optima for these instances were obtained by Dynamic Lattice Search [23] – a heuristic based on spherical deformations of a molecular cluster. Table 4 lists experimental data for some of the selected instances. We were able to obtain all known optima for Morse in range 1-100 atoms all known optima for Lennard-Jones clusters in the range 1-150 and all optimal Dzugutov clusters with up to 50 atoms. Experiments showed that general purposed algorithms can be very efficient for solving this problem provided that sufficient computational resources are involved.

Table 4. Exprimental results for molecular conformation problem

Potential	Number of atoms	Number of initial points	Maximal noimprove	Total computing time	Number of hits	Obtained minima	Best known minima
Lennard Jones	98	512	8192	43	8	-543.665361	-543.665361
Morse $\rho = 14$	80	1024	8192	244	3	-340.811371	-340.811371
Morse $\rho = 14$	85	1024	8192	188	5	-363.891261	-363.893075
Morse $\rho = 14$	90	1024	8192	266	2	-388.401652	-388.401652
Morse $\rho = 14$	100	1024	8192	232	8	-439.070547	-439.070547
Dzugutov	50	1024	8192	175	2	-104.366189	-104.366189
Dzugutov	100	1024	32758	371	1	-218.744395	-219.523265

RELATED WORK

Paper [24] discusses the FATCOP tool aimed at solving mixed integer programming problems by a Branch-and-Bound method on a network of workstations (NOW). FATCOP is built on top of Condor-PVM message passing library. This library is a part of Condor[18] – a system for distributed computing on NOWs. Two most notable features of Condor are the ability to detect idle workstations and to provide inter-host task migration. FATCOP follows a master working paradigm and a simple centralized load balancing strategy. To cope with unexpected failures the master process saves work assigned to a node in a pool and in the case of failure resubmits it to another node.

Another Condor based infrastructure for master-worker computing on the Grid called MW is proposed in [26]. This framework has been successfully applied to different optimization problems [27, 28]. MW is built on top of Condor. Using flocking and glide-in mechanisms Condor is able to harness thousands of geographically distributed workstations and processors of different computational clusters. MW uses pure master-working paradigm: there is a single point of control that coordinates computations of numerous CPUs involved. As authors state correctly there are many problems and resolution methods that can be efficiently implemented in this centralized approach. Nevertheless there are lots of problems that require tight cooperation of nodes where pure master-worker approach is inefficient.

Unlike FATCOP that focuses on mixed integer programming problems MALLBA [29] is aimed at solving arbitrary global optimization problems by exact heuristic and hybrid methods. To be independent on a particular middleware MALLBA uses own set of communication and process management routines. Different optimization algorithms are implemented as different skeletons with the common interface. Such approach reduces efforts needed to implement new problems. Successful results for some problems were reported. These results were obtained on local network or computational clusters and from papers it is not clear whether MALLBA can efficiently work in wide-area networks.

The solution for distributed systems consisting of several clusters connected via wide-area networks (WAN) is proposed in papers [10, 30]. Branch-and-bound algorithms are implemented via Ninf-G [31] middleware which provides secure communication over WANs and LANs. The system efficiently utilizes the hierarchical nature of distributed systems: good results are reported for different optimization problems. This approach is close to ours in the sense the work distribution is managed on two levels. At the top level the work is assigned to master processes while at the second level master processes distribute the work among their slaves. The difference is that we use MPI for communication within a single cluster while in [10, 31] the intra-cluster communication is done via Ninf middleware.

BNB-Grid combines best features of the approaches listed above: fault tolerance, hierarchical load balancing, separating problem-specific from problem-independent parts. Unlike other approaches we use different communication mechanisms at the bottom and top levels of hierarchy. Namely we use TCP/IP and ICE on the upper and MPI or PTHREADS on the bottom levels respectively. We believe that such an approach is more efficient because native communication mechanisms allow complete utilization of computing element network resources. For shared-memory machines threading is in general significantly outperforms other approaches. Another reason is that the direct connection from cluster nodes to the outside may be very slow or even forbidden.

CONCLUSION

In this paper we described BNB-Solver and BNB-Grid tools that form a layered software infrastructure for solving optimization problems in heterogeneous distributed computing environment. Related work analysis and experimental study suggested the following principles crucial for efficient resolution of optimization problems in the Grid:

1. modular structure that separates problem-specific and problem-independent parts;
2. hierarchy-aware work distribution;
3. fault-tolerance;
4. hierarchy-aware communications, i.e. using different communication mechanisms on different levels of hierarchy.

All this features are implemented in the presented infrastructure. In the future we plan to run more experiments with different optimization problems and resolution methods as well as to enlarge the number of processors involved in computations.

REFERENCES

[1] R. Horst and P.M. Pardalos (eds.), *Handbook of Global Optimization*, Kluwer, Dordrecht, 1995.

[2] E. Alba, F. Almeida, M. Blesa et al. Efficient Parallel LAN/WAN Algorithms for Optimization. The MALLBA Project. *Parallel Computing* 32(5-6):415-440, 2006.

[3] T. Ralphs, Parallel branch and cut. In: *Parallel Combinatorial Optimization*. JohnWiley & Sons, New Jersey, pp. 53-103, 2006.

[4] J. Eckstein, C. Philips, W. Hart, PEBBL 1.0 User Guide. *RUTCOR Research Report* RRR 19-2006.

[5] S. Tschöke, N. Holthöfer, A new parallel approach to the constrained two-dimensional cutting stock problem. In: *Parallel Algorithms for Irregularly Structured Problems*, LNCS 980, pp. 285-300, 2005.

[6] L. Casado, J. Martínez, I. García et al. Branch-and-Bound interval global optimization on shared memory multiprocessors. *Optim Methods and Softw.* 2008. Doi: 10.1080/10556780802086300

[7] M. Henning. A New Approach to Object-Oriented Middleware. *IEEE Internet Computing*, Jan 2004.

[8] H. Trienekens, A. Bruin, Towards a taxonomy of parallel branch and bound algorithms. *Report EUR*-CS-92-01, Erasmus Universisty. Rotterdam, 1992.

[9] B. Gendron, T.G. Grainic, Parallel branch-and-bound survey and synthesis//*Operations Research*. V. 42. № 6. P. 1042-1066, 1994.

[10] K. Aida, W. Natsume, Y. Futakata, Distributed Computing with Hierarchical Master-worker Paradigm for Parallel Branch and Bound Algorithm, *Proc. 3rd IEEE/ACM International Symposium on Cluster Computing and the Grid* (CCGrid 2003), pp.156-163, 2003.

[11] M.A. Posypkin, I.Kh. Sigal, Investigation of Algorithms for Parallel Computations in Knapsack-Type Discrete Optimization Problems. *Computational Mathematics and Mathematical Physics*, Vol. 45, No. 10, 2005, pp. 1735-1742.

[12] M.A. Posypkin, I.Kh. Sigal, Application of Parallel Heuristic Algorithms for Speeding up Parallel Implementations of the Branch-and-Bound Method. *Computational Mathematics and Mathematical Physics*, Vol.4, No. 9, 2007, pp. 1524-1537.

[13] S.A. Smirnov. A distributed programming environment for molecular structure modeling. In *Proc. of Third International Conference "Contemporary Information Technologies and IT Education."* pp. 521-528, 2008 (in Russian).

[14] Avogadro Editor. http://avogadro.openmolecules.net/wiki/Main_Page

[15] H. Kellerer, U. Pfershy, D. Pisinger, *Knapsack Problems.* Springer Verlag, 546 p., 2004.

[16] A. Afanasiev, O. Sukhoroslov, M. Posypkin, A High-Level Toolkit for Development of Distributed Scientific Applications// *Proceedings of Parallel Computing Technologies 9th International Conference*, PaCT 2007, Pereslavl-Zalessky, Russia, September 3-7, p. 103-110, 2007.

[17] D. Wales,J. Doye. Global Optimization by Basin-Hopping and the Lowest Energy Structures of Lennard-Jones Clusters Containing up to 110 Atoms. *J. Phys. Chem. A*, 101, 5111-5116, 1997.

[18] P.M. Pardalos, D. Shalloway, and G. Xue. Global Minimization of Nonconvex Energy Functions: Molecular Conformation and Protein Folding, *DIMACS Series* Vol. 23. American Mathematical Society, 1996.

[19] *The Cambridge Cluster Database.* http://www-wales.ch.cam.ac.uk/CCD.html.

[20] C. D. Maranas, C. A. Floudas. A Global Optimization Approach for Lennard-Jones Microclusters // *Journal of Chemical Physics*, Vol. 97, P. 7667-7677, 1992.

[21] R. H. Leary. Global Optimization on Funneling Landscapes. *J. of Global Optimization* 18, 4 (Dec. 2000), 367-383, 2000.

[22] A. Grosso, M. Locatelli, and F. Schoen. A population based approach for hard global optimization problems based on dissimilarity measures. *Mathematical Programming*, 110(2):373-404, 2007.

[23] L. Cheng, J. Yang, Global Minimum Structures of Morse Clusters as a Function of the Range of the Potential: 81 <= N <= 160 // *Journal of Physical Chemistry*, 111, P. 5287-5293, 2007.

[24] Q. Chen, and M. C. Ferris, FATCOP: A Fault Tolerant Condor-PVM Mixed Integer Programming Solver. *SIAM J. on Optimization* 11, 4 (Apr. 2000), 1019-1036, 2000.

[25] M. Litzkow, M. Livny, and , M. W. Mutka, Condor - A Hunter of Idle Workstations, *Proceedings of the 8th International Conference of Distributed Computing Systems*, San Jose, California, June, 1988, pp. 104-111.

[26] J.-P Goux, S. Kulkarni, J. T. Linderoth, and M. E. Yoder, Master-Worker: *An Enabling Framework for Applications on the Computational Grid, Cluster Computing* 4, pp. 63-70, 2001.

[27] K. Anstreicher and N. Brixius and J.-P. Goux and J. T. Linderoth, *Solving Large Quadratic Assignment Problems on Computational Grids, Mathematical Programming*, Series B, 91, pp. 563-588, 2002.

[28] J. Linderoth, F. Margot, and G. Thain, The Tera-Gridiron: A Natural Turf for High-Throughput Computing, Technical Report 07T-001, *Industrial and Systems Engineering*, Lehigh University, 2007.

[29] E. Alba et al.. MALLBA: A Library of Skeletons for Combinatorial Optimisation (Research Note). In *Proceedings of the 8th international Euro-Par Conference on Parallel Processing*, pp. 927-932, 2002.

[30] K. Aida, Y. Futakata, T. Osumi. Parallel Branch and Bound Algorithm with the Hierarchical Master-Worker Paradigm on the Grid, *IPSJ Trans. on Advanced Computing Systems*, Vol.47, No.SIG.12(ACS 15), 2006.

[31] H. Nakada, Y. Tanaka, S. Matsuoka, S. Sekiguchi, Ninf-G: a GridRPC system on the Globus toolkit, Grid Computing: *Making the Global Infrastructure a Reality*, John Wiley & Sons Ltd, pp. 625-638, 2003.

In: Horizons in Computer Science Research, Volume 4
Editor: Thomas S. Clary
ISBN: 978-1-61324-262-9

Chapter 7

IMPLEMENTATION MODELS FOR FUNCTION BLOCK AND FUNCTION BLOCK APPLICATION IN DISTRIBUTED INTELLIGENT CONTROL NETWORK BASED ON WORLD FIP PROTOCOL

Geng Liang[1]

School of Control and Computer Engineering,
North China Electric Power University, Beijing 102206, China

ABSTRACT

Configuration platforms based on function blocks and links such as Function Block Diagram (FBD) are used widely in designing and implementing distributed intelligent control network (DICN). Traditionally, FBD and Ladder Diagram (LD) are two completely different programming languages with different data models and compilation algorithms to generate different data and instructions for field intelligent nodes. Essential difference exists between implementation methods of control strategies with the two programming languages for data exchange within and between different nodes, which make it difficult for unification of programming languages in configuration platform, hybrid programming and improvement of control systems' openness and compliancy. Besides, products and systems developed based on WorldFIP technology are all above control level. No fully distributed intelligent control system based on field intelligent nodes is implemented. In the first part of this chapter, a kind of generalized FBD model for distributed intelligent control network is described. Scheme for implementing such model in field intelligent node is presented in detail. Transformation models for language elements in LD are presented based on the described model. The model is flexible and widely applicable. Application of the proposed model in design and development of configuration platform software for distributed intelligent system show the effectiveness of the model. In the second part of this chapter, a practical and general-purposed FBA model is presented. Data storage segmentation model for field intelligent nodes are expounded in detail. Concept of user layer in WorldFIP communication model is described and data model for user layer is defined. The schedule algorithms for the proposed FBA

---

[1] E-mail address: liangeng1976@163.com

model are presented in detail. Guided by the FBA model, design and implementation of distributed intelligent system based on Function Block and FBA is achieved.

Keywords: Network protocol, Fieldbus, WorldFIP, Function Block, Function Block Application, Distributed Intelligent System.

PART I. A IMPLEMENTATION MODELS FOR FUNCTION BLOCK IN DISTRIBUTED INTELLIGENT CONTROL NETWORK BASED ON WORLDFIP PROTOCOL

1. INTRODUCTION

In recent years, distributed intelligent control networks (DICN) symbolized by fieldbus technology and fieldbus control system (FCS), wireless communication network, sensors network developed fast to become the development trend for larg-scale measurement and control system. tho These systems are characterized by parallel computation and complete danger-distribution with their control and measurement function in these systems are distributed in each field node. Implementation of DICN are mainly based on upper-level configuration platform whose principal programming languages are Function Block Diagram (FBD) and ladder diagram (LD) conformed to norm IEC61131-3, remote communication between field intelligent nodes and local control function. All or parts of the 5 programming languages are to be supported by upper-level configuration platform according to norm IEC61131. FBD and LD are more widely used in DICN [1-5]. Completely different data model and compilation algorithm are used in traditional FBD and LD that are 2 completely different and independent languages in user's configuration. In the meantime, implementation methods for data exchange locally and between nodes dealing with control strategies written in the 2 programming languages are different essentially [6], which make it very difficult to realize uniform in the programming languages and hybrid programming in a same programming platform. In this part of the chapter, a kind of Generalized Function Block Diagram (GFBD) model and implementation scheme for the model in field intelligent nodes is described. The transform model for Ladder Diagram based on the GFBD is also presented. The proposed model is with strong flexibility and wide application range and independent of sorting algorithms in compilation of configuration written in GFBD, which resolved the above mentioned problems. Based on the proposed GFBD model, traditionally different programming languages can be used together in a same configuration platform and the same compiler and compilation algorithm can be used to compile user's program written in the both FBD and LD languages, which improved the re-usage and production efficiency of software and shorten the time in configuration software development and programming in configuration platform. In the meantime, the related thought can be extended, expanded and used in the capsulation of configuration modules written in other programming languages such as instruction list (IL) and structured text (ST).

2. GENERALIZED FUNCTION BLOCK DIAGRAM MODEL

The fundamental thought in constructing GFBD is that any a kind of diagram system composed of "block" and "link" can be discomposed into 2 fundamental elements, i.e. generalized function blocks (GFB) and links. Therefore, the applicable premise included in the thought in modeling is loose, which makes the model more flexible and wider in usage.

In the proposed GFB model, all characteristics in standard FB specified by IEC61131-3 are included. Furthermore, number in inputs and outputs specified by the norm are extended, which means the number of inputs and outputs can be 0~n (n >=1).

GFBD can be described as:

1. GFBD is composed of multi GFBs and links. Multi starting and ending GFBs are allowable in GFBD. Starting GFB is defined as a GFB without input, with more than 1 output and linked with other GFBs. Ending GFB is defined as a GFB without output, with more than 1 input and linked with other GFBs;

2. Each GFB can be viewed as a module including input and output terminals, contained parameters and instruction operation;

3. Each Link can be viewed as "copy" operation to copy the data from output terminal of one GFB to input terminal of the other GFB;

4. GFB and Link are independent from each other in operation and function. Operational field of GFB is within the function block itself and has nothing to do with Link. Data are drawn out from the input terminal of GFB and processed with certain algorithm and written out to the output of the GFB. Data transmission between different GFBs are handled by Link. The location information for both upper-reach GFB and lower-reach GFB are stored in a Link which linking the starting GFB and ending GFB. Only location information for output terminals are stored in starting GFB. Only location information for input terminals are stored in ending GFB.

The proposed GFB model is illustrated with Fig.1.

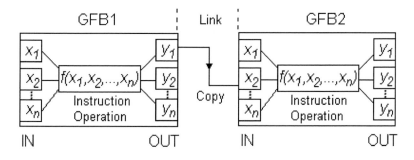

Figure 1. Generalized Function Block Diagram Model.

3. CONSTRUCTION AND IMPLEMENTATION OF GFBD MODEL IN FIELD INTELLIGENT NODES IN DICN

Form and structure of field intelligent nodes are relatively simple and with small-sized memory. In the meantime, the performance of processors in them are lower than that in upper level PC. These facts make it necessary that the data storage are to be continuous and can be accessed quickly.

In the proposed GFBD model, data after compilation of GFBD are stored into 4 segments which are GFB instruction codes segment, GFB input terminals segment, GFB output terminals segment, GFB contained parameters segment. All GFB instruction codes are stored in the GFB instruction codes segment. All GFB input terminals are stored in the GFB input terminals segment. All GFB output terminals are stored in the GFB input terminals segment. All GFB contained parameters are stored in GFB contained parameters segment. Data storage structures in 4 segments are different from each other [7].

3.1. Data Storage Structure in GFB Instruction Codes Segments

Two kinds of instruction code, which are GFB and Link instruction respectively, are stored in GFB instruction segment in field intelligent node. The structure of GFB instruction code is shown in Fig.2. Meaning of each field are as following:

Flag: instruction flag;
GFB_type: GFB types indicating algorithms or functions implemented with the GFB, such as PID control function;
In_index: starting index for input terminals of the GFB in input terminal segment;
Out_index: starting index for output terminals of the GFB in output terminal segment;
Offset: offset in number of byte of contained parameters in the FB in contained parameters segment.

| flag | GFB_type | in_index | out_index | offset |

Figure 2. Structure of GFB instruction code in field intelligent node.

The structure of Link instruction code is shown in Fig.3. Meaning of each field are as following:

Flag: instruction flag;
Out_index: starting index in FB output terminal segment in local node for the output terminal of upper-reach FB linked by starting point of Link instruction;
Addr: physical address of the remote field intelligent node in which the lower-reach GFB linked by ending point of Link instruction. The field value is 255 if the GFB is local;
In_index: starting index of input terminal of FB linked by Link instruction in FB input terminal segment in object node.

flag	out_index	addr	in_index

Figure 3. Structure of Link instruction code in field intelligent node.

Each GFB instruction and Link instruction are stored together with the same memory size. The first byte of each instruction is instruction flag. When the instruction is scanned with the instruction segment by the intelligent node, the instruction is differently interpreted and processed and pointer in instruction segment is moved backwards with different memory size span. The whole process is repeated continuously until the flag in current instruction indicates the end of the segment.

3.2. Data Storage Structure in FB Input/Output Segments

Four-byte unit are used universally as input/output storage structure for that operations dealing with float number are mainstream in field intelligent nodes and the uniform in data storage. The numbers of Four-byte units in memory for the input/output segment are generated in time of compilation of user's configuration in upper-level computer. Initialization of input/output segments in memory are done by field intelligent nodes autonomously when configuration downloads are finished.

3.3. Data Storage Structure in GFB Contained Parameter Segments

It is difficult even impossible to construct a universal data storage unit which is economic and flexible for many variety of GFB contained parameters. Therefore, 1-byte unit is chosen as the data storage unit for GFB contained parameters segment. Each parameter are aligned adjacently and offset in bytes and data length are used in identification of each parameter.

To summarize, the data storage segmentation and linkage orienting field intelligent nodes are shown as Fig.4, in which a PID control is set as an example. In Fig.3, number "(4)" indicates number of bytes.

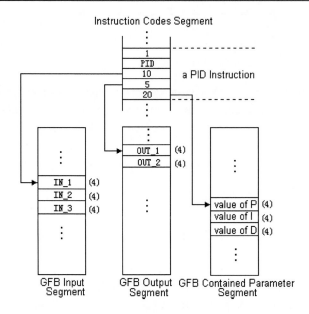

Figure 4. Data storage segmentation model in field intelligent nodes.

Data in each segment is stored compactly in field intelligent nodes. Array is used as the storage forms for all data in each segment except data in contained parameters segments in which byte-unit is used to store data. Array elements in input/output segment are of double-word type. Instruction codes in instruction segment is stored with the same memory size using following data structure [8]:

```
typedef union COMMAND_FOR_DEVICE
{
FBINFO_FOR_DEVICE fbinfo_for_device;
LINKINFO_FOR_DEVICE linkinfo_for_device;
};
typedef struct FBINFO_FOR_DEVICE
{
BYTE flag ;
BYTE fb_type;
WORD in_index;
WORD out_index;
WORD offset;
};
typedef struct LINKINFO_FOR_DEVICE
{
BYTE flag;
WORD out_index;
BYTE addr;
WORD in_index;
};
```

4. LADDER DIAGRAM ANALYSIS MODEL BASED ON GFBD MODEL

LD conforms to the application condition for GFBD model. Therefore, LD diagram elements can be analysed and transformed into GFBD elements. The transformation is as follows:

① Left vertical bar: equivalent to a kind of GFB with 0 input and multi outputs. Its operational logic can be described as the output values of the GFBD equal to constant 1. Equivalent transformation is shown in Fig.5.

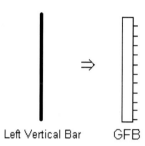

Figure 5. Equivalent transformation from left vertical bar to GFB.

② Contact and coil: equivalent to a kind of GFB with 1 input and 1 output. Their operational logics are dependent on the types of specified diagram elements. For example, equivalent transformation from normally open contact/ normally closed contact to a GFB is shown in Fig.6.

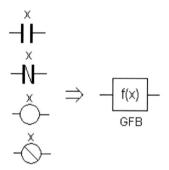

Figure 6. Equivalent transformation from contacts and coils to GFB.

③ Horizontal link: equivalent to a kind of GFB with 1 input and multi outputs. Its operational logic can be described as logical operation "OR";

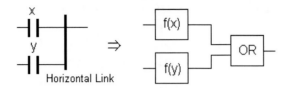

Figure 7. Equivalent transformation from horizontal link to GFB.

④ Lin@ks in LD: equivalent to link element in GFBD.

CONCLUSIONS

In this part of the chapter, a kind of Generalized Function Block Diagram (GFBD) model and implementation scheme for the model in field intelligent nodes is described. The transformation model for Ladder Diagram based on the GFBD is also presented. The described model is with strong flexibility and wide application range and independent of sorting algorithms in compilation of configuration written in GFBD, which resolved the above mentioned problems. Based on the GFBD model, traditionally different programming languages can be used together in a same configuration platform and the same compiler and compilation algorithm can be used to compile user's program written in the both FBD and LD languages, which improved the re-usage and production efficiency of software and shorten the time in configuration software development and programming in configuration platform. In the meantime, the related thought can be extended, expanded and used in the capsulation of configuration modules written in other programming languages such as instruction list (IL) and structured text (ST)[9-11]. The GFBD model has been applied in design and development of configuration software platform conforming to norm IEC61131-3 for DICN. The developed configuration platform is stable, efficient, flexible and extensible, which showed great effectiveness of the model.

PART II. A IMPLEMENTATION MODELS FOR FUNCTION BLOCK APPLICATION IN DICN BASED ON WORLDFIP PROTOCOL

1. INTRODUCTION

Products and systems developed based on WorldFIP are above control level and DICN based on intelligent nodes are not implemented yet. Function Block (FB) and Function Block Application (FBA), which are the most important means to implement fully distributed intelligent control network based on field intelligent nodes and communication in field, are the kernel parts in the implementation of DICN [12-15]. A kind of practically feasible FBA model is described in this part of the chapter based on independently developed WorldFIP DICN. Field intelligent nodes oriented data segmentation and structure for data segments in the described model are expounded. Concept of user layer in WorldFIP communication model is described and data sub-model in user layer in WorldFIP communication model, which serving as the base for implementation of the proposed FBA model in WorldFIP communication protocol. The proposed model is easy to implement and with good real time, certainty and transplantation in control. Good validity of the presented FBA model is shown by operational practice of the developed intelligent network control system.

2. Data Storage Segmentation Model for Field Intelligent Nodes

It is relatively simple in structure for field intelligent nodes in distributed intelligent control network. Memory in the nodes is small-sized; furthermore, performance of processor in the nodes are much lower than that in the PC. These facts make it necessary that the data storage are to be continuous and can be accessed quickly [16, 17].

In the described FBA model, the memory in field intelligent nodes is divided into 4 segments, which are FB instruction codes segment, FB input terminals segment, FB output terminals segment, FB contained parameters segment, to store the compiled and downloaded users' configuration data. All FB instruction codes are stored in the FB instruction codes segment. All FB input terminals are stored in the FB input terminals segment. All FB output terminals are stored in the FB input terminals segment. All FB contained parameters are stored in FB contained parameters segment. Data storage structures in 4 segments are different from each other.

2.1. Data Storage Structure in FB Instruction Codes Segments

Two kinds of instruction code, which are FB and link instruction respectively, are stored in FB instruction segment in field intelligent node. The structure of FB instruction code is shown in Fig.8. Meaning of each field are as following:

Flag: instruction flag;
FB_type: FB types indicating algorithms or functions implemented with the FB, such as PID control function;
In_index: starting index for input terminals of the FB in input terminal segment;
Out_index: starting index for output terminals of the FB in output terminal segment;
Offset: offset in number of byte of contained parameters in the FB in contained parameters segment.

flag	FB_type	in_index	out_index	offset

Figure8. Structure of FB instruction code in field intelligent node.

The structure of Link instruction code is shown in Fig.9. Meaning of each field are as following:

Flag: instruction flag;

Out_index: starting index in FB output terminal segment in local node for the output
terminal of upper-reach FB linked by starting point of Link instruction;

Addr: physical address of the remote field intelligent node in which the lower-reach FB
linked by ending point of Link instruction. The field value is 255 if the FB is local;

In_index: starting index of input terminal of FB linked by Link instruction in FB input
terminal segment in object node.

flag	out_index	addr	in_index

Figure 9. Structure of Link instruction code in field intelligent node.

Each FB instruction and Link instruction are stored together with the same memory size.
The first byte of each instruction is instruction flag. When the instruction is scanned with the
instruction segment by the intelligent node, the instruction is differently interpreted and
processed and pointer in instruction segment is moved backwards with different memory size
span. The whole process is repeated continuously until the flag in current instruction indicates
the end of the segment.

2.2. Data Storage Structure in FB Input/Output Segments

Four-byte unit are used universally as input/output storage structure for that operations
dealing with float number are mainstream in field intelligent nodes and the uniform in data
storage. The numbers of Four-byte units in memory for the input/output segment are
generated in time of compilation of user's configuration in upper-level computer.
Initialization of input/output segments in memory are done by field intelligent nodes
autonomously when configuration downloads are finished.

2.3. Data Storage Structure in FB Contained Parameter Segments

It is difficult even impossible to construct a universal data storage unit which is economic
and flexible for many variety of FB contained parameters. Therefore, 1-byte unit is chosen as
the data storage unit for FB contained parameters segment. Each parameter are aligned
adjacently and offset in bytes and data length are used in identification of each parameter.

To summarize, the data storage segmentation and linkage orienting field intelligent nodes
are shown as Fig.3, in which a PID control is set as an example. In Fig.10, number "(4)"
indicates number of bytes.

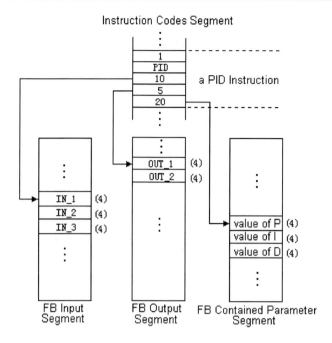

Figure 10. Data storage segmentation model in field intelligent nodes.

Data in each segment is stored compactly in field intelligent nodes. Array is used as the storage forms for all data in each segment except data in contained parameters segments in which byte-unit is used to store data. Array elements in input/output segment are of double-word type. Instruction codes in instruction segment is stored with the same memory size using following data structure:

```
typedef union COMMAND_FOR_DEVICE
{
FBINFO_FOR_DEVICE fbinfo_for_device;
LINKINFO_FOR_DEVICE linkinfo_for_device;
};
typedef struct FBINFO_FOR_DEVICE
{
BYTE flag;
BYTE fb_type;
WORD in_index;
WORD out_index;
WORD offset;
};
typedef struct LINKINFO_FOR_DEVICE
{
BYTE flag;
WORD out_index;
BYTE addr;
WORD in_index;
```

Meaning of each variable can be referred to Fig.8 and Fig.9.

3. DATA MODEL IN USER LAYER IN WORLDFIP COMMUNICATION

Physical layer, data linkage layer and application layer in ISO/OSI 7-layer reference model are adopted in reference model for WorldFIP fieldbus communication.

Composition of WorldFIP communication protocol is shown in Fig.11.

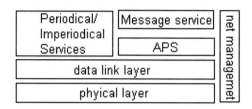

Figure 11. Composition of WorldFIP communication protocol.

WorldFIP communication is master-slave typed. The whole network is composed of bus schedulers which serves as master and field intelligent nodes which are subordinate. Value exchange between periodical and non-periodical variables and messages exchange are scheduled with bus schedulers. Two types of data exchange are used in network: data exchanges based on variable exchanges, which are usually used to transmit real-time and periodical data, and message exchange based on physically addressing. Detailed information can be referred to related reference. The following types of frames are used to exchange data over WorldFIP network.

The following is based on variables exchange:

ID_DAT: sent by bus scheduler and used to initialize a variable exchange process;
RP_DAT: sent by a field intelligent node and used to respond to ID_DAT to realize the data transmission based on variable exchange.

The following is based on message transmission:

ID_MSG: sent by bus scheduler and used to initialize a message transmission process;
RP_MSG: sent by a field intelligent node and used to respond to ID_MSG to realize the message transmission.
RP_MSG_ACK: sent by bus scheduler and used to acknowledge the data sent by field intelligent node;
RP_FIN: sent by a field intelligent node and used to respond to RP_MSG_ACK to finalize a message transmission process.

In the described model, RP_MSG_ACK is used to assure the reliable data transmission. Format of WorldFIP message frame is shown in Fig.12.

FSS	CON	PDU-T	LOM	AOD	AOS	MSG	FCS	FES

Figure 12. Format of WorldFIP message frame.

FSS: frame starting series;
CON: control
PDU_T: type of protocol data unit;
LOM: length of message;
AOD: address of destination;
AOS: address of source;
MSG: user's message;
FCS: frame check series:
FES: frame ending series;

In above frame format, all fields except "MSG" field are specified by WorldFIP protocol and have nothing to do with user layer in WorldFIP protocol. Therefore, "MSG" are the only field users can control use freely. Although physical layer, data link layer and application layer in WorldFIP communication reference model are standard, it is noticeable that there is no concept of user layer in the reference model. Norm for user layer are not specified yet. No universal norm is specified for user's data wrapped by application layer. A kind of user layer model in WorldFIP communication protocol is described according to "MSG" field in Fig.12 with process control as its application object.

For those field intelligent nodes using WorldFIP FULLFIP2 chips in communication, the maximum length of message is 256 bytes; for those using MICROFIP chips, the maximum length of message is 128 bytes. In the proposed user layer model, user's data are divided into several sub-fields illustrated by Fig.13, which relates closely to the data storage segmentation model in field intelligent nodes.

Figure 13. User layer model in WorldFIP communication protocol.

ID code: the field is set for system extension in future. Currently, ID code bears only 1 value that means "link operation" corresponding to the data transmission between FBs in different field intelligent nodes;

Input_index: index for the input terminal in input segment of lower-reach FB in remote linkage between FBs in different field intelligent nodes.

Data (float type): data wrapped in message.

5. FBA SCHEDULE ALGORITHM

4.1. "Passive Schedule" Based on Compel Data

Control strategies specified by users through configuration are executed in field intelligent nodes. Data and instructions are downloaded from users' PC to field nodes over network link scheduler. A "passive" schedule algorithm are used, which is different from "active" schedule algorithm in local nodes. In this mode, only compel data (CD) are transmitted between bus scheduler and element intelligent nodes. The compel data can be defined as a constant instruction execution in element nodes is scheduled by bus scheduler. Current instruction pointed by instruction pointer is to be executed only after receipt of compel data from bus scheduler. Field element nodes wait until the next compel data are received after finishing executing current instruction. The data, which are not constant, transmitted between different field intelligent nodes are those needed by remote FBs in FBA. FBs are executed repeatedly. Each repetition is a macro cycle. Any instruction executions within field intelligent nodes are under full-time schedule in each macro cycle. The "passive" schedule algorithm based on compel data are described as follows:

Bus scheduler sends compel data to field element intelligent nodes over network in periodical variable exchange form at certain time-tick specified by schedule table. Instructions are executed in the element nodes after the compel data are received. Detailed implementation is described as follows.

1. production variables corresponding to each element node are established in bus scheduler before startup of the whole control system. For example, 0x0501 is a consuming variable in element node N1, 0x0502 is a consuming variable in element node N2. Then 2 production variables 0x0501 and 0x0502 corresponding to the 2 consuming variables are established in bus scheduler;
2. CD are written into the production variables in bus scheduler;
3. scheduling item dealing with variable exchange, which are {0x0501, ID_DAT}and {0x0502,ID_DAT} in this example, are added to bus schedule table.

Thus, variable exchange can be implemented conforming to the time-tick specified by the schedule table over WorldFIP network, illustrating in Fig.14. After the CD is received as a consuming variable by element node, current instruction pointed by a pointer in FB instruction segment are executed. The pointer is moved backwards to next instruction after the execution of current instruction.

When MicroFIP chips are used in field intelligent nodes, data exchange can not be implemented between field intelligent nodes and can only be implemented by forwarding of bus scheduler, which make the communication less efficient. In the proposed model, periodical message exchanges between nodes are chosen to solve the problem. The data to be transmitted are wrapped in a message frame based on the above mentioned "data model in user layer", which ensures direct data exchange between element nodes and real-time in communication.

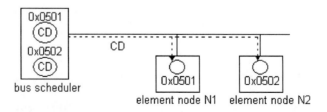

Figure 14. "Passive Schedule" based on compel data.

There are 2 types of FBA that are single-task FBA, which means that only one set of linkage from starting FB to ending FB, named FB task here, is included in whole FBA, and multi-task FBA which means 2 or more sets of linkage from starting FB to ending FB is included in whole FBA and each task is executed nearly at the same time. Unlinked FBs are not treated as a valid FBA. in single-task FBA. Unlinked FBs are not treated as a valid FBA. FBA schedule for single-task FBA and multi-task FBA are included in FBA schedule under "passive" schedule mode. Any FBA can be classified as the following 4 types:

4.2. Single-task FBA Schedule

① FB schedule for local linkage;

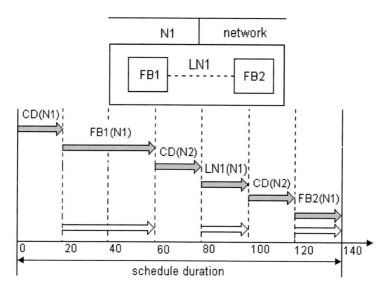

Figure 15. FB schedule for local linkage in single-task FBA.

Horizontal coordinate does not indicate time but the offset to absolute starting time in bus schedule. CD(N1) indicates bus scheduler sends CD to element node N1; FB1(N1) indicates execution of FB instruction FB1 in node N1; LN(N1) indicates execution of Link instruction in node N1, i.e. the output value of FB1 is sent to the input of FB2. In Fig.15, white empty arrows indicate schedule for non-periodical variable exchange or message transmission.

② FB schedule for remote linkage;

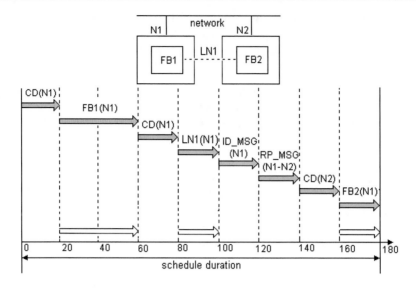

Figure 16. FB schedule for remote linkage in single-task FBA.

In Fig.16, the Link instruction is identified as remote link by node N1 when LN(N1) is executed. The value of output of local FB FB1 is wrapped in the response frame FR1 according to the above mentioned "data model in user layer" to prepare for the transmission of the response frame; ID_MSG(N1) indicates bus scheduler sends ID_MSG frame to node N1 to initialize message transmission between node N1 and N2 in order to transmit output of FB1 to input of FB2; RP_MSG(N1-N2) indicates responding message frame FR1 is sent by node N1 to N2.

4.3. Multi-task FBA Schedule

① FB schedule for local linkage

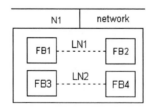

Figure 17. Continued on next page.

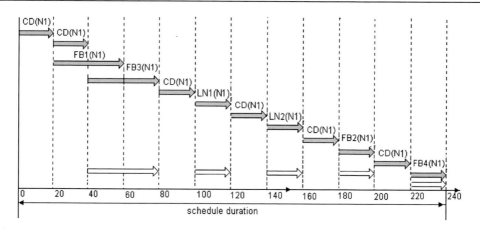

Figure 17. FB schedule for local linkage in multi-task FBA.

② FB schedule for remote linkage

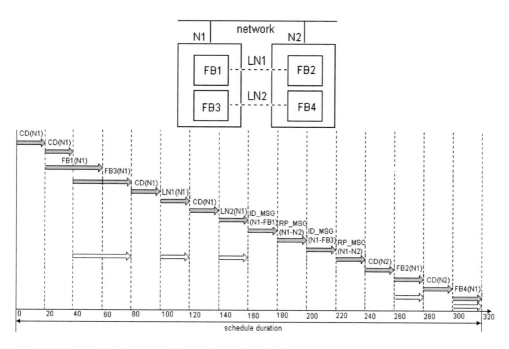

Figure 18. FB schedule for remote linkage in multi-task FBA.

In Fig.11, ID_MSG(N1-FB1) indicates bus scheduler sends frame ID_MSG to node N1 to prepare for message transmission between N1 and N2 in order to put value of output of FB1 in N1 into input of FB2 in N2.

Example: Data transmission process between node N1 and N2 illustrated by Fig.16 can be described as follows:

1. In periodical communication, CD is sent to node N1 by bus scheduler by means of production variable ox0501; instruction is executed in N1 on its receipt of CD; value of output of FB1 is wrapped in responding frame to prepare for frame transmission if current instruction in N1 is a "remote Link";
2. Frame (ID_MSG, 0x0601) is sent to N1 by bus scheduler to initialize a message transmission;
3. N1 identifies itself with variable 0x0601 as its producer and respond to the frame (ID_MSG, 0x0601) by sending frame (RP_MSG, 2, 1) which includes the wrapped data over network. In the frame, 2 is for the physical address of N2, 1 is for source address, i.e. address of node N1;
4. Frame (RP_MSG, 2, 1) is received by node N2 and data is drawn out frame the frame and put the data into the specified input terminal of FB2.

CONCLUSIONS

Now, products and systems developed based on WorldFIP are above control level and DICN based on intelligent nodes are not implemented yet. FBA is the kernel parts in DICN. Concept of user layer and norm for user layer in WorldFIP protocol are not dealt with yet. A kind of practically feasible FBA model is proposed in this part of the chapter based on independently developed WorldFIP DICN. Guided by the propose model, main problems in design and implementation of DICN based on FB and FBA in field control network can be resolved effectively and DICN with high reliability and good real-time property can be realized. Operational practice of the developed DICN by author's research team shows the effectiveness of the propose model and algorithms.

REFERENCES

[1] Laihua Fang, Research on the Key Technology of Configuration Software, *Control and instruments in chemical industry*, Vol.31, No.3, 33-38, 2004.
[2] Shuyu Sun, Researching and Realization of Embed Intelligent Control Software in Man Machine Interface Software, *Journal of Tianjin Science and Technology University*, Vol.15, No.4, 45-46,2002.
[3] Guangqing Xi, Visual System Simulation Method, *Journal of System Simulation*, Vol.10, No.1, 27-32, 1998.
[4] Zhenhua Hu, An Algorithm of Graphics Configuration Based on Distributed Control System, *Computer Application and Software*, Vol.14, No.7, 10-11,2002.
[5] Fuzhen Xu, Simulation Software of Control System Diagram Configuration Based on Elements, *Journal of System Simulation*, Vol.14, No.7, 855-857,2002.
[6] Chen Yang, Development of Visual Configurating Simulation Software for DCS, *Journal of System Simulation*, Vol.11, No.4, 261-264, 1999.
[7] Geng Liang, Design and Implementation of Control Strategy Configuration Software for WorldFIP Fieldbus Control System, *Proceedings of CSEE*, Vol.24, No.2, 150-156, 2005.

[8]   Geng Liang, *Research and development of function block application of the fieidbus intelligent device based on WorldFIP fieldbus*, Vol.27, No.6 (suppl), 902-904, 2006.

[9]   Zhang, Wei, Specification of function block applications with UML, *Proceedings of the 2005 IEEE International Conference on Robotics and Automation*, Vol.1, 4002-4007, 2005.

[10] Diedrich, Christian, "Function block applications in control systems based on IEC 61804", *ISA Transactions*, vol.43, no.1, , pp.123-131, 2004.

[11] Hagge, Nils, A new function block modeling language based on petri nets for automatic code generation, *IEEE Transactions on Industrial Informatics*, Vol.1, No.4, 226-237, 2005.

[12] Xianhui Yang, *Fieldbus Technology and Application*, Tsinghua University Press, Beijing, China, 1999.

[13] Yaping Wu, *WorldFIP fieldbus communication protocol*, WorldFIP Technology promotion center, Beijing, 2001.

[14] Geng Liang, Development of Scheme Configuration Software for WorldFIP FCS Based on Object Model, *Journal of Scientific Instruments*, Vol.26, No.12, 1293-1297, 2005.

[15] D. Z. Cheng, Controllability of switched bilinear systems, *IEEE Trans. on Automatic Control*, Vol.50, No.4, 511-515, 2005.

[16] Neumann, Habil P, "Free configurable function block application software in distributed control systems", *IEEE International Symposium on Industrial Electronics*, Vol.1, No.1, 293-298,1996.

[17] Yu Zhang, *Performance Analysis of Distributed Function Block Control Application, Computer Science*, Vol.34, No.4, 265-269, 2007.

In: Horizons in Computer Science Research, Volume 4   ISBN: 978-1-61324-262-9
Editor: Thomas S. Clary   © 2011 Nova Science Publishers, Inc.

Chapter 8

THE ITALIAN NETWORK SPIN-UTI: PROTOCOL DESIGN AND VALIDATION FOR ACTIVE SURVEILLANCE OF ICU-ACQUIRED INFECTIONS

Antonella Agodi[1,2] and Ida Mura[3]

[1]Department GF Ingrassia, University of Catania, Italy
[2]LaPoSS, Laboratorio di Progettazione,
Sperimentazione e Analisi di Politiche Pubbliche e Servizi alle Persone,
University of Catania, Italy
[3]Hygiene and Preventive Medicine Institute, University of Sassari, Italy

ABSTRACT

The Italian Nosocomial Infections Surveillance in Intensive Care Units (ICUs) (SPIN-UTI) project of the Italian Study Group of Hospital Hygiene (GISIO – SitI), was implemented to ensure standardisation of definitions, data collection and reporting procedures coherently with the HELICS-ICU benchmark. Before starting surveillance, participant ICUs were gathered in order to involve the key stakeholders in the project through participated planning. Four electronic data forms for web-based data collection, were designed. The six-months patient-based prospective survey was performed from November 2006 to May 2007. The SPIN-UTI network included 49 ICUs, 3,053 patients with length of stay longer than two days and 35,498 patient-days.

Furthermore, since validity is one of the most critical factors concerning surveillance of nosocomial infections (NIs). A validation study was performed after the end of the surveillance survey. For each selected ICU, all medical records including all clinical and laboratory data were retrospective reviewed by the trained physicians of the validation team and a positive predictive value, a negative predictive value, sensitivity and specificity were computed. The results of this study are useful to identify methodological problems within the surveillance program and they have been used to plan and perform training for surveillance personnel and to design and implement the second edition of the SPIN-UTI project.

The SPIN-UTI project showed that introduction of ongoing surveillance does seem to be possible in many Italian hospitals. The study provided the opportunity to participate in the HELICS project using benchmark data for comparison and for better understanding of factors that impact on associated risks.

BACKGROUND

Intensive care units (ICUs) worldwide are encountering the highest density of nosocomial infections (NI) and the spread of antibiotic-resistant pathogens responsible for emerging infection problems in the hospital (Edwards et al., 2009; Suetens et al., 2007). In fact, patients in ICUs are at high risk of health-care-associated infections (HCAIs) because of intrinsic (eg, severity of illness or impaired immunity) and extrinsic (eg, mechanical ventilation or central line catheterization) risk factors (Lambert et al., 2011). Several patient and pathogen-specific risk factors are associated with acquisition of microbial pathogens in ICUs, such as length of stay, severity of underlying disease and exposure to invasive procedures, on the one hand (Vincent et al., 1995; Rello et al., 2002), and virulence, adherence, and antimicrobial drug resistance on the other (Bertrand et al., 2001; Aloush et al., 2006). The hospital environment, particularly moist sites, are known reservoirs of microbial strains, often multidrug resistant (MDR) due to intrinsic and acquired determinants (Deplano et al., 2005). Although one possible explanation of the spread of antibiotic-resistant strains in ICUs is the selection exerted by extensive use of antibiotics, increased spread of MDR strains may be due to transmissions of resistant clones between patients (Meyer et al., 2010). Furthermore, it has been suggested that infection represents merely the tip of an iceberg, and that colonization, considered in case of patients with positive clinical specimens in the absence of clinical data confirming infection, reflects the submerged part. Colonization may be the first step of an endogenous infection, while the colonized patients represent a continuous exogenous source of microorganism for colonization/infection of other patients (Bertrand et al., 2001). The relative importance of both colonization and infection pathways, essential to design appropriate prevention strategies, has rarely been exploited by active surveillance studies (Agodi et al., 2007).

Surveillance of NIs in ICUs is an important tool of internal quality management in hospitals (Zuschneid et al., 2010). The Study on the Efficacy of Nosocomial Infection Control (SENIC study) demonstrated that NI surveillance, together with appropriate infection control activities, can decrease NI rates significantly (Haley et al., 1985). This provided the basis for the development of the National Nosocomial Infections Surveillance (NNIS) system in the USA and also stimulated the establishment of national NI surveillance systems in various European countries.

THE NATIONAL HEALTHCARE SAFETY NETWORK

Despite modern infection control is grounded in the work of Ignaz Semmelweis, who in the 1840s demonstrated the importance of hand hygiene for controlling transmission of infection in hospitals in Austria, however, infection control efforts were spotty for almost a century. In 1976, the Joint Commission on Accreditation of Healthcare Organizations published accreditation standards for infection control, creating the impetus and need for hospitals to provide administrative and financial support for infection control programs.

The National Healthcare Safety Network (NHSN) is a voluntary, secure, internet-based surveillance system that integrates patient and healthcare personnel safety surveillance systems managed by the Division of Healthcare Quality Promotion (DHQP) at Centers for

Disease Control and Prevention (CDC). During 2008, enrollment in NHSN was opened to all types of healthcare facilities in the United States, including acute care hospitals, long term acute care hospitals, psychiatric hospitals, rehabilitation hospitals, outpatient dialysis centers, ambulatory surgery centers, and long term care facilities (http://www.cdc.gov/nhsn/).

The NHSN was established in 2005 to integrate and supersede three surveillance systems at the CDC: the NNIS system, the Dialysis Surveillance Network (DSN), and the National Surveillance System for Healthcare Workers (NaSH). Similar to the NNIS system, NHSN hospitals and/or wards voluntarily report their HCAI surveillance data for aggregation into a single national database for the following purposes: 1. estimation of the magnitude of HCAIs; 2. monitoring of HCAI trends; 3. facilitation of inter-hospital and intra-hospital comparisons with risk-adjusted data that can be used for local quality improvement activities; and 4. assistance in developing surveillance and analytical methods that allow timely recognition of patient safety problems in order to define appropriate interventions (Edwards et al., 2009). NHSN data collection, reporting, and analysis are organized into four components: Patient Safety, Healthcare Personnel Safety, Biovigilance, and Research and Development. Data for the Patient Safety Components are collected using standardized protocols, methods and definitions (CDC, 2009; Horan et al., 2008).

In 1997 a national NI surveillance system was established in Germany (Krankenhaus Infektions Surveillance System - KISS). The KISS is a web-based national surveillance system for NI in Germany. The KISS methodology is almost identical to that in the NNIS system (Gastmeier et al., 2003; Emori et al., 1991) and uses the CDC definition of NI (Garner et al., 1988; Horan et al., 1992). Two surveillance components were chosen—the intensive care department and patients undergoing operation. Hospital participation in KISS is voluntary and results are handled confidentially. NIs are mainly registered by infection control practitioners but also by intensive care specialists, surgeons and other medical personnel. Data from the German KISS surveillance system from the period January 1997 through June 2008, comparing the first and third surveillance years of each period, report a significant reduction of NI rates between the first and third years of participation independently from the calendar year in which the surveillance activities started (Gastmeier et al., 2009).

THE HOSPITAL IN EUROPE LINK FOR INFECTION CONTROL THROUGH SURVEILLANCE PROJECT

Methods for national surveillance of NI applied in the different European member States have for a long time been too heterogeneous to allow for meaningful comparisons of results (Suetens et al., 2007). Since 2003, however, several member states have adapted their national protocols to comply with the DG Public Health co-funded Hospital in Europe Link for Infection Control through Surveillance (HELICS) protocol in order to standardize surveillance methods, while others, as Italy, have used the protocol to start or pilot new surveillance networks (HELICS, 2004; Agodi et al., 2010). The process of extending ICU-acquired infection surveillance in Europe will be further supported by HELICS-ICU as a work package of the IPSE project (Improving Patient Safety in Europe) and, for patient-based surveillance, as a work package within the BURDEN project (Burden of Resistance and

Disease in European Nations) whose main objective is to study the burden of antimicrobial resistance in HCAI (Frank U, 2007) and which was financed by the European Union (EU), and followed previous EU-funded projects that developed and implemented a common protocol for the surveillance of infections associated with health care across Europe (eg, HELICS and IPSE) (HELICS and IPSE, 2010).

In July 2008, the coordination of the network for the surveillance of HCAI in Europe IPSE network was transferred to the European Centre for Disease Prevention and Control (ECDC). The surveillance of surgical site infection surveillance (HELICS-SSI) and the surveillance of NIs in ICUs (HELICS-ICU) continued without changes to the surveillance protocols as in the HELICS network, collecting data from the national surveillance networks for HCAI based on common protocols. ECDC also continues providing support to Member States to set up such hospital surveillance networks in their countries by making available free software for hospitals and network coordination centers, training courses on HCAI surveillance and through country visits. The main objectives of the HCAI surveillance are to analyze inter-country differences, to work towards comparable surveillance methods, to support the use of European reference tables for inter-hospital comparisons of risk-adjusted HCAI rates and to contribute to the extension of HCAI surveillance in the EU (ECDC, 2009).

THE ITALIAN NOSOCOMIAL INFECTIONS SURVEILLANCE IN INTENSIVE CARE UNITS PROJECT

The Italian Nosocomial Infections Surveillance in Intensive Care Units project, *Sorveglianza Prospettica delle Infezioni Nosocomiali nelle Unità di Terapia Intensiva* (SPIN-UTI), was established in Italy by the Italian Study Group of Hospital Hygiene (GISIO) of the Italian Society of Hygiene, Preventive Medicine and Public Health (SItI). It was implemented to build a surveillance network of ICUs, to share standardized definitions, data collection and reporting procedures following the HELICS-ICU protocol, in order to participate in the European benchmark (HELICS, 2004; Agodi et al., 2010).

The first edition of the SPIN-UTI project was implemented from October 2006 to March 2007 (Agodi et al., 2010), the second edition from October 2008 to March 2009, and the third one is already in progress.

The Italian network SPIN-UTI was included as a collaborating partner of the IPSE project to build a benchmark in a European context, and, for patient-based surveillance, as a partner in the BURDEN project, work package 6 "Impact of AMR and appropriate antimicrobial treatment in ICU-acquired infections". In addition, the Italian network, has been acknowledged by the Italian CCM (Centro per il Controllo delle Malattie, Ministry of Health) to contribute to the development of a national database, in the framework of the INF-OSS Project (Prevenzione e controllo delle infezioni associate all'assistenza sanitaria e sociosanitaria) (http://asr.regione.emilia-romagna.it/wcm/asr/aree_di_programma/rischioinfettivo/gr_ist/ pr_inf_ccm/1-progetto/pr_inf-oss.htm).

METHODS FOR SURVEILLANCE

For the surveillance of HCAI the HELICS protocol includes a unit-based module (level 1) and a patient-based component (level 2). The level 1 (unit-based surveillance) is proposed for continuous surveillance and represents the minimal data to be collected. The denominator is collected at the level of the unit and consists in the number of patient-days for patients staying longer than 2 days in the ICU. Indicators issued by level 1 are appropriate for monitoring indicators in time within the same unit and for regional, national and international evaluation of trends for pathogen-specific infection rates. They offer relatively low inter-unit comparability, when stratified according to the type of unit. The level 2 is proposed for advanced risk-adjusted comparison of infection rates between ICUs as a measure of quality of care (benchmarking), in terms of infection control. Risk factors are collected for every patient staying more than 2 days in the ICU, infected or not (patient-based surveillance). In order to obtain sufficient validity of indicators, a surveillance period of 6 months is recommended (HELICS, 2004).

The Italian Steering Committee chose the level 2 module as a measure of quality of care in terms of infection control at the national level. Moreover, the surveillance indicators generated from the SPIN-UTI surveillance can be compared at the European level with the HELICS benchmarks. The indicators obtained from surveillance included cumulative incidence and incidence density (number of infections per 1000 patient-days) of NIs (overall and stratified by ICU type), device-associated infection rates (number of infections per 1000 device-days) and distribution of micro-organisms by infection site (Agodi et al., 2010).

The surveillance protocol was described in greater detail elsewhere (Agodi et al., 2010).

A planning phase involving participant ICUs was developed, conforming to HELICS methodology and adjusted to take into account the final SPIN-UTI project structure, in order to share and further refine the Italian version of the protocol and the data collection tools.

Hospitals were invited to join the SPIN-UTI project and, before starting surveillance, participant ICUs were gathered in a meeting session all the key stakeholders (hospital managers, epidemiologists, intensive care personnel, nurses, microbiologists). Thus, the final SPIN-UTI protocol and tools were produced, integrating the conclusions from discussions and the analysis of the methods used in the existing national surveillance protocols.

The first six-month patient-based prospective survey was from November 2006 to May 2007, preceded by a one-month surveillance pilot study to assess the overall feasibility of the project, and to determine the required time and resources for participant hospitals.

Pneumonia, bloodstream infections, central venous catheter-related bloodstream infections and urinary tract infections, were validated using the definitions proposed by the HELICS-ICU protocol (HELICS, 2004).

Patients were prospectively included, and all data were collected for each patient staying longer than two days in the ICU. A web-based data collection procedure was introduced into the SPIN-UTI project. Four electronic data forms were designed using SPSS Data Entry Enterprise Server (SPSS Inc.), presented and discussed during the participated planning session. Furthermore, to comply with confidentiality, codes for hospitals, ICU and patient identifiers were anonymous at the level of the surveillance network. The web-based data collection procedure used in the SPIN-UTI project is reported in Figure 1.

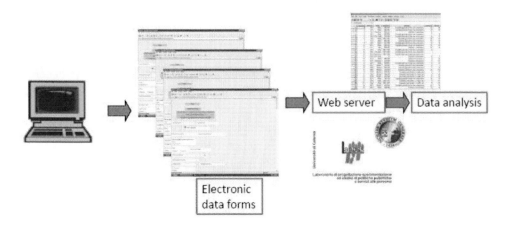

Figure 1. Web-based data collection procedure used in the SPIN-UTI project.

Characteristics of hospital and of ICU were collected: hospital and ICU codes, hospital and ICU size (number of beds), hospital and ICU type, and percentage of intubated patients over the last year in the ICU.

For each enrolled patients data were recorded as follows: ICU stay information, ICU admission and discharge and type of admission; patient ; age and origin, general severity scores, onset date and duration of device (intubation, central venous catheter and urinary catheter) exposure, antimicrobial use and patient discharge status.

Infection data, if any during the surveillance study, were recorded, date, site, and micro-organisms.

Further micro-organism-associated infection data were recorded in a separate electronic form.

Indicators were calculated as rates and incidence densities and their centile distribution was used to identify 'low and high outliers' (Edwards, 2009; Agodi et al., 2010) respectively as values <10th centile and >90th centile. The SPIN-UTI project showed that introduction of ongoing surveillance does seem to be possible in many Italian hospitals. The study provided the opportunity to participate in the HELICS project using benchmark data for comparison and for better understanding of factors that impact on associated risks.

VALIDATION OF ICU-ACQUIRED INFECTION SURVEILLANCE

One of the most critical factors relating to surveillance data is their validity and, especially in surveillance networks, validation studies are essential to ensure data reliability and validity (Gastmeier P, 2007; Houtari et al., 2007). Therefore, the surveillance staff must collect data accordingly, accurately and consistently. As such, in order to evaluate the quality and reliability of data, sensitivity and specificity of surveillance should be validated regularly (Gastmeier et al., 2008; Mannien et al., 2007).

The validation study on the first edition SPIN-UTI surveillance data was conducted with the main aim of validating infections data and thus to determine the sensitivity, specificity, and positive and negative predictive value of NIs data reported on patients in the ICUs participating in the SPIN-UTI network against the validated NIs data.

The validation study within the SPIN-UTI network was performed after the end of the surveillance survey adapting the retrospective approach adopted in the German survey (Zuschneid et al., 2007). The validation protocol was described in greater detail elsewhere (Masia et al., 2010). In brief, the inclusion criterion for the ICUs was contribution in the SPIN-UTI network, that is three months minimum. ICUs participating in the SPIN-UTI project were randomly chosen, from a list of all SPIN-UTI ICUs, to participate in the validation study. For each ICU selected and for each patient included, all medical records including all clinical and laboratory data were retrospective reviewed by the trained physicians of the validation team. Diagnoses were made by the trained physicians, one for each participating ICU, of the validation team which were blinded to the patient's infection status as recorded by the surveillance personnel prior to the validation study. In cases of discrepancy with the diagnosis of the surveillance personnel, a supervising epidemiologist from the Steering Committee was consulted and discrepant files were discussed to determine sources of discordance. After validation, for each ICU, medical records were discussed between the validation team and the surveillance staff, to highlight possible factors for misreports.

From the charts reviewed, a positive predictive value (PPV) was determined by calculating the proportion of the number of confirmed NIs among all infections identified by routine surveillance and a negative predictive value (NPV) by calculating the proportion of the number of confirmed patients without NI reported among all patients identified as not infected by routine surveillance.

Finally, validation data from a representative sample of the SPIN-UTI patients, showed a high quality level of surveillance, in terms of sensitivity, specificity and predictive values, thus providing evidence that the SPIN-UTI surveillance data are consistent, robust and precise enough to be used as a benchmark for inter-hospital and for European comparisons.

As found by other Authors (Zuschneid et al., 2007) an important reason for reporting incomplete data and thus an higher number of false-negative infections is that surveillance personnel may fear the consequences of detecting high infection rates, even though in the SPIN-UTI network, voluntary and confidential participation is ensured. In our study we found that discrepancies in NIs identification usually were related to interpretation of case definitions and deviations from the protocol and thus improving understanding of NI definitions and applying the criteria is essential in order to identify NI accurately and consistently. In fact, training of surveillance personnel is important to ensure that NIs are accurately and consistently reported (Gastmeier et al., 2008). Our validation study underlines common and specific methodological problems within the surveillance protocol. This protocol evaluation approach proved essential in order to plan and perform appropriate training for the surveillance team and to design and implement the second edition of the SPIN-UTI project that has been conducted in 2008 - 2009.

An Integrated Approach: Patient-based and Laboratory-based Surveillance

An alternative comprehensive approach integrating patient-based surveillance data, intended for advanced risk-adjusted comparison of infection rates between ICUs, with laboratory data, for molecular typing data has been adopted in order to investigate the clonality patterns sustaining the endemic *versus* the epidemic mode of transmission for acquisition of emerging multi-resistant pathogens (Agodi and Barchitta, 2010).

The surveillance protocol was described in greater detail elsewhere (Agodi et al., 2007; Barchitta et al., 2009). Briefly, during the study period all patients who stayed for ≥48 h at the ICU were enrolled into the patient-based surveillance conducted using the HELICS protocol (HELICS, 2004). Patterns of microorganism acquisition were: carriage on admission, colonization of sterile sites, and infections during ICU stay. Standard definitions of carriage, colonization and NI were used (Agodi et al., 2007; Bertrand et al., 2001; Suetens et al., 2007). Particularly, patients with screening cultures testing positives on admission in the absence of, or before isolation of, positive clinical specimens were considered to be carriers. Patients with positive clinical specimens were considered to be colonized in the absence of clinical data confirming infection. When both clinical and screening cultures were positive on the same day, the patient was considered as colonized. The following NI sites: pneumonia, bloodstream infections, central venous catheter-related bloodstream infections and urinary tract infections, following the HELICS definitions (HELICS, 2004), were included. Incidence rates of colonization and of infections were calculated both in terms of cumulative incidence and incidence density. Furthermore, all isolates were collected and identified by standard and molecular methods. Molecular typing by pulsed-field gel electrophoresis (PFGE) of the digested genomic DNA was performed using different protocols for each bacterial species. Definition of a cross-transmission episode was based both on the pathogens' PFGE pattern and the patient time of stay in the ward: a cross-transmission episode was assumed when two patients had indistinguishable isolates (Weist et al., 2002) and were treated in the ICU during intervals that overlapped or were no more than 7 days apart.

In conclusion, integrating laboratory data with prospective epidemiological studies does provide both patient rates of infections and microorganism clonality data, leading to the construction of appropriate indicators of the epidemiological *scenario* of cross-transmission of HCAI. These findings provide a framework for further investigation of the role of alert pathogens and/or high-risk clones together with patients' risk factor profiles for appropriate design of effective control strategies especially addressed to ICU patients (Agodi and Barchitta 2009).

Conclusion

In a recent European symposium on hospital infection prevention and control, the following topics were identified as European methodological challenges and research priorities for quality improvement and specifically for control of HCAI: i) isolation and screening for control of multidrug-resistant organisms; ii) impact of the environment on HCAI and iii) new technologies to control infection (Dettenkofer M et al., 2011).

There has been much progress made, especially in the field of HCAI prevention, following the establishment of the ECDC, Stockholm, in 2005. Strengthening research cooperation between different networks and scientific teams in the different healthcare settings - based on coherent protocols - will be critical in order to make progress in controlling HCAI in the next future.

REFERENCES

[1] Agodi A, Barchitta M, Cipresso R, Giaquinta L, Romeo MA, Denaro C. Pseudomonas aeruginosa carriage, colonization, and infection in ICU patients. *Intensive Care Med* 2007; 33: 1155-1161.

[2] Agodi A, Barchitta M. Assessment of Patient-To-Patient Transmission of Healthcare-Associated Infections: Integrating Laboratory Data with Patient-Based Surveillance. In *Cross Infections: Types, Causes and Prevention*. Hauppauge, NY: Nova Science Publishers, Inc, 2009.

[3] Agodi A, Auxilia F, Barchitta M, Brusaferro S, D'Alessandro D, Montagna MT, Orsi GB, Pasquarella C, Torregrossa V, Suetens C, Mura I et GISIO. Building a benchmark through active surveillance of ICU-acquired infections: the Italian network SPIN-UTI. *J. Hosp. Infect.* 2010; 74: 258-265.

[4] Aloush V, Navon-Venezia S, Seigman-Igra Y, Cabili S, Carmeli Y. Multidrug-resistant Pseudomonas aeruginosa: risk factors and clinical impact. *Antimicrob Agents Chemother* 2006; 50:43–48.

[5] Barchitta M, Cipresso R, Giaquinta L, Romeo MA, Denaro C, Pennisi C, Agodi A. Acquisition and spread of Acinetobacter baumannii and Stenotrophomonas maltophilia in intensive care patients. *Int. J. Hyg Environ Health*. 2009; 212: 330–337.

[6] Bertrand X, Thouverez M, Talon D, Boillot A, Capellier G, Floriot C, Helias JP. Endemicity, molecular diversity and colonisation routes of Pseudomonas aeruginosa in intensive care units. *Intensive Care Med* 2001; 27:1263–1268.

[7] *Centers for Disease Control and Prevention*. Outline for healthcare associated infection surveillance. Available from: http://www.cdc.gov/ncidod/dhqp/pdf/surveillance/ OutlineForHAISurveillance.pdf. Accessed October 5, 2009.

[8] Deplano A, Denis O, Poirel L, Hocquet D, Nonhoff C, Byl B, Nordmann P, Vincent JL, Struelens MJ. Molecular characterization of an epidemic clone of panantibiotic-resistant Pseudomonas aeruginosa. *J. Clin. Microbiol* 2005; 43:1198–1204.

[9] Dettenkofer M, Ammon A, Astagneau P, Dancer SJ, Gastmeier P, Harbarth S, Humphreys H, Kern WV, Lyytikäinen O, Sax H, Voss A, Widmer AF. Infection control - a European research perspective for the next decade. *J. Hosp. Infect.* 2011;77:7-10.

[10] Edwards JR, Peterson KD, Mu Y, Banerjee S, Allen-Bridson K, Morrell G, Dudeck MA, Pollock DA, Horan TC. National Healthcare Safety Network (NHSN) report: Data summary for 2006 through 2008, issued December 2009. *Am. J. Infect Control* 2009; 37:783-805.

[11] Emori TG, Culver DH, Horan TC, et al. National Nosocomial Infection Surveillance System (NNIS): description of surveillance methodology. *Am. J. Infect Control* 1991; 19:19-35.

[12]   European Centre for Disease Prevention and Control. *Annual Epidemiological Report on Communicable Diseases in Europe* 2009. Stockholm, European Centre for Disease Prevention and Control.

[13]   Frank U. The BURDEN project Assessing the burden of resistance and disease in Europe. *Eur. Surveill* 2007;12: E070111.5.

[14]   Garner JS, Emori WR, Horan TC, Hughes JM. CDC definitions for nosocomial infections. *Am. J. Infect Control* 1988;16: 128-140.

[15]   Gastmeier P, Geffers C, Sohr D, Dettenkofer M, Daschner F, Ruden H. Five years working with the German Nosocomial Infection Surveillance System KISS. *Am. J. Infect Control* 2003; 31:316-321.

[16]   Gastmeier P. European perspective on surveillance. J Hosp Infect 2007; 65: 159–164.

[17]   Gastmeier P, Sohr D, Schwab F, et al. Ten years of KISS: The most important requirements for success. *J. Hosp. Infect* 2008; 70: 11–16.

[18]   Gastmeier P, Schwab F, Sohr D, Behnke M, Geffers C. Reproducibility of the Surveillance Effect to Decrease Nosocomial Infection Rates. *Inf. Control Hosp Epidemiol.* 2009; 30: 993-999.

[19]   Haley RW, Culver DH, White JW, et al. The efficacy of infection control programs in preventing nosocomial infections in U.S. hospitals. *Am. J. Epidemiol.* 1985; 212:182-205.

[20]   HELICS-ICU working group. *Surveillance of Nosocomial Infections in Intensive Care Units. Protocol*, version 6.1. Brussels: Scientific Institute of Public Health; 2004, IPH/EPI reports D/2004/2505/48.

[21]   HELICS-ICU working group. *Surveillance of nosocomial infections in intensive care units*. HELICS implementation phase II. HELICS-ICU statistical report 2000-2004. Brussels: Scientific Institute of Public Health; 2005.

[22]   Horan TC, Gaynes RP, Martone WJ, Jarvis WR, Emori TG. CDC definitions of surgical site infections: a modification of CDC definitions of surgical wound infections. *Infect Control Hosp. Epidemiol* 1992; 13: 606-608.

[23]   Horan TC, Andrus M, Dudeck MA. CDC/NHSN surveillance definition of health care–associated infection and criteria for specific types of infections in the acute care setting. *Am. J. Infect Control* 2008; 35: 309-332.

[24]   Hospitals in Europe Link for Infection Control through *Surveillance (HELICS) and Improving Patient Safety in Europe (IPSE)*. http://www.ecdc.europa.eu/IPSE/home.htm (accessed Sept 25, 2010).

[25]   Huotari K, Agthe N, Lyytikainen O. Validation of surgical site infection surveillance in orthopedic procedures. *Am J Infect Control* 2007; 35:216-221.

[26]   Lambert ML, Suetens C, Savey A, Palomar M, Hiesmayr M, Morales I, Agodi A, Frank U, Mertens K, Schumacher M, Wolkewitz M. Clinical outcomes of health-care-associated infections and antimicrobial resistance in patients admitted to European intensive-care units: a cohort study. *Lancet Infect Dis.* 2011; 11:30-38.

[27]   Mannien J, van der Zeeuw AE, Wille JC, van den Hof S. Validation of Surgical Site Infection Surveillance in The Netherlands. *Infect Control Hosp Epidemiol* 2007; 28: 36-41.

[28]   Masia MD, Barchitta M, Liperi G, Cantù AP, Alliata E, Auxilia F, Torregrossa V, Mura I, Agodi A et GISIO. Validation of intensive care unit-acquired infection surveillance in the Italian SPIN-UTI network. *J. Hosp Infect.* 2010; 76:139-142.

[29] Meyer E, Schwab F, Schroeren-Boersch B, Gastmeier P. Dramatic increase of third-generation cephalosporin-resistant E. coli in German intensive care units: secular trends in antibiotic drug use and bacterial resistance, 2001 to 2008. *Critical Care* 2010, 14:R113.

[30] Rello J, Ollendorf DA, Oster G, Vera-Llonch M, Bellm L, Redman R, Kollef MH, VAP Outcomes Scientific Advisory Group. Epidemiology and outcomes of ventilator-associated pneumonia in a large US database. *Chest* 2002; 122:2115–2121.

[31] Suetens C, Morales I, Savey A, et al. European surveillance of ICU-acquired infections (HELICS-ICU): methods and main results. *J. Hosp. Infect* 2007; 65:171-173.

[32] Vincent JL, Bihari DJ, Suter PM, Bruining HA, White J, Nicolas-Chanoin MH, Wolff M, Spencer RC, Hemmer M. The prevalence of nosocomial infection in intensive care units in Europe. Results of the European Prevalence of Infection in Intensive Care (EPIC) Study. EPIC International Advisory Committee. *JAMA* 1995; 274:639–644.

[33] Weist, K. Pollege, K. Schultz, I. Ruden, H. Gastmeier, P. How many nosocomial infections are associated with cross-transmission? A prospective cohort study in a surgical intensive care unit. *Infect. Control Hosp. Epidemiol* 2002; 23, 127–132.

[34] Zuschneid I, Geffers C, Sohr D, Kohlhase C, Schumacher M, Ruden H, Gastmeier P. Validation of Surveillance in the Intensive Care Unit Component of the German Nosocomial Infections Surveillance System. *Infect. Control Hosp Epidemiol* 2007; 28:496-499.

[35] Zuschneid I, Rucker G, Schoop R, Beyersmann J, Schumacher M, Geffers C, Ruden H, Gastmeier P. Representativeness of the Surveillance Data in the Intensive Care Unit Component of the German Nosocomial Infections Surveillance System. *Infect Control Hosp. Epidemiol* 2010; 31: 934-938.

In: Horizons in Computer Science Research, Volume 4　　ISBN: 978-1-61324-262-9
Editor: Thomas S. Clary　　© 2011 Nova Science Publishers, Inc.

Chapter 9

A REVIEW OF THE INTELLECTUAL PROPERTY RIGHTS IN THE FIELD OF WEARABLE SENSORS AND SYSTEMS

Giuseppe Andreoni[1], Massimo Barbieri[2,2] and Luca Piccini[1]
[1]Dip. INDACO, Politecnico di Milano, Via Durando, 38/A – 20158 Milan, Italy
[2]Technology Transfer Office - Politecnico di Milano,
Piazza L. da Vinci, 32 - 20133 Milan, Italy

ABSTRACT

Wearable Biomedical Systems (WBS) integrate a complexity of components and technologies which are all crucial even though, sometimes, extremely simple: sensors, actuators, materials, data communication, power control units, user interfaces, new algorithms for signal processing, mechanical components, washability, characteristics and stability of the sensors and their placement on the body. Moreover those factors could change according to the activities or actions monitored and anthropometric characteristics of subjects. It's worth noting that is a very high number of features but each essential for the proper functioning of the entire system (without discussing the ethical and legal aspects of measuring and process sensitive personal data). From here we can identify many strategic areas for the development of WBS. In order to correctly address the research, especially the industrial one and its potential exploitation, it is fundamental a rigorous analysis of the state of the art both scientific and especially about the Intellectual Property Rights (IPR) and related issues. In this context, in recent years the result of innovations supported by the international research has primarily focused on IPR issues about textile sensors and electronic systems. This chapter offers an overview of this knowledge.

---

[1] E-mail address: giuseppe.andreoni@polimi.it.
[2] E-mail address: massimo.barbieri@polimi.it.

1. INTRODUCTION

Wearable computing is an emerging concept building upon the success of today's mobile computing and communication devices. Due to rapid technological progress it is currently making a transition from a pure research stage to practical applications. Many of those applications are in health related domains, in particular, health monitoring, mobile treatment and nursing. This research field is particularly pushed by the strong need of new healthcare approaches to reduce social expense and increase quality of care.

Wearable biomedical systems can be broadly defined as mobile electronic devices that can be unobtrusively embedded in the user's outfit as part of the clothing or an accessory. In particular, unlike conventional mobile systems, they can be operational and accessed without or reducing the hindrance to the user activity. To this end they are able to model and recognize user activity, state, and the surrounding situation: a property, referred to as context sensitivity. Wearable systems range from micro sensors seamlessly integrated in textiles through consumer electronics embedded in fashionable clothes and computerized watches to belt worn PCs with a head mounted display. The wearable computing concept is part of a broader framework of ubiquitous computing that aims at invisibly enhancing our environment with smart electronic devices.

The integration of electronics and clothing is an emerging concept that has led to the development of textile and wearable electronics for multifunctional applications that integrate monitoring of body functions, the implementation of actions on the subject, communication and data transfer and environmental monitoring too.

The term *wearable medical systems* or *devices* (or *wearable health systems*) describes autonomous devices that are worn by a person and provide medical monitoring or support over a prolonged period of time. Their peculiar characteristic is that they are worn either as an accessory or are embedded into clothing. Such devices normally incorporate noninvasive physiological sensors, data processing modules, medical feedback, and wireless data transmission capabilities. They are small, light, unobtrusive, and designed for operation by unskilled users. Current developments include real-time feedback, alerting mechanisms, medical decision support, and wireless access to information. Wearable medical devices offer the supporting hardware for dealing with the emerging medical trend of delivering point-of-care service, unconfined medical monitoring and support, and assisting in the remote management of medical conditions for rehabilitating patients, the chronically ill, and the disabled.

Within the next years wearable systems and more general ubiquitous computing will introduce relevant changes and new application types to health related systems. In particular they will prove useful in improving the quality and reducing the cost of caring for the aging population.

For this reason market's interest is potentially enormous and together with the technological development (which can produce a certain advantage and gap among competitors) also application for significant patents could be a relevant issue.

2. BUILDING BLOCKS OF WEARABLE BIOMEDICAL DEVICES

Up to now, several research groups have reached a significant level of expertise in terms of body sensor networks both in terms of miniaturized electronics for distributed micro-sensors and / or production of fabrics integrating conductive fibers for realizing a structured network of sensors. Indeed, so far, the research on wearable devices for medical applications makes available several solutions for the monitoring of specific parameters that are significant indicators of health and well being status. Furthermore, it is already possible to figure out the opportunity of active systems, that is to intervene through systems incorporated in the garments or from the fabric itself, to deliver drugs or other substances or to change the personal comfort feeling.

Up to now, monitoring of physiological parameters with WBS has dealt primarily with measurement of vital signs like ECG, heart rate, respiratory rate and skin temperature. There is a need to extend monitoring capabilities to biochemical variables. The analysis of biological samples and their analytes / metabolites (such as glucose, lactate and other proteins or substances) will enable a more complete clinical frame of individual health. There are many promising techniques to achieve this type of examination in a non-invasive, painless, and integrated in the WBS way.

In addition, through various types of actuators (primarily mechanical or transdermal) the WBS could incorporate techniques for controlled release of drugs: This innovation allows you to create an intelligent system of administration of drugs only if clearly needed and in doses appropriate to the symptoms. We can imagine the strategic impact of such a system, with enormous benefits that can be applied to the management of chronic diseases. A typical example is the management of diabetes, based on the use of transdermal glucose sensors and release actuators such as the micropump for insulin infusion. Such a system could have a sufficient intelligence to automatically adjust the time and dose of insulin infusion. If the conceptual and technological feasibility has been already demonstrated, some critical open issues (about reliability, accuracy and clinical and legal responsibility) still remain, before the industrial development of systems and its introduction to market.

Finally, the use of wearable sensors for monitoring motor functions has significantly grown in recent years thanks to the availability of miniaturized and low consumption technologies (MEMS gyroscopes and accelerometers).

To better understand the IPR-related issue, we must rely upon the following short description of WBS.

The first component is the first Human-Machine-Interface layer constituted by a transducer capable to sense bio-electrical/chemical/physical properties or signals from the human body, or otherwise to deliver to the body itself electrical (e.g. small currents or voltages or electro-magnetic field), or chemical drugs or other substances, or physical signals/actions (e.g. mechanical vibrations, heating, etc.). For these purposes different solutions are applied: from woven/knitted/embroidered textile electrodes for sensing, to micro/mini actuators for mechanical actions (such as vibrations at different frequencies) or chemical delivery of substances.

The second part is the wires-connector that is the input way to the case of the WBS where electronic is inserted. In its simplicity this is a crucial point, up-to-now poorly studies in WBS but just looking to already available solutions among industrial mini-connectors. The ongoing systems' miniaturizations will push this research towards new solutions.

The third component is the case that is directly related both to the electronics that it has to contain, and to the body location where it is placed onto, and to the body support or fixing element to the body itself. About this issue, to define body positions, case dimensions, and fixing/support elements some interesting studies and experiences where carried out by Gemperle et. al a decade ago. Instead new technological trends push technology towards textile integration and flexible electronics.

In fact the next component of the system is the technological one, i.e the electronics which can be divided in the analogue front-end for signal sensing and pre-processing, or for the conditioning circuits of the micro-actuators, and the digital part for data pre-processing and firmware hosting.

Finally the last element is related to output signal/information and this is done through two integrated layers: the first one is the second physical Human-Machine-Interface, i.e. buttons, display, LEDs, icons and any other kind of interface commands; the second layer is related in particular to the communication facilities which the electronics is equipped with. In this last we consider the firmware to pre-process data and the communication transmitter/transceiver, where several option could be adopted: from mobile GSM/UMTS device, to satellite modules, from standard or dedicated ISM radio chipset, to commercial Bluetooth/WiFi embedded or integrated radio, up to ZigBee (particularly interesting to build up distributed body sensors networks) or Wireless USB options.

3. CATEGORY AND HISTORY OF IPR IN WEARABLE BIOMEDICAL SYSTEMS

According to the previously described macro-elements (macro in functional sense but micro in dimensions) of the WBS, we can distinguish the following IPR issues:

1) wearable sensors, generally comprising garments as support to a plurality of sensors;
2) textile sensors, in terms of production techniques of textile elements that can be used to collect bio-physiological signals;
3) technological circuitry or components, e.g. innovative hardware solutions for data recording and processing;
4) wearable systems and related functions, i.e. a complete solution comprising a garment and a connected device capable to measure, process and transmit signals or information about the health status of a subject / patient.

Often the single patent could not be strictly associated just to one single class.

In the following of this paragraph, some examples of the patent categorization are presented through the "historical IPR" in WBS.

A first significant patent is no. US4729377 filed in 1988 which first introduced the concept of clothing that includes elements / fibers or embedded conductive pathways to be used for monitoring signals from the body or the stimulation of the same. It can be classified as a patent belonging to the category 4 - Wearable systems and related functions; it can be also assumed as partially relevant for the category 1 - Wearable Sensors.

This first example had the honor to introduce the concept of sensorized garment but we had had to wait about 10 years before seeing again this line of research.

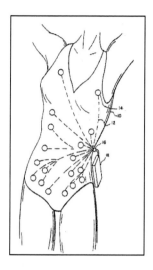

In fact, research from MIT-DARPA-GeorgiaTech, jointly developed since the second half of the 90s, produced the following patents.

Patent No.: WO9964657

Title: Fabric or Garment with Integrated Flexible Information Infrastructure

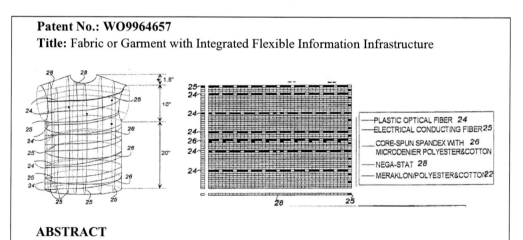

ABSTRACT

This invention is a fabric, in the form of a woven or knitted fabric or garment, including a flexible information infrastructure integrated within the fabric for collecting, processing, transmitting and receiving information concerning a wearer of the fabric. The fabric allows for plugging in chips/sensors from the fabric thus creating a wearable, mobile information infrastructure. The fabric can be provided with sensors for monitoring the vital signs of a wearer such as EKG, pulse, respiration rate, temperature, as well as penetration of the fabric.

The first one recorded in 1999 is no. WO9964657 and describes a structure or a textile fabric made also according to different techniques (woven, embroidered, knitted, etc.) that integrates sensors and pathways for transmission of signals into the warp and weft, thus allowing the retrieval of relevant and reliable information of the health status of who was wearing it. This patent can be classified in category *1 - Wearable Sensors* but also present element of the category *2 - Textile Sensors*.

The fabric consists of a base fabric; and an information infrastructure component consisting of a penetration detection component of optical fibers (24) and/or an electrical conductive component comprising conductive fibers (25). A fabric, in the form of a woven or knitted fabric or garment, including a flexible information infrastructure integrated within the fabric for collecting, processing, transmitting and receiving information concerning - but not limited to - a wearer of the fabric. The fabric allows a new way to customize information processing devices to "fit" the wearer by selecting and plugging in (or removing) chips/sensors from the fabric thus creating a wearable, mobile information infrastructure that can operate in a stand-alone or networked mode. The fabric can be provided with sensors for monitoring physical aspects of the wearer, for example body vital signs, such as heart rate, EKG, pulse, respiration rate, temperature, voice, and allergic reactions, as well as penetration of the fabric. The fabric consists of a base fabric ("comfort component"), and an information infrastructure component which can consist of a penetration detection component, or an electrical conductive component, or both. The preferred penetration detection component is a sheathed optical fiber. The information infrastructure component can include, in addition to an electrically conductive textile yarn, a sensor or a connector for a sensor. A process is provided for making an electrical interconnection between intersecting electrically conductive yarns. Furthermore, a process is established for sheathing the plastic optical fiber and protecting it.

(Source: Espacenet, accessed 23.08.2010)

The infrastructure also includes a textile system for the detection of possible penetration of the fabric or garment by other elements, like a bullet. In this case the purpose of a medical-military research is particularly evident.

Together with this one, the next patent no. WO0240091 (filed in 2002) describes the technique for manufacturing textile sensors. This is an example of a specific patent belonging to category *2 - Textile Sensors*.

Patent No.: WO0240091

Title: A Novel Fabric-based Sensor for Monitoring Vital Signs

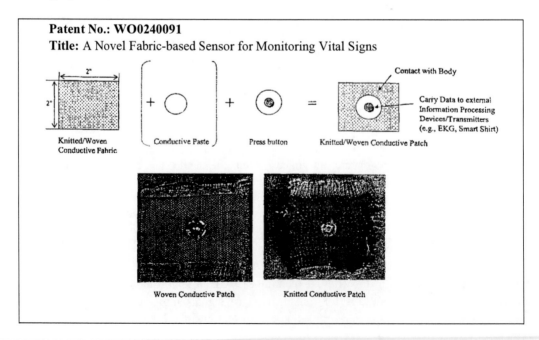

ABSTRACT

The present invention comprises a fabric-based sensor for monitoring vital signs or other electrical impulses of a subject. The sensor is woven or knitted from conductive fibers and, when in contact with the body, receives signals from the wearer and transmits them to a processing or monitoring device through a data-output terminal. The sensor may be integrated into the fabric of a garment or used independently as a conductive patch. Additionally, the sensor may provide bi-directional communication by both monitoring electrical impulses and sending them.

(Source: Espacenet, accessed 23.08.2010)

This document is a first comprehensive description of how the implementation of the conductive areas that can serve as electrode in contact with the human body for monitoring biological signals.

On the same topic, i.e. about the realization of textile sensors, the patent WO0102052 was filed in 2001, which has a similar method of construction of electrodes and fabrics that include the concept of flexibility and elasticity for the optimization of the garment-body contact and above all of the textile electrode with the skin. Also this patents is a typical example of category *2 - Textile Sensors*.

Patent No.: WO0102052
Title: Garment Comprising Electrode

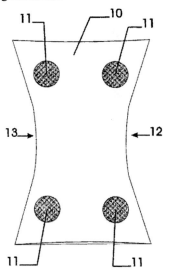

ABSTRACT

The invention relates to a garment, adapted to be used as a medical electrode. The garment comprises a tubular body, which comprises at least two different zones. One of these zones is an electrically conductive zone, to be used as the electrode surface of the medical electrode. Another zone is an elastic zone, which comprises electrically non-conductive yarns. This elastic zone assures the position of the electrically conductive zone on the corpus on which the medical electrode is to be used.

(Source: Espacenet, accessed 23.08.2010)

So far the bioelectrical signals were the only ones related to the wearable applications. In 1998 the patent no. WO9841279 was filed; it presented a very effective technique (the inductive plethysmography) applied to a garment for continuous monitoring of respiratory function (time parameters and volume of inhalation / exhalation possibly in combination with standard ECG electrodes and a patient unit can record and / or transmit those signals where necessary.

This patent can be classified in category *3 - Technological circuitry or components*, but also present element of the category *4 - Wearable systems and related functions*.

Patent No.: WO9841279
Title: Physiologic Signs Feedback System

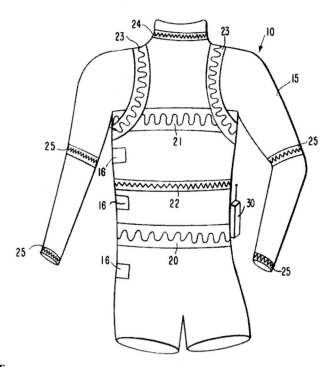

ABSTRACT

A non-invasive physiological signs monitoring device (10) includes a garment with electrocardiogram electrodes (26) and various plethysmographic sensors (20-25) sewn, embroidered, embedded, or otherwise attached to the garment with an adhesive. The garment is in the form of a shirt. When the garment is fitted over the torso of the patient (15) to be monitored, the electrodes and sensors generate signals in response to the physiological signs of the patient. The signals are transmitted to a recording/alarm device where they are monitored for adverse conditions and logged. When an adverse condition or other preprogrammed condition occurs, a message is communicated to the patient by either an audio message or a display. The recording/alarm unit is also connectable to a remote receiving unit for monitoring by a health care professional or other machine.

(Source: Espacenet, accessed 23.08.2010)

A key aspect for the detection of non-intrusive biopotentials is the capability to use not conventional sensors, made with materials now common in the textile industry or in other areas. Using these sensors, the an electrode-skin quality coupling is not comparable to that one of standard sensors because of the predominance of a capacitive coupling between sensor and skin. Although both this phenomenon is partially solved with an accurate design of the garment, to improve the stability of the electrode-skin contact and the quality of the sensor to reduce noise, to ensure performance comparable to conventional biomedical systems in terms of resistance, potential offset, common mode rejection ration and dynamic performance, innovative circuit topologies have been studied, developed and patented. They are based on the active compensation using multiple feedback loops.

An example of this technological innovation is reported by the patent no. WO9964657, filed in 2007 and classified in category *3 - Technological circuitry or components.*

Patent No.: WO9964657
Title: Signal Conditioning Circuit

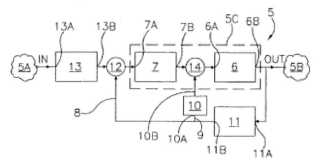

ABSTRACT
The present invention relates to a signal conditioning circuit, comprising: an amplification and filtering chain (5C) having amplifier means (6) and filter means (7), each with an input connection (6A, 7A) and an output connection (6B, 7B); a first feedback path (8) for providing feedback to said amplification and filtering network (6, 7), including a first phase-shifting network (11) having an input connection (HA) and an output connection (11B). The circuit (5) is characterized in that it comprises a second feedback path (9) for providing feedback to said amplifier means (6), including a second phase-shifting network (10) having an input connection (10A) and an output connection (10B); said input connection (11A) of said first phase-shifting network (11) being connected with said output connection (6B) of said amplifier means (6); said output connection (HB) of said first phase-shifting network (11) being connected with the input connection (10A) of said second phase-shifting network (10) and with said input connection (7A) of the filter means (7); said first phase-shifting network (11) being designed to compensate for errors in said output connection (6B) of said amplifier means (6) or to operate when said output connection (6B) of said amplifier means (6) is in a saturated condition.
(Source: Espacenet, accessed 23.08.2010)

Towards the development of active systems for transdermal drug delivery (micro- or mini-pumps are already been widely used), industrial innovation is looking with interest at iontophoretic solutions that can be joint with wearable sensors. An example of such a system is shown in the patent no. US20030028170 filed in 2003 by Birch Point Medical Inc..

Patent No.: US20030028170
Title: Controlled Dosage Drug Delivery

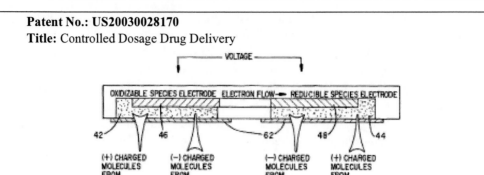

ABSTRACT

A planar disposable transdermal iontophoretic delivery system is disclosed which includes amounts of an oxidizable species and a reducible species connected by a common conductor forming a galvanic battery for serving as the sole source of power and control for the system, an amount of a therapeutic agent is provided to be driven through the skin of a patient solely through the use of the galvanic battery. The galvanic battery is provided with a lot-tested coulombic capacity rating to predict dosage.

(Source: Espacenet, accessed 23.08.2010)

Also this patent can be classified in category *3 - Technological circuitry or components.*

4. SURVEY OF IPR IN WEARABLE BIOMEDICAL SYSTEMS

The patent database used for the search is QPAT/ORBIT .

QPAT/ORBIT is a global portal for searching patent documents and it allows for accessing two different typologies of databases:

1) FamPat, a worldwide database structured in families, containing more than 55 millions of documents, 25 millions of summaries (in original language or in English) and 17 millions of pictures, from more than 80 countries, with temporal coverage from the 19th century. In FamPat there are available:
   - bibliographical data, titles, summaries and "key content" (object of the invention, advantages from the invention, disadvantages of the previous inventions, independent claims);
   - international classification codes (US, european and japanese);
   - citations (AU, BE, CH, CY, DE, DK, EP, ES, FI, FR, GB, IT, JPA, JPB, NL, PCT, TR, US);
   - legal status (Inpadoc e Patolis);

2) Full-text: Europe (AT, BE, CH, DE, DK, EP, ES, FI, FR, GB, SE), PCT, America: (BR, CA, US), Asia (CN, JP);

QPAT/ORBIT offers several functions; the main ones are:

   - documents download from more than 30 countries databases;
   - refined search;

- define and save search strategies;
- results exporting;
- national registry access
- automatic alert set up
- save the search results in an on-line archive to share it with other users;
- integrated procedures for statistical analysis and graphical display.

The used analysis software is INTELLIXIR. INTELLIXIR System is a web application allowing its users to analyze references of patents and non-patent literature exported from commercial or private databases. Statistical measures are graphically represented through dynamic and interactive web pages.

Firstly, to better focus the research into the patent database we looked at the most representative classes for all the patents (granted and applications) regarding wearable and textile sensors in the International Patent Classification System (IPC), which is used by patent offices to classify the subject matter of patent applications and by examiners for carrying out patentability searches.

IPC is a hierarchical classification in which several levels are distinguished. The highest level is that of Sections: there are 8 sections (A – H), which are further subdivided into classes. Each class comprises one or more subclasses; each subclass consists of several groups, which are further divided intro subgroups.

Another classification system is ECLA (which stands for European Classification), developed by European Patent Office (EPO).

ECLA is based on IPC, but it's more finely subdivided; it's more precise, containing about twice as many classification groups (137000 vs. 70000).

In this research IPC classification was used, because it's better for high recall searches, due to it's broad time and country coverage.

According to the provided descriptions, the selected IPC groups for further research were A61B5 and G06F19 (and all the related subgroups).

In particular A61B5 group relates to "Human Necessities" (Section A), "Medical or veterinary Science; Hygiene" (Class A61), "Diagnosis; Surgery; Identification" and specifically "Diagnosis; Psycho-physical tests" (Subclass A61B) and "Detecting, measuring or recording for diagnostic purposes" (Group A61B5).

Instead the G06F19 group relates to "Physics" (Section G), "Computing, Calculating, Counting" (Class G06), "Electrical Digital Data Processing" (Subclass G06F), "Digital computing or data processing equipment or methods, specially adapted for specific functions" (Group G06F19).

For the new Drug-Delivery systems based on wearable technology, we also looked in the Y01N ECLA subclass which specifically tags nanoscience and technology.

If we define the search criteria to the keyword and IPC groups as follows:

1. "wearable" (in the Claims section) and "sensor/system" (in the description)
2. IPC groups: A61B5 and G06F19

we obtain 533 items. Among these, the most relevant considered as the most cited ones are shown in figure 1.

(((WEARABLE)/ICLMS AND (SENSOR? OR SYSTEM?)/DESC) AND (A61B-005 OR G06F-019)/IC)

	Title	Documents having most citations — PN	Citations
1	System for remote monitoring of personnel	US6198394B1 EP0846440A2 EP0846440A3 JP10295652A CA2222337A1	19
2	Wireless internet bio-telemetry monitoring system and method	US6899339GB2 US2001027384A1 US6443890B1 US200020195884A1	13
3	PATIENT MONITORING SYSTEM	US6544173B2 EP1404213A4 US2002013517A1 WO200189362A3 US2003206116A1 US6544417B2 US2002013518A1 AU6465401A AU2001264654B2 US6616606B1 US200060307S9A1 WO200189362A2 EP1404213A2 US7390299B2 US698898982	9
4	ANALYTE MONITOR	WO2002001101A3 EP1296587A4 JP2004500948T US2002087056A1 WO200200101A2 EP1296587A2 US6923764B2 US6540675B2 US2003135333A1	7
5	TELEMEDICAL EXPERT SERVICE PROVISION FOR INTENSIVE CARE UNITS	WO200079466A3 CA237800S0C AU7638340B2 US7256700B2 US2006071797A1 CA237800SA1 US7475019B2 AU5764000A EP120092442 US2004111296A1 US6804655B1 WO200079466A2 EP204018BA1	7
6	Posture and body movement measuring system	US2005126026A1 US2002170193A1 US7210240B2 US6834436B2	6
7	SYSTEM FOR MONITORING HEALTH, WELLNESS AND FITNESS	IL15347BA US7689437B1 ES225339T3 US200603110241 EP1292217A2 KR2003001524A EP129221781 WO200196986A2 US2008171758A1 JP2004512061T AT310444T US660S038B1 IL15347800 WO200196986A8 WO200196986A3 CA2413220C DE6011523D1 AU6708301A CA2413220A1 DE6011523AT2 EP16399339A1 MXPA02012482A KR100831036B1 BR0111995A	5
8	PHYSIOLOGICAL MONITOR AND ASSOCIATED COMPUTATION, DISPLAY AND COMMUNICATION UNIT	CA2385573A1 US6790117B1 AU77155004 WO200128416A1 EP121794241	5
9	TELE-DIAGNOSTIC DEVICE	US6540673B2 EP1079729A4 CA23328902C WO9960919A1 US622454B81 US6248064G1 EP1079729A1 US2001000526A1 CN1309546A BR9910708A CA23328892A1 IL139781D0 JP200251613AT AU4191599A	5
10	Intelligent wearable monitor systems and methods	US2005240086A1	4
11	Home-based system and method for monitoring sleep state and assessing cardiorespiratory risk	JP2001522266T GB23399476A GB23394768 WO9843536A1 GB9922315B00 US5902250A DE1988226T0	4
12	PROCEDURE FOR DERIVING RELIABLE INFORMATION ON RESPIRATORY ACTIVITY FROM HEART PERIOD MEASUREMENT	WO3009119114A1 EP1507474A1 DE60326139D1 US7460901B2 US2005209521A1 AT422327T EP1507474B1 AU20032408 90A1 F120025029D0	3
13	SYSTEM FOR MONITORING HEALTH, WELLNESS AND FITNESS HAVING A METHOD AND APPARATUS FOR IMPROVED MEASUREMENT OF HEAT FLOW	WO207853BA2 CA2441962A1 US659592982 JP200453206ST EP1743571A3 EP1743571A2 BR020853 0A IL15806700 WO020785 3A8 EP13724 70A2 KR20030086337A US2002183 646A1 KR100885030B1 MXPA030089 00A IL158067A JP412513282	3
14	WIRELESS INTERNET BIO-TELEMETRY MONITORING SYSTEM AND INTERFACE	AU200225554SA1 EP1410206A4 WO200671 22A1 EP1410206A1	3
15	SYSTEM AND METHOD FOR WIRELESS COMMUNICATION OF SENSED DATA TO A CENTRAL SERVER	WO200227640A3 AU1182202A WO200227640A2	3
16	APPARATUS FOR MONITORING HEALTH, WELLNESS AND FITNESS	US2004034289A1 US200612 2474A1 US200201 9586A1 IL1160079A JP42836 72B2 IL1160079D0 EP141143 40A2 WO03015 005A3 US72616 9082 JP2004538 060T CA2454655A1 BR021176 0A AU20023 30965A1 WO30150 05A2 MXPA040 01005A	3
17	Wearable apron for use in egg and other medical tests	IL124900D0 AU4286699A US6341229B1 WO9965379A2 WO9965379A3	3
18	Medical communication system for ambulatory home-care patients	US5902234A	3
19	Method and apparatus for detecting, analyzing and recording cardiac rhythm disturbances	US5027824A	3
20	Respiration Motion Detection and Health State Assesment System	WO2005044090A2 WO2005046433A2 WO2005046433A3 US2007293781A1 US2009131759A1 WO2005044090A3	2

Figure 1. The first 20 most cited documents having the keywords "wearable" (in the Claims section) and "sensor/system" in the description, belonging to the A61B5 and G06F19 IPC groups.

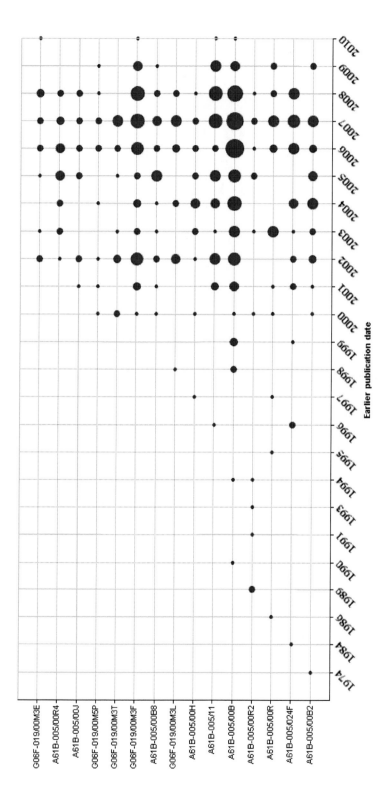

Figure 2. Time distribution of patents containing the words "wearable" (in the Claims section) and "sensor/system" (in the Description), belonging to the A61B5 and G06F19 IPC groups and split in ECLA subgroups.

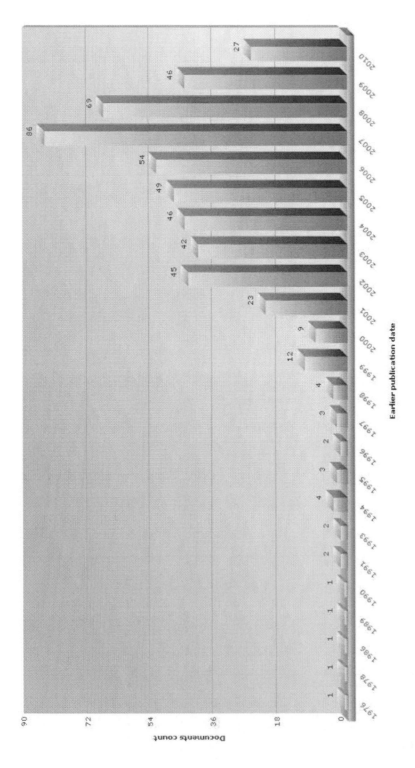

Figure 3. Total patents by publication date containing the words "wearable" (in the Claims section) and "sensor/system" (in the description) belonging to the A61B5 and G06F19 IPC groups.

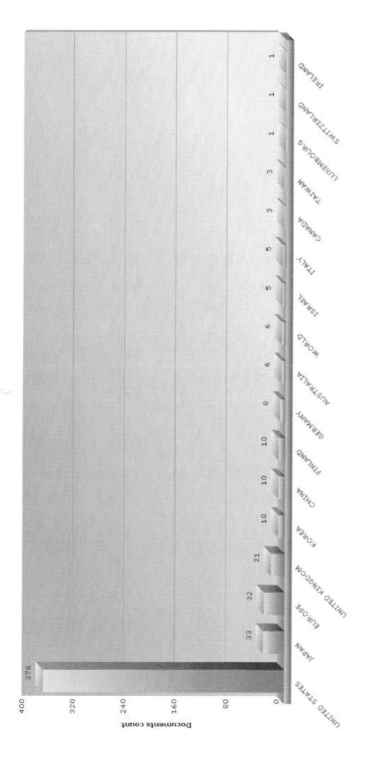

Figure 4. Geographical distribution of patents containing the words "wearable" (in the Claims section) and "sensor/system" (in the description), belonging to the A61B5 and G06F19 IPC groups.

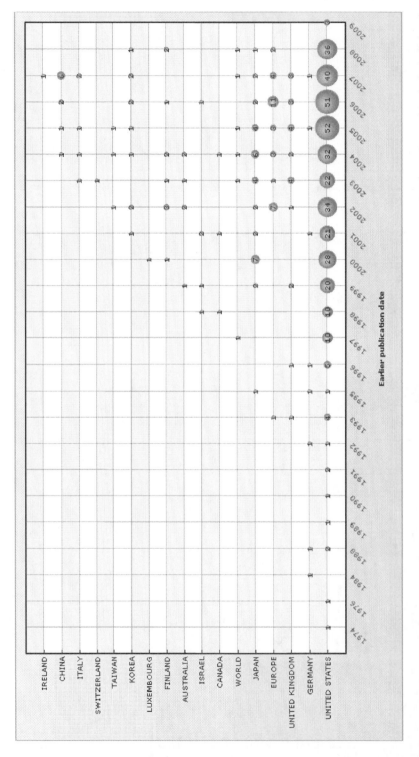

Figure 5. Geographical distribution of patents containing the words "wearable" (in the Claims section) and "sensor/system" (in the description), belonging to the A61B5 and G06F19 IPC groups split by earlier publication date.

It is also interesting to show the time evolution of the IPR: from the first experiences before 1995, the real interest of research and corresponding innovation protection started in 2000.

Instead it is significantly evident how USA is the leading country in this research field: more than 70% of patents come from United States, while Europe and Japan have only 6% each.

Refining the criteria according to the following rules, results are summarized in the following findings (Figure 6):

1. The search for patents into the A61B subclass with the key-words "textile" and "electrod+" found 73 documents
2. The search for patents into the A61B subclass with the key-words "smart cloth+ or dress+" found only the patent no. US20090048493.
3. The search for patents into the Y01N classification tag with the key-word "wearable sensor" found only 2 documents, both of them in USA.

Search history
Manage your current session and combine strategies

Collection: FAMPAT

N°	Answer(s)	Query	Assist
12	6	((WEARABLE AND (SENSOR? OR SYSTEM?))/CLMS AND (Y01N+)/ICO)	Script
11	7	(((WEARABLE)/CLMS AND (SENSOR? OR SYSTEM?)/DESC) AND (Y01N+)/ICO)	Script
10	1	((WEARABLE SENSOR+)/CLMS AND (Y01N+)/ICO)	Script
9	73	((TEXTILE AND ELECTROD+)/CLMS AND (A61B-005+)/IC)	Script
8	1	((SMART CLOTH+ OR SMART DRESS+)/CLMS AND (A61B+)/IC)	Script
7	15	((SMART AND (CLOTH+ OR DRESS+))/CLMS AND (A61B+)/IC)	Script
6	1	((SMART CLOTH+)/CLMS AND (A61B+)/IC)	Script
5	15	(SMART CLOTH+)/CLMS	Script
4	1	((SMART CLOTH+)/CLMS AND (A61B-005+)/IC)	Script
3	73	((TEXTILE AND ELECTROD+)/CLMS AND (A61B-005+)/IC)	Script
2	11	(TEXTILE ELECTROD+)/CLMS	Script
1	0	((TEXTILE ELECTROD+)/CLMS AND (Y01N+)/ICO)	Script

Figure 6. General IPR survey in A61B05 IPC group and Y01N ECLA subclasses.

Among these, the most relevant considered as the most cited ones are listed in figure 7.

No superimposition are shown between the item of two lists.

Finally we report also the patent citations by companies, dividing between self-citations and other ones. In figure 8, the citations for "textile electrod+" patents are shown, while in figure 9 the citations for "wearable sensor(s)" are reported.

	Title	PN	Citations
		Documents having most citations	
1	Garment apparatus for delivering or receiving electric impulses	US4585547A JP600051170A US4580572A US4729377A	5
2	Sensory for measuring of signals on the surface of the skin and method for producing of the sensory	FI12118181 HK109234+A1 GB060079E8D0 FI2003147600 US200061835900A1 DE112004J0192115 WO2C0503236GA1 GB242278SB 3B242278SA FI200314756A	3
3	TEXTILE ARTICLE HAVING ELECTRICALLY CONDUCTIVE PORTIONS AND METHOD FOR PRODUCING THE SAME	EP1509128A1 WO030947+7A1 AU200322550ZA1 CN1652720A JP4334467B2 JP200552547?T US20006234584A1 AT435209T CN100366213C DE60323087D1 EF1509123B1 GB021J88BD0	3
4	ELECTRODE ARRANGEMENT	CN100525856C JP2036512128T CN17320Z9A WO2004058346A1 G30230361D0 KR2005C08848DA EP157348ZA1 JS752295182 AU20032E8586A1 US200609494BA1	2
5	SQUEEZABLE ELECTRODE ASSEMBLY	EP148071781 US664011882 CN1638337A WO03070119A3 AU2C03206067A1 JP429984182 EF1480717A2 WO03070319A2 AT419895T JP2005517511T US200316303SA1 DE60325700D1	2
6	E-hanced pickup-electrode	US200407310+A1	2
7	Apparatus for equipping a garment for the emission or reception of electric pulses.	GB841387ZD0 DE12E103T1 EP0123103B1 CA126371DA1 EP0:2E103A1 GB21431353 NO842222A G62143135A IL71968A DK268984C0 AT47C38T DK268584A DE34E005501	2
8	Body electrode for electro-medical use	DE2552197A1 US0972329A FR2291732A1 US40929B5A ES442916A1 FR22917328J 4U3675975A GB152548?A BE835843A1 NL751353ZA BR75077736A JP51074486A	2
9	ELECTRODES FOR ELECTRO-MEDICAL USE	NL7012672A DE2041392A1 F2060727A5 GB1328111A DK:22258B	2
10	Sensor arrangement	GB243E953A FI12048261 CN101084826A GB07104480D FI2006539100 US2007288868A1 FI20065391A	2
11	CONTACT SENSORS	US200520039841 GB051939360D0 GB080469100 CA262317.A1 WO20C7036741A1 EP197642941 GB24442051 AU200629639SA1	1
12	TEXTILE-BASED ELECTRODE	WO2006171748A3 CA259870SA1 WO200610174881 EP1858581A2 IN6675/DELNP/2007A US22062-1934A1 WO200611748A2 EP185858181 ES231753373 CE6023060418ED1 KR2007011238?A US730829482 JP200852654Z? US74749106Z US20080458DBA1 US20071271B7A: AT41681ET	1
13	MONITORING SYSTEM FOR MONITORING OF A PHYSIOLOGICAL PARAMETER OF A RECIPIENT	WO2006054447A2 WO2006060644447A3	1
14	ENHANCED PICKUP-ELECTRODE	CA243E683A1 WO0206590441 WO0206590SA1	1
15	APPARATUS FOR BLOCKING FLOW THROUGH BLOOD VESSELS	IL125417A EP009324Z6A4 DE69663?411T? IL125-17D0 EP116672lA2 J20005045-94T US6709444B1 IL-25416D0 EP116672lA3 US6190053B1 JP11514269T AU184729?A CN1218414A CA223-3€1A1 EP095424B4A W097134634A1 US665538681 AU7333232 DE69633411D1 EP1707233A3 AU7431696A EP087906JA1 IL124C38A JP2J00505316T CA22408DA1 AU72671332 EP095424B81 EP17072339A2 WC927?393A1 US637931981 WO981615lA1 US633287581 AT27588DT CA224407A1 JP2006181370A AU1E47397A IL15.563C0 EP09324Z641 US628395181 EP037906BA4 CN1216929A AU1275997A EF095424A1 W09727B9EA1 US705533081 AU723785B2 JP434833882	1

Figure 7. The first 20 most cited documents having the keywords "textile and electrod+" (in the Claims section).

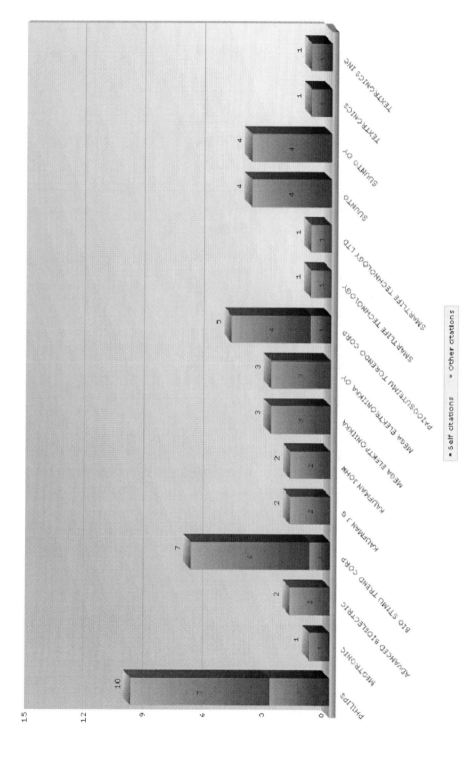

Figure 8. The citations of patents having the keywords "textile and electrod+" (in the Claims section) split by Assignees.

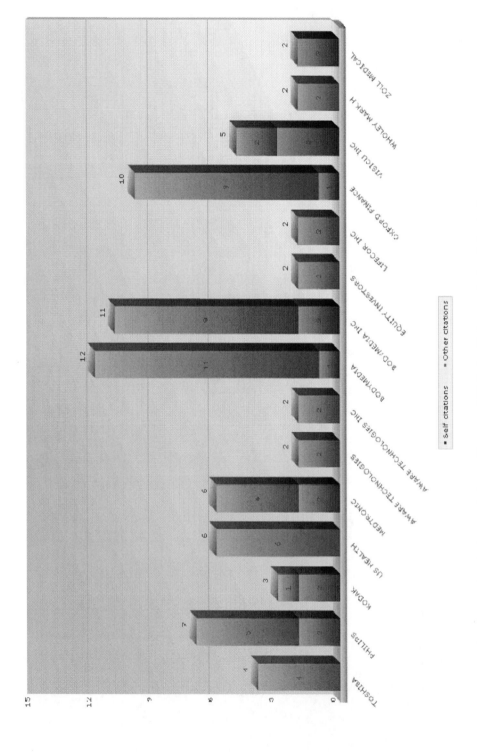

Figure 9. The citations of patents having the keywords "wearable sensor(s)" (in the Claims section) split by Assignees.

CONCLUSION

Nowadays, the wearable monitoring systems are still under development and validation to support monitoring of biophysical conditions of subjects. They can be successfully used in many situations: from in-hospital clinical monitoring, to (and more significantly) home management of several diseases or rehabilitation processes. Management of personal health and prevention are crucial applications of these technologies with immediate benefit both economically and in the quality of provided services (and consequently of the quality of life of the citizen-patient).

Today Wearable Biomedical Systems are at the beginning of the transition from research and development prototypes to full commercialization with significant number of sold units to support their integration into the clinical practice and healthcare processes.

Innovation and related IPR is expected to concern both technological aspects to be crystallized and further developments (e.g. the introduction of micro-and nano-technologies, the power and autonomy of scavenging devices, techniques for low power transmission and broadband and reconfigurable wearable sensor networks), the textile human interface (from production of materials and fibers with higher conductivity to the development of industrial processes of production of fabrics or clothing with integrated sensors and connectors, and guaranteed in terms of duration and stability of properties also after several washing and ironing cycles), and design (for obtaining and ensuring a high quality signal, equal or similar to the traditional diagnostic methods and a full acceptance by the clinical world, up to the ergonomic factors and comfort that determine the acceptance of the system by the user).

REFERENCES

De Rossi D., Lymberis A. (eds), *Wearable eHealth Sysyems for Personalised Health Management*, IOS Press, Amsterdam, 2004.

De Rossi D., Lymberis A., Guest Editorial, IEEE Trans Inf Tech Biomed, Special Section on *New Generation of Smart Wearable Health Systems and Applications*, Guest Editors D. De Rossi, A. Lymberis, vol. 9(3): 293-294, 2005.

Doughty K., Cameron K., Garner P., *Three generations of telecare of the elderly, Journal of Telemedicine and Telecare*, Vol 2: 71-80, 1996.

Gemperle et.al. Design for Wearability. *Proceedings of the ISWC O2, IEEE Computer.* Computer Society, 1998.

Lymberis A., Gatzoulis L., Wearable Health Systems: from smart technologies to real applications. *Conf. Proc. IEEE Eng. Med. Biol. Soc.*: 6789-92, 2006.

VDC Research Group (Main analyst: Krebs David), Wearable Electronics Systems Global Market Demand Analysis: Health Care Solutions, *Research Report # VDC6520, 2007.

Bonfiglio A., Cerutti S., De Rossi D., Magenes G. (eds), *Sistemi indossabili intelligenti per la Salute e la Protezione dell'Uomo*, ed. Patron, 2008, pp. 357-384. ISBN 978-88-555-2994-5.

Gilsoo Cho, Yonsei University, Seoul, South Korea, *Smart Clothing: Technology and Applications*, CRC Press, December 23, 2009, ISBN: 9781420088526.

Analytical Review of World Biosensors Market, Frost&Sullivan market report, 2010, pp.83.

Vijvers W.G., The International Patent Classification as a Search Tool. World Patent Information: Vol 12, No 1, 26-30, 1990.

Goebel M.W.E., *Mirror, mirror on the wall, squishy and soggy, 2 Nanos Tall: Strategies, methods and tools for searching homogeneous catalysts – An EPO perspective* Vol 32, Issue 1, 39-52, 2009.

In: Horizons in Computer Science Research, Volume 4   ISBN: 978-1-61324-262-9
Editor: Thomas S. Clary   © 2011 Nova Science Publishers, Inc.

Chapter 10

INTERNET INFRASTRUCTURE RESILIENCE ASSESSMENT

Rytis Rainys

Telecommunications Engineering Department,
Vilnius Gediminas Technical University, Lithuania

ABSTRACT

The present article examines the infrastructure of the Lithuanian Internet network and the possibilities to develop an Internet monitoring system, which would provide the environment for the regulatory authorities to monitor the state of the network and disruptions of communication. Assessment of Lithuanian Internet network infrastructure identified that are significantly important for the functioning of the entire country Internet network. It is proposed to perform monitoring of the network at the critical nodes level, which would help to collect data on the node status and errors, communication interruptions or register specific packet flows, generated by cyber attacks.

Keywords: Internet Network, Infrastructure Resilience, Autonomous Systems, Critical Node, Monitoring.

INTRODUCTION

The Internet is being continuously developed, new Internet service providers (hereinafter referred to as ISP) and local area networks come into existence, network interconnection tables are also changing dynamically. Cyber attacks against the Estonian networks and servers in 2007 and the 2008 incidents, which left more than 340 Lithuanian Internet websites damaged, are influencing necessity to investigate countries Internet networks infrastructure resilience. The present article examines the infrastructure of the Lithuanian Internet network and the possibilities to develop an Internet monitoring system, which would provide the environment for the regulatory authorities to monitor the state of the network and disruptions of communication, which would allow for, if necessary, to respond properly by way of redistributing the national communication resources. For the purpose of reaching the said overarching objectives, it is necessary to analyze the existing Internet network, identify the critical network interconnection nodes and develop the methods and tools for network monitoring.

The Internet is based on a network of interconnected autonomous systems (hereinafter referred to as AS). The total number of AS in the Internet reaches 50000 [1], therefore analysis of such complex network would be very complicated and the deficiencies identified would be difficult to eliminate due to the inertness of the Internet. As shown in related works [2, 3], there is shift to the fragmented analysis of certain Internet areas. Taking the aforementioned into consideration, a subdivision of the Internet network is a rational approach when performing an individualized and thorough analysis of the reliability of activities of a structural unit, defined by territorial, organizational or some other principles. The present analysis is focused on a structural separation and examination of the network of AS, operated on the territory of the country (Lithuania) as well as its relations with other AS, outside the territory of the country.

In order to reach the objective of the study, the following tasks must be resolved:

- collection of data of the Lithuanian Internet network;
- identification of critical network interconnection nodes;
- development of the core of Lithuanian Internet monitoring model.

RESULTS

113 ISPs [4] provide their services in Lithuania. However, not all of them arrange their activities by employing AS. Small ISPs usually connect to larger ASs by purchasing communication services. Therefore it could be argued that such ISPs do not play an important role in the common Lithuanian Internet network infrastructure. Taking the aforementioned circumstances and the examples of similar studies [2, 3] into consideration, the study of resilience of Lithuanian Internet infrastructure is performed on the AS level. It has been identified that 36 ISPs, which performed their activities in Lithuania at the moment of the study, arranged their activities through created AS.

In order to describe the structure of simplified Lithuania's Internet network (see Figure 1), the assumption that the structure is of a hierarchical character was used. Computers are connected into a local area network, which has an interconnection (interconnections) with other (usually larger) networks, some of which have gateways to the international Internet via foreign AS, which implies that the following can be logically distinguished:

a) the lowest local area networks level, on which an insignificant number of network interconnections is managed by AS and ISP without any AS identifiers, which actually are purchasers of services from the AS of a higher level;
b) the level of the networks, managing the main flows of Internet exchange points, to which the AS, selected according to the criteria and specified bellow;
c) foreign AS with which Lithuanian AS have communication lines and via which the international Internet network is reachable.

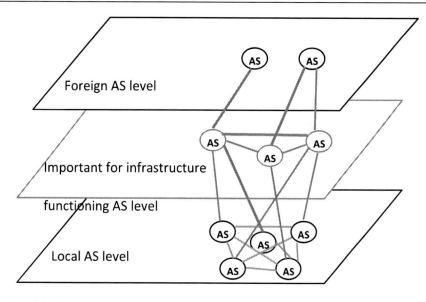

Figure 1. Simplified hierarchical network structure.

The data on the AS, operated in Lithuania, the identifiers they use, the transmission capacity, supported among AS, the communication technology and the number of subscribers, served by each individual AS according to the information of the Communications Regulatory Authority [4], collected during the study, are provided in Table 1. Comparing the data, the network nodes can be ranked in terms of their importance, as shown in Table 1. The AS, having more than 1000 subscribers, more than 10 network interconnections with other AS and the AS, having at least one communication line with foreign AS, were selected subjectively. The AS, which satisfied two or more of the aforementioned criteria, have been included into Table 1.

The data shows right away that Lithuanian Internet network has a rather limited number of gateways to international networks (15 communication lines with 11 foreign AS), and the number of AS, managing the said communication lines is even smaller – only six. It was identified that the total international gateway transmission capacity of Lithuanian Internet network during the study (at the beginning of 2009) reached 65.1 Gbps, and the largest transmission capacity to foreign countries is available at three AS, while the transmission capacity of the international gateway to foreign countries, managed by one of the said AS amounts to 53% of the country's total transmission capacity (see Figure 2). AS1, by managing the largest share of the international Internet traffic, may become the main target of cyber attacks, since a successful attack would result in Lithuania's loss of a half of the country's international Internet channels. The conclusion can be drawn that the resilience of Lithuania Internet network gateway to foreign countries actually depends on the resilience of the international gateway, held by one AS, as well as on the said AS's experience to rapidly ensure availability of alternative channels and capacity to arrange speed rate extensions, in case of, for instance, damage of a submarine cable.

Table. 1. Important for infrastructure functioning AS

AS No.	Quantity of accessible AS	Number of end users	Conections to foreign AS	Joint Access Capacity, Gb/s
AS1	32	298650	5	70
AS2	21	94193	1	2,6
AS3	23	22706	4	8,48
AS4	29	1115	-	6
AS5	32	1457	2	19
AS6	19	5713	-	2,5
AS7	24	17411	1	7
AS8	25	30	2	47,5
AS9	19	29459	-	4
AS10	28	26342	-	8
AS11	28	25738	-	7
AS12	23	15359	-	7

The total volume of international Lithuania's Internet gateway (65.1 Gb/s) may be insufficient to withstand sweeping cyber attacks. For instance, the presently operated major botnets (a network made up of a big number of infected computers, remotely managed by one or several controllers and intended for performing attacks), during a DDoS (Distributed Denial of Service Attack) might generate a data packet traffic, which could not possibly be processed by employing the transmission capacity of all the existing Lithuania's communication channels.

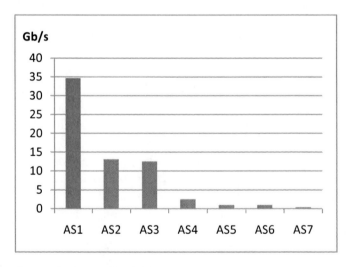

Figure 2. AS throughput to the international AS.

If, considering that an average botnet computer generates a 256 Kb/s data flow, it can be calculated that a botnet with 254297 computers would be sufficient to fully jam all Lithuanian international gateway channels. This is quite realistic scenario, since at present major botnets include 300 thousand computers and even more [5]. In the event of such an attack an ISP should immediately take rather complex measures: increase the transmission capacity of communication channels, divert data flows, detect the botnet IP addresses and block them, etc. Currently there is a shortage of implemented nationwide measures, able to organize management of flow priority or block addresses.

In addition, the total managed channel transmission capacity of each critical node was calculated (see Figure 3). The study has shown that on the critical infrastructure level two nodes, the total joint access capacity of which amounts to 64.5 % of the total of the transmission capacity of all the AS, stand out. The conclusion can be drawn that the damage of AS1 and AS8 due to systems overload, cyber attacks or router faults would have an impact to a bigger part of the infrastructure of the Lithuanian Internet network interconnections.

It has also been observed that 5 ISP, having the largest numbers of subscribers, serve approximately 70 per cent of all Lithuania's Internet users. When analyzing their interrelations it was identified that the said ISPs are connected to other critical nodes, highlighted in Table 1, by at least three lines.

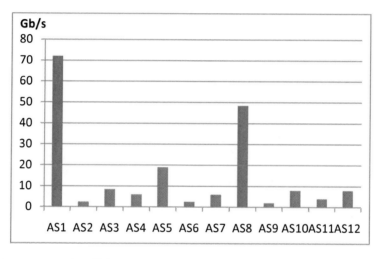

Figure 3. Joint access capacity, Gb/s.

DATABASE

For the purpose of development of the model of Lithuanian Internet network a significant amount of technical data was collected, for processing of which a database was decided to be developed. The database must systemize the data and simplify their operation. The SQL (Structured Query Language) supported structure with MySQL implementation was selected for the database. SQL is widely used and has proven as a fast and easily administered tool, which allows for remote updating of the data entries in the future.

The functioning of the database is based on entering of data into tables. Each table is divided into rows and columns. Each row corresponds to one entry, which may have information of several types, which depends on the types and names of columns. The data can be manipulated in several ways: by using a command line, browser or programming languages such as PHP, C, Perl, Java, Python, etc. When compiling the database the network interconnection data, obtained directly when examining the AS, were used and for international network registry databases ROBTEX [6] and RIPE [7] were used to fill in the missing information.

The structure of the developed database (see Figure 4) includes:

- The main Table No. 1 via which all the remaining tables are accessible. Table No. 1 contains the network interconnection data, such as the AS interconnectors, the technology used, the speed rate, the country, with which the connection is arranged and the node, in which the interconnection is implemented (if there is a case of peering at the IXP node);
- Table No. 2, containing the data on the AS: name, number, the supported number of the Internet service users, and notes;
- Table No. 3, containing the information on the location of the AS, the country;
- Table No. 4, containing the information on the types of connection (peering or other);
- Table No. 5, containing the contact information on the responsible person, administering the network of the AS;

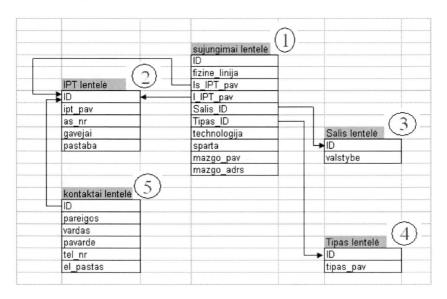

Figure 4. Data base structure.

For the purpose of entering the data into the tables as well as for presentation of the data a PHP Internet webpage was developed, which provides a possibility for quick presentation of different data, obtained from the MySQL database by processing them by PHP, for instance: AS peering connections scheme; the total speed rate or the speed rate of the international gateway of a specific AS; the number of AS, connected via the specific Internet Exchange Point (hereinafter referred to as the IXP), etc. One of the aspects of the use of the database, most relevant to an operator, is a graphic representation of the scheme of the Lithuanian Internet network.

When analyzing the scheme of the Lithuanian Internet network (see Figure 5), the conclusion can be made that the distributed connection scheme prevails in the country. The most important Lithuanian Internet network nodes are densely interconnected, and any interconnection interruptions at one or several points would result in an insignificant impact on interconnections between other points, thus on the functioning of the Internet, since a significant number of alternative communication channels is in existence. However, a disruption of the nodes themselves (especially the routers with a significant number of connections, listed in Table 1) would have more negative consequences. In order to find out the extent of the impact on the functioning of the network infrastructure which would result from damage to interconnection nodes, a further development of the model is necessary.

MONITORING

During the study the structure of the Internet network was drawn up and divided into three hierarchical levels, among which the interim level is defined as a critical one for the functioning of the entire infrastructure. We propose to perform monitoring of the network at the said level, which would help to collect data on the node status and errors, communication interruptions or register specific packet flows, generated by cyber attacks. When drawing up the monitoring strategy, the following must be defined:

- the parameters to be registered by sensors;
- the points in the infrastructure, where the sensors would be placed;
- the points, where the sensor collected data would be sent.

The simplest way to perform monitoring would be routine checks carried on network switching nodes. Those could be simple *ping, tracepath, pathping* or *traceroute* commands, which would continuously (for instance, at 10 minute intervals) check the response from all the critical nodes and the process itself would be automated. In case any network node fails to respond to the verification command, a fault warning would appear on the network topology map, supervised by the operator, and the periodicity of checks of the node would be made more frequent (for instance, at 1 s intervals) until the node reports on its vitality. The positive characteristic of such a method is its independence, since there would be no need for agreements with router administrators regarding placement of sensors. However, the method itself lacks flexibility. In addition, some ISP prohibit reception of the said commands in their networks.

Another method for monitoring of critical infrastructure nodes could be based by Simple Network Management Protocol (hereinafter referred to as SNMP) [8]. SNMP is an application level protocol, integrated into the majority of the modern network equipment supporting TCP/IP therefore it can be used to arrange centralized monitoring. The functioning of SNMP is based on the collection of data defined by a set of certain variables from remote equipment (network routers in this case) into the management system. The necessary variables can be specified from the control system or pre-set in advance. The software components, the so-called agents, function in each of the monitored nodes, register and send the data via the SNMP to the control system. It is important that the SNMP allows for performing active network management, for instance, it is possible to update or change the network configuration by exchanging commands between the control system and the network nodes. Such method of monitoring is more flexible, it allows for collection of a larger volume of technical information. However, agreements with the ISP, managing the critical nodes, are necessary for its implementation. SNMP is a standardized protocol with possibilities for multiple applications, therefore is can practically be adapted for registration of any network equipment parameters.

The monitored nodes are controlled by the SNMP protocol and the main commands *read*, *write* and *trap*. When arranging monitoring of critical infrastructure nodes, the *read* command is going to be used for periodic reading of data, and *trap* – for asynchronous reporting to the control system on any extra events, such as interruptions of communication, critical level of data flow, etc. The information to be collected by the agent at the monitored network equipment depends on the management information base (hereinafter referred to as the MIB). For the monitoring purposes the agents must be entered into the network routers. In such way the MIB text file (the data table) would describe the following parameters: communication errors, possible to occur in the network and the changes of flow in each channel. In case of necessity to register other data at the network node, the MIB text file may be changed. For this purpose the *traversal* command, which shows the variables, which routers are capable of supporting, would be used. The MIB file can be changed according to the needs of the operator of the management system by using the *write* command.

Taking into consideration that the data between the management system and the agents in the SNMPv1 protocol are sent unencrypted, for the security assurance purposes it is recommended to select the SNMPv3 version, using cryptography in order to ensure confidentiality.

The monitoring of critical nodes would virtually reflect the state of the entire Internet network, since the said nodes house the major share of network interconnections and the absolute majority of data communication. The principle scheme of such monitoring model is presented in Figure 5. The programmed critical node routers with the loaded agents will collect the identified data via the SNMP. For instance, this could be registration of network interconnections fault reports. As highlighted in red color in the scheme, in case a remote network is not available due to a fault of the communication line, a TCP packet, that the data of 443 port fails to reach the addressee, is formed at the critical node router. The agent registers the information and transmits a warning to the monitoring server. The applications of the monitoring server with the Internet network topology simulator would quickly present the location of the fault graphically and provide the information on possible reasons. The monitoring operator would react in accordance with the information received and arrange alternative data communication routes, making adjustments to the line loads, etc.

In addition, it could be possible to establish that the critical node routers would register the increase of certain data packet flows during a predefined time period, thus detecting the commencement of security attacks in their early phase. Availability of such information would be very relevant for the national security incidents investigation team CERT-LT [9].

When implementing the monitoring of critical infrastructure nodes or all main AS network nodes, the MySQL database would also be used for storing the data, received via the SNMP protocol. During the periodic checks of nodes by the SNMP protocol (for instance, network load), the data would be recorded into the database, from which the network load could be presented graphically or manipulated in another way. In addition, certain criteria could be established and in case they are exceeded the supervisory authorities, such as CERT-LT, would be informed.

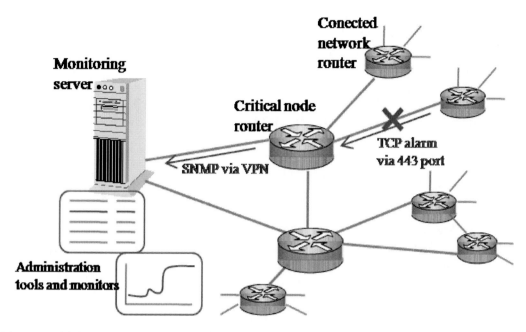

Figure 5. Priciple scheme of network monitoring model.

Increasing data communication demands of consumers, the reduction of costs and optimization of networks influence a continuous development of the Internet networks therefore in 2010 new data on the Internet infrastructure will be collected in order to assess the reliability of the network one more time. When continuing the studies the data on peering network interconnections will be collected and attempts will be made to identify the particularities of the physical and logical network interconnection schemes.

In addition, practical development and testing of the described monitoring method is planned. An MIB, adapted to network reliability monitoring will be developed and implemented into several routers. The data will be collected from agents and graphically represented by a dedicated server.

An SQL database will be developed in order to systematize the data on the Internet network infrastructure. With the database in place, the attempts will be made to develop a model for evaluation of the impact, which may be brought to the network infrastructure by a fault of a specific communication line.

FUTURE ASSESMENTS

Increasing data communication demands of consumers, the reduction of costs and optimization of networks influence a continuous development of the Internet networks therefore in a future new data on the Internet infrastructure will be collected in order to assess the reliability of the network one more time. When continuing the studies the data on peering network interconnections will be collected and attempts will be made to identify the particularities of the physical and logical network interconnection schemes.

In addition, practical development and testing of the described monitoring method is planned. An MIB, adapted to network reliability monitoring will be developed and implemented into several routers. The data will be collected from agents and graphically represented by a dedicated server.

An SQL database will be developed in order to systematize the data on the Internet network infrastructure. With the database in place, the attempts will be made to develop a model for evaluation of the impact, which may be brought to the network infrastructure by a fault of a specific communication line.

REFERENCES

[1]   *The Internet Assigned Numbers Authority* (IANA) http://www.iana.org, 2008.

[2]   Dohoon Kim, *Reliability and Risk Analysis of the Internet: Case of Korean Internet Interconnections.* College of Business Administration, Kyung Hee University 1 Hoegi-Dong, Dongdaemoon-Gu, Seoul 130-701, South Korea.

[3]   Danny Dolev, Sugih Jamin, Osnat (Ossi) Mokryn, Yuval Shavitt, Internet resiliency to attacks and failures under BGP policy routing, *Computer Networks*, 2006.

[4]   *RRT ataskaita apie Elektroninių ryšių veiklą* 2008 m. I ketv. http://www.rrt.lt.

[5]   David Barroso Botnets – The Silent Threat, *ENISA Position Paper* No. 3, November 2007 (p. 2).

[6]   *ROBTEX tarptautinė AS numerių duomenų bazė* http://www.robtex.com.

[7]   *RIPE Database*, http://www.ripe.net/db/index.html.

[8]   Internet Engineering Task Force, RFC 1157 - *A Simple Network Management Protocol* (SNMP), 1990.

[9]   R. Rainys, Network and Information Security. Assessments and Incidents Handling, *Electronics and electrical engineering*, Nr. 6(70), 2006.

In: Horizons in Computer Science Research, Volume 4
Editor: Thomas S. Clary

ISBN: 978-1-61324-262-9
© 2011 Nova Science Publishers, Inc.

Chapter 11

CHAOS-BASED 2D VISUAL ENCRYPTION MECHANISM FOR ECG MEDICAL SIGNALS

*Chin-Feng Lin**

Department of Electrical Engineering,
National Taiwan Ocean University, Taiwan, R.O.C.

ABSTRACT

Encryption is a necessary mechanism for secure data storage and transmission. Chaos-based encryption is an important encryption mechanism that is used for audio, image, video, electroencephalograms (EEG), and electrocardiographs (ECG) multimedia signals. Chaos sequences are popular because they increase unpredictability more than other types of random sequences. We have developed a two-dimensional (2D) chaos-based encryption scheme that can be applied to signals with transmission bit errors in clinical electroencephalography (ECG) and mobile telemedicine. We used a 2D chaotic scrambler and a 2D permutation scheme to achieve ECG visual encryption. The visual encryption mechanism was realized by first scrambling the input ECG signal values, then multiplying a chaotic 2D address scanning order encryption to randomize reference values. Simulation results show that when the correct deciphering parameters are entered, ECG signal with a transmission bit error rate of 10^{-7} are completely recovered; furthermore, the percent root-mean-square difference values for clinical ECG signals is 0.2496%. However, when there is an input parameter error, for example, an initial point error of 0.00000001%, these clinical ECG signals become unrecoverable. The proposed chaos-based 2D encryption is well suited for applications to clinical ECG signals.

Keywords: Chaos, 2D, visual encryption mechanism, ECG medical signal.

I. INTRODUCTION

Chaos-based encryption mechanism is an interesting research topic and has been examined in many previously studies [1-4]. In contrast to block encryption algorithms such as

---

* E-mail address: lcf1024@ mail.ntou.edu.tw.

the data encryption standard (DES) algorithm, Rivest, Shamir, and Adleman (RSA) algorithm, and advanced encryption standard (AES) algorithm, a chaos sequence is continuous; hence, it is suitable for data encryption in continuous media such as audio, video, electrocardiogram (ECG) and electroencephalography (EEG) signals, and in large block files such as image signals. This is because the unpredictability when chaos sequences are used is higher than when other types of random sequences are used. In addition, chaos-based encryption algorithms have certain advantages such as sensitivity to changes in the initial conditions and parameters, random-like behavior, and unstable periodic orbits with long periods. Moreover, it is possible to develop a robust encryption mechanism by using a large set of parameters. A visual image encryption concept using chaos sequence has been proposed in [5]. Its main principle is the use of the susceptibility of human vision to encrypt images in such a manner that privacy or confidentiality is maintained; such techniques make it impossible for people to clearly see the primitive encoded image. Visual image encryption can be implemented by (i) pixel address (position) permutation, (ii) transformation of pixel values and, (iii) a combination of (i) and (ii). Friedrich *et al.* [6] initially applied chaos theory to rearrange the addresses (positions) of pixels, making it difficult for human vision to distinguish the original and encrypted images. Yen *et al.* [7, 8] also utilized chaos theory to generate a binary digit array, which achieves conversion of pixel values. Li *et al.* [9, 10] proposed a chaos-based binary-digit decryption sequence, which enables brute-force searching method to decipher the sequence. A new video-streams encryption algorithm for H.264, which uses a chaos pseudo sequence, has also been discussed [11].

Chaos-based visual encryption mechanisms, mobile telemedicine, and HHT-based time frequency analysis of EEG signals have been extensively discussed studied in our earlier researches [12]-[24]. In particular, in [12], we performed chaos-based pixel address (position) permutation and transformation of pixel values in order to encrypt X-ray images. We used all-pass filtering to scramble the phase spectra of the most-important low-resolution sub-images in the following manner. In the pre-filtering step, we added 2D chaotic signals to randomize the reference phase spectra; subsequently, in the post-filtering step, we subtracted the same reference phase spectra to recover the original phase spectra of the image. In [13], we proposed one-dimensional (1D) chaos-based bit-stream ciphers for use in mobile telemedicine systems. In [14], we scrambled the signal values of the input EEG signals by using a 1D chaotic signal to randomize the EEG signal values; furthermore, we applied chaotic address scanning order encryption to achieve visual encryption. In [15], we made improvements to 1D chaos-based encryption and proposed a 2D chaos-based visual encryption scheme based on parallel processing for applications to clinical EEG signals.

In the chapter, we discuss the possibility of applying 2D chaos-based cipher to simultaneously encrypt N clinical ECG signals using a parallel architecture. An essential feature of the 2D encryption scheme is that signal mapping of a 2D chaotic scrambler as well as a permutation scheme are used to obtain the clinical ECG information requiring high-level encryption. Simulation results show that when the correct deciphering parameters are input, signals with a transmission bit error rate (BER) of 10^{-7} are completely recovered. However, signal recovery is not achieved if there is an error in the input parameters, for example, an input point error of 0.00000001%.

II. A 2D Chaos-based Encryption Scheme for Clinical ECG Signals

Figure 1 shows the architecture of the proposed 2D chaos-based encryption scheme for clinical ECG signals. In this scheme, a 2D chaos-based encryption scrambler and a 2D chaotic address permutation method are used. First, N multichannel clinical ECG signals are input to the 2D chaos-based cipher and then processed by a 2D chaos-based encryption scrambler to generate 1st 2D chaotically encrypted ECG signals. In addition, 2D chaotically encrypted sequences are generated, which are multiplied by N multichannel clinical ECG signals to obtain the 1st 2D chaotically encrypted ECG signals. The 1st 2D chaotically encrypted ECG signals are then processed by the 2D chaotic address permutation method to generate 2nd 2D chaotically encrypted ECG signals. Figure 2 shows the flow chart of the proposed 2D visual chaos-based encryption scheme for clinical ECG signals. Furthermore, in order to increase the robustness of the encryption system, we use the chaotic index address assignment process F_{CIAX} and the chaotic candidate point generator process G_{CCSX} to represent values in the x-axis, and to generate 1D chaotically encrypted sequences (CEX) of length L_F. The process is similarly repeated to generate 1D chaotically encrypted sequences (CEY) of length N in the y-axis. The vector inner product of CEX and CEY is used to generate 2D chaotically encrypted sequences, and chaotically encrypted signals $CECG1$ are generated from the vector inner product of $CEXY$ and N channel clinical ECG signals. In order to decrease the correlation between the encrypted and original ECG signals, we use 2D chaotic address permutation encryption to generate 2nd 2D chaotically encrypted ECG signals $SGECGN$. The steps involved in the implementation of our 2D chaos-based encryption scrambler are summarized as follows:

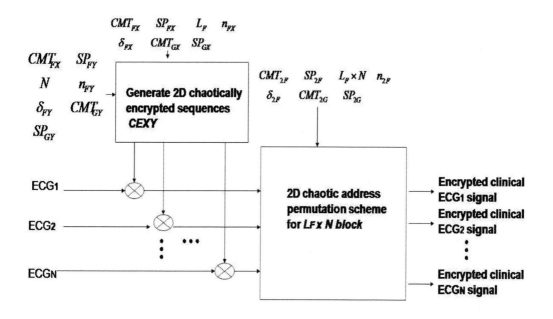

Figure 1. Proposed 2D chaos-based encryption scheme for clinical ECG signals.

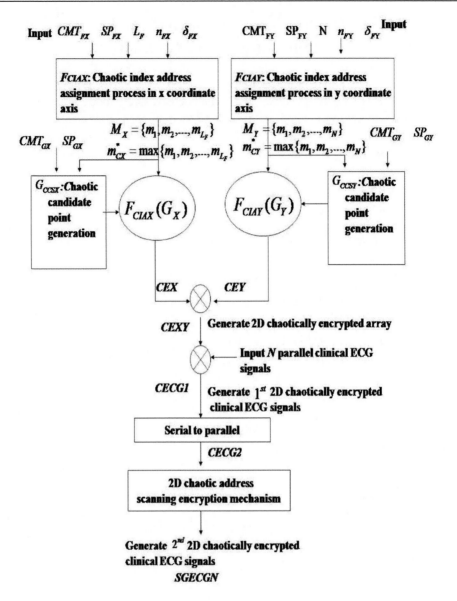

Figure 2. Flow chart of the proposed 2D visual chaos-based encryption scheme for clinical ECG signals.

Step 1: Select a chaotic logistic map type CMT_{FX} of F_{CIAX}, where the starting point is SP_{FX}, and L_F is the length of an encrypted clinical ECG signal. The parameters n_{FX} and, δ_{FX} denote the security level.

Step 2: Generate a chaotic sequence of length n_{FX}.

$$x_{n+1} = CMT_{FX}(x_n) \, ; x_0 = SP_{FX} \, ; \, n = \{1, 2, ..., n_{FX}\} \tag{1}$$

Step 3: Discard the previous n_{FX} chaotic sequence.

Step 4: Generate a new chaotic sequence

$$x_n = CMT(x_{n_{FX}+1}) ; n = \{n_{FX} + 1,...\}$$

Step 5: If $x_n > \delta_{FX}$, discard x_n and go to step 4.

Else, go to step 6.

Step 6:

$$m_k = \left\lceil \frac{1}{x_n} \right\rceil \qquad (2)$$

If $m_k \notin M_X$; $M_X = \{m_1,..., m_{k-1}, m_k\}$, go to step 7. Else, go to step 4.

Step 7: If $k = L_F$,

$$M_X = \{m_1, m_2,..., m_{L_F}\} ; m_{CX}^* = \max\{m_1, m_2,..., m_{L_F}\} \qquad (3)$$

Else, go to step 4.

Step 8: Deliver m_{CX}^* to the chaotic candidate point generator G_{CCSX} .

Step 9: Deliver a chaotic logistic map of the type CMT_{GX} for G_{CCSX} , where the starting point is SP_{GX} .

Step10: Generate a chaotic sequence of length m_C^* . $g_{n+1} = CMT_{GX}(g_n)$; $g_0 = SP_{GX}$; $n = \{1,2,..., m_C^*\}$;

$$G_X = \{g_1,..., g_{m_C^*}\} \qquad (4)$$

Step 11: Deliver M to the chaotic candidate point generator G_{CCSX} .

Step 12: Generate an encrypted chaotic signal CEX in the x-axis.

$$M_X = \{m_1, m_2,..., m_{L_F}\} ; G_X = \{g_1,..., g_{m_C^*}\} ; \qquad (5)$$

$$CEX = \{g_{m_1}, g_{m2},..., g_{m_{L_F}}\} = \{cex_1, cex_2,..., cex_{L_F}\}$$

Step 13: Repeat steps 1-12 to generate an encrypted chaotic signal CEY in the y-axis. The length of the CEY signal is N .

Step 14: Generate a 2D chaotically encrypted sequence $CEXY$.

$$CEX = \{cex_1, cex_2,..., cex_{L_F}\} , \qquad (6)$$

$$CEY = \{cey_1, cey_2,..., cey_{L_F}\} ,$$

$$CEXY = \begin{bmatrix} cex_1 \times cey_1 & cex_2 \times cey_1 & \cdots & cex_{L_{FX}} \times cey_1 \\ cex_1 \times cey_2 & cex_1 \times cey_2 & \cdots & cex_{L_{FX}} \times cey_2 \\ \vdots & \vdots & \vdots & \vdots \\ cex_1 \times cey_N & cex_2 \times cey_N & \cdots & cex_{L_{FX}} \times cey_N \end{bmatrix}$$

$$= \begin{bmatrix} cexy_{11} & cexy_{12} & \cdots & cexy_{1L_F} \\ cexy_{21} & cexy_{22} & \cdots & cexy_{2L_F} \\ \vdots & \vdots & \vdots & \vdots \\ cexy_{N1} & cexy_{N2} & \cdots & cexy_{NL_F} \end{bmatrix}$$

Step 15: Input N parallel clinical ECG signals. The length of the clinical ECG signal sequences is L_F. The N clinical ECG signals are defined as follows:

$$ECG = \begin{bmatrix} ecg_{11} & ecg_{12} & \cdots & ecg_{1L_F} \\ ecg_{21} & ecg_{22} & \cdots & ecg_{2L_F} \\ \vdots & \vdots & \vdots & \vdots \\ ecg_{N1} & ecg_{N2} & \cdots & ecg_{NL_F} \end{bmatrix} \tag{7}$$

Step 16: Generate 1st 2D chaotic clinical ECG signals $CECG1$, which are given as follows:

$$CECG1 = ECG \times CEXY = \begin{bmatrix} cecg1_{11} & cecg1_{12} & \cdots & cecg1_{1L_F} \\ cecg1_{21} & cecg1_{22} & \cdots & cecg1_{2L_F} \\ \vdots & \vdots & \vdots & \vdots \\ cecg1_{N1} & cecg1_{N2} & \cdots & cecg1_{NL_F} \end{bmatrix} \tag{8}$$

Finally, input the N parallel 1st 2D chaotic clinical ECG signals $CECG1$ to a serial-to-parallel converter and generate $N \times L_F$ chaotic clinical ECG signals $CECG2$, as follows:

$$CECG1 = \{ cecg1_{11} \quad cecg1_{12} \quad \cdots \quad cecg1_{1L_F} \quad \cdots \quad cecg1_{NL_F} \}$$
$$CECG2 = \{ cecg2_1 \quad cecg2_2 \quad \cdots \quad cecg2_{N \times L_F} \} \tag{9}$$

Process $CECG2$ by using the 2D chaotic address permutation method, and thus output the 2nd 2D chaotically encrypted clinical ECG signals.

The 2D chaotic address permutation encryption scheme is described as follows.

Steps 1 to 5 are the same as those described for the 1st 2D chaos-based encryption scheme.

Step 6:

$$m_{kl} = \left\lceil \frac{1}{x_n} \right\rceil \tag{10}$$

If $m_{kl} \leq N \times L_F$; $m_{kl} \notin \{ m_1, ..., m_{k-1} \}$;

$M = \{m_1,..., m_{k1-1}, m_{k1}\}$;go to step 7.

Else, go to step 4;

Step 7: If $k1 = N \times L_F$

$M = \{m_1, m_2,..., m_{N \times L_F}\}$; else, go to step 4.

Step 8: Deliver M to the encrypted output of the signal processor.

Step 9: Deliver the encrypted clinical ECG signals $CECG2$ to output the encrypted signals.

Step 10: Perform chaotic address permutation of the encrypted clinical ECG signal $SGECG$.

$$GECG = \{gecg_1,..., gecg_{N \times L_F}\}; M = \{m_1, m_2,..., m_{N \times L_F}\} \tag{11}$$
$$SGECG = \{gecg_{m_1}, gecg_{m_2} ..., gecg_{m_{N \times L_F}}\}$$
$$= \{sgecg_1, sgecg_2,..., sgecg_{N \times L_F}\}$$

Step 11: Input $SGECG$ to a serial-to-parallel converter, and generate 2nd 2D chaotically encrypted clinical ECG signals $SGECGN$.

$$SGECGN = \begin{bmatrix} sgecg_1 & sgecg_2 & \cdots & sgecg_{L_F} \\ sgecg_{L_F+1} & sgecg_{L_F+2} & \cdots & sgecg_{2L_F} \\ \vdots & \vdots & \vdots & \vdots \\ sgecg_{(N-1) \times L_F+1} & sgecg_{(N-1) \times L_F+2} & \cdots & sgecg_{N \times L_F} \end{bmatrix} \tag{12}$$

Note that if the abovementioned process is performed in the reverse order, N parallel clinical ECG signals are decrypted. Table I lists the parameters of the proposed 2D chaos-based visual clinical ECG signals.

Table I. The parameters of the proposed 2D chaos-based visual clinical ECG signals

F_{CIAX}	chaotic index address assignment process in x coordinate axis
CMT_{FX}	a chaotic logistic map type of F_{CIAX}
SP_{FX}	a initial value of chaotic logistic map CMT_{FX}
x_n	chaotic sequences which was generated by chaotic logistic map type CMT_{FX} and initial value SP_{FX}
n_{FX}	security level parameter discard previous n_{FX} chaotic sequences (x_n) to increase encryption robustness.
δ_{FX}	security level parameter If x_n is larger than δ_{FX}, discard the chaotic point x_n to increase encryption robustness.

Table I. Continued

G_{CCSX}	chaotic candidate point generation in x coordinate axis
CMT_{GX}	a chaotic logistic map type of G_{CCSX}
SP_{GX}	a initial value of chaotic logistic map CMT_{GX}
G_X	chaotic sequences which was generated by chaotic logistic map type CMT_{GX} and initial value SP_{GX}
F_{CIAY}	chaotic index address assignment process in y coordinate axis
CMT_{FY}	a chaotic logistic map type of F_{CIAY}
SP_{FY}	a initial value of chaotic logistic map CMT_{FY}
y_n	chaotic sequences which was generated by chaotic logistic map type CMT_{FY} and initial value SP_{FY}
n_{FY}	security level parameter discard previous n_{FY} chaotic sequences (y_n) to increase encryption robustness.
δ_{FY}	security level parameter If y_n is larger than δ_{FY} , discard the chaotic point y_n to increase encryption robustness.
G_{CCSY}	chaotic candidate point generation in y coordinate axis
CMT_{GY}	a chaotic logistic map type of G_{CCSY}
SP_{GY}	a initial value of chaotic logistic map CMT_{GY}
G_Y	chaotic sequences which was generated by chaotic logistic map type CMT_{GY} and initial value SP_{GY}
L_F	the number of input clinical ECG samples per channel
N	the number of input parallel clinical ECG channels.
CEX	1D chaotically encrypted sequence in the x coordinate axis
CEY	1D chaotically encrypted sequence in the y coordinate axis
$CEXY$	2D chaotically encrypted array
$CECG1$	1st 2D chaotically encrypted clinical ECG signals
$SGECGN$	2nd 2D chaotically encrypted clinical ECG signals
γ	Pearson correlation coefficient

III. SIMULATION RESULTS

Figure 3 shows four parallel ECG signals in the clinical ECG database [25]. The sampling rate of each clinical signal channel is 360 samples/s. The following parameters are used in the proposed 2D chaos-based encryption scheme. The starting points are as follows: $SP_{FX} = 0.100011$, and $SP_{FY} = 0.200011, m_C^* = 256$, $N=8$, $n_{FX} = n_{FY} = 25600$, and $\delta_{FX} = \delta_{FY} = 0.1$. The chaotic equation $x_{n+1} = rx_n(1-x_n)$ is applied to all types of chaotic logistic maps. Figure 4 shows the 1st 2D chaotically encrypted clinical EEG signals generated by using the proposed chaotic scrambler. We discuss the differences between the original and chaotically encrypted ECG signals by using the Pearson correlation coefficient r, which is given as follows:

$$r = \frac{\sum XY - \frac{\sum X \sum Y}{Z}}{\sqrt{(\sum X^2 - \frac{(\sum X)^2}{Z})(\sum Y^2 - \frac{(\sum Y)^2}{Z}}} \qquad (13)$$

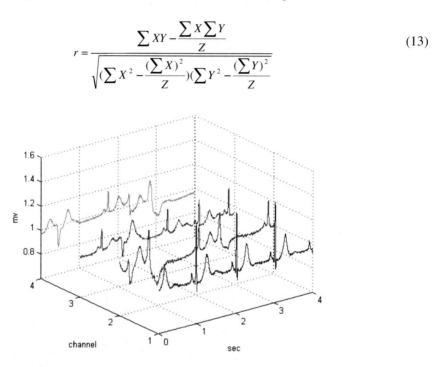

Figure 3. Four parallel clinical ECG signals.

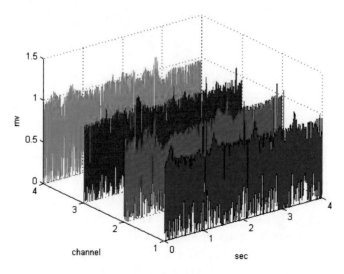

Figure 4. The 1st 2D chaotically encrypted clinical ECG signals generated by using the proposed chaotic scrambler. (BER=10^{-7} and r=0.08).

Here, X and Y are the amplitudes of the original and encrypted ECG signals, respectively; and Z is the total number of sampled ECG signals. The r value of the signals A and B is 1, which indicates that A and B are identical and completely correlated. The r value is 0.08 for the original clinical ECG signals and the chaotically encrypted signal (transmission BER of 10^{-7}) generated by using the proposed chaos-based encryption scrambler. Figure 5 shows the 2D ECG signals that are chaotically encrypted by the proposed encryption scrambler and the 2D chaotic address permutation method. The transmission BER is 10^{-7}. The r value of the original clinical ECG signals and those encrypted using the proposed encryption scheme is 0.001; This implies that the encrypted clinical ECG signals are unreadable. Further, the percent root-mean-square difference (PRD) is used to evaluate the distortion of the decrypted signals. The PRD value is obtained using the equation

$$PRD = 100 \times \sqrt{\frac{\sum_{i=1}^{L}(X_{ori}(i) - X_{dec}(i))^2}{\sum_{i=1}^{L}X_{ori}^2(i)}} \tag{14}$$

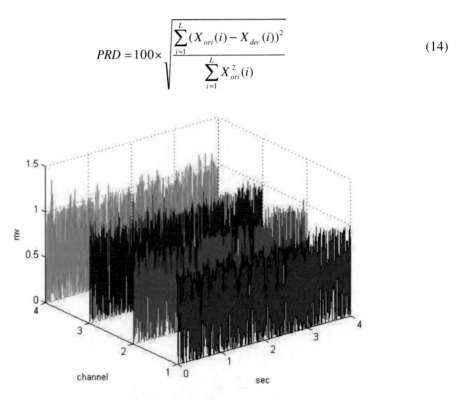

Figure 5. The 2nd 2D chaotically encrypted clinical ECG signals generated by using the proposed chaotic scrambler and 2D chaotic address permutation method. (BER=10^{-7} and r=0.001)

Here X_{ori} and X_{dec} are the original and decrypted clinical ECG signals, respectively. The correct decrypted clinical ECG signals are shown in Figure 6. We assume that the received ECG signals have a transmission BER of 10^{-7}. The PRD value of the correct decrypted ECG signals and original ECG signals is 0.2496%. Figure 7 shows that the error in the decrypted ECG signals and the decrypted parameter at the starting point is 0.00000001%. From these simulation results, we conclude that the proposed chaos-based 2D encryption is a superior scheme that is well suited for applications to clinical ECG signals.

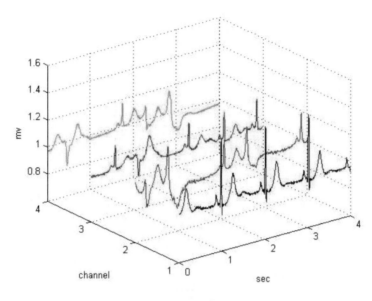

Figure 6. 2D ECG chaos decrypted signals. (BER=10^{-7} and PRD=0.2496%).

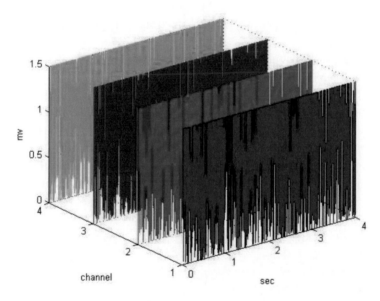

Figure 7. 2D decrypted ECG signals with error decryption parameter of an initial point error of 0.00000001%.

CONCLUSION

In this paper, we have developed a high-speed encryption scheme based on the chaos theory for applications to clinical ECG signals. Signal mapping of a 2D chaotic scrambler and a permutation scheme are used to perform high-level encryption of clinical ECG information. Simulation results show that when the correct deciphering parameters are input, the signals are completely recovered. This 2D encryption scheme can also be applied to mobile telemedicine systems in which the ECG signals have a transmission BER of 10^{-7}. However, signal recovery is not achieved if there is an appreciable error in the input parameters, for example, when the initial point error is 0.00000001%. The proposed encryption scheme can be used for the encryption of E-health and M-health biomedical signals.

ACKNOWLEDGMENTS

The author acknowledge the support of the North Center of Inter-Science Education Program of Ministry of Education, Taiwan, 99A1 Maritime Telemedicine, Taiwan, Center for Teaching and Learning in NTOU, Telemedicine Teaching and Learning Project, NSC 93-2218-E-019-024, and the valuable comments of the reviewers.

REFERENCES

[1]   L. Kocarev (2001), "Chaos-Based Cryptography: A Brief Overview," *IEEE Circuits and System Magazine,* 6-21.

[2]   M. Yang, N. Bourbakis and S. Li (2004), "Data, image, video encryption," *IEEE Potentials*, 28-34.

[3]   C. M. Ou(2009), "Design of Block Ciphers by Simple Chaotic Functions," *IEEE Computational Intelligence Magazine,* 54-59.

[4]   M. Naoki, J. Goce, A. Kazuyuki, and K. Ljupco (2006), "Chaotic Block Ciphers: From Theory to Practical Algorithms," *IEEE Trans. Circuits and Systems I*, 1341-1352.

[5]   M. Naor and A. Shamir (1994), "Visual cryptography," *Eurocrypt*, 1-12.

[6]   J. Friedrich (1997), "Image encryption based on chaotic maps," *IEEE International Conference on Computational Cybernetics and Simulation*, 1105-1110.

[7]   J. C. Yen and J. I. Guo (2000), "A new chaotic key-based design for image encryption and decryption", *IEEE International Symposium on Circuits and Systems,* 49-52.

[8]   J. C. Yen and J. I. Guo (2000), "Efficient hierarchical chaotic image encryption algorithm and its VLSI realisation, "*IEE Proc.-Vis. Image Signal Process.*, 167-175.

[9]   S. Li and X. Zheng (2002), "Cryptanalysis of a chaotic image encryption method," *IEEE International Symposium on Circuits and Systems,* 708-711.

[10]   S. Li and X. Zheng (2002), "On the security of an image encryption method, " *IEEE International Conference on Image Processing*, 925-928.

[11]   Li Y., Liang L., Su Z., and Jiang J. (2005): 'A new video Encryption Algorithm for H.264,' *IEEE ICICS,* 1121-1124.

[12]   C. F. Lin, W. T. Chang, and C. Y. Li (2007), "A Chaos-based Visual Encryption Mechanism in JPEG2000 Medical Images," *J. of Medical and Biological Engineering*, 27(3), 144-149.

[13]   C. F. Lin, C. H. Chung, Z. L. Chen, C. J. Song, and Z. X. Wang (2008), "A Chaos-based Unequal Encryption Mechanism in Wireless Telemedicine with Error Decryption, " *WSEAS Transactions on Systems*, 49-55.

[14] C. F. Lin, C. H. Chung, and J. H. Lin (2009), "A Chaos-based Visual Encryption Mechanism for Clinical EEG Signals," *Medical & Biological Engineering & Computing*, 757-762.

[15] C. F. Lin, and B. S. H. Wang, "A 2D Chaos-based Visual Encryption Scheme for Clinical EEG Signals," *appear to Journal of Marine Science and Technology.*

[16] C.F. Lin, "Mobile Telemedicine: A Survey Study," *Journal of Medical Systems.* (Online First)

[17] C.F. Lin, S. I. Hung, I. H. Chiang, "802.11n WLAN Transmission Scheme for Wireless Telemedicine Applications," *Proceedings of the Institution of Mechanical Engineers, Part H, Journal of Engineering in Medicine.* (Online First)

[18] C. F. Lin, and K. T. Chang (2008), "A Power Assignment Mechanism in Ka Band OFDM-based Multi-satellites Mobile Telemedicine," *J. of Medical and Biological Engineering,* 28(1), 17-22.

[19] C. F. Lin, W. T. Chang, H. W. Lee, and S. I. Hung (2006), "Downlink Power Control in Multi-Code CDMA Mobile Medicine System," *Medical & Biological Engineering & Computing*, vol.44, 437-444.

[20] C. F. Lin (2010), "An Advance Wireless Multimedia Communication Application: Mobile Telemedicine," *WSEAS Transactions on Communications,* 206-215.

[21] C. F. Lin and C. Y. Li (2008), "A DS UWB Transmission System for Wireless Telemedicine," *WSEAS Transactions on Systems,* July, 578-588.

[22] C. F. Lin, J. Y. Chen, R. H. Shiu, and S. H. Chang (2008), "A Ka Band WCDMA-based LEO Transport Architecture in Mobile Telemedicine," *Telemedicine in the 21st Century,* edited by Lucia Martinez and Carla Gomez, Nova Science Publishers, Inc, USA, 187-201.

[23] C. F. Lin, S. W. Yeh, Y. Y. Chien, T. I. Peng, J. H. Wang, S. H. Chang (20080, "A HHT-based Time Frequency Analysis Scheme in Clinical Alcoholic EEG Signals," *WSEAS Transactions on Biology and Biomedicine* ,249-260.

[24] C. F. Lin, S. W. Yeh, S. H. Chang, T. I. Peng, and Y Y. Chien (2010) "An HHT-based Time-frequency Scheme for Analyzing the EEG Signals of Clinical Alcoholics," *On line Book,* USA, Nova Science Publishers.

[25] EEG DataBase: *The MIT-BIH Malignant Ventricular Arrhythmia Database,* http://physionet.cps.unizar.es/physiobank/database/vfdb.

In: Horizons in Computer Science Research. Volume 4   ISBN: 978-1-61324-262-9
Editor: Thomas S. Clary   © 2011 Nova Science Publishers, Inc.

Chapter 12

PACKET CLASSIFICATION USING CROSS-PRODUCTING

Pi-Chung Wang

Department of Computer Science, National Chung Hsing University,
Taichung, Taiwan, R.O.C.

Abstract

Packet classification has become one of the most important application techniques in network security since the last decade. The technique involves a traffic descriptor or user-defined criteria to categorize packets to a specific forwarding class which will be accessible for future security handling.

In this chapter, we present two new schemes, Hierarchical Cross-Producting and Controlled Cross-producting, to achieve fast packet classification. The first scheme simplifies the classification procedure and decreases the distinct combinations of fields by hierarchically decomposing the multi-dimensional space based on the concept of telescopic search. Analogous to the use of telescopes with different powers, which is defined as the degree to which a telescope multiplies the apparent diameter of an object in optical terms, a multiple-step process is used to search for targets. In this scheme, the multi-dimensional space is endowed with a hierarchical property which self-divides into several smaller subspaces, whereas the procedure of packet classification is translated into recursive searching for matching subspaces. The required storage of our scheme could be significantly reduced since the distinct field specifications of subspaces are manageable. Next, we combine the technique of cross-producting with linear search to make packet classification both fast and scalable. The new algorithm, Controlled Cross-producting, could improve the scalability of cross-producting significantly with respect to storage, while maintaining the search latency. In addition, we introduce several refinements and procedures for incremental update.

The performance of both algorithms is evaluated based on both real and synthetic filter databases. The experimental results demonstrate the effectiveness and scalability of both schemes.

1. Introduction

The expansion of IP traffic has been fast growing due to the fact that business on the Internet has moved from a convenience to a mission-critical platform. At the same time, network security service has become much more difficult, as broadband networking technologies substantially increased the capacity of networking and enabled a wide-range of feature-rich high-speed communication services. Since the firewalls and network intrusion detection systems (NIDSs) are the most commonly used network security systems, their capability to manage a large amount of incoming traffic is critical. A serious problem would arise if the search performance of network security systems cannot keep pace with the incoming traffic: attackers may overload the systems by injecting worst-case traffic. This problem has been recognized and approached by improving the search performance of packet classification [1, 2].

The filters for packet classification consist of a set of fields and an associated action. Each field, in turn, corresponds to one field of packet headers. The value in each field could be a variable-length prefix, range, explicit value or wildcard. The five most common fields include source and destination IP address prefixes, source and destination port ranges of the transport protocol and a protocol type in a packet header [3]. Formally, we define a filter F with k fields as $F = (f_1, f_2, \ldots, f_k)$. While performing packet classification, a packet header P is said to match a particular filter F if for all i, the i_{th} field of the header satisfies f_i. Each action has a cost that defines its priority among the actions of the matching filters, and only the least-cost action from the matching filters is applied [4].

The problem of packet classification can be treated as a point location problem in a multidimensional space, i.e. finding the enclosing region of a point for a given set of regions. Unfortunately, even for non-overlapping regions, the bounds for N rules and k fields $(k > 3)$ are $O(\log N)$ in time with $O(N^k)$ space, or $O(\log^{k-1} N)$ time and $O(N)$ space [5]. Consequently, scalability is one of the major issues in packet classification. Since the performance of packet classification might degrade severely as the filters increase in number, several heuristic proposals have been proposed to deal with a large number of filters; for instance, the hash-based schemes [6] and the decision-based schemes [7, 8]. However, these algorithms do not perform well in either speed or space for certain filter databases and sometimes a tradeoff between time and storage is inevitable.

Crossproducting is a general mechanism which involves lookups of best matching prefixes on individual fields and the use of a pre-computed table to combine the results of individual prefix lookups [9]. A filter database with twelve filters and five fields is used as an example in Table 1. The distinct specifications of each field are listed in Table 2. There are 720 different combinations in total which means there are 60 combinations for each filter on average. In the worst case, every filter has different field specification, hence N filters would result in N^d combinations. [5] presents an algorithm, *recursive flow classification*, which can be considered as a generalization of crossproducting by performing crossproducting recursively. In each iteration, only a subset of the inspected fields is used to generate a crossproducting table and the unmatched entries are eliminated for storage saving. The algorithm improves the consumption of storage significantly, but its space complexity remains $O(N^d)$. Likewise, in the case of two-field filters, this scheme is identical to the crossproducting scheme and has a memory requirement of $O(N^2)$.

In this chapter, we present two algorithms for improving the performance of packet classification by using cross-producting. In the first algorithm, we present a new scheme, *Hierarchical Cross-Producting* (HCP). Our scheme improves storage efficiency by dividing a multidimensional space into multiple subspaces. Each subspace could be divided

Table 1. An Example with 12 Filters on Five Fields

Filter	f_1	f_2	f_3	f_4	f_5	Action
F_0	000*	111*	$[10:10]$	*	UDP	act_0
F_1	000*	111*	$[01:01]$	$[10:10]$	UDP	act_0
F_2	000*	10*	*	$[10:10]$	TCP	act_1
F_3	000*	10*	$[00:10]$	$[01:01]$	TCP	act_2
F_4	000*	10*	$[10:10]$	$[11:11]$	TCP	act_1
F_5	0*	111*	$[10:10]$	$[01:01]$	UDP	act_0
F_6	0*	111*	$[10:10]$	$[10:10]$	UDP	act_0
F_7	0*	1*	*	*	TCP	act_2
F_8	*	01*	$[00:10]$	*	TCP	act_2
F_9	*	0*	*	$[01:01]$	UDP	act_0
F_{10}	*	*	*	*	UDP	act_3
F_{11}	*	*	*	$[01:11]$	TCP	act_4

Table 2. The Distinct Specifications of Each Field

f_1	f_2	f_3	f_4	f_5
000*	111*	$[10:10]$	*	TCP
0*	10*	$[01:01]$	$[10:10]$	UDP
*	1*	$[00:10]$	$[01:01]$	
	01*	*	$[11:11]$	
	0*		$[01:11]$	
	*			

into smaller subspaces whose number is controllable. Therefore, the cost of searching for a matching subspace is much lower than that for a matching filter. For every target, the procedure of packet classification is recursive until a matching filter has been found. Our scheme extends the scalability of cross-producting based schemes [5, 9] and achieves fast lookup with minimum storage. Next, we describe another crossproducting-based algorithm with linear search to handle any filter databases undergone a size expansion as a result of new applications. The proposed algorithm, controlled crossproducting, is inspired by the following observation. Prior to performing crossproducting to derive the matching prefixes, d one-dimensional searches are carried out to derive the best matching prefix of each field. While the number of distinct prefixes in each field increases, the search performance of the one-dimensional searches is degraded along with an exponentially increased storage of crossproduct table. However, an increasing number of distinct prefixes also indicates that more filters can be categorized into individual groups by the prefixes of a field. The one-dimensional search derives the matching group. Then the filters in the matching group are accessed sequentially for possible matching. Therefore, these filters are excluded from inserting into the crossproduct table, and the overall storage performance can be improved by orders of magnitude. For each algorithm, we evaluate the performance with both real and synthetic filter databases of varying sizes and characteristics. The experimental results demonstrate that the new algorithms improve the speed and storage performance simultaneously.

2. Related Work

We provide a brief discussion of the existing algorithms by dividing them into three categories according to their methods of data structure construction. The algorithms in the first category build their data structures by considering all the filters from the outset. Srinivasan et al. [9] introduced *Cross-producting* which uses best matching prefix lookups and a pre-computed table to combine the results of individual prefix lookups in each header field. Gupta and McKeown presented *Recursive Flow Classification* that does cross-producting recursively and can be viewed as a generalization of cross-producting [5]. In each iteration, only a subset of the inspected fields is used to generate a cross-product table and the unmatched entries are eliminated for storage saving. In a recent work, *Distributed Cross-producting of Field Labels (DCFL)* [10] further improves the representation of cross-product entries in [5] with set-membership data structures to reduce storage space, although it relies heavily on hardware bit-parallelism. The algorithms presented in [11] and [7] are based on decision trees. Both schemes attempt to divide the filters into multiple linear search buckets by using the data structure of a decision tree. The cut rules of filter categorization may either be a value [11] or a bit [7] of any field. *HyperCuts* [8] is a well-known scheme that adopts multidimensional cut rules and whose performance is better than the decision-trees-based algorithms with single-dimensional cut rules. Another algorithm is *Extended Grid-of-Tries with Path Compression (EGT-PC)* evolved from *Grid-of-Tries (GT)* in [9] that supports filters with more than two fields [12] with a series of linear searches. *Independent Sets* also supports multidimensional search. The idea behind *Independent Sets* is to categorize multidimensional filters according to the specifications of one field [13]. The filters in each independent set are mutually disjoint; therefore, binary search can be used to derive the matching filter in each independent set. The number of independent sets thereby determines the search performance of the algorithm.

In contrast to the first category, the algorithms of the second category classify the filters into different groups at the outset. This category consists of mainly tuple-based algorithms. These algorithms store the filters with an identical prefix length combination in a hash table [6]. The prefixes can be concatenated to create a hash key for a hash table access. The matching filters can be found by probing each hash table alternately. Each hash table is also known as a tuple, and tuple space search aims at searching for the matching filters in the tuple space. Two well-known tuple-based algorithms are *Rectangle Search* and *Pruned Tuple Space Search*, both of which are designed to improve the performance of tuple space search [6]. A subsequent work in [14] further improves the speed and storage performance of the rectangle search by reducing the number of tuples. Another work is *Entry Pruned Tuple Search (EPTS)* [15] that enhances *Pruned Tuple Space Search* by storing pruning information of tuples containing non-conflicting filters in each filter in the form of a bit vector. However, inserting a new tuple might cause all tuple bit vectors in the filters to be updated. The performance of *Rectangle Search* has been improved by Wang et al. [16] who categorize the filters according to the prefix nested levels. Dharmapurikar et al. [17] also use the tuple-based approach to reduce the storage requirement of the Cross-producting scheme.

The third category of packet classification algorithms is based on hardware implementation. There are two subcategories of hardware-based solutions, ternary content-addressable memories (TCAMs) and bit vectors. TCAMs compare search data against a table of stored data and return the address of the first matching data. Each TCAM cell stores an extra "Don't Care" state to achieve arbitrary bit mask matches, such as IP address lookup and packet classification. TCAMs have been proven effective for packet classification with a high degree of parallelism [18]. The drawbacks of TCAMs include their smaller density, power dissipation and extra entries due to the range-to-prefix transformation [12, 19]. Moreover, TCAMs with a particular word width cannot be used when a flexible filter specification is required. It is also quite difficult to produce TCAMs with large word widths to fill all bits in a filter. Much effort has gone into improving the power and storage efficiency of TCAMs [20, 21, 22, 23]. In the other subcategory, the *Bit Vector* (*BV*) algorithm performs d one-dimensional searches to derive d lists of filters with at least one matching field. The filter list is in the form of bit vectors, meaning that the *BV* algorithm is suitable for hardware implementation. A later work, *Aggregate Bit Vector* [19], has demonstrated dramatic improvement in the speed performance of the *BV* algorithm.

In general, although a number of these algorithms, with the exception of TCAM-based ones, could support both single- and multi-match packet classification, some may not meet the standard in performance. For instance, the algorithms based on decision trees [24, 8] and bit vectors [25, 19] that usually sort the filters according to their priorities to improve the average search performance in the single-match classification can be extended to support multimatch. However, the search performance of these algorithms in the multimatch is usually worse than in the single-match. Although the original TCAM scheme cannot support multimatch packet classification, several algorithms have been proposed to address this issue with extra storage or slower speed as a tradeoff. For example, Yu et al. [1] presented an algorithm by generating all intersections between the filters to keep track of all possible matching conditions. This scheme is fast, but requires a large number of TCAM entries. Other algorithms also have been introduced to improve the TCAM storage in multimatch packet classification by decomposing filters [26] or adopting iterative searches [22].

3. Hierarchical Cross-producting

3.1. Telescopic Search

We start by introducing the concept of our telescopic search. Assume that we have a target in a distant landscape (Fig. 1(a)). The most effective way to find the target under the telescope would be first tuning to low-power to allow a quick scan of the entire landscape and to narrow down the search area. Then, we can switch to high-power to survey a small area with greater precision (Fig. 1(b)). The essence behind the concept is its temporary omission of every piece of information in the first step. We believe that the search could grant us with efficiency and accuracy when fishing from massive amount of information.

Now, let us apply telescopic search to packet classification. We use an example of two-field filters to show our design in Fig. 2. Assume that there are five filters in the filter database (Fig. 2(a)). For each field, there are *six* different ranges (including *wildcards*). The original cross-producting scheme would generate $36(= 6 \times 6)$ different range combinations.

(a) Viewing at low-power.   (b) Viewing at high-power.

Figure 1. While viewing at low-power, it is difficult to search for an inconspicuous target. After focusing in a specific area, the inconspicuous target in Fig. 1(a) can be viewed with enlarged size and increased clarity in Fig. 1(b).

Each combination will be associated with one or multiple blocks in Fig. 2(b). The blocks in the up-right (or bottom-left) corner are the cross-product of the vertical (or horizontal) ranges from the up-left corner and the horizontal (or vertical) ranges from the bottom-right corner. Since these blocks are not matched by any filter, a default action would be enacted for the matching packets. These blocks would lead to redundant entries and increase the memory consumption. Moreover, the condition gets worse as the number of fields increases.

We note that the redundant entries can be minimized when telescopic search is used in packet classification.Initially, we inspect the ranges which are fully covered only by *wildcards* and ignore the other ranges. Thus, only the ranges created by F_0 and F_3 in the horizontal axis are inspected. The other ranges are ignored since they are blurred at the current level of power. Similarly, two ranges created by F_2 and F_4 in the vertical axis are inspected. With the *wildcards* of both axes, *nine* blocks are formed, and two of them (i.e., block 2 and 3 in Fig. 2(c)) are redundant. For any given packet matches to the redundant blocks, the default action will be activated. If the packet matches to the other two blocks, the combinations of the previously ignored ranges will be extracted and browsed for further detail, as shown in Fig. 2(d). Although one extra search step is required, the number of range combinations is reduced. In this example, the number of range combinations is reduced from 36 to $22(= 3 \times 3 + 3 \times 3 + 2 \times 2)$. As a result, by ignoring the details early on, we can eliminate the storage requirement effectively.

3.2. Algorithm

In this section, our scheme, *HCP*, based on the telescopic search is presented. In our scheme, the ranges in the filters are represented by a series of prefixes. For example, the range from 1,024 to 65,535 would require *six* separate prefixes ($[1,024 - 2,047] =$ "000001*", $[2,048 - 4,095] =$ "00001*", $[4,096 - 8,191] =$ "0001 * ", $[8,192 - 16,383] =$ "001 * ", $[16,384 - 32,767] =$ "01 * " and $[32,768 - 65,535] =$ "1 * "). Once a range is converted into more than one prefix, the corresponding filter is duplicated as well [9]. To ease our description, we assume that all the inspected fields have been transformed into

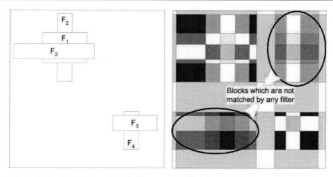

(a) A 2-D classifier with 5 filters.   (b) Original cross-product entries

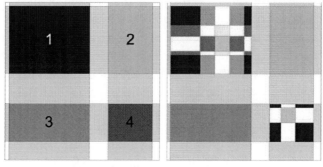

(c) Viewing at low-power   (d) Viewing at high-power

Figure 2. The Comparison of cross-producting with/without applying the concept of telescopic search. The original cross-producting scheme generates 36 combinations. Twelve of these combinations are redundant. The unnecessary combinations can be reduced to two after applying the new concept.

prefixes. We note that our approach of range to prefix transformation could support incremental updates. Although there are other approaches of range to prefix transformation, these approaches may not be suitable for software implementation [21, 22, 27].

We use the concept of *telescopic search* to divide the multidimensional space into several subspaces. Each subspace may contain one or more filters. Also, each filter might exist in several different subspaces. In each subspace, if the number of prefix combinations is too large, the subspace can be further decomposed into smaller subspaces. The search procedure starts from performing the lookup for the best matching prefix (BMP) of each field. What comes along with the BMP searches is the fragments of prefixes for indexing subspaces. Next, we cross-product the first fragments of all fields to derive the best matching subspace by referring to the cross-product table. If the matching subspace contains only one filter, the search procedure would be complete. Otherwise, next fragments are further cross-producted to index the smaller subspaces. The cross-producting is repeatedly executed until the matching filter is retrieved.

Our scheme is different from the existing cross-producting-based schemes. While the original cross-producting scheme generates all combinations at once and *RFC* selectively picks several fields for cross-producting, our scheme performs cross-producting for all dimensions simultaneously.

Our procedure of space decomposition starts from generating the sides of each sub-space. Since each side is expressed as a prefix, the generation of sides is analogous to generate prefixes of the sides (*sprefixes*) from the original prefixes. We note that the generated *sprefix* might be an existing prefix or a new one. The procedure of space decomposition consists of three steps: 1) generation of *sprefixes*, 2) subspace processing and 3) construction of the subspace cross-product tables. We describe each of the steps in further details in the following subsections.

3.2.1. Side Prefix Generation

First of all, we generate *sprefixes* to replace the original prefixes in the filters. The number of the *sprefixes* is controllable through adjusting the number of the original prefixes within a *sprefix*. First, the original prefixes of each field are extracted from the filters to construct a binary trie. Then, the *Side Prefix Generation Algorithm* shown in Fig. 3 is executed upon the constructed binary tries. The algorithm marks the nodes corresponding to the *sprefixes* according to a pre-defined threshold value α which indicates the number of prefixes to be included. The algorithm recursively traverses the binary trie with the order of depth first search. Each recursive instance returns an integer indicating the number of prefixes or *sprefixes* successive or corresponding to the current node. For a recursive event of $node_i$, the returned values from the instances of traversing the child nodes of $node_i$ are summed up. If the summed value is greater than or equal to α, a node of the *sprefix* is marked. Otherwise, the summed value is returned to the caller of the current instance.

```
Side Prefix Generation Algorithm
Input: The root of the binary tree
Output:The sprefixes
integer Prefix_Generator(Node) BEGIN
  IF (Node=NULL)
    return 0;
  Left_Count=Prefix_Generator(Node→Left);
  Right_Count=Prefix_Generator(Node→Right);
  Count=Left_Count+Right_Count;
  IF (Count≥ α) BEGIN
    Node→ sprefix =true;
    return 1;
  END
  ELSE BEGIN
    IF (Node→ prefix =true)
      return Count+1;
    ELSE
      return Count;
  END
END
```

Figure 3. Side prefix generation algorithm.

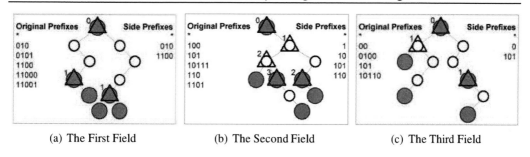

(a) The First Field	(b) The Second Field	(c) The Third Field

Figure 4. The generation of *sprefixes* for the filters in Table 3.

We use seven *three*-field filters[1] in Table 3 as an example to show the procedure of generating *sprefixes*. Assume that α (i.e., the number of included prefixes) is *two*. The prefixes extracted from the filters are used to construct *three* binary prefix tries, as shown in Fig. 4, where the dark-gray circles represent the nodes with the original prefixes. After executing our algorithm upon the prefix tries, *three sprefixes* for $field_1$, *five* for $field_2$ and *three* for $field_3$ are generated. The nodes corresponding to *sprefixes* are marked with triangles, where the number aside each triangle denotes the number of its nested *sprefixes*. The numbers of the nested *sprefixes* will be used in the procedure of generating subspaces in Section 3.2.2..

Table 3. A simple example with seven filters on three fields

Filter	$Field_1$	$Field_2$	$Field_3$
F_0	010*	10111	101*
F_1	11001	110*	0100*
F_2	*	100*	101*
F_3	0101*	101*	10110
F_4	11000	1101*	0100*
F_5	1100*	110*	00*
F_6	*	*	*

Intuitively, adjusting the value of α could change the number of *sprefixes*. The number of *sprefixes* is directly proportional to the number of subspaces. Therefore, a larger value of α would result in fewer *sprefixes* as well as subspaces, where each subspace is larger. In addition, the complexity of searching for the best matching subspaces would be decreased. However, a larger subspace would store more filters and increase the complexity of searching for the matching filters within a subspace. On the other hand, a smaller α would result in the increase of the number of smaller subspaces. Hence, the search for a matching subspace is complicated while the search procedure within a matching subspace could be simplified. Accordingly, we could achieve a better balance between the speed and storage performance by adjusting the value of α.

---

[1]We use the *three*-field filters due to the difficulty of illustrating a *five*-dimensional space.

3.2.2. Subspace Processing

Next, we use the *sprefixes* to generate multidimensional subspaces in the following procedure.

1. Each *sprefix* is labeled with the number of its nested *sprefixes*, i.e., the number of its shorter matching *sprefixes*. With the labels, the *sprefixes* are categorized into different nested levels. For example, the nested level of *sprefix* "110*" of $Field_2$ is 2 since there are two shorter *sprefixes*, "*" and "1*", that match "110*" in Fig. 4.

2. We cross-product the first- and second-level *sprefixes* of every field to generate subspaces, where each subspace corresponds to a combination of *sprefixes*. The first-level *sprefixes* are included in the cross-product table since the search key may not match any second-level *sprefixes*. Therefore, the first-level *sprefixes* must be used to generate the cross-product table to avoid the case where there is no matching subspaces. Next, each filter is categorized into one subspace which can fully cover the filter. If there are several candidate subspaces, the smallest one is chosen to store the filter. We note that there is only one such subspace since each filter has only one longest matching *sprefix* for each field. We call this subspace the best-matching subspace of the processed filter. Furthermore, the other subspaces which are covered by the best-matching subspace are checked to determine whether they are *partially overlapping*[2] with the processed filter. If *yes*, the subspace keeps a copy of the processed filter to maintain the accuracy of the search procedure since this subspace might be matched by a search key which matches to the best-matching subspace.

3. After the step of filter categorization is accomplished, the previous two steps are repeated for each generated subspace to further categorize the stored filters based on the second- and third-level *sprefixes*. We also include the second-level *sprefixes* in the cross-product table for the same reason as described above. Some fields of the subspaces may not have longer *sprefixes*. For these fields, a *wildcard* is used. The procedure is repeated until one of the following criteria is met. The first is when the subspace stores only one filter, since generating a smaller subspace for the filter is not necessary. Second, there is no smaller subspaces that can be generated through cross-producting *sprefixes*.

We use the filters in Table 3 to demonstrate the procedure. First, the *sprefix* "*" is labeled as 0, "010*" and "1100*" are labeled as 1 in Fig. 4(a). We also tag the number of shorter *sprefixes* for each *sprefix* node in Fig. 4(b) and 4(c). Since three *sprefixes* of $Field_1$, two of $Field_2$ and three of $Field_3$ are labeled with 0 and 1, $18(= 3 \times 2 \times 3)$ subspaces are resulted. Next, we examine the best-matching subspace for each filter in Table 4. Only *four* distinct subspaces contain at least one filter. Each filter is stored in its best-matching subspace. We list these subspaces with their stored filters in Table 5. The filter, F_6, is stored in S_0 which corresponds to the original space. Since F_6 completely covers the other subspaces, we do not duplicate F_6 in these subspaces according to **Step 2**. However, since F_2 partially overlaps with S_1, F_2 is duplicated by S_1, which is denoted by the parentheses.

---

[2]Two spaces are said to partially overlap with each other if they overlap with each other but have no superset-subset relationship, e.g., the spaces of F_0 and F_3 in Table 3.

Table 4. The best-matching subspace of each filter in the first iteration of subspace generation

Filter	Best-matching subspace
F_0	$(010*, 1*, 101*)$
F_1	$(1100*, 1*, 0*)$
F_2	$(*, 1*, 101*)$
F_3	$(010*, 1*, 101*)$
F_4	$(1100*, 1*, 0*)$
F_5	$(1100*, 1*, 0*)$
F_6	$(*, *, *)$

Table 5. The generated subspaces and the stored filters in the first iteration

Subspace	*sprefix* combination	Stored filters
S_0	$(*, *, *)$	F_6, S_1, S_2, S_3
S_1	$(010*, 1*, 101*)$	$F_0, F_3, (F_2)$
S_2	$(1100*, 1*, 0*)$	F_1, F_4, F_5
S_3	$(*, 1*, 101*)$	F_2

Next, we consider the filters F_0 and F_3 in S_1. Both filters have a longer matching *sprefix* "10*" in $Field_2$. Therefore, an extra subspace S_4 whose sides of $Field_1$ and $Field_3$ are equal to those of S_1 is generated in the second iteration. Consequently, F_0 and F_3 are removed from S_1 by inserting S_4. Similarly, F_1, F_4 and F_5 in S_2 are replaced by S_5, as shown in Table 6. In the third iteration, F_0 and F_3 are further categorized by using their third-level *sprefixes* of $Field_2$ to generate S_6. A three-dimensional view for the filters and subspaces in Table 6 is presented in Fig. 5.

3.2.3. Cross-product Table Construction

After generating the subspaces, we generate a cross-product table for each subspace by cross-producting the referred *sprefixes* and prefixes. We could assign a unique sequence number to each *sprefix* and prefix. We found that the array-based cross-product table is not feasible here. Because there are different *sprefixes* and prefixes in each subspace, the sequence number used in each cross-product table may not be consecutive. Therefore, the cross-product table is implemented as a hash table whose hash keys could be generated by concatenating the sequence numbers. Each cross-product entry may represent a subspace or a filter. In the first case, the starting address of the hash table of the corresponding subspace is recorded. In the second case, we directly store the *action* of the corresponding filter.

In Table 6, we generate *seven* cross-product tables. The number of the cross-product entries for S_0 is $18(= 3 \times 2 \times 3)$. The numbers of cross-product tables for subspaces $S_1 \sim S_6$ are $3(= 1 \times 3 \times 1)$, $2(= 1 \times 2 \times 1)$, $2(= 1 \times 2 \times 1)$, $2(= 1 \times 2 \times 1)$, $18(= 3 \times 2 \times 3)$ and $8(= 2 \times 2 \times 2)$, respectively. While the original cross-producting requires 180 entries, the proposed scheme requires only 53 entries.

With the proposed scheme, each filter is contained in at least one subspace and each subspace can be stored in at most W subspaces. For those filters stored in more than one

Table 6. The subspaces and their filters after the second and third iterations

Subspace	*sprefix* combination	Stored filters
	The second iteration	
S_0	$(*, *, *)$	F_6, S_1, S_2, S_3
S_1	$(010*, 1*, 101*)$	$S_4, (F_2)$
S_2	$(1100*, 1*, 0*)$	S_5
S_3	$(*, 1*, 101*)$	F_2
S_4	$(010*, 10*, 101*)$	$F_0, F_3, (F_2)$
S_5	$(1100*, 110*, 0*)$	F_1, F_4, F_5
	The third iteration	
S_0	$(*, *, *)$	F_6, S_1, S_2, S_3
S_1	$(010*, 1*, 101*)$	$S_4, (F_2)$
S_2	$(1100*, 1*, 0*)$	S_5
S_3	$(*, 1*, 101*)$	F_2
S_4	$(010*, 10*, 101*)$	$S_6, (F_2)$
S_5	$(1100*, 110*, 0*)$	F_1, F_4, F_5
S_6	$(010*, 101*, 101*)$	F_0, F_3

subspace, the extra storage are limited by the maximum size of the generated cross-product table, $(2\alpha)^k$. Therefore, the required storage is $2^k NW\alpha^k$ in the worst case.

3.2.4. Lookup Procedure

The lookup procedure consists of two parts. In the first part, we perform k BMP searches for the corresponding fields of the incoming packet to derive the sequence numbers of the matching *sprefixes* and BMP. For the fields of source and destination addresses, the existing BMP scheme can be easily accomplished within *two* to *five* memory accesses [28]. The search of the BMP in the other fields can be resolved by maintaining direct access arrays with 2^{16} entries (for source and destination ports) or 2^8 entries (for protocol field). Besides the algorithmic solutions, TCAM is also a feasible solution since the number of address prefixes in the classifiers are usually much less than that of routing tables.

Next, we cross-product the sequence numbers of the second-level *sprefixes* of every field to access the cross-product table corresponding to the original space (e.g., S_0 in Table 6). If there is no matching second-level *sprefixes*, the first-level *sprefixes*, "$*$", is used. If the fetched entry is a pointer to the cross-product table of a subspace, we further access the cross-product table by using the sequence number of the next-level *sprefixes*. Similarly, for the field without longer *sprefixes*, the current *sprefix* is used. The procedure is repeated until there is no matching subspaces. Then, the sequence numbers of the BMPs for each field are used to retrieve the matching filter.

We use the filters in Table 3 as an example to show the search procedure for a packet header, $\langle 11000, 11010, 00101 \rangle$. The first *sprefixes* for accessing the cross-product table are "$1100*$", "$1*$" and "$0*$". By concatenating their sequence numbers to generate a hash key, the cross-product entry which stores the pointer of S_2 is fetched. Since a subspace is retrieved, the *sprefixes* of the next level are used. However, there is no third-level *sprefixes* for

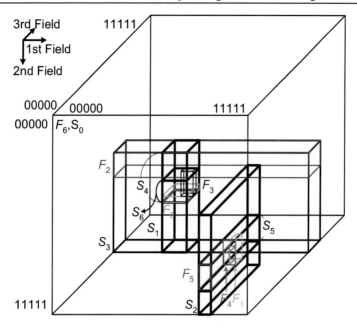

Figure 5. A three-dimensional view of the filters and subspaces derived from Table 6.

$Field_1$ and $Field_3$ for the incoming packet header, we still use the second-level *sprefixes*, "1100* and "0*". The sequence numbers of the *sprefix* combination, "1100*, 110*, 0*", are used to fetch the pointer of S_5. Since no smaller subspace is available in S_5, the sequence numbers of k BMPs are then used to access S_5 and derive the matching filter, F_5. The geometrical representation of the lookup procedure is illustrated in Fig. 6. With our procedure, the complex packet classification is divided into several simple cross-producting operation. As a result, the overall complexity is significantly reduced.

Since the number of *sprefixes* for each field is W at most, the maximum steps of cross-producting is W. The time complexity is O(Wk) by taking the k BMP searches into account. We can further improve the throughput with two aspects in the hardware implementation. First, the BMP searches could be performed in parallel. Second, we could adopt pipeline implementation by allocating cross-product tables into different processing elements according to their levels. With these improvements, one packet classification for every memory access is achievable.

3.2.5. Update Procedure

The filter update can be categorized into three categories: *change, deletion* and *insertion*. To ease our explanation, we treat changing a filter as the equivalent deleting the original filter and inserting a new one.

To perform filter deletion, the duplicated entries in every subspace should be removed. In the worst case, $W(2\alpha)^k$ cross-product tables are updated. However, our data structure consists of multiple cross-product tables which can be independently updated, and the use of hash-based cross-product tables also avoids table reconstruction. Moreover, the existing literature has reported that filter overlapping is quite rare [5, 19]; thus, the update cost is

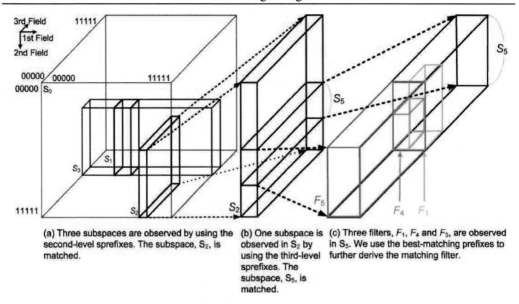

(a) Three subspaces are observed by using the second-level sprefixes. The subspace, S_2, is matched.

(b) One subspace is observed in S_2 by using the third-level sprefixes. The subspace, S_5, is matched.

(c) Three filters, F_1, F_4 and F_5, are observed in S_5. We use the best-matching prefixes to further derive the matching filter.

Figure 6. The geometrical representation of our search procedure for the filters in Table 3.

moderate in practice.

For filter insertion, the cross-product table of the subspaces, which are stridden by the inserted filter, are updated. The cost is identical to the cost of filter deletion. However, the entries in the updated cross-product tables might be larger than $(2\alpha)^k$.

Similar to the existing combination-based schemes, the update performance of our scheme is not good due to the cost of updating cross-product tables. However, our scheme only updates partial tables for most cases while the existing schemes must reconstruct their data structures [5, 9]. In addition, our scheme generates less cross-product entries than the existing schemes. Therefore, our scheme outperforms the existing combination-based schemes in the update performance.

3.3. Performance Evaluation

In this section, we use real and synthetic filter databases to investigate the performance of our scheme. The performance evaluation consists of two parts. In the first part, the performance of our scheme is evaluated based on real filter databases. We also relate our numerical results to other existing schemes in a performance study. The second part further tests the scalability of our scheme by using the synthetic databases. In both parts, the performance metrics include the required storage in kilobytes and the numbers of memory accesses in the worst case.

3.3.1. Real Filter Databases

We use three real filter databases that are publicly available in [29]. The numbers of filters vary from 283 to 1,702, and each filter has *five* fields. The numbers of the unique field values in the real databases are presented in Table 7. We also show the numbers of the cross-product entries of the original cross-producting scheme. The numbers of filters would affect the generated cross-product entries. Also, a raised number of distinct prefixes in one field can significantly affect the storage performance.

Table 7. Unique field values of the real filter databases

DBs	Filters	Unique Field Values					Cross-product Entries
		SA	DA	SP	DP	Prot	
ACL1	733	97	205	1	108	4	8,590,320
FW1	283	57	66	13	43	2	4,205,916
IPC1	1,702	152	128	34	54	7	250,048,512

DA: Destination Address, SA: Source Address, DP: Destination Port, SP: Source Port, Prot: Protocol.

We show the performance difference caused by different $alpha$ values ranging between 2 and 32 in Table 8, where the term "cross-product" is abbreviated as **CP**. For three real filter databases, we evaluate the numbers of subspace levels, cross-product tables, cross-product entries and the maximum sizes of the cross-product tables. The former three metrics show the effect of different α values, since a larger α would lead to fewer cross-product tables and vice versa. The last metric can present the geometrical properties of the filter databases by illustrating how **close** the filters are to each other. The probability is higher for storing filters close to each other in a subspace, which results in a large cross-product table.

As shown in Table 8, the total number of the required entries are largely reduced as compared to the original cross-product scheme, while the number of memory accesses retains acceptable values. The results support our scheme of space decomposition that categorizes the filters into different cross-product tables. Since each cross-product table stores less filters, the required storage is reduced as well. Our scheme is particularly effective for the filters which are sparsely distributed since the number of filter overlaps is decreased. On the other hand, our scheme cannot improve the case with volume filter overlaps since the field combinations of these filters cannot be eliminated through space decomposition. However, such filters are relatively low in current filter databases [12].

According to the different values of α, we can summarize three trends: 1) the numbers of memory accesses are inversely proportional to the value of α; 2) the numbers of cross-product tables are inversely proportional to the value of α; 3) the maximum size of the cross-product table is proportional to the value of α^k. However, the total cross-product entries are not proportionate to the values of α. With the α values 4 and 8, our scheme generates the fewest CP entries as compared to the other α values. This is due to a leverage between the number of cross-product tables and the number of the entries in each cross-product table.

We further illustrate the trade-off between storage and speed in Fig. 7. As described above, the α values 4 and 8 are the best configurations for our real databases. While $\alpha = 4$ can achieve better storage performance, $\alpha = 8$ leads to better speed performance. For other filter databases, a suitable α value can be determined by examining the filters for the best balance between speed and storage performance.

Next, we compare our scheme with several notable algorithms, including *ABV* [19], *HyperCuts* [8] and *RFC* [5]. The source codes for the existing algorithms are publicly

Table 8. Performance evaluation for real databases

DBs	α	Subspace Levels	No. of CP Tables	Max. CP Table	Total CP Entries
ACL1	2	22	6,875	72	29,222
	4	10	736	288	14,266
	8	7	600	1,344	68,970
	16	5	194	24,000	327,023
	32	3	51	273,000	1,286,277
FW1	2	13	5,573	243	40,868
	4	8	1,725	6,300	193,584
	8	6	336	57,915	478,537
	16	3	26	582,120	1,597,533
	32	3	12	5,755,520	6,628,004
IPC1	2	14	6,784	162	72,740
	4	7	3,967	1,280	301,454
	8	6	1,472	15,120	876,044
	16	3	314	380,016	4,205,470
	32	3	52	3,991,350	15,853,935

available in [29]. For *ABV*, the aggregate size is 32 bits, and the memory width is 256 bits. *Hypercuts* adopts the setting in which the space factor is 1 and bucket size is 32. The comparisons of storage and speed performance are listed in Table 9 and 10, respectively. For the storage performance, our scheme outperforms *ABV* and *HyperCuts* in most cases. However, our scheme has better search performance than these two algorithms. Contrarily, our scheme is slower than *RFC*, but has much better storage efficiency. Therefore, our scheme could achieve better search performance while maintaining storage performance.

Table 9. Storage Performance of the Existing Algorithms Using Real Databases

DBs	ABV	HyperCuts	RFC	HCP
ACL1	296.34	29.45	497.62	27.86
FW1	263.73	33.41	1,094.55	79.82
IPC1	331.46	142.18	8,984.18	142.07

Table 10. Speed Performance of the Existing Algorithms Using Real Databases

DBs	ABV	HyperCuts	RFC	HCP
ACL1	44	22	11	21
FW1	30	46	11	24
IPC1	50	49	11	25

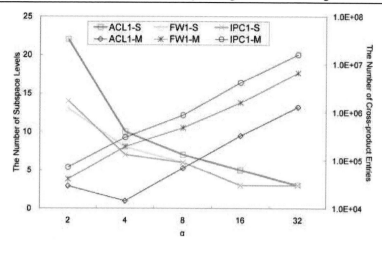

Figure 7. The Trade-off between Storage and Speed for Five-dimensional Real Databases. ACL1-M, FW1-M and IPC1-M indicate the required entries and ACL1-S, FW1-S and IPC1-S are the numbers of the worst-case memory accesses.

3.3.2. Synthetic Databases

To further evaluate the scalability of our scheme, we use *ClassBench* [30] to generate *five*-dimensional synthetic databases for further evaluation. Each database is initialized with 16,000 filters. After removing the redundant filters, the actual number of filters in each database is usually less than 16,000.

Table 11. Storage Performance of the Existing Algorithms Using Synthetic Databases

DBs	Filters	ABV	HyperCuts	HCP
ACL1	15,926	36,523.81	369.18	1,215.42
ACL2	15,447	55,141.81	1,359.68	2,033.18
FW1	14,898	32,494.13	23,883.84	9,136.81
FW2	15,501	39,885.48	10,859.94	1,886.66
IPC1	14,954	16,116.21	3,557.90	1,327.19
IPC2	16,000	44,405.32	12,450.29	250.49

The storage and speed performance are listed in Table 11 and 12, respectively. The experimental results of *RFC* are not included since it takes up too much storage. As compared to the existing schemes, our scheme features relatively stable storage requirements, except for the case of FW1. We observed that the filters in FW1 massively overlap with each other. Therefore, these filters cannot be categorized by using the technique of space decomposition, which also causes *HyperCuts* to have poor storage performance. In addition, our scheme yields better search performance than the existing algorithms, as shown in Table 12. From the results, we believe that our scheme achieves a better balance between storage and speed performance than the existing schemes.

Table 12. Speed Performance of the Existing Algorithms Using Synthetic Databases

DBs	ABV	HyperCuts	HCP
ACL1	44	56	18
ACL2	50	132	19
FW1	56	221	18
FW2	34	43	23
IPC1	65	87	22
IPC2	33	41	14

4.   Controlled Cross-producting

4.1.   Motivation

Our idea is inspired by the correlation between the number of distinct field specifications and the required storage of the crossproduct table. While the required storage increases with the number of distinct field specifications, the cross-producting-based schemes would suffer from severe degradation on storage performance when the size of filter database expands. In addition, the performance of one-dimensional search is also degraded with a larger data structure and slower speed. Interestingly, some algorithms perform well on such filter databases. Take the decision-tree-based algorithms as an example, the procedure of tree construction usually selects the field with more distinct specifications for space decomposition. Since the number of filters sharing the same specification in the selected field is reduced, the space decomposition could yield a better categorization of filters. As a result, the decision-tree-based algorithms would perform better on the filter databases with miscellaneous field specifications.

Another algorithm which could benefit from the miscellaneous filter specifications is the *independent sets* scheme [13]. As mentioned above, the filters are categorized into different independent sets, whose filters are disjoint on a selected field. With more distinct field specifications, each independent set could store more filters which results in fewer independent sets and yields a better search performance.

Based on the observation, we are motivated to combine the cross-producting-based schemes with the decision-tree-based algorithms or the *independent sets* scheme to achieve a better balance between storage and speed performance. In our scheme, we optimize the seminal cross-producting scheme by combining the concept of independent sets. The merge of the two schemes only requires moderate modification since both search procedures perform one-dimensional searches.

Overall, our idea is to divide the filters into two groups. The first group includes filters searched by one-dimensional search and the other group includes those searched by cross-producting. The selection procedure involves the use of field specifications. Take the filters in Table 1 as an example. The filters, F_1, F_4, F_7, F_8, F_9 and F_{11}, contain one field specification, which is not specified by other filters. Therefore, we can categorize these filters into the one-dimensional searched group. After the categorization, the rest of the filters would contribute to at most $162(= 3 \times 3 \times 3 \times 3 \times 2)$ combinations. As compared to the seminal cross-producting scheme which would result in 720 combinations, the new scheme could improve the storage efficiency by orders of magnitude. This procedure could be repeated until further reduction is achieved. For example, filter F_3 is selected into the one-dimensional search group in the second iteration and filter F_9 is selected in the third iteration. The number of the resulting combinations is further reduced to 72. An advantage of this procedure would be that the required storage of the proposed scheme could be easily adjusted.

However, there is a tradeoff in the proposed scheme. An additional search cost is necessary since the seminal cross-producting scheme needs one-dimensional searches, the cost lies in the extra comparison of the filters in one-dimensional search group. We believe that this extra cost is a reasonable tradeoff for storage saving. The experimental results would further demonstrate our point. In the following, we present the procedures of constructing the searchable data structure of the proposed scheme.

4.1.1. Algorithm

The first step of data structure construction in the proposed scheme is to transform ranges of the filters to prefixes. In the seminal cross-producting scheme, the ranges must be divided into primitive ranges that are mutually disjointed [20]. However, the primitive ranges are not updatable due to the new range insertion which might result in new primitive ranges. To support incremental updates, we transform the ranges into prefixes by splitting each range into multiple subranges, where each subrange uniquely corresponds to one prefix [9]. The main drawback of this approach is an increase in the number of filters and distinct field specifications.

Let us consider the example in Table 1. Each filter contains two range fields, f_3 and f_4, which are converted to the prefix form. As shown in Table 13, the original filter database is transformed into fifteen filters after performing the basic range to prefix transformation.

Table 13. The Converted Filters by Using the Range to Prefix Transformation

Filter	f_1	f_2	f_3	f_4	f_5	Action
F_a	000*	111*	10*	*	UDP	act_0
F_b	000*	111*	01*	10*	UDP	act_0
F_c	000*	10*	*	10*	TCP	act_1
F_d	000*	10*	0*	01*	TCP	act_2
F_e	000*	10*	10*	01*	TCP	act_2
F_f	000*	10*	10*	11*	TCP	act_1
F_g	0*	111*	10*	01*	UDP	act_0
F_h	0*	111*	10*	10*	UDP	act_0
F_i	0*	1*	*	*	TCP	act_2
F_j	*	01*	0*	*	TCP	act_2
F_k	*	01*	10*	*	TCP	act_2
F_l	*	0*	*	01*	UDP	act_0
F_m	*	*	*	*	UDP	act_3
F_n	*	*	*	01*	TCP	act_4
F_o	*	*	*	1*	TCP	act_4

After performing the range to prefix transformation, a prefix trie of each field is constructed based on the field specifications of the new filters. In addition, the index of each filter is inserted to the nodes corresponding to the field specifications of the filter. To decrease the number of distinct field specifications, our approach is to eliminate the number of associated filters in the nodes by moving these filters to the one-dimensional search group. When the filter count in a node decreases to zero, the field specification corresponding to the node could be removed to diminish the number of cross-producting combinations.

In the following, prefix trie with the maximal number of leaf nodes is used to select the filters to be searched in one-dimensional data structure. The purpose of this step is to maximize the number of filters in the one-dimensional search group. While the number of distinct field specification increases, the number of leaf nodes usually multiplies as well. As a result, the average number of filters associated with these leaf nodes is decreased, and a higher proportion of lowering the number of cross-producting combinations could be achieved. We note that there might be more than one associative filter in a leaf node. In this case, we select the filter whose corresponding nodes of its field specifications have the least number of filters. In addition, according to the definition of independent set as mention above, the selected filters in each iteration could belong to an independent set and the one-dimensional search group could be treated as a set of independent sets.

After moving the selected filters to the first independent set, all prefix tries are reformed based on the field specifications of the rest of the filters. The number of the cross-producting combinations of the remaining filters is calculated to decide whether the required storage is under a predefined threshold. If not, the above steps, including selecting the prefix trie with maximal leaf nodes and generating another independent set, are repeated before the procedure of filter categorization is completed.

We use the previous example to illustrate the procedure of filter categorization. The prefix tries of five fields are shown in Fig. 8. For an established binary trie, each prefix node is assigned with a unique identifier to ease the following description. We also list the associative filters of each prefix node. The number in the parentheses indicates the number of the associative filters.

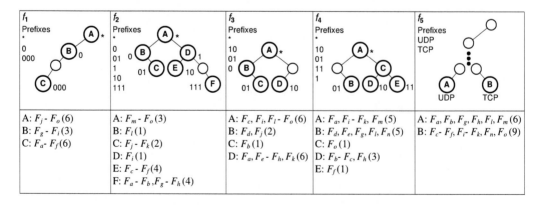

Figure 8. The Prefix Tries of the Filters in Table 13.

The first step is to select a prefix trie with the maximal number of leaf nodes. In this case, either the prefix trie of f_2 or f_4 can be selected, and we randomly choose the former. Next, the filters in each leaf node of the prefix trie of f_2 become the candidates, and one filter of each leaf node would be selected for the corresponding independent set. There are two candidates, F_j and F_k, in node **C**. For filter F_j, its specification of the third field corresponds to node **B** of prefix trie of f_3 which is associative to two filters. Since the corresponding nodes of F_k associate with at least five filters, F_j is selected and removed from its corresponding nodes, including node **A** of f_1, node **C** of f_2, and so on. Similarly, the filter F_f is selected in node **E** and F_b is selected in node **F**. After disassociating these selected filters from their corresponding nodes, both the numbers of distinct field specifications on f_3 and f_4 are decreased by one, and the number of the cross-producting combinations is reduced from 720 to 432. The resulting prefix tries are shown in Fig. 9 where the newly generated independent set is listed in the shaded grid.

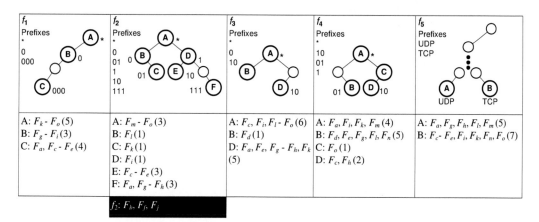

f_1	f_2	f_3	f_4	f_5
A: F_k - F_o (5)	A: F_m - F_o (3)	A: F_c, F_i, F_l - F_o (6)	A: F_a, F_i, F_k, F_m (4)	A: F_a, F_g, F_h, F_l, F_m (5)
B: F_g - F_i (3)	B: F_l (1)	B: F_d (1)	B: F_d, F_e, F_g, F_l, F_n (5)	B: F_c - F_e, F_i, F_k, F_n, F_o (7)
C: F_a, F_c - F_e (4)	C: F_k (1)	D: F_a, F_e, F_g - F_h, F_k	C: F_o (1)	
	D: F_i (1)	(5)	D: F_c, F_h (2)	
	E: F_c - F_e (3)			
	F: F_a, F_g - F_h (3)			

f_2: F_b, F_f, F_j

Figure 9. The Prefix Tries with One Independent Set.

When the number of the distinct cross-producting combinations is decreased to less than 100, the above steps are repeated. In the second and third iterations, the prefix trie of f_2 is still selected. Three filters, F_d, F_h and F_k, are taken in the second iteration and another three filters, F_c, F_g and F_l, are picked in the third one. After the third iteration, three independent sets are generated and the number of cross-producting combinations is reduced to 144. The resulting prefix tries are shown in Fig. 10.

In the fourth iteration, another prefix trie of f_4 is adopted, and two filters, F_e and F_o, are chosen. After the fourth iterations, the number of cross-producting combinations is dropped to 72 which causes the procedure to stop. The resulting prefix tries are shown in Fig. 11, where the ratio of storage reduction is 90%. There are four independent sets with nine filters. To perform packet classification, the filters of the independent sets are inserted into the one-dimensional data structure and the rest are inserted into the crossproduct table. In the following, we present the search procedure and the data structures of the proposed scheme.

The search procedure consists of two parts: d one-dimensional searches and one access to the crossproduct table. The seminal cross-producting scheme differs from the one-dimensional search in that extra comparisons to the filters in the independent sets would be needed. Therefore, the data structure for each one-dimensional search contains all field specifications of the filters for indexing the crossproduct table and the field specifications of the filters in the independent sets of the corresponding field. In our example, there is

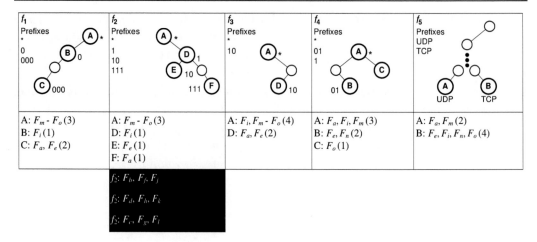

Figure 10. The Prefix Tries with Three Independent Sets.

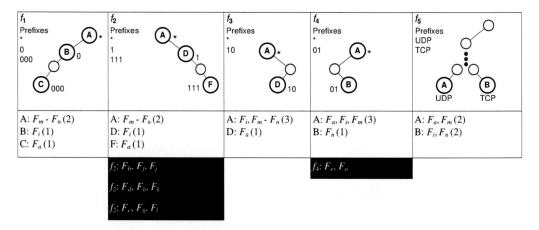

Figure 11. The Prefix Tries with Four Independent Sets.

no independent set on f_1, f_3 and f_5, hence the data structures of these three fields can be constructed based on the corresponding field specifications of the filters which are outside of the independent sets. For the field f_2, the data structure includes the field specifications of most filters, except F_e and F_o. The prefix tries for one-dimensional searches are shown in Fig. 12. In the prefix trie of f_2, there are four nodes, **B**, **C**, **E** and **F**, which contain the filters to be compared and three nodes, **A**, **D**, **F**, which are searched for the best matching prefixes. Since node **F** is served for two purposes, it is shaded in gray along with node **B** in field f_4.

While performing one-dimensional search on the prefix trie, the best matching node (unshaded) indicates that there is no filters of independent sets to be compared. In this case, the prefix corresponding to the best matching node is used to index the crossproduct table. If the best matching node is shaded in black, the associated filters are compared sequentially and the prefix corresponding to the last retrieved prefix node (unshaded) is used for cross-producting. In the last case, the best matching node in gray corresponds to the best matching prefix for cross-producting and a filter list of linear search. In the

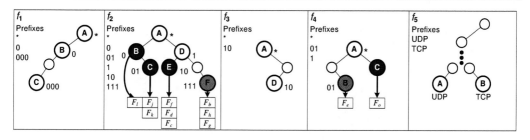

Figure 12. The Prefix Tries for One-dimensional Searches.

latter two cases, the associated filters in the parent of the best matching node should also be compared for possible matching.

In Fig. 12, a specification of f_2, "101", would match to node **E**, which indicates that the best matching prefix for cross-producting is $\langle 1* \rangle$ and three filters, F_f, F_d and F_c, are compared. Another f_2 specification "111" would match to node **F**, whose best matching prefix is $\langle 111* \rangle$ and another three filters, F_b, F_h and F_g, are compared. While node **C** is matched, the associated filters of node **C** and node **B** are compared sequentially.

We note that the data structure of prefix trie can be replaced by other advanced data structure to search for the best matching prefix, such as hash tables [28] or multiway search tree [31]. In this work, we adopt the data structure of multiway search tree for one-dimensional search. The main reason for such a selection is its scalability with respect to the number of prefixes and the prefix lengths. Although the data structure only supports local reconstruction, the side effect can be minimized since the filters usually share their field values [10, 32]. The time complexity of the proposed scheme is thus equal to $O(d \log N + \ell + 1)$, where ℓ is the number of independent sets.

4.2.   Refinements

In the following, we present two techniques to improve the search and storage performance. The first technique is an approach of approximate range to prefix transformation. The other technique is cache line alignment for optimize the access speed of linear search. In the following, we describe these two techniques in detail.

4.2.1.   Approximate Range to Prefix Transformation

As mentioned above, the range fields of a filter must be transformed to prefixes for supporting incremental updates. However, such an approach would result in more field specifications and lead to an increasing number of cross-producting combinations. In addition, the increasing number of filters would also cause more independent sets to be generated.

We propose a new approach to address the performance degradation caused by range to prefix transformation. Our approach is to represent a range by its smallest enclosure prefix. For the filters in Table 1, the ranges, [00:10] and [01:11], are both transformed to prefix $\langle * \rangle$. Since each range is represented by one prefix, there are no duplicated filters with the proposed approach. The transformed filters are listed in Table 14. These filters are then used to generate the prefix tries and derive the independent sets.

Table 14. The Converted Filters by using the Approximate Range to Prefix Transformation

Filter	f_1	f_2	f_3	f_4	f_5	Action
F_0	000*	111*	10*	*	UDP	act_0
F_1	000*	111*	01*	10*	UDP	act_0
F_2	000*	10*	*	10*	TCP	act_1
F_3	000*	10*	*	01*	TCP	act_2
F_4	000*	10*	10*	11*	TCP	act_1
F_5	0*	111*	10*	01*	UDP	act_0
F_6	0*	111*	10*	10*	UDP	act_0
F_7	0*	1*	*	*	TCP	act_2
F_8	*	01*	*	*	TCP	act_2
F_9	*	0*	*	01*	UDP	act_0
F_{10}	*	*	*	*	UDP	act_3
F_{11}	*	*	*	*	TCP	act_4

Next, three independent sets on field f_2 are generated. In the first iteration, three filters, F_1, F_4 and F_8, are selected, and another three filters, F_2, F_6 and F_9, are picked in the second iteration. In the last iteration, the filters, F_0 and F_3, are selected. Then the remaining four filters are used to generate the crossproduct table by performing the original range to prefix transformation. We depict the prefix tries for one-dimensional searches in Fig. 13. In this example, there are only three independent sets with 72 cross-producting combinations. Therefore, the required storage of the one-dimensional data structures could be reduced while the search performance is improved simultaneously.

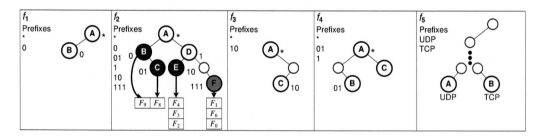

Figure 13. The Prefix Tries for One-dimensional Searches with Approximate Range to Prefix Transformation.

4.2.2. Cache Line Alignment

The other technique to improve the search performance is cache line alignment, which utilizes the property of processors where the entire cache line is fetched from dynamic random access memory (DRAM) even though only a single word is required. The access time is dominated by the latency of accessing the first word in the cache line; therefore, the remaining words come at a very low cost [33]. This technique has been used to speed up several algorithms [34, 31, 35, 33]. We apply this technique to increase the rate of accessing the linear-searched filters by fitting these filters into one or more cache lines. Currently, the size of each cache line in a modern processor could be as large as 64 or 128 bytes. Therefore, each cache line could hold three filters (20 bytes per filter). With this technique, we could merge several filter lists to achieve better search efficiency by reassociating the filters from a node to its parent node. For the example in Fig. 13, the filter lists of node **B** and node **C** can be merged to adhere to the size limit of a cache line. To achieve this, F_8 is reassociated to node **B** and ode **C** is no longer needed. As a result, all filters of a list can be read in one cache line access.

4.3. Incremental Updates

The update procedure of the proposed scheme could be divided into two portions. The first portion involves updating the one-dimensional data structures and the second is about updating the crossproduct table. Since the first portion has been studied extensively [36], we focus on the update procedure of crossproduct table.

The major issue of updating the crossproduct table is the new combinations caused by a newly inserted filter. When a new filter is inserted, the crossproduct table would also be inserted $(N + 1)^d - N^d$ new combinations of new intersections in the worst case. As mentioned above, the crossproduct table can be implemented as a direct access array or a hash table. The implementation using the direct access array can achieve faster access rate, but it is usually not updatable due to its consecutively allocated entries. Although the implementation using hash table can be inserted with new entries, the large number of insertions would severely degrade the search performance.

To address this problem, we replace the new prefix of the inserted filter with its longest existing enclosure prefix. After the replacement, there is no new combination for the crossproduct table of direct access array and at most, one for that of hash table. Yet, the existing combination might have corresponded to a matching filter. In this case, the new filter is appended to the existing filter and accessed by linear search. The other existing entries intersected by the new filter are also modified if necessary. Although all entries are still modified in the worst case, filter intersection is usually far less than in the worst case [5, 32, 10]. Hence the cost of inserting new filter can be greatly reduced with only moderate speed reduction.

Let us consider the insertion of a new filter, $\langle 01*, 11*, [10 : 10], [01 : 01], TCP \rangle$, into the proposed data structure of the filters in Table 1. Assume that the filter is not categorized into any independent set, hence this filter must be stored in the crossproduct table. According to Fig. 13, both $\langle 01* \rangle$ and $\langle 11* \rangle$ are new prefixes of f_1 and f_2, respectively. Therefore, the number of new combinations could be as many as 72. With the proposed approach, the new filter would be represented by $\langle 0*, 1*, 10*, 01*, TCP \rangle$. Since all field specifications are existent, no new combination is inserted and the reconstruction of the crossproduct table can be avoided.

4.4. Performance Evaluation

In this section we describe how the new algorithm performs on both real and synthetic databases in terms of its speed and storage. Our performance evaluation focuses on relating the numerical results of the proposed scheme to other existing schemes in a study of performance. The performance metrics include the required storage in kilobytes, and the numbers of memory accesses in the average case (AMA) and the worst case (WMA).

To begin with, the real databases are used in the evaluation. Table 15 shows the storage performance of the proposed scheme and other existing schemes, and Table 16 lists the speed performance. As compared to *RFC*, the search performance of the proposed scheme is slower as a tradeoff to yield better storage consumption and scalability. Although both schemes are based on cross-producting, the proposed scheme could reduce the required storage by eliminating the distinct field specifications. As a result, the scalability of the proposed scheme could be significantly improved.

Table 15. Storage Performance of the Existing Algorithms Using Real Databases

Real DBs	Original Filters	ABV	HyperCuts	RFC	Controlled Cross-producting
ACL1	752	296.34	29.45	497.62	417.72
FW1	269	263.73	33.41	1,094.55	262.11
IPC1	1,550	331.46	142.18	8,984.18	879.00

As compared to other non-cross-producting-based schemes, the proposed scheme seems not competitive in the storage performance, but the proposed scheme outperforms these schemes in both average and the worst case search performance. Both the storage disadvantage and speed advantage come from the crossproduct table. While the crossproduct table is superior in search speed, it also incurs extra storage.

Table 16. Speed Performance of the Existing Algorithms Using Real Databases

Real DBs	ABV		HyperCuts		RFC		Controlled Cross-producting	
	AMA	WMA	AMA	WMA	AMA	WMA	AMA	WMA
ACL1	35.13	44	14.79	22	11	11	13.02	15
FW1	20.49	30	21.37	46	11	11	9.90	14
IPC1	26.14	50	22.44	49	11	11	15.29	19

Next, we use synthetic databases for further evaluation. While the storage performance of the proposed scheme is not comparable to the existing schemes using the relatively small, real, filter databases, the side effect disappears when the size of filter database increases. As shown in Table 17, the memory consumption of the proposed scheme is superior than that of *ABV* and most cases of *Hypercuts*. In addition, the proposed scheme also surpasses both schemes in search performance, as shown in Table 18. The experimental results of *RFC* are not listed since the table construction would consume more than 4GB memory and cannot be completed in our 32-bit machine. Although a 64-bit machine might be able to complete the construction procedure, we believe that the required storage of *RFC* is unlikely to be acceptable even with the state-of-the-art hardware.

In sum, the proposed scheme could significantly improve the storage efficiency with moderate speed degradation as a tradeoff. By combining the advantages of cross-producting

Table 17. Storage Performance of the Existing Algorithms Using Synthetic Databases

Syn DBs	Original Filters	ABV	HyperCuts	Controlled Cross-producting
ACL1	15,926	36,523.81	369.18	827.55
ACL2	15,447	55,141.81	1,359.68	1,690.12
FW1	14,898	32,494.13	23,883.84	2,075.47
FW2	15,501	39,885.48	10,859.94	1,766.12
IPC1	14,954	16,116.21	3,557.90	1,519.83
IPC2	16,000	44,405.32	12,450.29	1,707.25

Table 18. Speed Performance of the Existing Algorithms Using Synthetic Databases

Syn DBs	ABV		HyperCuts		Controlled Cross-producting	
	AMA	WMA	AMA	WMA	AMA	WMA
ACL1	33.30	44	21.07	56	10.69	13
ACL2	36.55	50	21.72	132	8.47	11
FW1	47.33	56	22.52	221	9.05	10
FW2	33.28	34	21.12	43	2.78	3
IPC1	44.05	65	22.44	87	14.79	23
IPC2	32.34	33	17.14	41	2.73	3

and linear search, the proposed scheme achieves a better leverage between speed and storage performance.

5. Conclusion

Packet classification plays a crucial role in the applications of network security. Previous approaches tend to rely on hardware support to achieve fast classification. However, such prerequisite may not be always feasible for network applications; an example would be firewalls with large rule sets.

In this chapter, we present two algorithms to improve the feasibility of packet classification. The first algorithm, *Hierarchical Cross-Producting*, hierarchically decomposes the multidimensional space into smaller subspaces. For each subspace, a cross-product table, which is implemented by a hash table, is generated. Through controlling the number of distinct fields in each subspace, the required storage can be greatly reduced, especially for the sparse filters. We also demonstrated the speed and storage efficiency as compared with previously proposed algorithms. Our algorithm not only supports incremental updates but also improves the scalability of cross-producting by promoting space efficiency.

The second algorithm, *Controlled Cross-producting*, is inspired by the following observation that an increasing number of distinct prefixes also indicates that more filters can be distinguished simply by the specifications of one field. These distinguishable filters can be searched with one-dimensional data structures and excluded from the cross-product table. *Controlled Cross-producting* can adjust storage usage by controlling the number of filters that are distinguishable through one-dimensional searches. With more filters searched by one-dimensional data structures, the storage needed for the cross-product table could be further decreased while trading off search speed. In our experiments, we evaluate the performance of the new algorithm with filter databases of varying sizes and characteristics. Our results show that new algorithm can provide superior search performance while keeping the space requirement comparable with the prominent existing schemes.

In sum, the new algorithms are suitable for network applications with numerous filters or multifunction network devices that integrate routers, firewalls and network intrusion detection systems (NIDS). We believe that our proposed scheme will remain up-to-date with new network applications due to its insensitivity to filter databases with different characteristics. Therefore, we believe that the applications of network security can benefit from the new algorithms by the consolidation of data protection.

References

[1] Yu F, Katz RH, Lakshman TV. Efficient Multimatch Packet Classification and Lookup with TCAM. *IEEE Micro*. 2005;25(1):50–59.

[2] Song H, Lockwood JW. Efficient packet classification for network intrusion detection using FPGA. In: *FPGA '05*; 2005. p. 238–245.

[3] Kumar VP, Lakshman TV, Stiliadis D. Beyond best effort: router architectures for the differentiated services of tomorrow's Internet. *Communications Magazine, IEEE*. 1998 May;36(5):152–164.

[4] Taylor DE. Survey and Taxonomy of Packet Classification Techniques. *ACM Computing Survey*. 2005;37(3):238–275.

[5] Gupta P, McKeown N. Packet classification on multiple fields. In: *Proceedings of ACM SIGCOMM '99*; 1999. p. 147–160.

[6] Srinivasan V, Varghese G, Suri S. Packet classification using tuple space search. In: *Proceedings of ACM SIGCOMM '99*; 1999. p. 135–146.

[7] Woo T. A modular approach to packet classification: algorithms and results. In: *Proceedings of IEEE INFOCOM '00*; 2000. p. 1213–1222.

[8] Sumeet Singh GV Florin Baboescu, Wang J. Packet Classification Using Multidimensional Cutting. In: *Proceedings of ACM SIGCOMM '03*; 2003. p. 213–224.

[9] Srinivasan V, Varghese G, Suri S, Waldvogel M. Fast and scalable layer four switching. In: *Proceedings of ACM SIGCOMM '98*; 1998. p. 191–202.

[10] Taylor DE, Turner JS. Scalable Packet Classification using Distributed Crossproducting of Field Labels. In: *Proceedings of IEEE INFOCOM '05*; 2005. p. 269–280.

[11] Gupta P, McKeown N. Packet Classification using Hierarchical Intelligent Cuttings. In: *Proceedings of Hot Interconnects VII*; 1999. .

[12] Baboescu F, Singh S, Varghese G. Packet classification for core routers: Is there an alternative to CAMs? In: *Proceedings of IEEE INFOCOM '03*; 2003. p. 53–63.

[13] Sun X, Sahni SK, Zhao YQ. Packet classification consuming small amount of memory. *IEEE/ACM Transactions on Networking*. 2005;13(5):1135–1145.

[14] Wang PC, Chan CT, Hu SC, Lee CL, Tseng WC. High-speed packet classification for differentiated services in ngns. *IEEE Transactions on Multimedia*. 2004;6(6):925–935.

[15] Srinivasan V. A packet classification and filter management system. In: *Proceedings of IEEE INFOCOM '01*; 2001. p. 1464–1473.

[16] Wang PC, Lee CL, Chan CT, Chang HY. Performance improvement of two-dimensional packet classification by filter rephrasing. *IEEE/ACM Transactions on Networking*. 2007;15(4):906–917.

[17] Dharmapurikar S, Song H, Turner J, Lockwood J. Fast packet classification using bloom filters. In: *ANCS '06: Proceedings of the 2006 ACM/IEEE symposium on Architecture for networking and communications systems*; 2006. p. 61–70.

[18] Gupta P, McKeown N. Algorithms for packet classification. *IEEE Network Magazine*. 2001;15(2):24–32.

[19] Baboescu F, Varghese G. Scalable Packet Classification. In: *Proceedings of ACM SIGCOMM '01*; 2001. p. 199–210.

[20] van Lunteren J, Engbersen T. Fast and scalable packet classification. *IEEE Journal on Selected Areas in Communications*. 2003 May;21(4):560–571.

[21] Bremler-Barr A, Hendler D. *Space-Efficient TCAM-Based Classification Using Gray Coding*; 2007. p. 1388–1396.

[22] Lakshminarayanan K, Rangarajan A, Venkatachary S. Algorithms for advanced packet classification with ternary CAMs. In: *SIGCOMM '05: Proceedings of the 2005 conference on Applications, technologies, architectures, and protocols for computer communications*; 2005. p. 193–204.

[23] Liu H. Efficient Mapping of Range Classifier into Ternary-CAM. In: *Hot Interconnects X; 2002*. p. 95–100.

[24] McCanne S, Jacobson V. The BSD packet filter: a new architecture for user-level packet capture. In: *Proceedings of USENIX Technical Conference '93*; 1993. .

[25] Lakshman TV, Stidialis D. High-speed policy-based packet forwarding using efficient multi-dimensional range matching. In: *Proceedings of ACM SIGCOMM '98*; 1998. p. 203–214.

[26] Yu F, Lakshman TV, Motoyama MA, Katz RH. Efficient Multimatch Packet Classification for Network Security Applications. *IEEE Journal on Selected Areas in Communications*. 2006;24(10):1805–1816.

[27] Bremler-Barr A, Hay D, Hendler D, Farber B. Layered interval codes for tcam-based classification. In: *SIGMETRICS '08: Proceedings of the 2008 ACM SIGMETRICS international conference on Measurement and modeling of computer systems*; 2008. p. 445–446.

[28] Waldvogel M, Varghese G, Turner J, Plattner B. Scalable high speed IP routing lookups. In: *Proceedings of ACM SIGCOMM '97*; 1997. p. 25–36.

[29] Song H. *Design and evaluation of packet classification systems*. Dept. of Computer Science and Engineering, Washington University; 2006.

[30] Taylor DE, Turner JS. Classbench: a packet classification benchmark. In: *Proceedings of IEEE INFOCOM '05*; 2005. p. 2068–2079.

[31] Lampson B, Srinivasan V, Varghese G. IP lookups using multiway and multicolumn search. *IEEE/ACM Transactions On Networking*. 1999 June;7(4):323–334.

[32] Kounavis ME, Kumar A, Vin H, Yavatkar R, Campbell AT. Directions in packet classification for network processors. In: *Proceedings of Second Workshop on Network Processors (NP2)*; 2003. .

[33] Feldmann A, Muthukrishnan S. Tradeoffs for Packet Classification. In: *Proceedings of IEEE INFOCOM '00*; 2000. p. 1193–1202.

[34] Srinivasan V, Varghese G. Fast address lookups using controlled prefix expansion. *ACM Transctions On Computer Systems*. 1999 Febuary;17(1):1–40.

[35] Lu H, Sahni S. O(logW) multidimensional packet classification. *IEEE/ACM Transactions on Networking*. 2007;15(2):462–472.

[36] Miguel A Ruiz-Sanchez EWB, Dabbous W. Survey and Taxonomy of IP Address Lookup Algorithms. *IEEE Network Magazine*. 2001;15(2):8–23.

[37] Wang PC. Scalable packet classification with controlled cross-producting. *Computer Networks*. 2009;53(6):821–834.

[38] Lee CL, Chan CT, Wang PC. Packet Classification with Hierarchical Cross-producting. *IEICE Transactions on Information and Systems*. 2010;E93-D(5):1117–1126.

In: Horizons in Computer Science Research, Volume 4   ISBN: 978-1-61324-262-9
Editor: Thomas S. Clary   © 2011 Nova Science Publishers, Inc.

Chapter 13

PRINCIPLES OF DISTRIBUTED MODEL-BASED DIAGNOSIS OF ACTIVE SYSTEMS

Gianfranco Lamperti*and *Marina Zanella*[†]
Dipartimento di Ingegneria dell'Informazione
Università degli Studi di Brescia, Italy

Keywords: Distributed diagnosis, Model-based reasoning, Active systems, Discrete-event systems, Active algebra, Uncertainty.

1. Introduction

Active systems are a class of discrete-event systems (DESs) that has been the focus of the authors' research over the last decade [?, ?, ?, ?, ?, ?, ?]. Based on past work, by now the awareness has grown that, in order to cope with model-based diagnosis of DESs, it is not enough to model them as composite systems, as done by most approaches [?, ?, ?, ?], it is also necessary to process them in a stepwise, modular way. This is the reason for the proposal of a problem – decomposition, solution – composition paradigm for model-based diagnosis of active systems [?], and for an increasing use of *decentralized* features, such as the observation [?], or the diagnosis method [?] of other classes of DESs. All these contributions denote progressive attempts to pinpoint some major requirements of *distributed model-based diagnosis* (DMBD) of DESs.

   This chapter defines and substantiates the task of (general) DMBD of active systems with the support of six requirements. Specifically, Sections 2 through 7 introduce the requirements guiding the formulation of DMBD, and instantiate them in the domain of active systems. In particular, Section 6 emphasizes the issue of processing optimization by introducing Active Algebra and relevant equivalence rules, while Section 7 deals with a method

---

*E-mail address: lamperti@ing.unibs.it
[†]E-mail address: zanella@ing.unibs.it

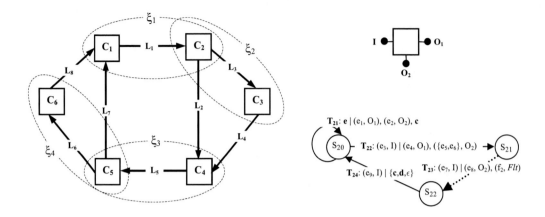

Figure 1. System Θ (left) and model M_2 of component C_2 (right).

for monotonically updating a complete set of candidate diagnosis during the processing. Related work is discussed in Section 8. Conclusions are drawn in Section 9.

2. Distributed System

DESs are modeled as networks of connected components, rather than as monolithic objects, where each component is characterized by a behavioral model, typically represented by a finite automaton. Transitions between states of behavioral models are triggered by events exchanged among components over the network.

Requirement 1. *The DMBD approach provides support for modeling each system to be diagnosed in terms of its topology, interconnecting components by means of connectors, and of the behavior of each component and connector.*

This requirement stresses the need for compositional modeling of active systems, as a necessary property for DMBD. Besides, it highlights that there are two structural types of elements in active systems, and both of them have to be behaviorally modeled.

Several approaches to model-based diagnosis of DESs exploit compositional modeling, however, most of them do not use explicit models for connectors, which are structural elements devoted to event exchange between components, where distinct connectors may transmit events according to different protocols. Instead, our approach provides ad hoc modeling primitives for representing connectors, thus enhancing the expressive power of system descriptions.

The characterization of active system fulfilled Requirement 1 also in previous work. To make the chapter self-contained, such a characterization is summarized below. Besides, the notion of active system is generalized and extended with new forms of nondeterminism.

Active systems are composite DESs whose *components* are endowed with input and output *terminals*, which are connected with each other through directed connection *links*.

Example 1. Shown on the left of Figure 1 is a system Θ, which includes components $C_1, \ldots, C_6$ and links $L_1, \ldots, L_8$. A *cluster* is a connected sub-graph which incorporates one or several system components and all the links among them. A system is a cluster itself. Four cluster are indicated in Figure 1, namely $\xi_1, \ldots, \xi_4$, where ξ_1 and ξ_2 share component C_2, and ξ_3 and ξ_4 share C_5. As a sample, shown on the right of the figure is the model M_2 of component C_2, in terms of topology (top) and behavior (bottom). The topology of M_2 incorporates one input terminal, I, and two output terminals, O_1 and O_2. Besides, each component is endowed with two *virtual terminals* for the interconnection with the external world: the *standard input* and the *standard output*. Identifiers of virtual terminals are omitted, and, in the pictorial representation, the relevant events are in bold.

The behavior of C_2 is composed of three states, S_{20}, S_{21}, and S_{22}, and four transitions, T_{21}, T_{22}, T_{23}, and T_{24}, where T_{23}, denoted by a dotted arrow, is the only faulty transition. For instance, T_{21} is triggered by event e received on the standard input, and generates the set of output events $\{(e_1, O_1), (e_2, O_2), c\}$, that is, event e_1 on terminal O_1, event e_2 on terminal O_2, and event c on the standard output. An event sent to the standard output is called a *message* and is *observable*[1]. A (possibly nondeterministic) fault is associated with each faulty transition. Such a fault is denoted as an output event sent to an implicit fictitious terminal, called the *fault terminal* and denoted by Flt. For instance, transition T_{23} is characterized by fault f_2. This means that transition T_{23} is performed just in case component C_2 is affected by fault f_2. Transition T_{21} is deterministic, insofar as it is the only transition exiting from state S_{20} that is triggered by event e on the standard input, and the sets of events associated with output terminals are singletons. By contrast, transition T_{22} is nondeterministic, as it involves the *disjunctive* output event $(\{e_5, e_6\}, O_2)$. This means that, when T_{22} is triggered, either e_5 or e_6 is generated at terminal O_2. The same applies to T_{24}, which generates $\{c, d, \epsilon\}$. This means that either message c, or d, or nothing is expected to be generated on the standard output.

Every event directed from a component to another is transmitted on a link, which is either *synchronous* or *asynchronous*. In the former case, the event is available to the neighboring component as soon as it is transmitted and is immediately consumed. In the latter case, the event is temporally saved in the link. Each link is characterized by a *capacity*, which is the (finite) maximum number of events that can be buffered within the link, by a management *policy*, such as LIFO (last-in, first-out), FIFO (first-in, first-out), etc., and by a *saturation mode*, which dictates the semantics for triggering a transition that generates an event to be buffered in the link when the link is full, and for buffering such an event, if the transition is allowed to be triggered.

A system can be either *quiescent* or *reacting*. When quiescent, no component changes its state and links are empty. The reaction is triggered by an external event, for instance, with reference to Example 1, e for C_2, which makes a component change its state. Since each state change may generate some output events directed to neighboring components, the system continues changing its state until it reaches a new quiescent state, where links are empty anew.

---

[1]As pointed out in Section 3, the observability of a message is only virtual, as, for the message to be actually observed, the availability of an appropriate observer is required.

3. Distributed Observation

As in other real-world contexts, where several agents may view the same phenomenon from different viewpoints, so in DMBD the observation of the system is not viewed by a single observer only but, rather, shared by multiples observers, with each observer perceiving a particular view of the system behavior.

Requirement 2. *The DMBD approach allows for the representation of each system observation as the composition of several views, where each view is what is observed by a distinct observer.*

Upon the reaction of an active system, a number of messages are likely to be generated. If (some of) these messages are observed, they constitute the *observation* of the active system. Typically, an observation, even if consisting of several fragments [?, ?], was not structured into distinct views, each pertaining to a single observer, as the concept of observer had not been defined yet.

Then, the notion of observation has been extended to fulfill the above requirement. Distinct observers may have different capabilities to observe each distinct system component, that is, each observer is able to detect a (sub)set of all the categories of messages generated by the component, called the *domain* of the observer. The domain of a specific observer may possibly be null or overlap that of another observer. If a category of messages of a component cannot be observed by any observer, then it is not observable at all.

The above characterization catches two orthogonal aspects that together determine the real ability to observe: the physical ability of an observer to detect certain events (and not others), and the communication between the system to be observed and the observer. In fact, even if an observer is potentially able to detect message c, a c generated by a component C can be detected only if it is received, that is, if there are some communication means that convey this message from C to the observer.

Example 2. With reference to Example 1, an observer, such as ω_2, is characterized as follows:

$$\omega_2 = \{(C_2, d), (C_4, d), (C_5, f), (C_6, \{a, b\})\} \tag{1}$$

this meaning that ω_2 can see message d generated by component C_2 (while no c generated by the same component can be observed), message d generated by C_4, message f generated by C_5, and messages a and b generated by C_6. Note that observer ω_2 cannot observe any message of components C_1 and C_3.

4. Uncertain Observation

When the system is large and distributed, as typically happens in real-world applications, the observation generated by its reaction is not perceived to the observer(s) as a totally-ordered sequence of observable labels. Rather, owing to possible noise and multiple communication channels, the observation is uncertain in nature.

Requirement 3. *The DMBD approach allows for the representation of each observation view as either logically or temporally uncertain, or both.*

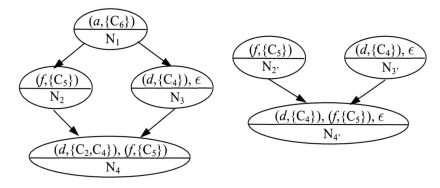

Figure 2. View graphs: $\gamma_2(\Theta)$ (left) and relevant restriction $\gamma_{2\langle\xi_3\rangle}(\Theta)$ (right).

The concept of uncertain observation was introduced in [?, ?]. Now this concept is applied to each observation view. Therefore, each view is represented by a *view graph*, accommodating, according to their (uncertain) emission order, the (uncertain) messages which have been observed by an observer.

Example 3. Considering system Θ in Figure 1, we may have

$$OBS(\Theta) = \{W_1, W_2, W_3, W_4\} \tag{2}$$

where each view W_i is a pair (γ_i, ω_i), with γ_i being the view graph relevant to observer ω_i. In other words, four different observers are assumed. Shown on the left-hand side of Figure 2 is the view graph $\gamma_2(\Theta)$, that is, what ω_2 has actually observed during the reaction of Θ. This graph involves nodes $N_1, \ldots, N_4$, where each node represents an observed message. Nodes N_1 and N_2 are marked by logically 'certain' messages, while N_3 and N_4 are uncertain in nature. In fact, N_3 is either label d of C_4 or the null label. Instead, the uncertainty of N_4 is twofold: either d or f has been observed, where d might have been generated either by C_2 or C_4. Moreover, the temporal relationships among messages is weak, as N_2 and N_3 are not temporally related to one another.

5. Distributed Processing

In order to speed up the diagnosis process, the reconstruction of the system behavior is required to be carried out in parallel by several processing units. This way, distinct projections of the system behavior are elaborated based on the partial views of the involved observers. In the end, however, the diagnosis output is expected to be sound and complete.

Requirement 4. *The DMBD approach enables the diagnosis process to be split into several independent processing units, which are virtually run in parallel on distinct processors.*

Within the diagnosis method proposed in [?, ?], the main task is to reconstruct the behavior of the system Θ to be diagnosed, based on a given diagnosis problem

$$\wp(\Theta) = (OBS(\Theta), \Theta_0) \tag{3}$$

where $OBS(\Theta)$ is the observation gathered during the reaction, and Θ_0 the state of the system, i.e. the composition of the states of all components, when the reaction started. The result is an *active space*, that is, a graph incorporating all (and only) the system *histories*, which represent the feasible behaviors of the system during the reaction, each history corresponding to a sequence of transitions from the initial state to a final quiescent state. In the active space, each transition is marked by the relevant component and transition identifiers, and by the message(s) it is assumed to have generated[2].

The reconstruction of the system behavior exploits a problem–decomposition, solution–composition paradigm [?] that fulfills the above principle.

6. Processing Optimization

Since, generally speaking, there exist different ways in which independent processing units cooperate to the diagnosis process, it is essential for the diagnosis engine to establish the best setting of parallel tasks so as to optimize the whole diagnosis process. Specifically, some optimization criteria should be envisaged, in a way similar to query optimization in relational database systems [?].

Requirement 5. *The independent processing units of the DMBD process are arranged so as to fulfill some computational optimization criteria.*

In order to satisfy this requirement, a number of operators for the manipulation of active spaces can be defined, giving rise to an *active algebra*. They are algebraic insofar as the application of each of them to active spaces results in a new active space. This set of operators is a formal means for the optimization of the reconstruction of the system behavior. Roughly, the reconstruction of the system behavior based on a given diagnosis problem may be specified in a (possibly large) variety of equivalent active-algebra expressions. What makes the difference between expressions is the computational cost, which depends on several parameters, such as the nature of component models and system observations.

6.1. Active Algebra

Operators

In what follows we refer to a generic system Θ and assume that each cluster referenced in the operator definitions belongs to Θ. Besides, we define the union $\xi_i \cup \xi_j$ of clusters ξ_i and ξ_j as the cluster that includes the union of the components of each one of the two given clusters (and, consequently, all the links among them).

The (possibly boundless) set of histories intensionally incorporated in an active space A is called the *extension* of A, denoted by $\|A\|$.

Definition 1. (*Set-theoretic operators*) Let A_1 and A_2 be two active spaces relevant to the same cluster ξ. The *union* $A_1 \cup A_2$ is an active space A such that $\|A\| = \|A_1\| \cup \|A_2\|$. The *intersection* $A_1 \cap A_2$ is an active space A such that $\|A\| = \|A_1\| \cap \|A_2\|$. The *difference* $A_1 - A_2$, is an active space A such that $\|A\| = \|A_1\| - \|A_2\|$. □

---

[2]According to the notion of active system, if there are events on several synchronous links, all the transitions enabled by these events are fired together and, therefore, they may generate several messages.

Definition 2. (*Projection*) Let A be an active space relevant to cluster ξ. The *projection* of A on a cluster $\xi' \subseteq \xi$, denoted by $\pi_{\xi'}(A)$, is the active space A' relevant to ξ' such that $\|A'\| = \{h' \mid h' \subseteq h, h \in \|A\|, \forall T(C) \in h, C \in \xi'(T(C) \in h'), \forall T(C) \in h'(C \in \xi')\}$, where $T(C)$ denotes a transition of component C.   □

Definition 3. (*Selection*) Let A be an active space relevant to cluster ξ. The *selection* of A based on an observation $OBS(\xi)$, denoted by $\sigma_{OBS(\xi)}(A)$, is an active space A' relevant to ξ such that $\|A'\| = \{h \mid h \in \|A\|, h \models OBS(\xi)\}$.   □

Definition 4. (*Composition*) Let $A_1, \ldots, A_n$, $n \geq 1$, be a set of active spaces relevant to clusters $\xi_1, \ldots, \xi_n$, respectively. A *composition* of $h_1, \ldots, h_n$, where $\forall i \in [1..n]$ ($h_i \in \|A_i\|$), is a history h such that:

(*a*) h includes all the sets of transitions in $h_1, \ldots, h_n$;

(*b*) The relative order of transitions in $h_1, \ldots, h_n$, respectively, is preserved in h;

(*c*) h is consistent with $\xi = \xi_1 \cup \cdots \cup \xi_n$.

By definition, $h \in \oplus(h_1, \ldots, h_n)$ means that h is a composition of $h_1, \ldots, h_n$. The *composition* of $A_1, \ldots, A_n$, denoted by $\oplus(A_1, \ldots, A_n)$, is the active space A relevant to ξ such that $\|A\| = \{h \mid h \in \oplus(h_1, \ldots, h_n), \forall i \in [1..n]$ ($h_i \in \|A_i\|)\}$.

The *selective composition* of $A_1, \ldots, A_n$, based on an observation $OBS(\xi)$, denoted by $\oplus_{OBS(\xi)}(A_1, \ldots, A_n)$, is the active space A relevant to ξ such that $\|A\| = \{h \mid h \in \| \oplus (A_1, \ldots, A_n)\|, h \models OBS(\xi)\}$.

In case there are just two operands for the composition operator (or for selective composition), then the infix syntactical form can be adopted, such as $A_1 \oplus A_2$.   □

Equivalence Rules

An *equivalence rule* establishes when two active-algebra expressions are equivalent, that is, when the active spaces A_l and A_r resulting from the two expressions have the same extensions, namely $\|A_l\| = \|A_r\|$. Equivalence rules can be exploited by an optimization algorithm to progressively transform expressions. Hereafter, a number of general equivalence rules holding on active-algebra expressions are listed.

(*a*) Union and intersection are commutative:

$$A_1 \cup A_2 = A_2 \cup A_1 \tag{4}$$
$$A_1 \cap A_2 = A_2 \cap A_1 \tag{5}$$

(*b*) Union and intersection are associative:

$$(A_1 \cup A_2) \cup A_3 = A_1 \cup (A_2 \cup A_3)$$
$$(A_1 \cap A_2) \cap A_3 = A_1 \cap (A_2 \cap A_3) \tag{6}$$

(c) Intersection can be expressed in terms of differences:

$$A_1 \cap A_2 = A_1 - (A_1 - A_2) \tag{7}$$

(d) A cascade of projections equals the outermost projection:

$$\pi_{\xi_1}(\pi_{\xi_2}(\cdots(\pi_{\xi_n}(A))\cdots)) = \pi_{\xi_1}(A) \tag{8}$$

(e) Projection distributes over union:

$$\pi_\xi(A_1 \cup A_2) = (\pi_\xi(A_1)) \cup (\pi_\xi(A_2)) \tag{9}$$

(f) Selection distributes over union, intersection, and difference:

$$\sigma_{OBS(\xi)}(A_1 \cup A_2) = \sigma_{OBS(\xi)}(A_1) \cup \sigma_{OBS(\xi)}(A_2)$$
$$\sigma_{OBS(\xi)}(A_1 \cap A_2) = \sigma_{OBS(\xi)}(A_1) \cap \sigma_{OBS(\xi)}(A_2) \tag{10}$$
$$\sigma_{OBS(\xi)}(A_1 - A_2) = \sigma_{OBS(\xi)}(A_1) - \sigma_{OBS(\xi)}(A_2)$$

Furthermore, for intersection and difference the following equivalences hold:

$$\sigma_{OBS(\xi)}(A_1 \cap A_2) = \sigma_{OBS(\xi)}(A_1) \cap A_2$$
$$\sigma_{OBS(\xi)}(A_1 - A_2) = \sigma_{OBS(\xi)}(A_1) - A_2 \tag{11}$$

(g) Selection based on union of observations can be deconstructed into a cascade of individual selections:

$$\sigma_{OBS_1(\xi) \cup OBS_2(\xi)}(A) = \sigma_{OBS_1(\xi)}(\sigma_{OBS_2(\xi)}(A)) \tag{12}$$

(h) Selection is commutative:

$$\sigma_{OBS_1(\xi)}(\sigma_{OBS_2(\xi)}(A)) = \sigma_{OBS_2(\xi)}(\sigma_{OBS_1(\xi)}(A)) \tag{13}$$

(i) Selections can be combined with (possibly selective) compositions:

$$\sigma_{OBS(\xi)}(A_1 \oplus A_2) = A_1 \oplus_{OBS(\xi)} A_2$$
$$\sigma_{OBS_1(\xi)}(A_1 \oplus_{OBS_2(\xi)} A_2) = A_1 \oplus_{OBS_1(\xi) \cup OBS_2(\xi)} A_2 \tag{14}$$

(j) Composition is commutative:

$$A_1 \oplus A_2 = A_2 \oplus A_1 \tag{15}$$

(k) Composition is associative:

$$(A_1 \oplus A_2) \oplus A_3 = A_1 \oplus (A_2 \oplus A_3) \tag{16}$$

(l) The composition of a single active space equals the active space:

$$\oplus(A) = A \tag{17}$$

(m) Selection of composition is equivalent to selective composition:

$$\sigma_{OBS(\xi)}(\oplus(A_1, \ldots, A_n)) = \oplus_{OBS(\xi)}(A_1, \ldots, A_n) \tag{18}$$

(n) Composition of compositions of several sets of active spaces is equivalent to a single composition of the union of all the sets of active spaces:

$$\oplus\left(\oplus(A_{11}, \ldots, A_{1k_1}), \oplus(A_{21}, \ldots, A_{2k_2}), \ldots, \oplus(A_{n1}, \ldots, A_{nk_n})\right) = \\ \oplus\left(A_{11}, \ldots, A_{1k_1}, A_{21}, \ldots, A_{2k_2}, \ldots, A_{n1}, \ldots, A_{nk_n}\right) \tag{19}$$

Active Algebra and Optimization

In the context of non-distributed diagnosis, the reconstruction process is supposed to be carried out in a single step. Accordingly, the active space $\mathbf{A}(\wp(\Theta))$ of the given diagnosis problem $\wp(\Theta) = (OBS(\Theta), \Theta_0)$, where Θ includes components $C_1, \ldots, C_n$, and $\Theta_0 = (C_{10}, \ldots, C_{n0})$, is made up by a monolithic algorithm, which accounts for all the constraints imposed by the component models, the link models, and the observation, as a whole. In active-algebra terms this can be specified by the following *canonical expression* (on the right-hand side):

$$\mathbf{A}(\wp(\Theta)) = \oplus_{OBS(\Theta)}(\mathbf{A}(C_{10}), \ldots, \mathbf{A}(C_{n0})) \tag{20}$$

where $\mathbf{A}(C_{i0})$ is the *atomic* active space of component C_i, i.e. the active space inherent to the problem $(null, C_{i0})$, where *null* denotes an unspecified observation, and C_{i0} is a state of the behavioral model of component C_i[3]. The canonical expression of a diagnosis problem inherent to the system Θ of Figure 1 is:

$$\mathbf{A}(\wp(\Theta)) = \oplus_{OBS(\Theta)}(A_1, \ldots, A_6), \tag{21}$$

where A_i, $i \in [1 .. 6]$, denotes the atomic active space $\mathbf{A}(C_{i0})$.

Considering distributed diagnosis, equivalence rules can be exploited to transform, for instance, the canonical expression into another which is likely to be evaluated more efficiently. Conceptually, given an expression, if any sub-expression matches one side of an equivalence rule, a new expression is generated, where the sub-expression is transformed to match the other side of the rule. In principle, this process continues until no more new expressions can be generated. Pragmatically, heuristic and/or cost-based techniques are to be envisaged to reduce the (time and space) complexity of this generation process. Transforming the canonical expression relevant to a diagnosis problem $\wp(\Theta)$ into a new one which can

---

[3]The atomic active space $\mathbf{A}(C_{i0})$ corresponds to the subsets of nodes and transitions of the behavioral model of C_i that are reachable from the initial state C_{i0}, where, by definition, each reachable state is a final state as well. Ideally, atomic active spaces can be compiled off-line from the behavioral models of components, so as to be directly available to the reconstruction process.

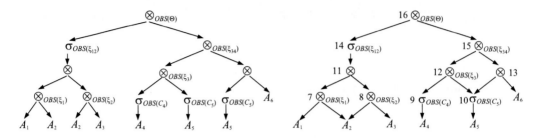

Figure 3. Evaluation plan (left) and corresponding reconstruction plan (right).

be evaluated more efficiently is called *(bottom-up) diagnosis optimization*. The expression resulting at the end of each step of the diagnosis optimization process is called *evaluation plan*.

Example 4. An evaluation plan obtained by progressively transforming the right-hand side of (**??**) is

$$(\sigma_{OBS(\xi_{12})}((A_1 \oplus_{OBS(\xi_1)} A_2) \oplus (A_2 \oplus_{OBS(\xi_2)} A_3)))\oplus_{OBS(\Theta)}$$
$$(((\sigma_{OBS(C_4)}(A_4) \oplus_{OBS(\xi_3)} \sigma_{OBS(C_5)}(A_5)) \oplus_{OBS(\xi_{34})} (\sigma_{OBS(C_5)}(A_5) \oplus A_6))) \tag{22}$$

where each cluster ξ_k is displayed in Figure 1, and each cluster ξ_{ij} denotes the unions $\xi_i \cup \xi_j$. Pictorially, an evaluation plan obtained by transforming the canonical expression is represented as a tree, where leaf nodes are atomic active spaces, while internal nodes are marked by active-algebra operators. Shown on the left of Figure 3 is the evaluation plan algebraically expressed by (**??**) relevant to a diagnosis problem $\wp(\Theta)$ of the system displayed in Figure 1. Leaf nodes are marked by the atomic active spaces $A_1, \ldots, A_6$.

The evaluation plan is then transformed into a *reconstruction plan* by means of a factorization criterion. This means that the evaluation plan, which is a tree, is transformed into a graph by factorizing all identical subtrees.

Example 5. Notice that both A_2 and $\sigma_{OBS(C_5)}(A_5)$ of the evaluation plan have been factorized in the corresponding reconstruction plan, shown on the right-hand side of Figure 3, where internal nodes are identified by numbers $7 \cdots 16$.

The reconstruction plan represents a possible way for performing the construction process. Such a process starts from the leaves and proceeds upward to the root. The reconstruction step inherent to a node takes as input the active spaces resulting from the reconstructions of its child nodes. The estimation of the cost of the relevant algebraic expression corresponds to the estimation of the computational cost of the whole reconstruction process in case it would be based on the derived reconstruction plan. The factorization of the evaluation plan is necessary for reducing the computational cost of the reconstruction process. In fact, if in the reconstruction plan there is no repetition of the same subtree, the reconstruction based on each (sub)tree is performed just once. This kind of factorization cannot be achieved at the algebraic level.

The observations of a cluster ξ in Θ can be obtained by restricting $OBS(\Theta)$ on ξ.

Example 6. Shown on the right-hand side of Figure 2 is the restriction of the view graph $\gamma_2(\Theta)$ on cluster ξ_3, denoted by $\gamma_{2\langle\xi_3\rangle}(\Theta)$. Accordingly, node N_1 is missing in the restriction, as the corresponding message is relevant to C_6, which is not in ξ_3. Besides, N_4 has been restricted into $N_{4'}$, where message d is now relevant to C_4 only and the null label ϵ has been added. The rationale behind the additional null label is that we do not know which component actually generated d. Thus, if such a component is C_2, in the context of ξ_3 no observable label has to be accounted for.

The reconstruction plan can be processed in several different ways, called *(reconstruction) plan instances*, determined by the order in which the operations corresponding to the nodes of the reconstruction plan terminate their processing.

Some of the concepts informally introduced above are formalized below.

Definition 5. (*Reconstruction plan*) Limiting our attention to bottom-up diagnosis optimization, an *evaluation plan* $\mathbf{E}(\wp(\Theta))$ is an active-algebra expression obtained, via equivalence rules, from the canonical expression inherent to a diagnosis problem $\wp(\Theta)$. A *reconstruction plan* $\mathcal{P}$ of $\wp(\Theta)$ is the DAG

$$\mathcal{P} = (\mathbb{N}, \Upsilon, N_0, \mathbb{N}_f) \tag{23}$$

such that $\mathbb{N}$ is the set of nodes, $\Upsilon : \mathbb{N} \mapsto 2^{\mathbb{N}}$ the set of edges, $N_0 \in \mathbb{N}$ the *root*, and $\mathbb{N}_f \subseteq \mathbb{N}$ the set of *leaves*, obtained by factorizing common sub-expressions in the tree of $\mathbf{E}(\wp(\Theta))$.

An *instance* $\widehat{\mathcal{P}}$ of $\mathcal{P}$ is a sequence $\langle N_1, \ldots, N_p \rangle$, where:

(a) $\{N_1, \ldots, N_p\} = \mathbb{N} - \mathbb{N}_f$;

(b) $\forall i \in [2 .. p], \forall N_i \mapsto N_j \in \Upsilon \; (N_j \in \{N_1, \ldots, N_{i-1}\})$. □

7. Stepwise Diagnosis-generation

When the system to be diagnoses is large and distributed, it may take a long time to complete the diagnosis process, even when the task is performed in parallel by different processing units. Therefore, it is of paramount importance providing some intermediate output, even if it embodies spurious candidate diagnoses (that is, candidates that are not part of the final diagnosis verdict).

Requirement 6. *Upon the completion of some processing units, the DMBD process updates the current set of candidate diagnoses.*

Based on this requirement, the set of candidate diagnoses is expected to be given incrementally, rather than in one shot at the end of the processing. In previous work, we introduced two concepts of diagnosis, namely *shallow* and *deep*, each featuring a different abstraction level. Besides, each reconstructed history of the considered system is an *explanatory diagnosis* [?]. In this chapter, the stepwise diagnosis-generation requirement is considered only for shallow diagnosis, whose definition is reported below.

Definition 6. (*Shallow diagnosis*) Let A be an active space. A history $h \in \|A\|$ which incorporates a faulty transition is a *faulty history* and the relevant component, a *faulty component*. A *(shallow) diagnosis* relevant to A is the set of faulty components relevant to a history in $\|A\|$. The whole set of diagnoses relevant to the histories in $\|A\|$ is the *diagnosis set* of A, denoted by $\Delta(A)$. $\qquad\qquad\square$

The fulfillment of the above requirement for shallow diagnosis is achieved by means of a completeness-based approach, where the diagnosis output is refined at each processing point by eliminating a subset of spurious candidate diagnoses. A processing point corresponds to the termination of the computation pertinent to a node of the reconstruction plan. At each processing point, a complete (but in general not sound) set of candidate diagnoses, called *diagnosis snapshot*, is output. The sequence of diagnosis snapshots gives rise to a *diagnosis evolution*, which terminates in a complete and sound set of candidate diagnoses.

Since each node N in a plan instance $\mathcal{P}$ is associated with the corresponding active space (fulfilling the specifications of the active-algebra operator placed in that node of the reconstruction plan), we can denote the relevant diagnosis set as $\Delta(N)$.

Definition 7. (*Diagnostic evolution*) Let $\widehat{\mathcal{P}} = \langle N_1, \dots, N_p \rangle$ be an instance of a reconstruction plan $\mathcal{P}$. The *processing point* $\widehat{\mathcal{P}}(i)$ of $\widehat{\mathcal{P}}$, $i \in [0..p]$, is the set of nodes defined as follows:

$$\widehat{\mathcal{P}}(i) \stackrel{\text{def}}{=} \begin{cases} \mathbb{N}_f & \text{if } i = 0 \\ \{N_1, \dots, N_i\} & \text{otherwise} \end{cases} \qquad (24)$$

The *frontier* of $\widehat{\mathcal{P}}(i)$, $Front(\widehat{\mathcal{P}}(i))$, is defined as follows:

$$Front(\widehat{\mathcal{P}}(i)) \stackrel{\text{def}}{=} \{N \mid N \in (\widehat{\mathcal{P}}(i) \cup \mathbb{N}_f), \nexists N'(N' \in \widehat{\mathcal{P}}(i), N' \mapsto N \in \Upsilon)\} \qquad (25)$$

The *diagnosis snapshot* $\mathbf{D}$ relevant to a processing point $\widehat{\mathcal{P}}(i)$, $\mathbf{D}(\widehat{\mathcal{P}}(i))$, is the set of diagnoses defined as follows:

$$\mathbf{D}(\widehat{\mathcal{P}}(i)) \stackrel{\text{def}}{=} \biguplus_{N \in Front(\widehat{\mathcal{P}}(i))} \Delta(N) \qquad (26)$$

where $\uplus$ is the *aggregation* operator, defined as follows. Let Δ_1 and Δ_2 be two diagnosis sets relevant to active spaces A_1 and A_2, respectively. Let $\mathbb{C}_1$ and $\mathbb{C}_2$ be the set of components in the clusters relevant to A_1 and A_2, respectively, and $\mathbb{C}_{12}$ denote the intersection $\mathbb{C}_1 \cap \mathbb{C}_2$. Then:

$$\Delta_1 \uplus \Delta_2 \stackrel{\text{def}}{=} \{\delta \mid \delta = \delta_1 \cup \delta_2, (\delta_1, \delta_2) \in (\Delta_1 \times \Delta_2), (\delta_1 \cap \mathbb{C}_{12}) = (\delta_2 \cap \mathbb{C}_{12})\} \qquad (27)$$

The *diagnosis evolution* $\mathbb{D}$ relevant to a plan instance $\widehat{\mathcal{P}}$, $\mathbb{D}(\widehat{\mathcal{P}})$, is the sequence of diagnosis snapshots relevant to the sequence of processing points $\widehat{\mathcal{P}}(i)$:

$$\mathbb{D}(\widehat{\mathcal{P}}) \stackrel{\text{def}}{=} \langle \mathbf{D}(\widehat{\mathcal{P}}(0)), \mathbf{D}(\widehat{\mathcal{P}}(1)), \dots, \mathbf{D}(\widehat{\mathcal{P}}(p)) \rangle \qquad (28)$$

$\qquad\qquad\square$

Table 1. Diagnostic sets relevant to nodes of the reconstruction plan displayed in Figure 3

N	$\Delta(N)$
N_1	$\emptyset, \{C_1\}$
N_2	$\{C_2\}$
N_3	$\emptyset, \{C_3\}$
N_4	$\emptyset, \{C_4\}$
N_5	$\emptyset$
N_6	$\{C_6\}$
N_7	$\{C_2\}, \{C_1, C_2\}$
N_8	$\{C_2\}$
N_9	$\{C_4\}$
N_{10}	$\emptyset$
N_{11}	$\{C_2\}$
N_{12}	$\{C_4\}$
N_{13}	$\{C_6\}$
N_{14}	$\{C_2\}$
N_{15}	$\{C_4, C_6\}$
N_{16}	$\{C_2, C_4, C_6\}$

Proposition 1. (Diagnostic relationships) *Let A denote an active space and $\Delta(A)$ the relevant diagnosis set. Then, the following relationships hold:*

$$\Delta(A_1 \cup A_2) = \Delta(A_1) \cup \Delta(A_2) \tag{29}$$

$$\Delta(A_1 \cap A_2) \subseteq \Delta(A_1) \cap \Delta(A_2) \tag{30}$$

$$\Delta(A_1 - A_2) \subseteq \Delta(A_1) \tag{31}$$

$$\Delta(\pi_{\xi'}(A)) = \pi_{\xi'}(\Delta(A)) \tag{32}$$

$$\Delta(\sigma_{OBS(\xi)}(A)) \subseteq \Delta(A) \tag{33}$$

$$\Delta(A_1 \oplus A_2) \subseteq \Delta(A_1) \uplus \Delta(A_2) \tag{34}$$

$$\Delta(A_1 \oplus_{OBS(\xi)} A_2) \subseteq \Delta(A_1) \uplus \Delta(A_2) \tag{35}$$

$$\Delta(\oplus(A_1, \ldots, A_n)) \subseteq \Delta(A_1) \uplus \cdots \uplus \Delta(A_n) \tag{36}$$

$$\Delta(\oplus_{OBS(\xi)}(A_1, \ldots, A_n)) \subseteq \Delta(A_1) \uplus \cdots \uplus \Delta(A_n). \tag{37}$$

Proposition 2. (Monotonic convergence) *Let $\wp(\Theta)$ be a diagnosis problem and Δ the diagnosis set corresponding to the active space yielded by the canonical expression relevant to $\wp(\Theta)$. Let $\widehat{\mathcal{P}} = \langle N_1, \ldots, N_p \rangle$ be an instance of a reconstruction plan $\mathcal{P}(\wp(\Theta))$. Then, the diagnosis evolution $\mathbb{D}(\widehat{\mathcal{P}})$ converges monotonically to Δ:*

$$\mathbf{D}(\widehat{\mathcal{P}}(0)) \supseteq \mathbf{D}(\widehat{\mathcal{P}}(1)) \supseteq \cdots \supseteq \mathbf{D}(\widehat{\mathcal{P}}(p-1)) \supseteq \mathbf{D}(\widehat{\mathcal{P}}(p)) = \Delta. \tag{38}$$

Example 7. Considering the reconstruction plan $\mathcal{P}$ shown on the right of Figure 3 as the basis for reconstruction, we assume the plan instance $\widehat{\mathcal{P}} = \langle N_9, N_{10}, N_7, N_8, N_{11}, N_{13},$

$N_{12}, N_{14}, N_{15}, N_{16}\rangle$. At each processing point, after performing the reconstruction inherent to the relevant node of $\mathcal{P}$, the diagnosis set for such a node of $\mathcal{P}$ is generated: we assume results for all the nodes of $\mathcal{P}$ be outlined in Table 1.

Table 2. Diagnostic evolution

i	$Front(\widehat{\mathcal{P}}(i))$	$\mathbf{D}(\widehat{\mathcal{P}}(i))$
0	$\{N_1, N_2, N_3, N_4, N_5, N_6\}$	$26, 246, 236, 2346, 126, 1246, 1236, 12346$
1	$\{N_1, N_2, N_3, N_5, N_6, N_9\}$	$246, 2346, 1246, 12346$
2	$\{N_1, N_2, N_3, N_6, N_9, N_{10}\}$	$246, 2346, 1246, 12346$
3	$\{N_3, N_6, N_7, N_9, N_{10}\}$	$246, 2346, 1246, 12346$
4	$\{N_6, N_7, N_8, N_9, N_{10}\}$	$246, 1246$
5	$\{N_6, N_9, N_{10}, N_{11}\}$	246
6	$\{N_9, N_{11}, N_{13}\}$	246
7	$\{N_{11}, N_{12}, N_{13}\}$	246
8	$\{N_{12}, N_{13}, N_{14}\}$	246
9	$\{N_{14}, N_{15}\}$	246
10	$\{N_{16}\}$	246

The diagnosis evolution $\mathbf{D}(\widehat{\mathcal{P}})$ is shown in Table 2, where for each index i of the instance plan, both the relevant frontier $Front(\widehat{\mathcal{P}}(i))$ and diagnosis snapshot $\mathbf{D}(\widehat{\mathcal{P}}(i))$ are given (diagnoses are represented concisely as strings of numbers, for example, 246 is a shorthand for $\{C_2, C_4, C_6\}$). At processing point $\widehat{\mathcal{P}}(0))$ atomic active spaces are considered; in particular, $N_i, \forall i \in [1..6]$, represents the leaf node of the reconstruction plan whose atomic active space is A_i.

It is worthwhile considering a computation of the aggregation operator $\uplus$. For example, the diagnosis snapshot corresponding to the processing point $\widehat{\mathcal{P}}(3)$, which is inherent to node N_7 of $\mathcal{P}$, consists of four diagnoses, namely $\{C_2, C_4, C_6\}$, $\{C_2, C_3, C_4, C_6\}$, $\{C_1, C_2, C_4, C_6\}$, and $\{C_1, C_2, C_3, C_4, C_6\}$. According to Definition **??**, the next diagnosis snapshot is calculated as follows:

$$\mathbf{D}(\widehat{\mathcal{P}}(4)) = \Delta(N_6) \uplus \Delta(N_7) \uplus \Delta(N_8) \uplus \Delta(N_9) \uplus \Delta(N_{10}). \tag{39}$$

However, since ξ_1 and ξ_2 share component C_2, we have to remove from the Cartesian product of $\Delta(N_7)$ and $\Delta(N_8)$ those pairs that do not share the same intersection with $\{C_2\}$, in other words, those pairs in which an element includes C_2 and the other does not. Thus, we have:

$$\Delta(N_7) \times \Delta(N_8) = \{(\{C_2\}, \emptyset), (\{C_2\}, \{C_2\}), (\{C_1, C_2\}, \emptyset), (\{C_1, C_2\}, \{C_2\})\} \tag{40}$$
$$\Delta(N_7) \uplus \Delta(N_8) = \{\{C_2\}, \{C_1, C_2\}\}. \tag{41}$$

Finally, notice that, if we are interested only in the final shallow diagnosis rather than in the whole reconstruction of the system behavior, the diagnosis task may stop at processing point $\widehat{\mathcal{P}}(5)$, as, incidentally, the diagnosis snapshot corresponds to a singleton. This example shows that stepwise shallow diagnosis depends on reconstruction scheduling; in fact, the process for obtaining the final diagnosis is more efficient if $\widehat{\mathcal{P}}(2)$ is skipped.

8. Related Work

In recent contributions to model-based diagnosis of DESs, terms such as 'distributed', 'decentralized', 'modular' and 'incremental' appear very often. Typically, *distributed* [?, ?] refers to the abstraction of the system to be diagnosed, just meaning that it supports compositional modeling. Instead, *decentralized* is used with multiple meanings: for referring either to the processing architecture [?], or to the observation [?], or to the diagnostic method [?]. Finally, in [?] *modular* refers to the diagnostic method, which is decomposed in subtasks, while *incremental* refers to the task decomposition strategy. The use of these terms, all related, either directly or indirectly, to the notion of distribution, denote several heterogeneous progressive attempts to underpin some major features and requirements of DMBD. Several other approaches somehow related to DMBD have been proposed, including [?, ?, ?, ?, ?, ?, ?, ?, ?]. By now the awareness has grown that, in order to cope with DESs, it is not enough to model them as composite systems, as done by most approaches, it is also necessary to process them in a way which is not monolithic. Moreover, it has been realized that, in the real world, the available observation of a given system usually is gathered by several observers. However, sometimes the concept of observer and that of processing site within a hardware architecture are mixed up: that is, a processing site carries out a diagnosis (according to a given diagnosing method) based on the observation of a single observer. What is highlighted here is that the concepts of system, observer, diagnosing method, and processing architecture are independent from one another and, therefore, the requirements of DMBD inherent to these concepts are orthogonal. Indeed, based on the principles stated in this paper, diagnosis may be distributed independently from the processing architecture. According to the given definition, making a DMBD basically means taking as input a distributed (i.e. compositionally modeled) system and processing it in a distributed (i.e. decomposed) way based on a distributed (i.e. gathered by multiple observers) observation. Moreover, a DMBD is general if the adopted notion of observation allows for the representation of uncertainty, and processing optimization criteria are exploited, and, at any processing point, a set of candidate diagnoses, meeting some constraints, is available.

9. Conclusion

This chapter has introduced the notion of DMBD by substantiating six stated requirements in the domain of active systems. Systems are distributed in nature, each of them being watched by several observers. Observations are sets of uncertain views taken by distinct observers. The diagnosis process is virtually distributed over several processing units and amenable to parallelism. Optimization criteria are envisaged to cope with the complexity of the main diagnosis step, the reconstruction of the system behavior. To this end, a special-purpose algebra has been introduced and relevant equivalence rules have been formulated. Candidate diagnoses are generated incrementally as a sequence of diagnosis snapshots, corresponding to subsequent processing points. The notion of DMBD can be easily instantiated in the broader domain of discrete-event systems and offers a conceptual platform for DMBD of general dynamic systems [?]. On the other hand, further work is required in order to provide heuristic and/or cost-based algebraic techniques for the automatic generation of the optimized reconstruction plan, and methods for adaptive run-time reconstruction scheduling, which are the real challenges of DMBD of active systems.

References

[1] A. Aghasaryan, E. Fabre, A. Benveniste, B. Boubour, and C. Jard. Fault detection and diagnosis in distributed systems: an approach by partially stochastic Petri nets. *Journal of Discrete Event Dynamical Systems: Theory and Application*, August:203–231, 1998.

[2] P. Baroni, G. Lamperti, P. Pogliano, and M. Zanella. Diagnosis of active systems. In *Thirteenth European Conference on Artificial Intelligence – ECAI'98*, pages 274–278, Brighton, UK, 1998.

[3] P. Baroni, G. Lamperti, P. Pogliano, and M. Zanella. Diagnosis of large active systems. *Artificial Intelligence*, **110**(1):135–183, 1999.

[4] P. Baroni, G. Lamperti, P. Pogliano, and M. Zanella. Diagnosis of a class of distributed discrete-event systems. *IEEE Transactions on Systems, Man, and Cybernetics – Part A: Systems and Humans*, **30**(6):731–752, 2000.

[5] R. Debouk, S. Lafortune, and D. Teneketzis. Coordinated decentralized protocols for failure diagnosis of discrete-event systems. *Journal of Discrete Event Dynamic Systems: Theory and Applications*, **10**:33–86, 2000.

[6] R. Debouk, S. Lafortune, and D. Teneketzis. A diagnostic protocol for discrete-event systems with decentralized information. In *Eleventh International Workshop on Principles of Diagnosis – DX'00*, pages 41–48, Morelia, MX, 2000.

[7] R. Debouk, S. Lafortune, and D. Teneketzis. On the effect of communication delays in failure diagnosis of decentralized discrete event systems. *Journal of Discrete Event Dynamic Systems: Theory and Applications*, **13**:263–289, 2003.

[8] E. Fabre, A. Benveniste, S. Haar, and C. Jard. Distributed monitoring of concurrent and asynchronous systems. *Journal of Discrete Event Dynamic Systems*, **15**(1):33–84, 2005.

[9] A. Grastien, M.O. Cordier, and C. Largouët. Extending decentralized discrete-event modelling to diagnose reconfigurable systems. In *Fifteenth International Workshop on Principles of Diagnosis –DX'04*, pages 75–80, Carcassonne, F, 2004.

[10] G. Lamperti, P. Pogliano, and M. Zanella. Modular diagnosis of distributed discrete-event systems by incremental clusterization techniques. In *International Conference on Control and Modeling of Complex Systems*, pages 12–20, Samara, Russia, 1999.

[11] G. Lamperti and M. Zanella. Uncertain discrete-event observations. In *Eleventh International Workshop on Principles of Diagnosis – DX'00*, pages 101–108, Morelia, MX, 2000.

[12] G. Lamperti and M. Zanella. Uncertain temporal observations in diagnosis. In *Fourteenth European Conference on Artificial Intelligence – ECAI'2000*, pages 151–155, Berlin, D, 2000. IOS Press, Amsterdam, NL.

[13] G. Lamperti and M. Zanella. Diagnosis of discrete-event systems from uncertain temporal observations. *Artificial Intelligence*, 137(1–2):91–163, 2002.

[14] G. Lamperti and M. Zanella. *Diagnosis of Active Systems – Principles and Techniques*, volume 741 of *The Kluwer International Series in Engineering and Computer Science*. Kluwer Academic Publisher, Dordrecht, NL, 2003.

[15] G. Lamperti and M. Zanella. A bridged diagnostic method for the monitoring of polymorphic discrete-event systems. *IEEE Transactions on Systems, Man, and Cybernetics – Part B: Cybernetics*, 34(5):2222–2244, 2004.

[16] G. Lamperti and M. Zanella. Flexible diagnosis of discrete-event systems by similarity-based reasoning techniques. *Artificial Intelligence*, 170(3):232–297, 2006.

[17] G. Lamperti and M. Zanella. Reactive diagnosis of active systems. *International Journal of Computer Research*, 18(1), 2010.

[18] S.A. McIlraith. Explanatory diagnosis: conjecturing actions to explain observations. In *Sixth International Conference on Principles of Knowledge Representation and Reasoning – KR'98*, pages 167–177, Trento, I, 1998. Morgan Kaufmann, S. Francisco, CA.

[19] Y. Pencolé. Decentralized diagnoser approach: application to telecommunication networks. In *Eleventh International Workshop on Principles of Diagnosis – DX'00*, pages 185–192, Morelia, MX, 2000.

[20] Y. Pencolé. Diagnosability analysis of distributed discrete event systems. In *Sixteenth European Conference on Artificial Intelligence –ECAI'2004*, pages 43–47, Valencia, E, 2004.

[21] Y. Pencolé and M.O. Cordier. A formal framework for the decentralized diagnosis of large scale discrete event systems and its application to telecommunication networks. *Artificial Intelligence*, 164:121–170, 2005.

[22] W. Qiu and R. Kumar. Decentralized failure diagnosis of discrete event systems. *IEEE Transactions on Systems, Man, and Cybernetics – Part A: Systems and Humans*, 36(2):384–395, 2006.

[23] L. Rozé. Supervision of telecommunication network: a diagnoser approach. In *Eighth International Workshop on Principles of Diagnosis – DX'97*, pages 103–111, Mont St. Michel, F, 1997.

[24] M. Sampath, R. Sengupta, S. Lafortune, K. Sinnamohideen, and D.C. Teneketzis. Failure diagnosis using discrete-event models. *IEEE Transactions on Control Systems Technology*, 4(2):105–124, 1996.

[25] A. Silberschatz, H. Korth, and S. Sudarshan. *Database System Concepts*. McGraw-Hill, 1998.

[26] P. Struss. Fundamentals of model-based diagnosis of dynamic systems. In *Fifteenth International Joint Conference on Artificial Intelligence – IJCAI'97*, pages 480–485, Nagoya, J, 1997. Morgan Kaufmann, S. Francisco, CA.

[27] R. Su and W.M. Wonham. Global and local consistencies in distributed fault diagnosis for discrete-event systems. *IEEE Transactions on Automatic Control*, **50**(12):1923–1935, 2005.

[28] L. Ye, P. Dague, and Y. Yan. A distributed approach for pattern diagnosability. In *20th International Workshop on Principles of Diagnosis – DX'09*, pages 179–186, Stockholm, S, 2009.

In: Horizons in Computer Science Research, Volume 4   ISBN: 978-1-61324-262-9
Editors: Thomas S. Clary   © 2011 Nova Science Publishers, Inc.

Chapter 14

CRYPTOGRAPHIC PUZZLES AND GAME THEORY AGAINST DoS AND DDoS ATTACKS IN NETWORKS

Antonis Michalas[1], *Nikos Komninos*[1] *and Neeli R. Prasad*[2]
[1]Athens Information Technology, GR-19002 Peania (Athens), Greece
[2]Aalborg University, DK-9220, Aalborg, Denmark

Abstract

In this chapter, we present techniques to defeat Denial of Service (DoS) and Distributed Denial of Service (DDoS) attacks. In the first part, we describe client puzzle techniques that are based on the idea of computationally exhausting a malicious user when he attempts to launch an attack. In the second part we are introducing some basic principles of game theory and we discuss how game theoretical frameworks can protect computer networks. Finally, we show techniques that combine client puzzles with game theory in order to provide DoS and DDoS resilience.

1. Introduction

Imagine a situation where Bob calls to a restaurant and make a reservation for four people in the name of $Mr.X$. After a while he calls again and make a new reservation for 5 persons in the name of $Mr.Y$. Lets assume that he keeps calling to the restaurant and making fake reservations until all the tables of the restaurant are booked. The result of that is that if Alice (a legitimate use) wants to go and eat to that particular restaurant she could not book a table since Bob have booked them all. So Alice would not be able to use the service that the restaurant offers to its clients. More precise Alice and every other legitimate customer would face a Denial of Service Attack (DoS).

Denial of Service attacks is considered to be one of the most important threats as well as one of the hardest problems in computer security nowadays. The main aim of a DoS attack is the interruption of services by attempting to limit access to a machine or service instead of subverting the service itself. This kind of attack aims at rendering a network incapable of providing normal service by targeting either the networks bandwidth or its connectivity. These attacks achieve their goal by sending at a victim a stream of packets that swamps his network or processing capacity denying access to his regular clients.

Protection against DoS attacks is a crucial component of any security system. While DoS has been studied extensively for the wired networks, there is lack of research for preventing such attacks in ad hoc networks. Because devices like PDA's and mobile phones have limited resources, like battery life and memory, the techniques that are implemented in wired networks are not suitable for ad hoc networks. Due to deployment in tactical battlefield missions these networks are susceptible to attacks of malicious intruders. These intruders might attempt to disrupt/degrade the performance of the whole network or may harm a specific node. Traditional DoS attacks involve overwhelming a particular host. However, in ad hoc networks, mobility, limited bandwidth, routing functionalities associated with each node, etc, resent many new opportunities for launching a DoS attack. These attacks might be at the routing layer or at the MAC layer [14].

The improvement of DoS attack is the so called Distributed Denial of Service (DDoS) attack. In the past years we saw lot of popular sites such as Yahoo, eBay, Amazon, CNN and many more to be under such attacks. DDoS attacks present a significant security threat to corporations, and the threat appears to be growing [26]. In the sixth of August (2009) the Social Networks world was under attack, in other words, we were in the middle of a planned attempt to take down two of the world's most popular social media sites: Facebook and Twitter. Even though that no user data was at risk, the sites were down for several hours. Distributed Denial of Service, is a relatively simple, yet very powerful technique to attack Internet resources. DDoS attacks add the many - to - one dimension to the denial of service (DoS) problem making the prevention and mitigation of such attacks more difficult and the impact proportionally severe. DDoS exploits the intrinsic weakness of the Internet system architecture, its open resource access model, which paradoxically, also happens to be its greatest advantage [9].

A solution to those threats is to authenticate the client before the server commits any resources to it. A technique that is mainly used is based on *Cryptographic Puzzles* which proposed by Merkle [20] to relay secret information between parties over an insecure channel. Client puzzles, a type of cryptographic puzzle, have been proposed by Juels and Brainard in [16] to defend a server against DoS attacks. The idea behind client puzzles is that each node in a network will be asked to first solve a puzzle, which is in fact a computational problem, and if the solution of the puzzle is the expected one then and only then this node will be served.

This chapter is organized in three parts. In Section 2. we describe client puzzle techniques that provide DoS and DDoS resistance. In Section 3. we first describe some basic concepts of game theory like how a game is mathematically defined etc and then we show how game theory is related with the network security and we also present some techniques that already exists. In Section 4. we describe game theoretics frameworks that have been proposed with main aim to defeat DoS and DDoS attacks. Finally we conclude in Section 5. by making a brief overview of the chapter.

2.   Client Puzzles

In the 1970's Diffe, Hellman, and Merkle began to challenge the accepted wisdom that two parties cannot communicate confidentially over an open channel without first exchanging a secret key using some secure means [5]. The original idea of cryptographic puzzles

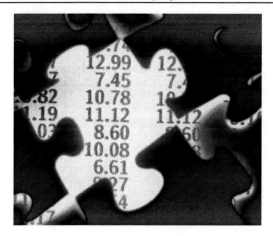

Figure 1. Puzzle.

belongs to Merkle who in 1974 constructed the first cryptosystem which introduces general concept of the public key cryptography. Merkle's protocol allows two parties Alice and Bob to agree on a random number k that will not be known to an eavesdropping adversary Eve [5]. However, Merkle used puzzles for key agreement, rather than access control. Based on cryptographic puzzles, Juels and Brainard proposed *Client Puzzles* [16] as a solution to defeat DoS attacks.

The basic idea behind client puzzles is to force the client to solve a computational problem such as the Discrete Logarithm Problem (see section 2.2.5.) before attending to a request. With this way the server ensures that the client spends sufficient resources before committing its own while at the same time exhausts attackers resources when they attempt to launch an attack.

Client Puzzles are divided into two categories. The CPU-bound puzzles and the MEMORY-bound puzzles. In the first case the client is required to perform a number of computations while in the second case the client is asked to search for specific information that is stored in the memory. A general idea of how a client puzzle protocol works is show in Figure 2.

2.1. Client Puzzle Properties

To prevent DoS attacks, each client puzzle needs to meet the following properties:

- Granularity represents the ability of the server to finely and easily adjust puzzle difficulty to different levels.

- Server's Cost must be efficient and significantly less expensive than the computational cost employed by the client in solving the puzzle. This property is divided into three subcategories. *Pre-Computation Cost*, *Construction Cost* and *Verification Cost*.

- Pre-computing puzzle solutions should be infeasible.

- If a client has solved previous puzzles will not have any advantage in comparison with other clients.

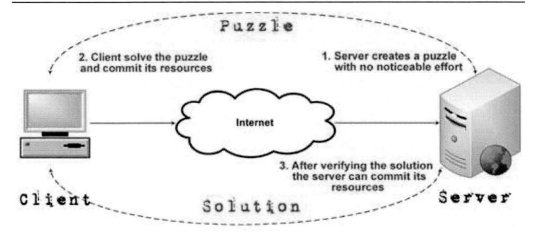

Figure 2. Simplified Client Puzzle Protocol.

In addition, Feng proposed in [12] three more properties that client puzzles should meet.

- The server should be able to successfully handle multiple requests at the same time. This means that the server will be able to generate multiple different puzzles (one for each request) without being flooded by the attacker(s).

- When a client receives a puzzle, should not be able to bypass the puzzle mechanism.

- The server should be able to generate puzzles with different difficulty, depending on the clients hardware. For example a PDA will receive an easier puzzle in comparison with a laptop.

2.2.   CPU-bound Puzzles

CPU-bound puzzles, are based on an amount of computational effort that each client has to do in order to solve the puzzle and therefore get access to the requested resource. Each puzzle has a level of difficulty. As the difficulty level of the puzzle is increasing, the computations that the client should do in order to find the solution are also increasing. In this section we will describe some of the most well known CPU-bound puzzles.

2.2.1.   Hash Reversal Puzzles:

Puzzles of this category, are based on *Cryptographic Hash Functions*[1], in which the client is requested to reverse a hash function. Reversing a hash function is computational hard and thus this technique by its own it would be inappropriate, since the clients of the network would need much time and resources in order to be served. A solution to this problem is to ask from clients to reverse only a part of the hash.

The main idea behind this technique is that the server generates hashes from which erase k $bits$. The client has to perform a brute force search on the erased bits by hashing

---

[1]From now on we will refer to Cryptographic Hash Function(s) as hash function(s).

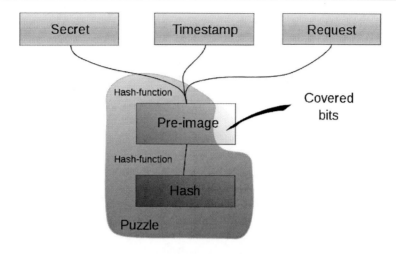

Figure 3. Client Puzzle Generation.

each pattern in the space, until it finds the remaining $k\ bits$. It is clear that the difficulty of these puzzles is increasing along with the erased bits.

More precise, the client solves X from the following equation:

$$H(params, X) = \overbrace{000\cdots000}^{first\ k\ bits}\ \underbrace{Y}_{rest\ bits} \tag{1}$$

This approach requires two hash operations. One at puzzle construction and one at the verification step. Apart from that the solution of the puzzle can be computed in parallel by multiple clients. This is a serious flaw since an attacker will probably compromise a number of other nodes in the network so as to work for him/her. Furthermore this technique has a lack of hardness granularity since the difficulty is increasing exponential.

2.2.2. Parallel Hash Puzzle

Juels and Brainard in [16] proposed an improvement of the previous mentioned technique in order to achieve better hardness granularity. More precise they proposed to use multiple hash puzzles in parallel where the client is responsible to find the missing bits of a pre-image of a hash function whose output is given. In other words, given part of h_1 and all h_2, find the missing bits of h_1 such that $h_2 = H(h_1)$, where H is a hash function. A graphical representation for the generation of such puzzles can be found in Figure 3

This scheme is basically the same as the previous one with the difference that the client has to solve more puzzles. This means that the number of required computations are multiplied by the number of puzzles that a client receives while the level of difficulty is the sum of the difficulty of each puzzle that the client needs to solve.

2.2.3. Hint-Based Puzzle

Feng *et al.* proposed in [7] some modifications to existing puzzle protocols that allow them to work on the network layer. They suggested that the server along with the puzzle would also provide the client with a range in which the solution of the puzzle would be. With this technique, the client would have to make exhaustive search only within the specified range.

The main difference with the hash reversal puzzle is the fact that the difficulty of the puzzle has become linear due to the limited range that the client has to search for the solution.

2.2.4. Chained Hash Puzzle

In [13] Groza and Petrica introduced the concept of chained cryptographic puzzle. They defined two kinds of chained puzzle constructions: linearly chained puzzles and randomly chained puzzles. The first construction prove to be very useful in some scenarios, from which the more general is in which a client may choose to solve only some of the puzzles that were sent by the server and gain resources from the server according to the amount of puzzles that he solved. Linearly chained puzzles offers more flexibility to the client since he may choose to solve only some of the puzzles that were sent by the server and gain resources according to the amount of puzzles that he solved.

Two hash operations must take place in order for the construction of the first puzzle while the rest of the puzzles in the chain require three hash operations. Each step in the chain depends on the solution of the previous step, however clients can still work together to speed up each individual step. Hardness granularity for this scheme follows the same line as for parallel hash puzzles [15].

2.2.5. Discrete Logarithm Puzzle

Waters *et al.* proposed in [27] a puzzle based on the discrete logarithm one way function. For the puzzle construction, server first generates a random prime number q and selects a generator g such that $g \in [2, q - 1]$. Then generates a random number x and calculates y from equation 2.

$$y = g^x mod\ q \tag{2}$$

At this step, server sends to client parameters y, g, q and then client is responsible to calculate x by brute forcing equation 2.

The DLP puzzle is computational expensive because of the modular exponentiation during the puzzle construction but the rest of the calculations are rather light. Apart from that, only a little storage space is needed and only one value should be stored for each new puzzle. Furthermore, the complexity is minimal as only three values needs to be sent in order to transmit the puzzle and only one to transmit the solution.

2.2.6. Subset Sum Puzzle

Tritilanunt *et al.* proposed in [25] to use the subset sum problem as a client puzzle. The subset sum problem is defined as follows:

Given a set of positive integers $S = \{a_1, a_2, \cdots, a_n\}$ and a positive integer s, determine whether or not there is a subset of the x_i that sums up to s. Equivalently, determine whether or not there exist $x_i \in \{0, 1\}$, $1 \le i \le n$ such that $\sum_{i=1}^{n} a_i x_i = s$

The creation and verification of the subset sum puzzle needs only one hash and a basic arithmetic operation while the complexity and the communication overhead of the scheme are minimal. Furthermore the subset sum problem is NP-complete while the computational version is NP-hard [19].

2.3. Memory-bound Puzzles

CPU-bound puzzles have been suggested as a defense mechanism against connection depletion attacks. However, the wide disparity in CPU speeds prevents such puzzles from being globally deployed. For example a system with many computational resources would solve such a puzzle really faster than a system with less resources. This problem can be addressed by using a different approach called memory-bound puzzles. This technique is based on memory usage and the client has to pre-compute a database of information, which will be used later in order to solve the puzzle. The client has to perform numerous queries to the database, and because the size of the database is large, memory handling should take place.

2.3.1. Function Look-up Puzzle

Abadi *et al.* proposed in [2] a way to speed up the reversing of a one-way function by using memory-bound computations. Many considerations may affect the acceptance of moderately hard functions, and of memory-bound functions in particular. The problems of large-scale deployment, such as software distribution and handling legacy systems, may be the most challenging.

2.3.2. Pattern Puzzle

Doshi *et al.* in [8] they further investigated the applicability of memory bound puzzles from a new perspective and proposed constructions based on heuristic search methods. Their constructions were derived from a more algorithmic foundation, and as a result, they managed to easily tune parameters that impact puzzle creation and verification costs. Moreover, unlike prior approaches, they addressed client-side costs and presented an extension that allows memory constrained clients to implement this construction in a secure fashion.

This approach is based on the sliding tile problem where there are several tiles on a grid that have to be set to a certain position and one blank space to slide to. Client is responsible for finding a particular (not necessarily optimal) path from a starting state to a goal state. Using pattern databases the computation time can be reduced by trading in memory. The grid must be large enough in order for not being stored in the cache memory.

Puzzle verification requires only one hash, light initial computations and a set of goal states that has to be created. This puzzle can be seen as game in which every move depends on the previous one and the client is forced to solve one layer at a time which means that different parts of the memory database should be used.

In general, game theory is a study of how to mathematically determine the best strategy for given conditions in order to optimize the outcome. While game theory was initially used in economics, it has been expanded to treat a wide class of fields such as politics, international negotiations, biology, military operations, networking, game programming,

Figure 4. Game Theory.

network security, sports and many more. In every case though, the main goal is the same: to analyze strategic interactions in which the outcome of one's choices depends upon the others choices. Furthermore, it assumes that all human interactions can be understood and navigated by presumptions.

In this paragraph we focus on how game theory can improve the security of networks. The communication between attackers and legitimate users is based on game theoretic models as a way to determine if a user is malicious or not and thus to protect the network from him. Network security involves decision making by both attackers and defenders in multiple levels and time scales using the limited resources available to them. Currently, most of these decisions are made instinctively and in an ad-hoc manner.

3.   Game Theory and Security

In such games, each node in the network is considered to be a player. Each player follows some strategies with main aim to win the game. The reward for winning the game usually is that this player's request will be served. The main idea behind security games is almost the same as with client puzzles. This is the allocation of resources from all players in the game. Each player will have to spend some resources in order to play the game but at the same time will have to find the best strategy in each case so as to win the game. Here is where the concept of *Optimum Strategy* and *Nash Equilibrium* are getting into the game.

3.1.   Types of Games & Basic Definitions

Before describing the types of games that we meet in game theory, we are going to give a mathematical definition and notation of games. Games are well defined objects with mathematical structure and in general they must have a set of players, a set of possible strategies for every player and a payoff for each combination strategies. Table 1 shows a list with all the elements that a game can have.

Definition 1. *An n-player ($P = \{P_1, P_2, \cdots, P_n\}$) normal game is defined as follows:*

$$\Gamma = (\{S_i\}_{i=1}^n, \{u_i\}_{i=1}^n) \tag{3}$$

Table 1. Elements of Games

Game Elements	Description
Players	Players of the game
Actions	The actions that a player can do.
Rules	States who can do what and when they can do it.
Strategies	A strategy is a plan of actions in each possible situations in the game.
Outcome	Possible results of the game.
Payoffs	The amount that the player wins or loses in a particular situation in a game.
Equilibria	A stable condition in which forces cancel one another

for each player P_i there is a set of possible actions (strategies) S_i and a utility function (payoffs) such that:

$$u_i : S_1 \times \cdots \times S_n \longmapsto \Re$$

Letting $S = S_1 \times \cdots \times S_n$, we refer to a tuple of actions: $s = (s_1, \cdots, s_n) \in S$ as an outcome. u_i of P_i expresses this player's preferences over outcome:

$$P_i \text{ prefers outcome } s \text{ to } s' \text{ iff} : u_i(s) > u_i(s').$$

Definition 2. *Let $\Gamma = (\{S_i\}_{i=1}^n, \{u_i\}_{i=1}^n)$ be a game presented in normal form and let $S = S_1 \times \cdots \times S_n$. A tuple $s = (s_1, \cdots, s_n) \in S$ is a Nash Equilibrium if for all i and for any $s_i' \in S$ it holds:*

$$u_i(s_i', s_i) \leq u_i(s) \tag{4}$$

Games studied in game theory are categorized in several ways: Whether an equilibrium strategy exists, whether players know other players' previous moves, whether players' decisions are simultaneous or sequential, and whether they are zero sum. Table 2 shows a pairwise list with the most popular categories of games.

3.1.1. Cooperative & Non-Cooperative Games

A cooperative game is one in which players are able to make enforceable contracts. Hence, it is not defined as games in which players actually do cooperate, but as games in

Table 2. Types of Games

Game Types		
Cooperative	**vs**	Non-Cooperative
Sequential	**vs**	Simultaneous
Single	**vs**	Repeated
Perfect Information	**vs**	Inperfect Information
Zero Sum	**vs**	Non-Zero sum

which any cooperation is enforceable by an outside party [1]. This kind of communication between the players is not possible in non-cooperative games. Furthermore, the sets of players are called coalitions and the game is a competition between coalitions and not between independent players.

Definition 3. *A coalition is simply a subset of the set of players which forms in order to coordinate strategies and to agree on how the total payoff is to be divided among the members.*

Lemma 1. *For every n players in a cooperative game, the the total number of coalitions is 2^n.*

Example: Let P be the set of players in a cooperative game. If we suppose that the number of players is 3 such that $P = \{P_1, P_2, P_3\}$ then based on the previous lemma, the number of coalitions for this game will be $2^3 = 8$.

- The empty coalition $\emptyset$

- $\{P_1\}$

- $\{P_2\}$

- $\{P_3\}$

- $\{P_1, P_2\}$

- $\{P_1, P_3\}$

- $\{P_2, P_3\}$

- The grand coalition $P = \{P_1, P_2, P_3\}$

Definition 4. *Given a coalition C the counter coalition is $C^c = \{P_i \in P : P_i \notin C\}$.*

3.1.2.   Sequential & Simultaneous Games

In sequential games, the player who made the last action has at least some knowledge about the actions that the previous player(s) made. In contrast, in simultaneous games players can do there movements in parallel and they are unaware of the actions that the rest of the players made before.

3.1.3. Single & Repeated Games

When a player acts in a given situation, he takes into account not only the implications of his actions for the current situation but also their implications for the future. If the players are patient and the current actions have significant implications for the future, then the considerations about the future may take over, and this may lead to a rich set of behavior that may seem to be irrational when one considers the current situation alone. Such ideas are captured in the repeated games, in which a "stage game" is played repeatedly. The stage game is repeated regardless of what has been played in the previous games. Furthermore, repeated games are considered to be extensive form games.[2]

3.1.4. Perfect & Inperfect Information

In perfect information games, all players in the game knows the moves of all other players that have been taken so far. A sequential game is one of perfect information if only one player moves at a time and if each player knows every action of the players that moved before him at every point. Technically, every information set contains exactly one node. Intuitively, if it is my turn to move, I always know what every other player has done up to now. All other games are games of imperfect information. [24]

3.1.5. Zero Sum & Non Zero Sum Games

In a zero-sum game the total benefit to all players in the game at the end is zero. Von Neumann and Oskar Morgenstern demonstrated mathematically that $n - person$ non-zero-sum game can be reduced to an $n + 1$ zero-sum game, and that such $n + 1$ person games can be generalized from the special case of the two-person zero-sum game. Von Neumann made a great contribution to game theory and especially to economics with the minimax theorem. This theorem says that in some zero sum games where there is perfect information for the players there exists one strategy for each player such that the lose of each player in the game will be minimal.

3.2. Secure Games

Network security can be seen as a game between administrators and attackers. Administrators try to protect there network from various attacks unlike attackers who try to find even a small security flaw in a system in order to successfully made an attack to it. As we mentioned before, game theory is a study of how to mathematically determine which is the optimum strategy so as to have the better outcome. This means that since an attack to a network is a game between the attacker and the administrator and each one of them "'play'" according to a set of strategies, game theory can provide models for defending computer networks against various attacks. In the beginning the defense of a network was based on the optimization of the defense resources of the network. Overtime, other methods of defense were implemented, where defensive mechanism can also predict the behavior of an

---

[2]A game in extensive form specifies the complete order of moves (along the direction of time), typically in a game tree, in addition to the complete list of payoffs and the available information at each point in time and under each contingency.

attacker. The elements that security games rely on are the same as the ones described in Table 1.

3.2.1. Intrution Detection Games

An intrusion-detection system (IDS) can be defined as a set of tools/mechanisms that can identify or sometimes even to predict a numerous of attacks in a network. Apart from that is in position of recognizing and reporting possible unauthorized access to the network. In general an IDS is a part of the security system of a network and it is not considered as a stand alone application.

Generally speaking, a game theoretic framework for an IDS takes part to the decisions that the system has to take in order for example to reallocate limited resources, or it can even help on redefining the security policies by given the severity attacks.

T. Alpcan and T. Basar in [4] presented a 2-player zero-sum stochastic (Markov) security game which models the interaction between malicious attackers to a system and the IDS who allocates system resources for detection and response. They captured the operation of a sensor network observing and reporting the attack information to the IDS as a finite Markov chain. Furthermore, they study limited information cases where players optimize their strategies offline or online depending on the type of information available, using methods based on Markov decision process and Q-learning.

In [22] Hadi Otrok *et al.* addresses the problem of increasing the effectiveness of an IDS for a cluster of nodes in ad hoc networks. To reduce the performance overhead of the IDS, a leader node is usually elected to handle the intrusion detection service on behalf of the whole cluster. However, most current solutions elect a leader randomly without considering the resource level of nodes. Such a solution will cause nodes with less remaining resources to die faster, reducing the overall lifetime of the cluster. It is also vulnerable to selfish nodes who do not provide services to others while at the same time benefiting from such services. Our experiments show that the presence of selfish nodes can significantly reduce the effectiveness of an IDS because less packets are inspected over time. To increase the effectiveness of an IDS in mobile ad hoc networks (MANET's), they proposed a unified framework that is able to:

1. Balance the resource consumption among all the nodes and thus increase the overall lifetime of a cluster by electing truthfully and efficiently the most cost-efficient node known as leader-IDS. A mechanism was designed using Vickrey, Clarke, and Groves (VCG) to achieve the desired goal.

2. Catch and punish a misbehaving leader through checkers that monitor the behavior of the leader. A cooperative game-theoretic model was proposed to analyze the interaction among checkers to reduce the false-positive rate. A multi-stage catch mechanism was also introduced to reduce the performance overhead of checkers.

3. Maximize the probability of detection for an elected leader to effectively execute the detection service. This was achieved by formulating a zero-sum non-cooperative game between the leader and intruder. The solution of the game was to find the Bayesian Nash Equilibrium where the leaders optimal detection strategy was determined.

Yu Liu *et al.* proposed in [17] game theoretic framework to analyze the interactions between pairs of attacking/defending nodes using a Bayesian formulation. Theye studied the achievable Nash equilibrium for the attacker/defender game in both static and dynamic scenarios. The dynamic Bayesian game is a more realistic model, since it allows the defender to consistently update his belief on his opponent's maliciousness as the game evolves. A new Bayesian hybrid detection approach was suggested for the defender, in which a lightweight monitoring system was used to estimate his opponent's actions, and a heavyweight monitoring system acts as a last resort of defense. Furthermore, they showed that the dynamic game produces energy-efficient monitoring strategies for the defender, while improving the overall hybrid detection power.

3.2.2.   Authorization Games

Authorization is the process of controlling users access to existing resources. A problem that rises with authorization models is the method that defines the privileges of each user. Current approaches, suffer from the assumption that users will not depart from the expected behavior implicit in the authorization policy. This assumption clearly is a critical security flaw. Farzad Salim *et al.* in [11] argued that the conflict of interest between insiders and authorization mechanisms is analogous to the subset of problems formally studied in the field of game theory. They proposed a game theoretic authorization model that can ensure users potential misuse of a resource is explicitly considered while making an authorization decision. The resulting authorization model is dynamic in the sense that its access decisions vary according to the changes in explicit factors that influence the cost of misuse for both the authorization mechanism and the insider.

3.2.3.   Cyber Security

Game Theory has been studied extensively as a way to protect many different kind of networks such as wired, ad hoc, heterogeneous, vehicular etc. Sajjan Shiva *et al.* went a step further and proposed in [23] a holistic Cyber Security scheme with the use of game theory. In their approach, they also considered the interaction between the attacks and the defense mechanisms as a game played between the attacker and the defender. Furthermore, they proposed a game theory inspired defense architecture in which a game model acts as the brain.

4.   Game Theory Can Defeat DoS & DDoS

As we saw in the previous section game theory has been successfully used in securing computer networks. One of the major threats as we mentioned in the beginning of this chapter, is DoS and DDoS attacks. In this section we are going to describe techniques that have been designed with main scope to defeat such attacks and their basic functionality rely on game theoretic aspects.

C. Meadows in [18] showed how some principles that have already been used to make cryptographic protocols more resistant to denial of service by trading of the cost to defender against the cost to the attacker can be formalized based on a modifcation of the

Gong-Syverson fail-stop model of cryptographic protocols, and indicates the ways in which existing cryptographic protocol analysis tools could be modified to operate within this formal framework.

Afrand Agah and Sajal K. Das in [3] formulate the prevention of DoS attacks in wireless sensor networks as a repeated game between an intrusion detector and nodes of a sensor network, where some of these nodes act maliciously. They proposed a protocol based on game theory which achieves the design objectives of truthfulness by recognizing the presence of nodes that agree to forward packets but fail to do so.

A game based analysis of the client puzzle approach in order to defend DoS attacks have been introduced by Boldizsar Bencsath *et al.* in [6], in which the optimal strategy is derived for the attacked server in order to respond to DoS attacks effectively. Furthermore, they modelled the situation faced by the DoS attacker and the attacked server as a two-player strategic game and they analyzed this game and gave useful insights into the client puzzle approach.

A DoS mitigation technique is proposed in [28] that uses digital signatures to verify legitimate packets, and drop packets that do not pass the verification. A network game is formulated in which nodes along a network path, are encouraged to act collectively to filter out bad packets in order to optimize their own benefits.

Mehran S. Fallah in [10] utilized game theory to propose a series of optimal puzzle-based strategies for handling increasingly sophisticated flooding attack scenarios. In doing so, the solution concept of Nash equilibrium was used in a prescriptive way, where the defender takes his part in the solution as an optimum defense against rational attackers. This study culminates in a strategy for handling distributed attacks from an unknown number of sources.

Antonis Michalas *et al.* in [21] created a new client puzzle technique for DoS ressistance in ad hoc networks. Inspired form Blotto 2-player game, they created a combination of the discrete logarithm puzzle with the blotto game taking the role of a computational problem. By combining computational problems with puzzles, improved the efficiency and latency of the communicating nodes and resistance in DoS attacks. A graphical representation of the puzzle steps are shown in Figure 5.

5.   Conclusions

Game theory is very promising for the future of Secure Networking. Until now, many techniques have been proposed to protect almost every kind of computer network. We believe that in the near future we are going to see much more techniques that will rely on secure games. Apart from that, game theory can enhance already used techniques in order to provide better and more efficient defense mechanisms. Furthermore, one of the biggest problems in computer security is the prediction of the moves of an attacker. Game theory seems to be very promising towards this direction since it can provide scientists with the appropriate tools.

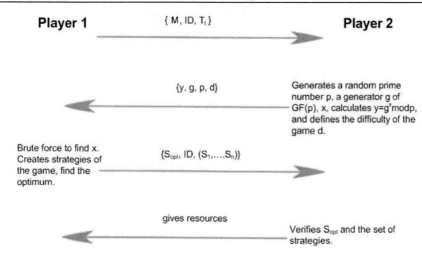

Player 1   { M, ID, T_1 }   **Player 2**

{y, g, p, d}   Generates a random prime number p, a generator g of GF(p), x, calculates y=g^{x}modp, and defines the difficulty of the game d.

Brute force to find x. Creates strategies of the game, find the optimum.   {S_{opt}, ID, (S_1,...,S_n)}

gives resources   Verifies S_{opt} and the set of strategies.

Figure 5. Client Puzzle [21].

References

[1] *Resource allocation for wireless networks : basics, techniques, and applications.* Cambridge University Press, 2008.

[2] M. Abadi, M. Burrows, M. Manasse, and T. Wobber. Moderately hard, memory-bound functions. *ACM Trans. Internet Technol.*, 5(2):299–327, 2005.

[3] A. Agah and S. K. Das. Preventing dos attacks in wireless sensor networks: A repeated game theory approach. *I. J. Network Security*, 5(2):145–153, 2007.

[4] T. Alpcan and T. Basar. An intrusion detection game with limited observations. In *12th Int. Symp. on Dynamic Games and Applications*, Sophia Antipolis, France, July 2006.

[5] B. Barak and M. Mahmoody-Ghidary. Merkle puzzles are optimal – an $o(n^2)$- query attack on any key exchange from a random oracle. In *CRYPTO '09: Proceedings of the 29th Annual International Cryptology Conference on Advances in Cryptology*, pages 374–390, Berlin, Heidelberg, 2009. Springer-Verlag.

[6] B. Bencsath, I. Vajda, and L. Buttyan. A game based analysis of the client puzzle approach to defend against dos attacks. In http://www.hit.bme.hu/ buttyan/publications/BencsathVB03softcom.pdf. *Proceedings of the 2003 International Conference on Software, Telecommunications and Computer Networks*, pages 763–767, 2003.

[7] W. chang Feng, W. chi Feng, and A. Luu. The design and implementation of network puzzles. In *In Proc. Annual Joint Conf. of IEEE Computer and Communications Societies (INFOCOM)*, pages 2372–2382, 2005.

[8] S. Doshi, F. Monrose, and A. D. Rubin. Efficient memory bound puzzles using pattern databased. In *In Proceedings of te 4 th Applied Cryptography and Network Security Conference (ACNS)*, pages 98–113, 2006.

[9] C. Douligeris and A. Mitrokotsa. *Ddos attacks and defense mechanisms: classification and state-of-the-art.* pages 643–666, Texas, USA, 2004.

[10] M. S. Fallah. A puzzle-based defense strategy against flooding attacks using game theory. *IEEE Transactions on Dependable and Secure Computing*, 7:5–19, 2010.

[11] U. D. Farzad Salim, Jason Reid and E. Dawson. Towards a game theoretic authorisation model. In *GameSec '10: 2010 Conference on Decision and Game Theory for Security*, Berlin, 2010.

[12] W.-c. Feng. The case for tcp/ip puzzles. *SIGCOMM Comput. Commun. Rev.*, **33**(4):322–327, 2003.

[13] B. Groza and D. Petrica. On chained cryptographic puzzles. In *3rd Romanian-Hungarian Joint Symposium on Applied Computational Intelligence*, pages 182–191, 2006.

[14] V. Gupta, S. Krishnamurthy, and M. Faloutsos. Denial of service attacks at the mac layer in wireless ad hoc networks. In *MILCOM - Network Security, Anaheim*, 2000.

[15] A. Jeckmans. *Practical client puzzle from repeated squaring*, August 2009.

[16] A. Juels and J. G. Brainard. Client puzzles: A cryptographic countermeasure against connection depletion attacks. In *In S. Kent, editor, Proceedings of NDSS '99 (Networks and Distributed Security Systems)*, pages 151–165, 1999.

[17] Y. Liu, C. Comaniciu, and H. Man. A bayesian game approach for intrusion detection in wireless ad hoc networks. In *GameNets '06: Proceeding from the 2006 workshop on Game theory for communications and networks*, page 4, New York, NY, USA, 2006. ACM.

[18] C. Meadows. A cost-based framework for analysis of denial of service in networks. *J. Comput. Secur.*, **9**(1-2):143–164, 2001.

[19] A. J. Menezes, P. C. V. Oorschot, S. A. Vanstone, and R. L. Rivest. *Handbook of applied cryptography*, 1997.

[20] R. C. Merkle. Secure communications over insecure channels. *Commun. ACM*, **21**(4):294–299, 1978.

[21] A. Michalas, N. Komninos, N. R. Prasad, and V. A. Oleshchuk. New client puzzle approach for dos resistance in ad hoc networks. In *ICITIS 2010: 2010 IEEE International Conference on Information Theory and Information Security*, Beijing, China, 2010. IEEE Computer Society.

[22] H. Otrok, N. Mohammed, L. Wang, M. Debbabi, and P. Bhattacharya. A game-theoretic intrusion detection model for mobile ad hoc networks. *Computer Communications*, **31**(4):708 – 721, 2008. Algorithmic and Theoretical Aspects of Wireless ad hoc and Sensor Networks.

[23] S. Shiva, S. Roy, and D. Dasgupta. Game theory for cyber security. In *CSIIRW '10: Proceedings of the Sixth Annual Workshop on Cyber Security and Information Intelligence Research*, pages 1–4, New York, NY, USA, 2010. ACM.

[24] M. Shor. Perfect information. *Dictionary of Game Theory Terms, Game Theory .net*, 2005.

[25] S. Tritilanunt, C. Boyd, E. Foo, and J. Gonzlez Nieto. Toward non-parallelizable client puzzles. In F. Bao, S. Ling, T. Okamoto, H. Wang, and C. Xing, editors, *Cryptology and Network Security*, volume 4856 of *Lecture Notes in Computer Science*, pages 247–264. Springer Berlin / Heidelberg, 2007. $10.1007/978 - 3 - 540 - 76969 - 9\_16$.

[26] J. Vijayan. Denial - of - service attacks still a threat. September 22 2004.

[27] B. Waters, A. Juels, J. A. Halderman, and E. W. Felten. New client puzzle outsourcing techniques for dos resistance. In *CCS '04: Proceedings of the 11th ACM conference on Computer and communications security*, pages 246–256, New York, NY, USA, 2004. ACM.

[28] X. Wu, Yau, and D. K. Y. Mitigating denial-of-service attacks in manet by distributed packet filtering: a game-theoretic approach. In *ASIACCS '07: Proceedings of the 2nd ACM symposium on Information, computer and communications security*, pages 365–367, New York, NY, USA, 2007. ACM.

In: Horizons in Computer Science Research, Volume 4   ISBN: 978-1-61324-262-9
Editor: Thomas S. Clary   © 2011 Nova Science Publishers, Inc.

Chapter 15

A NEW IDENTITY-BASED SIGNCRYPTION WITHOUT RANDOM ORACLES

Fagen Li[1,2,*], *Qi Xia*[1] *and Yong Yu*[1]
[1]School of Computer Science and Engineering,
University of Electronic Science and Technology of China,
Chengdu 610054, China
[2] State Key Laboratory of Information Security,
Graduate School of Chinese Academy of Sciences, Beijing 100049, China

Abstract

Signcryption is a cryptographic primitive that fulfills both the functions of digital signature and public key encryption simultaneously, at a cost significantly lower than that required by the traditional signature-then-encryption approach. In this chapter, we present a new identity-based signcryption scheme that is fully secure without random oracles. We prove its semantic security under the decisional bilinear Diffie-Hellman assumption and its unforgeability under the computational Diffie-Hellman assumption in the standard model. Our construction is based on Paterson and Schuldt's recently proposed identity-based signature scheme.

1. Introduction

Identity-based (ID-based) cryptography was introduced by Shamir in 1984 [1]. The distinguishing property of ID-based cryptography is that a user's public key can be any binary string, such as an email address that can identify the user. This removes the need for senders to look up the recipient's public key before sending out an encrypted message. ID-based cryptography is supposed to provide a more convenient alternative to conventional public key infrastructure. Several practical ID-based signature schemes have been devised since 1984, but a satisfying ID-based encryption scheme only appeared in 2001 [2]. It was devised by Boneh and Franklin and cleverly uses bilinear maps (the Weil or Tate pairing) over supersingular elliptic curves.

---

[*]E-mail address: fagenli@uestc.edu.cn

Confidentiality, integrity, non-repudiation and authentication are the important requirements for many cryptographic applications. A traditional approach to achieve these requirements is to sign-then-encrypt the message. Signcryption, first proposed by Zheng in
1997 [3], is a cryptographic primitive that fulfills both the functions of digital signature and
public key encryption simultaneously, at a cost significantly lower than that required by the
traditional signature-then-encryption approach. Several efficient signcryption schemes have
been proposed since 1997. The original scheme in [3] is based on the discrete logarithm
problem but no security proof is given. Zheng's original construction was only proven
secure in 2002 by Baek et al. [4] who described a formal security model in a multi-user
setting.

A recent direction is to merge the concepts of ID-based cryptography and signcryption
to design efficient ID-based signcryption schemes. Several ID-based signcryption schemes
have been proposed so far, e.g. [5, 6, 7, 8, 9, 10]. However, all of these ID-based signcryption schemes are provably secure in the random oracle model [11]. Random oracle model
is a formal model in analyzing cryptographic schemes, where a hash function is considered
as a black-box that contains a random function. However, it has been shown that security
in the random oracle model does not imply the security in the real world [12, 13]. So, it is
important to design provably secure ID-based signcryption schemes in the standard model.
Recently, Yu et al. [14] proposed an ID-based signcryption scheme in the standard model.
Yu et al.'s scheme is based on Waters' ID-based encryption scheme [15] and Paterson and
Schuldt's ID-based signature scheme [16]. However, Xia and Xu [17] showed that Yu et
al.'s scheme is not secure against adaptive chosen ciphertext attacks.

In this chapter, we propose a new ID-based signcryption scheme that is fully secure in
the standard model. We prove its semantic security under the decisional bilinear Diffie-
Hellman assumption and its unforgeability under the computational Diffie-Hellman assumption in the standard model. Our construction is based on Paterson and Schuldt's recently proposed ID-based signature scheme [16], which is obtained from Waters' ID-based
encryption scheme [15].

The rest of this chapter is organized as follows. Some preliminary works are given
in Section 2. The formal model of ID-based signcryption is described in Section 3. The
proposed ID-based signcryption scheme is given in Section 4. We analyze the proposed
scheme in Section 5. Finally, the conclusions are given in Section 6.

2. Preliminaries

In this section, we briefly describe the basic definition and properties of the bilinear
pairings. We refer the reader to previous literature [2] for more details.

Let G and G_T be groups of prime order p and g be a generator of G. The map $\hat{e}$:
$G \times G \rightarrow G_T$ is said to be an admissible map if the following three conditions hold true:

- $\hat{e}$ is bilinear, i.e. $\hat{e}(g^a, g^b) = \hat{e}(g, g)^{ab}$ for all $a, b \in Z_p$.

- $\hat{e}$ is non-degenerate, i.e. $\hat{e}(g, g) \neq 1$.

- $\hat{e}$ is efficiently computable.

The security of our scheme described here relies on the hardness of the following problems.

Definition 1. Given two groups G and G_T of the same prime order p, a bilinear map $\hat{e} : G \times G \to G_T$ and a generator g of G, the decisional bilinear Diffie-Hellman (DBDH) problem in $(G, G_T, \hat{e})$ is to decide whether $h = \hat{e}(P, P)^{abc}$ given (g, g^a, g^b, g^c) and an element $h \in G_T$. We define the advantage of a distinguisher against the DBDH problem like this

$$
\begin{aligned}
Adv(D) \;=\; & |P_{a,b,c,\in_R Z_p, h \in_R G_T}[1 \leftarrow D(g^a, g^b, g^c, h)] \\
& - P_{a,b,c,\in_R Z_p}[1 \leftarrow D(g^a, g^b, g^c, \hat{e}(g, g)^{abc})]|.
\end{aligned}
$$

Definition 2. Given a group G of prime order p and a generator g of G, the computational Diffie-Hellman (CDH) problem in G is to compute g^{ab} given $g, g^a, g^b \in G$ for some unknown $a, b \in Z_p$.

3. Formal Model of ID-Based Signcryption

3.1. Generic Scheme

A generic ID-based signcryption scheme consists of the following four algorithms.

Setup: Given a security parameter, the private key generator (PKG) generates the system's public parameters *params* and a master secret. PKG publishes *params* and keeps the master secret to itself.

Extract: Given an identity u, the PKG computes the corresponding private key d_u and transmits it to its owner in a secure way.

Signcrypt: To send a message m to the receiver Bob whose identity is u_B, Alice computes **Signcrypt**(m, d_A, u_B) to obtain the ciphertext σ.

Unsigncrypt: When receiving σ, Bob computes **Unsigncrypt**(σ, u_A, d_B) and obtains the plaintext m or the symbol $\perp$ if σ is an invalid ciphertext between identities u_A and u_B.

We make the consistency constraint that if

$$\sigma = \textbf{Signcrypt}(m, d_A, u_B),$$

then

$$m = \textbf{Unsigncrypt}(\sigma, u_A, d_B).$$

3.2. Security Notions

Malone-Lee [5] defines security notions for ID-based signcryption schemes. These notions are semantical security (i.e. indistinguishability against adaptive chosen ciphertext attacks) and unforgeability against adaptive chosen messages attacks. We modify their definitions slightly by adding the insider security for signcryption [18].

Definition 3. An ID-based signcryption scheme (IDSC) is said to have the indistinguishability against adaptive chosen ciphertext attacks property (IND-IDSC-CCA2) if no polynomially bounded adversary has a non-negligible advantage in the following game.

1. The challenger $\mathcal{B}$ runs the **Setup** algorithm with a security parameter and sends the system parameters to $\mathcal{A}$.

2. The adversary $\mathcal{A}$ performs a polynomially bounded number of queries (these queries may be made adaptively, i.e. each query may depend on the answer to the previous queries).

   - Key extraction queries:$\mathcal{A}$ chooses an identity u. $\mathcal{B}$ computes $d_u = \textbf{Extract}(u)$ and sends d_u to $\mathcal{A}$.

   - Signcryption queries: $\mathcal{A}$ chooses two identities u_i and u_j, and a plaintext m. $\mathcal{B}$ computes $d_i = \textbf{Extract}(u_i)$ and $\sigma = \textbf{Signcrypt}(m, d_i, u_j)$, and sends σ to $\mathcal{A}$.

   - Unsigncryption queries: $\mathcal{A}$ chooses two identities u_i and u_j, and a ciphertext σ. $\mathcal{B}$ generates the private key $d_j = \textbf{Extract}(u_j)$ and sends the result of **Unsigncrypt**(σ, u_i, d_j) to $\mathcal{A}$ (this result can be the $\perp$ symbol if σ is an invalid ciphertext)

3. $\mathcal{A}$ generates two equal length plaintexts m_0, m_1 and two identities u_A and u_B on which he wants to be challenged. He cannot have asked the private key corresponding to u_B in the first stage.

4. $\mathcal{B}$ takes a bit $b \in_R \{0, 1\}$ and computes $\sigma = \textbf{Signcrypt}(m_b, d_A, u_B)$ which is sent to $\mathcal{A}$.

5. $\mathcal{A}$ can ask a polynomially bounded number of queries adaptively again as in the first stage. This time, he cannot make a key extraction query on u_B and cannot make an unsigncryption query on σ to obtain the corresponding plaintext.

6. Finally, $\mathcal{A}$ produces a bit b' and wins the game if $b' = b$.

The advantage of $\mathcal{A}$ is defined as $Adv(\mathcal{A}) = |2P[b' = b] - 1|$, where $P[b' = b]$ denotes the probability that $b' = b$.

Notice that the adversary is allowed to make a key extraction query on the signcrypting identity u_A in the above definition. This condition corresponds to the stringent requirement of insider security for confidentiality of signcryption [18]. On the other hand, it ensures the forward security of the scheme, i.e. confidentiality is preserved in case the sender's private key becomes compromised.

Definition 4. An ID-based signcryption scheme (IDSC) is said to have the existential unforgeability against adaptive chosen messages attacks (EUF-IDSC-CMA) if no polynomially bounded adversary has a non-negligible advantage in the following game.

1. The challenger $\mathcal{B}$ runs the **Setup** algorithm with a security parameter and sends the system parameters to $\mathcal{A}$.

2. The adversary $\mathcal{A}$ performs a polynomially bounded number of queries just like in the Definition 3.

3. Finally, $\mathcal{A}$ produces a new triple (u_A, u_B, σ)(i.e. a triple that was not produced by the signcryption oracle), where the private key of u_A was not asked in the second stage and wins the game if the result of **Unsigncrypt**(σ, u_A, d_B) is not the $\perp$ symbol.

The advantage of $\mathcal{A}$ is defined as the probability that it wins.

Note that the adversary is allowed to make a key extraction query on the identity u_B in the above definition. Again, this condition corresponds to the stringent requirement of insider security for signcryption [18].

4. Construction

In this section, we present a new ID-based signcryption scheme based on the bilinear pairings. Our scheme is motivated by Paterson and Schuldt's recently proposed ID-based signature scheme [16]. In our scheme, all identities and messages will be assumed to be bit strings of length n_u and n_m, respectively. To construct a more flexible scheme which allows identities and messages of arbitrary lengths, collision-resistant hash functions, $H_u : \{0,1\}^* \rightarrow \{0,1\}^{n_u}$ and $H_m : \{0,1\}^* \rightarrow \{0,1\}^{n_m}$, can be defined and used to create identities and messages of the desired length. The following shows the details of our scheme.

Setup: Given a security parameter, the PKG chooses groups G and G_T of prime order p, a generator g of G, and a bilinear map $\hat{e} : G \times G \rightarrow G_T$. The PKG chooses a secret $\alpha \in Z_p$ randomly, computes $g_1 = g^\alpha$ and chooses $g_2 \in G$ randomly. Additionally, the PKG chooses a random value $u', m' \in G$ and vectors $\boldsymbol{U} = (u_i)$, $\boldsymbol{M} = (m_i)$ of length n_u and n_m, respectively, whose elements are chosen at random from G. The PKG publishes system parameters $params=\{G, G_T, \hat{e}, g, g_1, g_2, u', \boldsymbol{U}, m', \boldsymbol{M}\}$ and keeps the master secret g_2^α to itself.

Extract: Let u be an n bit string representing an identity and $u[i]$ be the ith bit of u. Define $\mathcal{U} \subseteq \{1, \ldots, n_u\}$ to be the set of indicies i such that $u[i] = 1$. To construct the private key d_u of the identity u. The PKG chooses $r_u \in Z_p$ randomly and computes

$$d_u = \left(g_2^\alpha \left(u' \prod_{i \in \mathcal{U}} u_i \right)^{r_u}, g^{r_u} \right).$$

Signcrypt: Let u_A be the n_u bit string representing Alice's identity, u_B be the n_u bit string representing Bob's identity, and m be a n_m bit string representing a message. As in the **Extract** algorithm, let $\mathcal{U}_A \subseteq \{1, \ldots, n_u\}$ be the set of indicies i such that $u_A[i] = 1$ and $\mathcal{U}_B \subseteq \{1, \ldots, n_u\}$ be the set of indicies i such that $u_B[i] = 1$. To send m to Bob, Alice computes the ciphertext $\sigma = (U, W, c, V, X)$ as follows:

$$\sigma = \left(g^t, \left(u' \prod_{i \in \mathcal{U}_B} u_i \right)^t, \hat{e}(g_1, g_2)^t m, g_2^\alpha \left(u' \prod_{i \in \mathcal{U}_A} u_i \right)^{r_A} \left(m' \prod_{j \in \mathcal{C}} m_j \right)^t, g^{r_A} \right).$$

In the above equation, $C \subseteq \{1, \ldots, n_m\}$ is the set of indicies j such that $c[j] = 1$, where $c[j]$ is the jth bit of c.

Unsigncrypt: When receiving $\sigma = (U, W, c, V, X)$, Bob firstly verify the signature by the following equation:

$$\hat{e}(V, g) = \hat{e}(g_2, g_1)\hat{e}\left(u' \prod_{i \in \mathcal{U}_A} u_i, X\right) \hat{e}\left(m' \prod_{j \in C} m_j, U\right). \tag{1}$$

If the above equation holds, then Bob recovers plaintext m using his private key by the following equation:

$$m = c \frac{\hat{e}\left(g^{r_B}, W\right)}{\hat{e}\left(g_2^\alpha \left(u' \prod_{i \in \mathcal{U}_B} u_i\right)^{r_B}, U\right)}.$$

The consistency of the scheme is easy to verify. Any third party can be convinced of the message's origin by checking if the Eq.(1) holds. The knowledge of the plaintext m is not required for the public verification of a message's origin. Therefore, our scheme provides the ciphertext authenticity [7] which is very useful in firewalls [19]. Unlike Yu et al.'s scheme [14], our scheme does not need the message m in signature verification. So a attacker cannot verify the signature on plaintexts m_0 and m_1 produced during the IND-IDSC-CCA2 game and find out which one matches to the challenge ciphertext.

5. Analysis of the Scheme

In this section, we analyze the security and efficiency of the proposed scheme.

5.1. Security

Theorem 1. In the standard model, we assume that we have an IND-IDSC-CCA2 adversary called $\mathcal{A}$ that is able to distinguish ciphertext during the game of Definition 3 with an advantage ϵ when running in a time t and asking at most q_k key extraction queries, q_s signcryption queries and q_u unsigncryption queries. Then, there exists a distinguisher $\mathcal{B}$ that can solve the decisional bilinear Diffie-Hellman problem in a time $O(t + (q_s + 6q_u)T_{\hat{e}})$ with an advantage

$$Adv(\mathcal{B}) > \frac{\epsilon}{16(q_s + q_u)(q_k + q_s + q_u)(n_u + 1)(n_m + 1)},$$

where $T_{\hat{e}}$ denotes the computation time of the bilinear map.

Proof. We assume the distinguisher $\mathcal{B}$ receives a random instance (g, g^a, g^b, g^c, h) of the decisional bilinear Diffie-Hellman problem. His goal is to decide whether $h = \hat{e}(g, g)^{abc}$ or not. $\mathcal{B}$ will run $\mathcal{A}$ as a subroutine and act as $\mathcal{A}$'s challenger in the IND-IDSC-CCA2 game. Our approach is based on that of Paterson and Schuldt [16]. We assume that ciphertext returned from a signcryption query will not be used by $\mathcal{A}$ in an unsigncryption query. We describe the simulation as follows.

$\mathcal{B}$ sets $l_u = 2(q_k + q_s + q_u)$ and $l_m = 2(q_s + q_u)$, and randomly chooses two integers k_u and k_m, with $0 \leq k_u \leq n_u$ and $0 \leq k_m \leq n_m$. We assume that $l_u(n_u + 1) < p$ and $l_m(n_m + 1) < p$ for the given values of q_k, q_s, q_u, n_u and n_m. $\mathcal{B}$ then chooses an integer $x' \in Z_{l_u}$ randomly and a vector $\mathbf{X} = (x_i)$ of length n_u, whose elements are chosen at random from Z_{l_u}. Likewise, $\mathcal{B}$ chooses an integer $z' \in Z_{l_m}$ randomly and a vector $\mathbf{Z} = (z_j)$ of length n_m, whose elements are chosen at random from Z_{l_m}. Lastly, $\mathcal{B}$ chooses two integers $y', w' \in Z_p$ and vectors $\mathbf{Y} = (y_i)$, $\mathbf{W} = (w_j)$ of length n_u and n_m, respectively, whose elements are chosen at random from Z_p.

Again, for an identity u we let $\mathcal{U} \subseteq \{1, \ldots, n_u\}$ be the set of all i for which $u[i] = 1$. For a ciphertext c we let $\mathcal{C} \subseteq \{1, \ldots, n_m\}$ be the set of all i for which $c[i] = 1$. For ease of analysis, we define the following two pairs of functions for an identity u and a ciphertext c respectively:

$$F(u) = x' + \sum_{i \in \mathcal{U}} x_i - l_u k_u \quad \text{and} \quad J(u) = y' + \sum_{i \in \mathcal{U}} y_i,$$

$$K(c) = z' + \sum_{j \in \mathcal{C}} z_j - l_m k_m \quad \text{and} \quad L(c) = w' + \sum_{j \in \mathcal{C}} w_j.$$

Now, $\mathcal{B}$ constructs a set of public parameters for the ID-based signcryption scheme by making the following assignments:

$$
\begin{aligned}
g_1 &= g^a \\
g_2 &= g^b \\
u' &= g_2^{-l_u k_u + x'} g^{y'} \\
u_i &= g_2^{x_i} g^{y_i} \quad 1 \leq i \leq n_u \\
m' &= g_2^{-l_m k_m + z'} g^{w'} \\
m_j &= g_2^{z_j} g^{w_j} \quad 1 \leq j \leq n_m
\end{aligned}
$$

From the perspective of the adversary, the distribution of the public parameters is identical to the real construction. Furthermore, this assignment means that the master secret will be $g_2^\alpha = g_2^a = g^{ab}$ and that for any identity u and ciphertext c, the equations

$$u' \prod_{i \in \mathcal{U}} u_i = g_2^{F(u)} g^{J(u)} \quad \text{and} \quad m' \prod_{j \in \mathcal{C}} m_j = g_2^{K(c)} g^{L(c)}$$

hold. All public parameters are passed to $\mathcal{A}$.

When $\mathcal{A}$ asks key extraction queries, signcryption queries and unsigncryption queries, $\mathcal{B}$ answers these in the following way:

- Key extraction queries: when $\mathcal{A}$ asks a query for the private key of an identity u, if $F(u) \neq 0 \bmod p$, $\mathcal{B}$ chooses a random $r_u \in Z_p$ and computes

$$d_u = (d_0, d_1) = \left(g_1^{\frac{-J(u)}{F(u)}} \left(u' \prod_{i \in \mathcal{U}} u_i \right)^{r_u}, g_1^{\frac{-1}{F(u)}} g^{r_u} \right).$$

Let $\tilde{r}_u = r_u - \frac{a}{F(u)}$. Then we can see that d_u is a valid private key of u, since:

$$
\begin{aligned}
d_0 &= g_1^{\frac{-J(u)}{F(u)}} \left(u' \prod_{i \in \mathcal{U}} u_i \right)^{r_u} \\
&= g_2^a \left(g_2^{F(u)} g^{J(u)} \right)^{\frac{-a}{F(u)}} \left(g_2^{F(u)} g^{J(u)} \right)^{r_u} \\
&= g_2^a \left(g_2^{F(u)} g^{J(u)} \right)^{r_u - \frac{a}{F(u)}} \\
&= g_2^a \left(u' \prod_{i \in \mathcal{U}} u_i \right)^{\tilde{r}_u}
\end{aligned}
$$

and

$$
d_1 = g_1^{\frac{-1}{F(u)}} g^{r_u} = g^{r_u - \frac{a}{F(u)}} = g^{\tilde{r}_u}.
$$

On the other hand, if $F(u) = 0 \bmod p$, the above computation cannot be performed and the simulator will abort. To make the analysis of the simulation easier, we will force the simulator to abort whenever $F(u) = 0 \bmod l_u$. Given the assumption $l_u(n_u + 1) < p$ which implies $0 \leq l_u k_u < p$ and $0 \leq x' + \sum_{i \in \mathcal{U}} x_i < p$, it is easy to see that $F(u) = 0 \bmod p$ implies that $F(u) = 0 \bmod l_u$. Hence, $F(u) \neq 0 \bmod l_u$ implies $F(u) \neq 0 \bmod p$, so the former condition will be a sufficient requirement to ensure that a private key for u can be constructed.

- Signcryption queries: at any time $\mathcal{A}$ can perform a signcryption query for a plaintext m and identities u_i and u_j. If $F(u_i) = 0 \bmod l_u$, then $\mathcal{B}$ fails and stops. Otherwise, $\mathcal{B}$ computes the private key d_i corresponding to u_i by running the key extraction query algorithm and then can simply run the algorithm **Signcrypt**(m, d_i, u_j).

- Unsigncryption queries: when $\mathcal{A}$ observes a ciphertext $\sigma = (U, W, c, V, X)$ for identities u_i and u_j, he may want to ask $\mathcal{B}$ for the unsigncryption of σ. Then $\mathcal{B}$ checks if the following equation hold:

$$
\hat{e}(V, g) = \hat{e}(g_2, g_1) \hat{e} \left(u' \prod_{i \in \mathcal{U}_i} u_i, X \right) \hat{e} \left(m' \prod_{j \in \mathcal{C}} m_j, U \right).
$$

If the above equation does not hold, $\mathcal{B}$ notifies $\mathcal{A}$ that the ciphertext is invalid. Otherwise, $\mathcal{B}$ checks if $F(u_j) = 0 \bmod l_u$ holds. If $F(u_j) = 0 \bmod l_u$, then $\mathcal{B}$ fails and stops. Otherwise $\mathcal{B}$ computes the private key d_j corresponding to u_j by running the key extraction query algorithm and then can simply run the algorithm **Unsigncrypt**(σ, u_i, d_j).

At the end of the first stage, $\mathcal{A}$ outputs two plaintexts m_0 and m_1 together with two identities u_i^* and u_j^* on which he wishes to be challenged. $\mathcal{B}$ chooses a random bit $b \in_R \{0, 1\}$ and signcrypts m_b. If $F(u_i^*) = 0 \bmod l_u$, then $\mathcal{B}$ fails and stops. Otherwise, he computes the private key d_i^* corresponding to u_i^* by running the key extraction query algorithm. If

$F(u_j^*) \neq 0 \bmod l_u$ and $K(c_b) \neq 0 \bmod l_m$, then $\mathcal{B}$ fails and stops. Otherwise, the ciphertext $\sigma^* = (U^*, W^*, c_b, V^*, X^*)$ of m_b can be constructed as follows:

$$\sigma^* = \left(g^c, g^{cJ(u_j^*)}, hm_b, g_2^\alpha \left(u' \prod_{i \in \mathcal{U}_i^*} u_i \right)^{r_i^*} g^{cL(c_b)}, g^{r_i^*} \right),$$

where, h is $\mathcal{B}$ candidate for the DBDH problem. $\mathcal{B}$ sends the ciphertext σ^* to $\mathcal{A}$

$\mathcal{A}$ then performs a second series of queries which is treated in the same way as the first one. At the end of the simulation, he produces a bit b' for which he believes the relation $\sigma^* = \mathbf{Signcrypt}(m_b, d_i^*, u_j^*)$ holds. At this moment, if $b' = b$, $\mathcal{B}$ then answers 1 as a result because his candidate h allowed him to produce a σ^* that appeared to $\mathcal{A}$ as a valid signcrypted text of m_b. If $b' = b$, $\mathcal{B}$ then answers 0.

This completes the description of the simulation. It remains to analyze the probability of $\mathcal{B}$ not aborting. For the simulation to complete without aborting, we require that all key extraction queries on an identity u have $F(u) \neq 0 \bmod l_u$, that all signcryption queries (u_i, u_j, m) have $F(u_i) \neq 0 \bmod l_u$, that all unsigncryption queries (u_i, u_j, σ) have $F(u_j) \neq 0 \bmod l_u$, and that $F(u_i^*) \neq 0 \bmod l_u$, $F(u_j^*) = 0 \bmod l_u$ and $K(c_b) = 0 \bmod l_m$. Similarly to [16], we have

$$Adv(\mathcal{B}) > \frac{\epsilon}{16(q_s + q_u)(q_k + q_s + q_u)(n_u + 1)(n_m + 1)}.$$

Regarding the time complexity, it can be verified by counting the number of pairing operations required to answer all queries.

Theorem 2. In the standard model, if there exists an adversary $\mathcal{A}$ that has a non-negligible advantage ϵ against the EUF-IDSC-CMA security of the scheme when running in a time t, making q_k key extraction queries, q_s signcryption queries and q_u unsigncryption queries, then there exists an algorithm $\mathcal{B}$ that can solve the computational Diffie-Hellman problem in a time $O(t + (q_s + 6q_u)T_{\hat{e}})$ with an advantage

$$Adv(\mathcal{B}) > \frac{\epsilon}{8(q_s + q_u)(q_k + q_s + q_u)(n_u + 1)(n_m + 1)},$$

where $T_{\hat{e}}$ denotes the computation time of the bilinear map.

Proof. $\mathcal{B}$ receives a random instance (g, g^a, g^b) of the computational Diffie-Hellman problem. $\mathcal{B}$ uses $\mathcal{A}$ as a subroutine to solve that instance and plays the role of $\mathcal{A}$'s challenger in the game of Definition 4. The simulation process is the same as that described in Theorem 1.

At the end of the game, $\mathcal{A}$ produces a ciphertext $\sigma' = (U', W', c', V', X')$ and two identities u_i' and u_j'. If $F(u_i') \neq 0 \bmod p$ and $K(c') \neq 0 \bmod p$, then $\mathcal{B}$ fails and stops. Otherwise, $\mathcal{B}$ computes and outputs

$$\frac{V'}{X'^{J(u_i')}U'^{L(c')}} = \frac{g_2^\alpha \left(u' \prod_{i \in \mathcal{U}_i'} u_i \right)^{r_i'} \left(m' \prod_{j \in \mathcal{C}'} m_j \right)^t}{g^{J(u_i')r_i'} g^{L(c')t}} = g^{ab}$$

which is the solution to the given CDH problem. This completes the description of the simulation. It remains to analyze the probability of $\mathcal{B}$ not aborting. For the simulation to complete without aborting, we require that all key extraction queries on an identity u have $F(u) \neq 0 \mod l_u$, that all signcryption queries (u_i, u_j, m) have $F(u_i) \neq 0 \mod l_u$, that all unsigncryption queries (u_i, u_j, σ) have $F(u_j) \neq 0 \mod l_u$, and that $F(u_i') = 0 \mod l_u$ and $K(c') = 0 \mod l_m$. So, we have

$$Adv(\mathcal{B}) > \frac{\epsilon}{8(q_s + q_u)(q_k + q_s + q_u)(n_u + 1)(n_m + 1)}.$$

Regarding the time complexity, it can be verified by counting the number of pairing operations required to answer all queries.

5.2. Efficiency

We compare the major computational cost and communication overhead (the length of the ciphertext) of our scheme with those of Yu et al.'s scheme and the simple signature-then-encryption approach based on Paterson and Schuldt's ID-based signature scheme [16] and Waters's ID-based encryption scheme [15] (PS+W for short) in Table 1. We consider the costly operations which include multiplications in G (G Mul), exponentiations in G (G Exp), exponentiations in G_T (G_T Exp), and pairing operations (Pairing). In the table, we

Table 1. Efficiency comparison

	G Mul	G Exp	G_T Exp	Pairing	Ciphertext size
Yu et al. scheme	$2n_u + n_m$	3	1	5(+1)	$4|G| + |G_T|$
PS+W	$2n_u + 2n_m$	4	1	5(+1)	$5|G| + |G_T|$
Our scheme	$2n_u + n_m$	3	1	5(+1)	$4|G| + |G_T|$

represent the total number of pairing computations in the form of $x(+y)$ where y is the number of operations that are independent of the message and can be pre-computed and cached for subsequent uses. From Table 1, we can see that the proposed scheme is more efficient than PS+W approach. Our scheme is as efficient as the Yu et al.'s scheme.

6. Conclusions

We have presented a new ID-based signcryption scheme that is provably secure in the standard model. We have proved its semantic security under the decisional bilinear Diffie-Hellman assumption and its unforgeability under the computational Diffie-Hellman assumption. An interesting work is to design an more efficient ID-based signcryption scheme than ours that is secure in the standard model.

Acknowledgements

This work is supported by the National Natural Science Foundation of China (Grant Nos. 60803133, 60873233 and 61073176), the Specialized Research Fund for the Doctoral Program of Higher Education (Grant No. 200806140010), the State Key Laboratory of

Information Security, the Fundamental Research Funds for the Central Universities, and the Youth Science and Technology Foundation of UESTC.

References

[1] A. Shamir. "Identity-based cryptosystems and signature schemes", in *Proc. Advances in Cryptology-CRYPTO'84*, LNCS 196, Springer-Verlag, pp. 47–53, 1984.

[2] D. Boneh and M. Franklin. "Identity-based encryption from the weil pairing", In *Proc. Advances in Cryptology-CRYPTO 2001*, LNCS 2139, Springer-Verlag, pp. 213–229, 2001.

[3] Y. Zheng. "Digital signcryption or how to achieve cost (signature & encryption) $\ll$ cost (signature) + cost(encryption)", In *Proc. Advances in Cryptology-CRYPTO'97*, LNCS 1294, Springer-Verlag, pp. 165–179, 1997.

[4] J. Baek, R. Steinfeld, and Y. Zheng. "Formal proofs for the security of signcryption", In *Proc. Public Key Cryptography-PKC 2002*, LNCS 2274, Springer-Verlag, pp. 80–98, 2002.

[5] J. Malone-Lee. "Identity based signcryption", *Cryptology ePrint Archive*, Report 2002/098, 2002.

[6] B. Libert and J.J. Quisquater. "A new identity based signcryption schemes from pairings", In *Proc. 2003 IEEE Information Theory Workshop*, Paris, France, pp. 155–158, 2003.

[7] S.S.M. Chow, S.M. Yiu, L.C.K. Hui, and K.P. Chow. "Efficient forward and provably secure ID-based signcryption scheme with public verifiability and public ciphertext authenticity", In *Proc. Information Security and Cryptology-ICISC 2003*, LNCS 2971, Springer-Verlag, pp. 352–369, 2004.

[8] X. Boyen. "Multipurpose identity-based signcryption: a swiss army knife for identity-based cryptography", In *Proc. Advances in Cryptology-CRYPTO 2003*, LNCS 2729, Springer-Verlag, pp. 383–399, 2003.

[9] L. Chen and J. Malone-Lee. "Improved identity-based signcryption", In *Proc. Public Key Cryptography-PKC 2005*, LNCS 3386, Springer-Verlag, pp. 362–379, 2005.

[10] P.S.L.M. Barreto, B. Libert, N. McCullagh, and J.J. Quisquater. "Efficient and provably-secure identity-based signatures and signcryption from bilinear maps", In *Proc. Advances in Cryptology-ASIACRYPT 2005*, LNCS 3788, Springer-Verlag, pp. 515–532, 2005.

[11] M. Bellare and P. Rogaway. "Random oracles are practical: a paradigm for designing efficient protocols", In *Proc. 1st ACM Conference on Computer and Communications Security*, Fairfax, Virginia, USA, pp. 62–73, 1993.

[12] M. Bellare, A. Boldyreva, and A. Palacio. "An uninstantiable random-oracle-model scheme for a hybrid-encryption problem", In *Proc. Advances in Cryptology-EUROCRYPT 2004*, LNCS 3027, Springer-Verlag, pp. 171–188, 2004.

[13] R. Canetti, O. Goldreich, and S. Halevi. "The random oracle methodology, revisited", *Journal of the ACM*, vol. 51, no. 4, pp. 557–594, 2004.

[14] Y. Yu, B Yang, Y. Sun, and S. Zhu. "Identity based signcryption scheme without random oracles", *Computer Standards & Interfaces*, vol. 31, no. 1, pp. 56–62, 2009.

[15] B. Waters. "Efficient identity-based encryption without random oracles", In *Proc. Advances in Cryptology-EUROCRYPT 2005*, LNCS 3494, Springer-Verlag, pp. 114–127, 2005.

[16] K.G. Paterson and J.C.N. Schuldt. "Efficient identity-based signatures secure in the standard model", In *Proc. Information Security and Privacy-ACISP 2006*, LNCS 4058, Springer-Verlag, pp. 207–222, 2006.

[17] Q. Xia and C. Xu, "Cryptanalysis of two identity based signcryption schemes", in *Proc. 8th International Conference on Dependable, Autonomic and Secure Computing*, Chengdu, China, pp. 292–294, 2009.

[18] J.H. An, Y. Dodis, and T. Rabin. "On the security of joint signature and encryption", In *Proc. Advances in Cryptology-EUROCRYPT 2002*, LNCS 2332, Springer-Verlag, pp. 83–107, 2002.

[19] C. Gamage, J. Leiwo, and Y. Zheng. "Encrypted message authentication by firewalls", In *Proc. Public Key Cryptography-PKC'99*, LNCS 1560, Springer-Verlag, pp. 69–81, 1999.

In: Horizons in Computer Science Research, Volume 4   ISBN: 978-1-61324-262-9
Editor: Thomas S. Clary   © 2011 Nova Science Publishers, Inc.

Chapter 16

CHAOTIC MAP CRYPTOGRAPHY AND SECURITY

Alexander N. Pisarchik[1,*] ***and Massimiliano Zanin***[2]
[1]Centro de Investigaciones en Optica, Loma del Bosque 115, Lomas del
Campestre, 37150 Leon, Guanajuato, Mexico
[2]Universidad Autónoma de Madrid, 28049 Madrid, Spain

Abstract

In the last decade, chaos has emerged as a new promising candidate for cryptography because many chaos fundamental characteristics such as a broadband spectrum, ergodicity, and high sensitivity to initial conditions are directly connected with two basic properties of good ciphers: confusion and diffusion. In this chapter we recount some of the saga undergone by this field; we review the main achievements in the field of chaotic cryptography, starting with the definition of chaotic systems and their properties and the difficulties it has to outwit. According to their intrinsic dynamics, chaotic cryptosystems are classified depending on whether the system is discrete or continuous. Due to their simplicity and rapidity the discrete chaotic systems based on iterative maps have received a lot of attention. In spite of the significant achievements accomplished in this field, there are still many problems, basically speed, that restrict the application of existing encoding/decoding algorithms to real systems. The major advantages and drawbacks of the most popular chaotic map ciphers in terms of security and computational cost are analyzed. The most significant cryptanalytic techniques are considered and applied for testing the security of some chaotic algorithms. Finally, future trends in the development of this topic are discussed.

Keywords: Cryptography, iterative maps, chaos.

PACS 05.45.Gg, 89.20.Ff, 05.45.Vx.

Introduction

In recent years, the transmission of a large amount of data over communication media, such as computer networks, mobile phones, TV cable, etc. was highly developed, making it a security problem in storage and transmission of confidential information and therefore

---

*E-mail address: apisarch@cio.mx

research in this area is growing in importance to give the required solutions for pay TV, video conferences, medical and military databases, etc. Most conventional secure ciphers, such as Data Encryption Standard (DES), International Data Encryption Algorithm (IDEA), Advanced Encryption Standard (AES), linear feedback shift register (LFSR), etc. [1, 2] consider plaintext as either block cipher or data stream and are not suitable for fast encryption of a large data volume (for example, color images and video) in real time. Their implementation, when they are realized by software, of traditional algorithms for image encryption is even more complicated because of high correlation between image pixels. Therefore, there is still a lot of work to be done for the development of nontraditional encryption methods.

Many researchers have pointed out the existence of a strong relationship between chaos and cryptography. Actually, in real systems, chaos and noise are two natural irregular behaviors, therefore the utilization of these motions in cryptography is also natural. The greatest advantage of a chaotic system over a noisy one is that the chaotic system is deterministic, so that the exact knowledge of initial conditions and system parameters enables one to recover a message. This property of chaos significantly facilitates the decryption process. The idea of chaotic cryptography can be traced back to Shanon [3] yet in 1949. Although he did not explicitly use the word "chaos", he did mention that well-mixing transformations in a good secrecy system can be constructed on the base of the stretch-and-fold mechanism, which is really a chaotic motion. The two basic properties of a good cipher, *confusion* and *diffusion*, are strongly related to the fundamental characteristics of chaos, such as a broadband spectrum, ergodicity (almost all points of a chaotic attractor are eventually visited in infinitely long time), and high sensitivity to initial conditions, so that any good cryptosystem has to present properties of chaos or pseudo-randomness. In Shannon's original definitions [3], diffusion was associated with the dependence of the output on input bits, i.e. it referred to the property that redundancy in the statistics of plaintext is dissipated in the statistics of ciphertext, whereas confusion was guaranteed by making the relationship between the key and the ciphertext as complex and involved as possible, i.e. the data sequence has to be permuted.

In the first scientific paper on chaotic cryptography that appeared in 1989, Matthews [4] came up with the idea of a stream cipher based on one-dimensional chaotic map. One year later, Pecora and Caroll [5] published the pioneer work on synchronization of chaotic systems, a great tool for secure communications [6]. Afterwards, chaotic cryptography has taken two distinct paths with almost no interaction between them: digital chaotic ciphers [7, 8, 9, 10] and chaos synchronization [11, 12, 13, 14, 15]. The principal difference between these two approaches is that in the former case a cryptosystem requires a predetermined secret key(s), while the key in the latter is the system itself. Still, the main advantage of chaotic synchronization schemes is its easy analog implementation for secure communication. Traditionally, encryption is based on discrete number theory, so that data has to be digitized before any encryption process can take place. In order to encrypt a continuous voice or a video in the old fashion way, digitalization and encryption can pose a heavy computational burden. Using chaotic communication enables to encrypt the message waveform without a need to digitalize it. Furthermore, chaotic encryption can be implemented using fast analog components (electric/optical).

A very important feature of any encryption scheme is its security. The traditional approach based on integer number theory has proven to be reliable, while the security of chaotic encryption still poses some problems. The incorporation of chaotic dynamics in cryptology, the science that puts together cryptography and cryptanalysis, is a relatively new approach initiated only last decade. Different cryptanalytic techniques have been developed to estimate the security of proposed chaotic ciphers [16, 17, 18, 19, 20] and of most chaotic synchronization schemes [21, 22, 23], many of which have already been broken. Until now, the security of chaotic communication has often relied on a mixture of analytic methods and intuition. However, we may positively state that no cryptosystem, with the exception maybe of quantum systems [24], is forever secure; better ways to cryptanalyze are always popping up. At present quantum cryptography is still unacceptable for modern secure communication, because of serious drawbacks: first, it is too slow and second, it can only be used over point-to-point connections and not through networks where data has to be routed.

The goal of any cryptosystem is to convert plaintext to ciphertext with the use of a secure algorithm. Generally, in any cryptosystem, the confusion and diffusion processes are repeated several times, as schematically shown in Fig. 1, and described mathematically as [25]

$$\mathbf{R} = D^{\alpha}(C^{\beta}(\mathbf{P}, K_C), K_D),\tag{1}$$

where $\mathbf{P}$ and $\mathbf{R}$ are respectively plaintext and ciphertext, C and D are the confusion and diffusion functions, K_C and K_D are the confusion and diffusion keys, and α and β are numbers of rounds for total encryption and for confusion, respectively. Equation (1) determines the cryptosystem's security; the more sensitive the functions C and D are to their keys K_C and K_D and the larger the key space, the higher the security. The cryptosystem's key space in Fig. 1 is defined as

$$S = (S_C^{\beta} S_D)^{\alpha},\tag{2}$$

where S_D and S_C are key spaces of the confusion and diffusion keys, that are determined by the key spaces for initial conditions and parameters in the confusion and diffusion processes. As seen from Eq. (2), the higher the powers α and β, the bigger the key space and hence the higher the security. However, the encryption+decryption time (EDT) also increases as α and β are increased. Therefore, when designing new cryptosystems, cryptographs should always balance security and speed.

A good chaotic cryptosystem should also comply with the two requirements mentioned by Shannon [3]: diffusion and confusion, both processes should be based on chaotic systems whose high sensitivity to initial conditions and parameters make the cryptosystem extremely secure and robust against cryptographic attacks. Although chaos is a irregular motion, it is a deterministic phenomenon, and therefore the plaintext can be completely recovered if the secret keys are exactly known. Moreover, EDT should be very short enabling the real-time application, this entails that the length of ciphertext must be the same as the length of plaintext. In spite of the significant achievements already accomplished, there are still too many problems to be solved in the field of chaotic cryptography, further investigation is needed to develop new efficient algorithms for real applications.

Among various chaotic cryptosystems we can distinguish the ciphers based of discrete systems (iterative maps) [8, 26, 27, 28], continuous systems (modeled by differential equa-

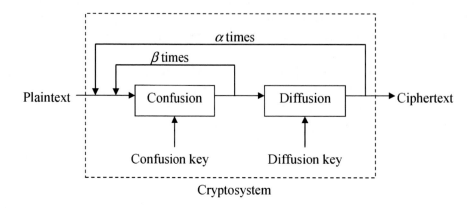

Figure 1. General scheme of a cryptosystem.

tions) [29, 30, 31, 32, 33, 34], and combined algorithms which use jointly discrete and continuous systems [35, 36, 37, 38]. In this chapter we restrict our review to the first class of chaotic cryptosystems, i.e. to the ciphers based on iterative maps. Even if they do not display generic behavior from a physical point of view, these systems are intrinsically interesting: they confirm the main assertion that dynamical instability is the root of irreversibility. Furthermore, chaotic cryptography based on iterative maps is simple and fast.

An iterative map is specified by a dynamical law that determines how an initial point $\mathbf{x}_0$ evolves with time. The phase space dimension (the number of system variables) associated with $\mathbf{x}$ may be higher than 1, e.g., for three-dimensional map $\mathbf{x} = \{x, y, z\}$. The map function describes the evolution after one time step, to obtain it after n steps we apply an iterative procedure:

$$\mathbf{x}_n = \mathbf{M}(\mathbf{x}_{n-1}) = \mathbf{M}(\mathbf{M}(\mathbf{x}_{n-2})) = \dots = \mathbf{M}^n(\mathbf{x}_0), \tag{3}$$

where $\mathbf{M}$ is the vector map function that yields a discrete time series and a system trajectory in phase space. The principal characterization of chaotic trajectory dynamics is given by the values of the positive Lyapunov exponents, which determine the rate of exponential divergence of nearby trajectories. The ergodic properties of chaos[1] and its high sensitivity to initial conditions and parameters are crucial for designing new chaotic algorithms with good confusion and diffusion properties.

Many different iterative maps do generate chaotic series for certain parameters. Table 1 displays the list of the most popular ones. Note, that only few maps have been put to test in cryptography so far.

The complex motion in chaotic systems naturally defines densities in phase space. An initial nonequilibrium density may correspond to some uncertainty in the initial condition specifications or may be thought of as representing an ensemble of systems with different initial conditions. For cryptographic applications, a smooth density is desirable; since it can be maintained on a finite region of phase space, whose evolution can shade a light on some non-local information that otherwise will be missing in a point dynamical description. Thus,

---

[1]In an ergodic system, long time averages may be replaced by phase space averages.

Table 1. List of most popular chaotic maps

Map name	Space dimension	Cryptosystem
Arnold cat	2	[9, 35, 73, 74]
Baker	2	[9, 69, 72, 97, 98]
Bernoulli shift	1	[99, 100, 101, 102]
Bit shift	1	
Bogdanov	2	
Circle	1	
Complex squaring	1	
Chebyshev	1	[63, 103, 104]
Chrossat-Golubitsky	2	
Cubic	1	[46, 57]
Curry-Yorke	2	
Double rotor	2	
Duffing	2	
Dyadic transform	1	
Exponential	1 and 2	
Gauss	1	
Gingerbreadman	2	
Gumowski-Mira	2	
Hénon	2	[105]
Hitzl-Zele	3	
Horseshoe	1	
Ikeda	2	[106]
Infinite Collapses	1	[104]
Interval exchange	1	
Kaplan-Yorke	2	[106]
Lissajous	2	[107]
Logarithm	1	
Logistic	1	[8, 57, 63, 77, 79, 108]
Lozi	2	
Markov	1	[99, 100, 101]
Tangent logistic	1	[81]
Nordmark	2	
Piecewise linear	1	[19, 27, 65, 80, 109]
Piecewise nonlinear	1	[110, 111]
Polynomial	1	[111, 112]
Pomeau-Manneville	1 and 2	
Rulkov	2	
Sawtooth	1	
Shobu-Ose-Mori	1	
Sinai	2	
Sine	1	[57]
Skew tent	1	[104, 109, 113]
Standard	2	[9, 25, 87, 114]
Tangent	1	
Tent	1	[7, 57, 106]
Tinkerbell	2	
Torus automorphism	2	[63]
Trigonometric	1	[115]
"V"	1	
Zaslavskii	2	

the natural description for the time evolution in chaotic systems is, in terms of densities, irreducible to phase space trajectories. This yields an intrinsically irreversible distribution for systems that nevertheless have time-reversible trajectory dynamics.

To understand the basics of how a chaotic encryption algorithm works, let us choose a number of iterations n that depends on the number of precision decimal points that are carried through the computing iterations of $\mathbf{M}$. Concretely, with a given decimal precision d, the continuous interval of interest $(0,1)$ (0 being fixed, and 1 being eventually fixed) is transformed into a discrete set whose elements expressed with the same precision are also in $(0,1)$. So, if d decimal places are carried through computations, then n should be equal to 10^d. In fact, due to the chaotic nature of the calculations, after a finite number of iterations which carry more than d decimal places we will begin to see drastic deviations between the more and less precise computations. It should be noted that for a given key length, there is a minimum d that can be used, so that only keys of that size are available. For example, for binary key length k, d has to satisfy the relation $10^d \geq 2^k$ to give us the maximum possible number of keys. While this indicates a lower bound for the desired d, increasing d will provide better security but incurring in a higher computational cost. Simple computations show that, to get all 64-bit keys, at least 20 decimal places should be carried out. Therefore, before using a common chaotic map algorithm, sender and receiver must agree at least on the following information: (i) initial values $\mathbf{x}_0$, (ii) system parameters, (iii) a decimal precision d to be used, and (iv) a number of iterations n. With this information at hand, one can simply compute a key by selecting the k least significant digits of $\mathbf{M}^n(\mathbf{x}_0)$, expressed as a binary code calculated with precision d. This key generation process is in itself fairly secure for a sufficiently large n (in fact, not extremely large). A very small variation either in $\mathbf{x}_0$ or in d will lead to a drastically different key, and of course, due to the strong divergence of the chaotic trajectory a single extra (or fewer) iteration will also yield a completely different key. In typical applications of symmetric key cryptography, it is wise to have a large number of secret keys.

Based on strengths and weaknesses of already existing algorithms, Kelber and Schwarz [39] formulated ten general rules to design a good chaos-based cryptosystem:

1. Either use suitable chaotic maps which preserves important properties during discretization for block cipher or use a balanced combining function and a suitable key stream generator for a stream cipher.

2. Use a large key space.

3. Do not use initial conditions of an inverse system as part of the key.

4. Avoid simple permutations of identical system parameters.

5. Use the same precision for subkey values and their corresponding system parameters.

6. Use a complex input key transformation.

7. Use a dynamical system.

8. Use complex nonlinearities.

9. Modify nonlinearities in terms of key and signal values.

10. Use several rounds of operation for block ciphers.

In the remainder of this chapter we review the most significant achievements in the history of chaotic encryption based on chaotic maps, a novel field of cryptography. In section 2 we consider the encryption of standard messages (text), while in section 3 we analyze chaotic cryptosystems used for image and video. Section 4 describes major advantages and drawbacks of the more popular chaotic ciphers in terms of security and computational cost using the most important cryptanalytic techniques. Finally, in section 5 conclusions and future trends in the development of this topic are presented.

Encryption of Standard Messages

Ergodicity of Chaotic Logistic Map

The logistic map is one of the simplest and thus more widely used chaotic maps. Introduced first in 1845 by Verhulst [40, 41] as a model for the population growth of a species, it is expressed as a recurrence equation:

$$x_{n+1} = r x_n (1 - x_n), \tag{4}$$

where the parameter r belongs to the interval $[0, 4]$ and determines the map behavior, while n is the iteration number that discretizes time. Figure 2 shows the bifurcation diagram where, starting at a certain initial value x_0, every iteration value x_n of the map Eq. 4 is plotted as a function of r. The right-hand side of the diagram clearly exhibits that for most values of r between 3.57 and 4.0 the system is in a chaotic regime, i.e. the variable x_n can take any value within a certain interval, where the system dynamics is very sensitive to the initial condition. In Fig. 3 we plot two time series obtained for the same parameter $r = 3.995$ but for two slightly different initial conditions ($x = 0.500$ and $x' = 0.501$). One can see that after only 25 iterations the two trajectories are completely different.

Baptista [8] was the first to explore the usefulness of the logistic map ergodicity in the realm of digital cryptography. To encrypt a message, he assigned to every alphabetic character a certain range of the variable x_n. Starting from a particular initial value x_0 (which was part of the secret key), he iterated the logistic map until x_n fell within the region corresponding to the first character of the plaintext. He then represented the corresponding number of iterations as the first character of ciphertext. For the second character of the message, this procedure was executed again taking x_n as the new initial condition. Another parameter $\eta \in (0, 1)$ was chosen to define the probability of discarding a value x_n: each time x_n falls within the range of the character to be encoded, a random number is drawn from a uniform distribution between zero and one; if this number is less than η, then the sender keeps iterating the map until x_n falls again in the required range. Since $\eta > 0$, a single initial character can be encoded in different ciphertexts, thus increasing the security of the algorithm. Note that the receiver does not need to know the value of η, nor the value of the random number generated by the sender; he/she needs only to iterate the chaotic

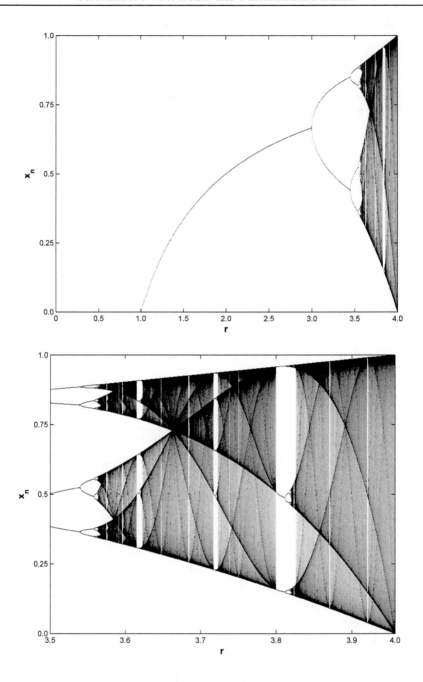

Figure 2. Bifurcation diagram of logistic map Eq. 4.

map according to the received value, and the result of such iterations will be the decoded character, independently of how the sender did generate that value.

As many chaos-based cryptosystems, Baptista's method [8] is both slow and insecure. The computational cost problem was first tackled by Wong, *et al.* [42]. Instead of generating a random number each time x_n falls in the target range, only a single random integer number R is drawn; the logistic map is then iterated R times prior to the encryption process.

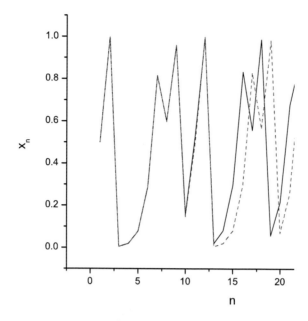

Figure 3. Time series generated with the same parameter $r = 3.995$ but with slightly different initial values ($x_0 = 0.5$ and 0.501).

However, even with only one random number, this modified algorithm is still too slow to be used in most applications. Wong, *et al.* [42] reported in 2001 that in order to encrypt with a state-of-the-art PC 4 KB of information, 4 seconds were required, meaning 8 KB processed processed every second in an up-to-date system, and therefore to encrypt the content of a CD-ROM it would take almost a whole day.

The second attempt to take advantage of chaos ergodicity in cryptography was made by Alvarez, *et al.* [10], who suggested to use a chaotic function of the form

$$x_{n+1} = f(x_n, x_{n-1}, \dots), \qquad (5)$$

as a construction block of the chaotic cryptosystem. The logistic map is then just a particular case of Eq. 5 when the function $f(x) = rx(1 - x)$. By iterating the map Eq. 5 and using a threshold U, a sequence of bits b_n is generated as follows

$$b_n = \begin{cases} 1, & x_n > U, \\ 0, & x_n \le U. \end{cases} \qquad (6)$$

When the bits sequence generated by the chaotic map is equal to the first part of the message to be transmitted, that part is encoded by the triplet (n, x_0, U), i.e. by the number of iterations n needed to generate the correct sequence, the initial value of the map x_0, and the threshold U.

Both algorithms, the one proposed by Baptista [8] and the other by Álvarez [10] were cryptoanalyzed some years later by Jakimoski and Kocarev [43]. They first noted that the security of the second algorithm relies on the assumption that the attacker does not know the actual chaotic function, i.e. the map Eq. 5 is secret. This assumption is contrary of one of the fundamental principles of cryptography, known as the *Kerckhoffs' principle* [44] which states that **the security of an encryption process should only be guaranteed by secret key(s), and never by the algorithm itself.** Jakimovski and Kocarev [43] also showed that both algorithms are vulnerable to known-plaintext attacks. By feeding the systems with a limited number of predefined messages (4000 for the Baptista's and 1000000 for the Álvarez's algorithms), and by recording the output of the encryption process, an attacker can construct an almost complete decryption vocabulary.

In the following years, many different modifications of the original Baptista's algorithm have been proposed (see, for example, [45, 46, 47, 48]), but all of them have been cryptanalyzed using similar techniques (e.g., [49]). Intuitively, a single logistic map cannot provide a complex enough dynamics to be used in cryptographic applications; therefore, for chaotic encryption, more sophisticated systems have to be conceived such as combinations of two or more different chaotic maps.

Stream Ciphera Using Logistic Map

The use of the chaotic logistic map in cryptography takes advantage of its ergodic property. So do, other new interesting algorithms whose aim is to create stream ciphers. In these encryption schemes, a plaintext is mixed with a keystream; when the mixing process is performed by some suitable bitwise operators (such as XOR or XNOR) and the keystream is a random sequence of bits, we expect that the encryption process to be completely secure. The security problem is therefore reduced to the creation of a pseudo-random bit generator with good statistical properties.

The first such method was proposed by Bianco, *et al.* [50, 51], who described the bit generation process by the following equation

$$b = \begin{cases} 0, & x_n \in [x_l, x_m], \\ 1, & x_n \in [x_m, x_r]. \end{cases} \tag{7}$$

When the logistic map is iterated n times, a value x_n is obtained, the algorithm has to check whether x_n falls within the interval $[x_l, x_r]$ to stop, otherwise the number is discarded and another iteration of the map is executed. The previously defined interval is further divided into two equal sub-intervals; if the accepted x_n falls in the left sub-interval (i.e., $x_n \in [x_l, x_m]$) 0 is added to the output stream, 1 otherwise. This is a very slow process to obtain a bit sequence that will pass the usual statistical randomness tests; to improve their statistical characteristics, the interval $[x_l, x_r]$ should be quite narrow, leading to discard a great part of the map's iterations, and therefore slowing its velocity.

Another approach was developed later by Phatak, *et al.* [52], who introduced the following change of variable:

$$x_n = \frac{1 - \cos\theta_n}{2} = \sin^2\frac{\theta_n}{2}. \tag{8}$$

When applied to the logistic map for $r = 4$, Eq. 4 is transformed into

$$\theta_{n+1} = 2\theta_n, \qquad \theta_n < \pi/2, \theta_{n+1} = 2\pi - 2\theta_n, \ \theta_n > \pi/2. \tag{9}$$

In other words, the application of the logistic map is stretching a closed circle by a factor of two and then collapsing it back to the original circle. This dynamics is periodic if and only if the initial value θ_0 is a rational fraction of π. In all other cases, the correlation between values of the sequence $\theta_n, \theta_{n+\tau}, \theta_{n+2\tau}, \ldots$ is lost for $\tau > 23$.

Instead of discarding values from the series generated by the logistic map, Lee, *et al.* [53] proposed to use just the lower bits of each obtained number, i.e. an integer number in the range $[0, S]$ is obtained at each iteration by means of the following transformation:

$$B_n = A x_n \bmod S, \tag{10}$$

where A is an arbitrary constant. In spite of its efficiency, this approach is not very functional since it strongly relies on the computer internal binary representation of the number generated by the logistic map; the obtained random sequence of B_n will depend on the hardware used, so that two different processors will generate different outputs.

All these methods share a common drawback inherent to the logistic map: the main secret key is a single parameter, i.e. r. Therefore, the resulting key space is small leaving the door open to a brute force attack. To avoid this problem, Li, *et al.* [54] suggested to build a coupled map lattice (CML) of different logistic maps, both the complexity of the cryptosystem and the number of secret keys were ameliorated. Every map $j = 1, \ldots, L$ in CML is defined by the following equation

$$x_{n+1}^j = (1 - \varepsilon) f(x_n^j, a_j) + \varepsilon f(x_n^{j-1}, a_{j-a}), \tag{11}$$

where ε is a coupling coefficient between different maps and $f(x, a)$ is the logistic map function described by Eq. 4 with parameter a. All maps are finally combined sequentially to create the output keystream

$$K_n^j = \mathrm{int}\left[2^u x_n^j\right] \bmod 2^v, \tag{12}$$

where u and v are arbitrary constants.

Rhouma and Belghith [55] recently criticized this approach with arguments that can hold for all stream ciphers based on chaotic maps. Namely, since the keystream is just a function of the system key(s) and does not vary when the plaintext changes, it is quite easy to retrieve this keystream by getting temporary access to the encryption machine and encrypting or decrypting an all zero message. For instance, if the keystream corresponding to a given keys combination is $K = (1, 0, 0, 1, 0, 1)$, when combined through a XOR operation with text $M = (0, 0, 0, 0, 0, 0)$, the output will be $C = (1, 0, 0, 1, 0, 1)$, i.e. the keystream itself. Any subsequent message will be decrypted as long as the keys remain unchanged. The algorithm security is thus totally violated.

Other Approaches Using Chaotic Maps

As previously stated, all approaches to chaotic cryptography using only one logistic map have proven to be insecure, mainly because the secret keys of the system are either the parameter r or the number of iterations or both. In this context, the approach of Pareek, *et al.* [26] has to be mentioned. They proposed to generate the system parameters in a non-trivial way, namely, by using an external secret key.

The method starts with a secret key of 128 bits split into groups of 8 bits: $K = K_1 K_2 K_3 \ldots K_{16}$. The initial conditions X_S and the number of iterations X_N are obtained as follows

$$
\begin{aligned}
X_S &= (K_1 \oplus K_2 \oplus \cdots \oplus K_{16})/256, \\
N_S &= (K_1 + K_2 + \cdots + K_{16}) \bmod 256.
\end{aligned}
\tag{13}
$$

The parameter r of the logistic map is also generated deterministically by a modified linear congruent random number generator initialized with an initial secret key. The map so defined is iterated and the output value X_{new} is used to encrypt the first message symbol P_0 as

$$
C_0 = (P_0 + \lfloor 256 X_{new} \rfloor) \bmod 256.
\tag{14}
$$

Then, subsequent symbols of the message are codified in a similar way, using the obtained X_{new} as the seed for the next iteration.

Unfortunately, in the same year Álvarez, *et al.* [56] managed to break down this algorithm. The generation of the parameter r of the map was the weakest point. According to Pareek's method, r can be taken among only 81 different values; and to make it worse, some of these possible values correspond to period-3 orbits. These limitations narrow the system dynamical range, allowing a very cheap brute-force attack: only three plaintexts of the approximately 1000-symbol length are needed.

This last failure in creating a secure algorithm using only a single logistic map was the trigger to change the paradigm; complexity had to be guaranteed in order to improve security. Therefore, combinations of chaotic maps appeared as a possible solution of this problem. Based on the previously published algorithm [26], Pareek *et al.* [57] constructed a cryptosystem by putting together four different chaotic maps: logistic, tent, sine, and cubic maps expressed, respectively, by the following four equations:

$$
\begin{aligned}
x_{n+1} &= \lambda x_n (1 - x_n), &(15) \\
x_{n+1} &= \begin{cases} \lambda x_n, & \text{if } x_n > 0.5, \\ \lambda(1 - x_n), & \text{if } x_n \le 0.5, \end{cases} &(16) \\
x_{n+1} &= \lambda \sin(\pi x_n), &(17) \\
x_{n+1} &= \lambda x_n (1 - x_n^2). &(18)
\end{aligned}
$$

The parameter λ for all maps is defined at the beginning of the encryption process, independently of the secret keys, and it is publicly shared with the receiver: in other words, the security is not dependent on the maps' parameters, but rather on their initial conditions previously generated with a certain simple equation from the secret keys. Before encryption, the plaintext is divided into blocks of different lengths, which are calculated from the secret keys with the help of a linear congruent random number generator, and are assigned to each chaotic map with the help of the same generator. In this way, different fragments of the plaintext are encoded with different chaotic maps; the receiver can easily undo the operation, by also calculating the initial conditions and blocks lengths from the secret keys.

To overcome the security problem with known plaintext attack, Wei, *et al.* [58] proposed further modifications of this algorithm, nevertheless, even their improved version was successfully cryptanalyzed one year later again by the Álvarez's group [59]; only 120 plain-bytes in one known plaintext were needed to recover the secret key.

Furthermore, the speed of this class of algorithms still remains a big challenge. Although Pareek, *et al.* [26, 57] claimed that their methods are faster than other alternative ciphers based on chaotic maps, to encrypt the content of a CD-ROM their algorithms use up 132 [26] and 95 [57] minutes.

Chaotic Maps for Public-key Cryptography

Only recently, public-key encryption algorithms based on chaotic systems have taken an important place back in the main stream of cryptography research. To illustrate how they work, suppose that a user called Bob wants to transmit a private message to another user, say Alice. Secret keys transmission is forbidden to insure security. Alice then creates a pair of keys, say d and e, so that computing d from e is computationally infeasible. d is a *private key* and Alice must keep it secret, while e is a *public key* that may be shared with everyone, particularly with Bob. Anyone wishing to send a message to Alice should encrypt it with the public key e, but the only way to decrypt it would be using the private key d, therefore Alice is the only one capable to do it. Thus, the public key serves only for encryption, while the private key serves only for decryption.

The first public-key chaotic algorithms implied neural networks coupled with chaotic maps [60, 61]. Meaning, both sender and receiver have identical neural networks driven by the same external sequence of random bits acting as the public key, while the internal connections' weight is used as the private key. The receiver uses the public key to synchronize his/her own network with the sender's and the private key to decrypt the message. When using chaotic synchronization, as the complexity of the neural networks increases, so do both the security and the computational cost (the time needed to synchronize the two networks grows up). While the system is apparently safe from an individual attack, it has been shown that a breach in security can be brought about with a *majority flipping attack*, that is, a group of attackers cooperate throughout the synchronization process [62].

Kocarev, *et al.* [63] proposed to put in the same category a wide class of chaotic encryption algorithms together with more classical approaches, such as RSA, ElGamal, or Rabinusing, describing them with the generalized map:

$$Y = T_p(X) \bmod N, \tag{19}$$

where p and N are integer numbers and $X \in \{0, 1, \ldots, N-1\}$. T_p are the Chebyshev polynomials of order p, defined by the following recurrent relation:

$$T_0(x) = 1, \tag{20}$$
$$T_1(x) = x, \tag{21}$$
$$T_2(x) = 2x^2 - 1, \tag{cuadmap}$$
$$T_{p+1}(x) = 2xT_p(x) - T_{p-1}(x). \tag{22}$$

Under this mapping, the interval $[-1, 1]$ is invariant, furthermore, for $p > 0$ the map is chaotic with an unique absolute continuous invariant measure with positive Lyapunov exponent $\ln p$. Moreover, for $p = 1$, the Chebyshev map reduces to the logistic map of Eq. 4. Since the map Eq. cuadmap is used as a generalization of the RSA algorithm to construct a public-key encryption algorithm [63], one might expect that, taking advantage of the intractability of the integer factorization problem, it will inherit its security. However, as was recently shown [64], the Chebyshev map alone cannot provide a good enough security.

Finally, one of the latest approaches to this class of problems was proposed in 2005 by Wang, *et al.* [65] through so-called "Merkle's puzzles" [66]. In this method the receiver first generates a large number (for instance, one million) of puzzles (messages) in the form: "This is puzzle number x and its secret key is y", where x and y are just a random number and a random secret key. All these messages are encrypted with a low security algorithm (for instance, with 20-bit keys) and sent to other users. The receivers of all these messages (including the one sending the secret message) chooses one of them at random, and performs a brute force attack on this message, in order to retrieve the pair (x, y). After that, he encrypts the message with y and send it back to the original user along with x. The target receiver now can easily decrypt this communication by just remembering which key was associated to the random number x, whereas a nonautorized user should perform a brute-force attack for each one of the original puzzles, thus facing an extremely high computational cost. Here, the main drawback is that the receiver has to keep all transmitted messages, to be able to retrieve the key once he gets the associated random number x. Security is only maintained with a large enough number of puzzles. To circumvent this difficulty, Wang, *et al.* [65] proposed to substitute the pair (x, y) by pseudo-random values generated with a one-way coupled map lattice composed by chaotic logistic maps. So that the receiver can instantaneously calculate the associated secret key from his knowledge of the puzzle identification code. The memory and computation time needed are therefore considerably reduced. One can keep its expectations high, since no attack has been successful so far.

Encryption of Images and Video

While classical cryptosystems (like IDEA, AES, DES or RSA) were originally designed to encrypt standard messages, mainly text, in the last decade a new kind of content in great need of attention (images, video, and multimedia information) has gained in importance. Graphical contents have some intrinsic characteristics which require special considerations when designing cryptographic algorithms. First of all, they are associated to large information quantities; as an extreme example, movies are stored in several GB of information, and second, they have to be decrypted in real time for a smooth viewing experience, therefore, velocity is a major requirement. Furthermore, images are characterized by an high redundancy of data, because of a strong correlation among adjacent pixels; the encryption algorithm should therefore be efficient in destroying any original pattern, no matter how broad, otherwise the human eye may be able to reconstruct part of the graphical information.

It is in this context that chaos-based cryptography has the most to offer, this is evident from the growing number of works devoted to image encryption [25, 9, 73, 72, 35, 74]. In chaotic block cryptosystems, chaotic maps are usually used to encrypt a plaintext[2] block by

---

[2]In some works on image encryption, plaintext and ciphertext are referred to as "plain image" and "cipher

block, whereas chaotic stream cryptosystems utilize a chaotic map for bit-by-bit encryption. Parameters and/or initial values of the diffusion function (chaotic map) normally serve as diffusion and confusion keys to modify sequentially pixel values and change pixel positions. Fridrich [9] was the first one to suggest a permutation of the pixel positions in a chaotic fashion, using either the Baker map or the cat map for chaotic confusion. However, Lian, *et al.* [25] pointed out that not all map parameters are secure enough to be used as encryption keys. Therefore, they designed a symmetric block cipher based on the chaotic standard map for a confusion process, plus a diffusion function and a key generator.

Since chaotic stream ciphers that utilize only one chaotic system to generate a pseudo-random sequence for image encryption, are not secure enough to withstand powerful cryptographic attacks, Guan, *et al.* [35] designed a more complex system which combines both discrete and continuous chaotic systems. At the confusion stage, pixel positions are shuffled by the Arnold cat map while at the diffusion stage, pixel values of the shuffled image are encrypted by the continuos Chen's chaotic system. Recently, Pareek, *et al.* [75] proposed an image encryption scheme which exploits two chaotic logistic maps and an external 80-bit key. The initial conditions for both logistic maps are derived from the external secret key. The first logistic map is used to generate numbers in the range between 1 and 24 and the initial condition of the second logistic map is modified by the numbers generated by the first logistic map. The authors showed that by modifying the initial condition of the second logistic map in this way, its dynamics becomes more unpredictable.

Unfortunately, in the majority of known algorithms based on a block cipher encryption technique, plaintext files are represented as blocks of bits. The encryption speed of such cryptosystems is relatively slow; the necessary number of iterations of the chaotic map for encrypting an 8-bit symbol is at least 200 and can reach 29617 [47]. A large block of plaintext, such as 128-bit, usually used in conventional cryptosystems, requires significantly higher velocity [58]. Since the length of ciphertext is often larger than the plaintext length, the size of encrypted multimedia files is enormous.

A completely different approach to image encryption has been proposed in Ref. [77]. Every image pixel is considered as a chaotic map on its own, in separating the colors (red, green, blue) the whole image is now represented by three chaotic map lattices, one for each color. Since the logistic map is noninvertible, to recuperate the original image all the maps (pixels) of the plain image should be coupled, so that every encrypted pixel contains some information on the original color of a neighboring pixel. In other words, all pixels are somehow mixed. For example, in the algorithm developed in Ref. [77] all maps are coupled (pixel by pixel) by initial conditions, providing a good diffusion property. Note, that the main problem in modern communication technology is not the security of an encryption algorithm, as much as its good dynamic properties, i.e. its robustness against noise or other external disturbances. It is in this sense, that unidirectional coupling of all image pixels worsens the dynamic properties, since the image cannot be recovered if even one pixel undergoes a small error.

To overcome this drawback, the novel cryptosystem instead of neighboring pixel coupling utilizes chaotic coupling or chaotic mixing of pixel's colors [79]. This allows a significant security enhancement, while decreasing the encryption time. From the topological

---

image" [25, 77].

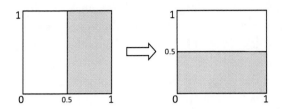

Figure 4. Graphical representation of the transformation performed by the 2D Baker map.

point of view, *mixing* in phase space means the system evolves over time in such a way that any given region or open set will eventually overlap with any other given region; the colored dyes mixing and turbulent fluids are prototypes of chaos.

2D and 3D Chaotic Maps

One of the first attempts to create an efficient cryptographic algorithm designed specifically for images was made by Fridrich [67], followed by the works of Pichler and Scharinger [68, 69]. The family of algorithms they proposed is based on bidimensional chaotic maps, i.e. a square interval (usually, the unit square $I \times I$, $I = [0, 1]$) maps onto itself in a one-to-one manner. Among all 2D chaotic maps, the standard map, the cat map, and the Baker map are most prevalent. When used on an $N \times N$ image, these maps can be written, respectively, in their discretized forms as:

$$\left\{ \begin{array}{l} x_{j+1} = (x_j + y_j) \bmod N, \\ y_{j+1} = (y_j + k \sin \frac{x_{j+1}N}{2\pi}) \bmod N, \end{array} \right. \tag{23}$$

$$\left[\begin{array}{c} x_{j+1} \\ y_{j+1} \end{array} \right] = \left[\begin{array}{cc} 1 & u \\ v & uv+1 \end{array} \right] \left[\begin{array}{c} x_j \\ y_j \end{array} \right] (\bmod N), \tag{24}$$

$$\left\{ \begin{array}{l} x_{j+1} = \frac{N}{k_i}(x_j - N_i) + y_j \bmod \frac{N}{k_i}, \\ y_{j+1} = \frac{k_i}{N}(y_j - y_j \bmod \frac{N}{k_i}) + N_i \end{array} \right. \quad \text{with} \quad \left\{ \begin{array}{l} k_1 + k_2 + \ldots + k_t = N, \\ N_i = k_i + \ldots + k_{i-1}, \\ N_i \le x_j < N_i + k_i, \\ 0 \le y_j < N. \end{array} \right. \tag{25}$$

Here, x_j and y_j are the coordinates of an image pixel at j iteration, u and v in the cat map Eq. 24 and $K = [k_1, k_2, \ldots, k_t]$ in the Baker map Eq. 25 are the parameters to be used as secret keys.

In the Fridrich's encryption scheme [67] based on the Baker map Eq. 25, the transformation represented in Figure 4 divides the image into two (or, more generally, into n) vertical strips, which are vertically stretched and horizontally compressed in order to be rearranged horizontally. The proposed encryption scheme, which has been widely used since, can be summarized as follows:

1. Define a suitable 2D chaotic map, mapping the unit square $I \times I$, $I = [0, 1]$ onto itself in a one-to-one manner; generalize that map by introducing some parameter

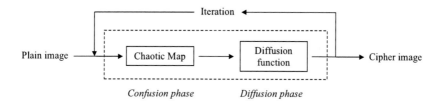

Figure 5. Image encryption scheme proposed by Fridrich [67].

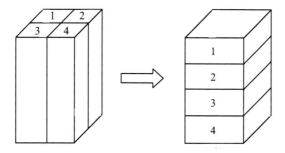

Figure 6. Graphical representation of the transformation performed by the 3D Baker map.

that alters its standard behavior and discretize it. At the end, what is obtained is a map which takes each pixel and assigns it to some other pixel in a bijective manner (the discretized version is a permutation of pixels).

2. Extend the previous 2D map to a 3D map, where the third dimension will be used to permute the gray-scale value of each pixel. In this way, the actual color content of each pixel is also changed. An efficient and secure cipher applied to a black square should result in a uniform histogram.

3. Compose the previous map with a simple diffusion mechanism to spread the information of one pixel over different pixels.

4. Repeat steps 2 and 3 as many times as needed.

This process is schematically represented in Figure 5.

Due to its extremely high efficiency, the method proposed by Fridrich [67] has been widely explored afterward. It allows encoding more than 16 MB of information in one second with a standard 1GHz processor. Analyzing the security of the Fridrich's algorithm, Lian, *et al.* [25] found it relies mostly on the diffusion process, so that once broken, the remaining part (the confusion process) can be easily attacked with almost any known plaintext strategy at a relatively low computational cost.

Later on, several modifications (evolutions) to the Fridrich's approach have been proposed (see, for instance, Refs. [70, 71]). New algorithms for image encryption based on 3D chaotic maps have also been developed (see, e.g., Refs. [72, 73]). The previously introduced 2D Baker map was expanded to the third dimension [72], as shown in Figure 6. Such 3D maps have at least two advantages: first, the third dimension is directly used in the confusion phase computation, hence lowering the computational cost of the algorithm; and second, the 3D map is a more complex system than the equivalent 2D map, if two of the three dimensions have positive Lyapunov exponents, the system becomes hyper-chaotic.

Image Encryption with Multiple Maps

In principle, a single map either 2D or 3D has a small key space dimension, to improve security several attempts had to be made to use multiple unidimensional maps coupled together. In a new effort Li, *et al.* [76] proposed a single chaotic map to generate two vectors of 2^n values to be iterated them 2×2^n times. These two vectors are then used to define the initial value and the control parameter of other 2^n chaotic maps (called $ECS(i)$, $i \in [1, 2^n]$). In order to increase the computational speed of the system, as well as to reduce the cost of the hardware implementation, all calculations are performed in fixed-point arithmetic with a precision of L bits.

However, some new problems arise, the most important being that there are only 2^L values available to represent any value in the chaotic orbits, and therefore the cycle length of any chaotic orbit cannot be larger than 2^L. In other words, the dynamics is no longer chaotic, because it is being trapped in closed periodic orbits. The solution for this drawback is to perturb the dynamics of the chaotic map with a small signal $\xi(i)$ produced by a pseudo-random number generator. Once all the 2^n chaotic maps have been initialized, the plaintext is divided into groups of L bits; for each one of these groups, the main map is iterated and the obtained value i gives the label of the map to be used (from the 2^n possible maps). This map is then also iterated, and the value obtained is used to encrypt the group of bits with a bitwise XOR operation. After this operation, one last encryption step is performed: the 2^n chaotic maps are sorted, and all indices of the sorted states and the original states are used for a substitution process (S-Box). Due to the fixed-point arithmetic, this algorithm is extremely fast; its final speed is about 1/10 of the CPU frequency, therefore a 2.0 GHz processor can encrypt up to 200 MBytes each second [76].

A set of chaotic maps was also used in Ref. [77], where to each and every pixel a different logistic map is associated, these maps are then coupled in a sequential fashion. To encode the i-pixel value x_i, the algorithm takes the encrypted value x_{i-1} of the previous pixel $i - 1$, applies the logistic map n times and sums the result of the iteration to the actual pixel value; the end result is the encrypted value for pixel i. Clearly this algorithm has a great sensitivity to initial conditions: small changes in one pixel of the plain image propagates through all the maps, changing completely the cipher image. The weak point of this algorithm was highlighted two years after by Arroyo, *et al.* [78]; different maps of the lattice, i.e. different pixels of the image, are coupled pixel-by-pixel, reducing the complexity of the algorithm. Moreover, some of the parameters, like the number of iterations of the logistic map, may be obtained with a timing attack by measuring the time needed to encrypt an image of known size.

The problem related with the unidirectional coupling was overruled in Ref. [79]; instead of coupling a pixel i with pixel $i - 1$, a new logistic map is used to generate a number k_i for each pixel ($k \in [0, m]$, where m is the total number of pixels in the image); pixel i is now coupled with pixel k_i. Moreover, it was shown that many operations, especially the ones concerning the logistic map, can be pre-calculated and memory stored; and last but not least, this is the fastest chaotic algorithm ever proposed: a 2.0 GHz processor allows a velocity of about 280 MBytes of information per second.

Different chaotic maps have also been applied to two main stages of the encryption process, that is, the permutation and substitution (P-Box and S-Box). In the following, we will review several works where the design of both boxes calls for different chaotic functions.

In this context, Zhang, *et al.* [80] tackled the creation of a P-Box algorithm suitable for image encryption (with a low computational cost) with chaotic maps. The aim was, as in the already described work [76], to avoid floating-point arithmetic. Their proposal was to use a discrete exponential chaotic map defined as:

$$x_{n+1} = g(x_n) = \begin{cases} a^{x_n} (\mathrm{mod}\, 257) & if \ \ x_{n+1} < 256, \\ 0 & if \ \ x_{n+1} = 256, \end{cases} \tag{26}$$

where $x \in 0, 1, \ldots, 255$. Parameter a is chosen so that the map g does generate a multiplicative group of nonzero elements of the Galois field of order 257; for any of the 128 possible values of a fulfilling this condition, the associated map g performs a one-to-one transformation.

A different approach was proposed by Gao, *et al.* [81], subsequently adopted by other authors, like Xiao and Xia [82]. Since many cryptosystems based on the logistic map had already been cryptanalyzed, they tried to design a custom made chaotic map that had to fulfill certain requirements. First of all, this new map has to present a chaotic behavior in the whole range of parameters, then it must also have a good balance between zeros and ones, zero cross-correlations, and high nonlinearity. In other words, the output of this new map should be as similar as possible to a random binary sequence. The recursive function that gets the job done is the following:

$$x_{n+1} = \left(1 - \beta^{-4}\right) ctg \left(\frac{\alpha}{1+\beta}\right) \left(1 + \frac{1}{\beta}\right)^{\beta} tg\left(\alpha x_n\right) \left(1 - x_n\right)^{\beta}, \tag{27}$$

where $x_n \in (0, 1)$. Three distinct chaotic regions in the (α, β)-parameter space can be exploited: either $\alpha \in (0, 1.4]$, $\beta \in [5, 43]$, or $\alpha \in (1.4, 1.5]$, $\beta \in [9, 38]$, or $\alpha \in (1.5, 1.57]$, $\beta \in [3, 15]$. The permutation process takes place as follows [82]. To exclude transitions the map Eq. 27 is first iterated K times, and then $N \times N$ times to create an array $X = x_K, x_{K+1}, \ldots, x_{K+N^2}$ (N being the image size); finally, X is arranged in an ascending order to form a permutation vector Y.

However, the function of Eq. 27 entails at least two distinct problems. First, too many calculations are needed to compute each term of the array because of the use of powers of fractional numbers and trigonometric functions whose implementation in standard hardware is not yet optimized. Second, there is a breach of security. Álvarez and Shujun Li [83] have shown that the values distribution in the sequence of x_n is not flat, as could be expected from a pseudo-random number generator. The left-hand side of Figure 7 shows the time series obtained from 1000 iterations of the map, and the right-hand side displays the corresponding histogram. The clear asymmetric distribution does indeed invalidate the security of any cryptosystem built upon it, because an attacker may infer some information from the values with higher probability.

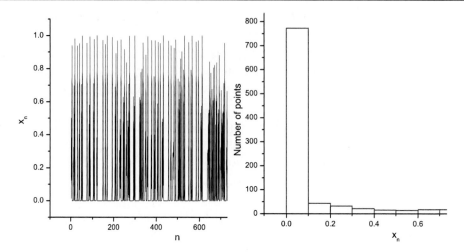

Figure 7. (Left) Time series of 1000 iterations of the chaotic map proposed by Gao *et al.* [81], at parameters $\alpha = 0.7$ and $\beta = 10$. (Right) Corresponding histogram showing that the distribution of x_n is not flat.

Later, to achieve a more complex permutation pattern Sun, *et al.* [84] devised another strategy taking advantage of the inherent structure of any 2D image. To illustrate their method, suppose we have a 2D $m \times n$ image, or data array in orthogonal Dekart coordinates with X and Y axes. The algorithm first creates two linear arrays M and N of sizes m and n, respectively, and fills these arrays using a chaotic map; then, both columns and rows are permuted, depending on the values originally stored in M and N, by applying a given rule. In their work Sun's, *et al.* use the logistic map in order to fill both arrays with unique integer numbers. As an example, suppose that the output of the logistic map is $x = \{0.1208, 0.8457, 0.1210, 0.4835, \ldots\}$; these values are multiplied by the array size (m or n) and rounded to the next integer (e.g., with $m = 10$), the result is $x' = \{2, 9, 2, 5, \ldots\}$. Since no repeated values could be accepted, the third number is discarded, i.e. $M = \{2, 9, 5, \ldots\}$. Although the process of permuting both rows and columns does effectively improve security, the computational cost largely increases because repeated values have to be discarded; each time a value is generated, it must be compared with all previous values. This is the main shortcoming of this approach.

The use of a simple digital function as a chaotic map can alleviate this problem [85]. Such a function is the Gray code named after Frank Gray [86]. It has the property that the representation of two successive values differs in one bit only. To transform a binary number into its Gray representation, it should be multiplied by $Q = q \times q$ matrix defined as follows: (i) 1 in the main diagonal, (ii) 1 along the upper/minor diagonal, and (iii) 0 elsewhere, with every operation performed in $mod\ 2$. For example, the matrix Q for $q = 4$ bits would be

$$Q = \begin{bmatrix} 1 & 1 & 0 & 0 \\ 0 & 1 & 1 & 0 \\ 0 & 0 & 1 & 1 \\ 0 & 0 & 0 & 1 \end{bmatrix}. \tag{28}$$

A more efficient conversion algorithm for a software or hardware implementation is given by

$$G = B \oplus (B \gg 1), \tag{29}$$

where G is the resulting Gray number, B is the original number (in a binary representation), $\oplus$ is the binary XOR operation, and $\gg$ represents the binary right shift. Using this Gray code, a simple nonlinear transformation T may be defined: given a binary number x in a q-bits code, calculate its Gray representation with Eq. 29, and then read the result in a standard binary representation. The proposed T-transformation has several advantages, namely, it is a bijective map in the whole 2^q space, the output is nonlinear, especially for high values of q, and finally the software implementation is extremely fast, since it does not require any floating-point calculation.

The ideas of many researchers discussed in this chapter are still the corner stone of many publications, only in 2009 the most important Refs. [87, 88, 89, 90] should be mentioned. In spite of all the efforts, many problems of chaotic cryptography still remain, and some of these difficulties will be probed in the following section.

Limitations of Chaotic Cryptography

Even though, in recent years there is been a tremendous boom in chaos-based cryptography research, there are still some limitations that prevent its wider application. Emphasizing, a big drawback is its relatively slow speed. While many of the proposed chaotic algorithms (see, for instance [8, 42]) can encrypt with as much speed as 10-50 Kbps (kilobits per second), standard nonchaotic algorithms have velocities three order of magnitude higher (AES ranges from 50 to 200 Mbps using a 1 GHz Pentium ®processor). Many factors can explain such poor performance. First, chaotic maps usually operate with floating-point numbers, i.e. with decimal numbers whose manipulation is never as efficient as integer or bitwise representations. For instance, a 64-bits Intel processor uses 6 times more clocks to add floating-point numbers than integer values [91]. To take full advantage of a chaotic map ergodicity, a lot of iterations are required and many values have to be discarded, for example, in his work [8] Baptista should perform around 30000 iterations for every encoded symbol.

The use of floating-point variables not only generates a speed problem but also gives birth to other issues related to the computer numbers representation. Clearly, the internal precision cannot be infinite, and a convention about internal representation or a way to execute operations or roundings had to be defined. Such a convention does already exist, this is a set of rules called **IEEE 754** [92]. However, while most standard computer processors, such as Intel Pentium IV or i7 ®, follow this set of rules, the use of some new, fast and efficient processors like Cell BroadBand Engine ®system developed by IBM [93] that do not adhere to these rules, is spreading for high demanding computational and multimedia applications. The reason they do not obey the IEEE 754 rules is that the required way of performing round-offs is very expensive, while the introduction of some small modifications to the process (leaving the final result practically unchanged) increases substantially the computational power [94]. Nevertheless, these small differences become very important

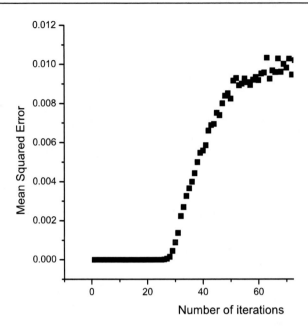

Figure 8. Mean Squared Error between two time generated by the same logistic map in a 32 bits representation, calculated with the Intel chip-set and the IBM processor. Note, that only for series smaller than 30 values, the different rounding algorithm does not affect the final result.

when computing chaotic maps, because of their high sensitivity to small variations in their parameters, and/or initial conditions.

Figure 8 shows the Mean Squared Error between two time series generated by the same logistic map Eq. 4 (the same parameter r and the same initial value), but calculated with two different computers, the Pentium IV ®processor and the Cell BroadBand Engine ®processor.

While high sensitivity to initial conditions is indeed a great theoretical asset for cryptographic applications, practically it is also its main weakness, since after as little as 30 iterations the series generated by two different processors have nothing in common. This means that a message encoded with one processor cannot be correctly decoded by a different processor; thus chaotic cryptography is still very limited in real-world applications. Even if the use of identical processors by both the sender and the receiver can be guaranteed, the differences in software implementation can provoke similar problems; such as the calculation precision of the floating-point representation, i.e., the number of bits used to characterize a number, for instance, standard processors offer 32-bits (called *float*), 64-bits (*double*), and 80-bits (*long double*) representations.

Suppose we create a series with a logistic map and that the values are rounded at some decimal digit. The important question is: How many significant digits can we trust, if the original floating-point precision is unknown? To answer this question, pairs of series have been generated with the same initial value and parameter, but using different floating-point representations (32 and 64 bits). Afterward, values in both series of a pair have been rounded at the same decimal digit, and the number of identical value has been calculated. In

Table 2. Mean, maximum, and minimum numbers of equal values obtained with two logistic maps; every map has the same initial value and the same parameter a, the only difference is the floating-point precision, 32 and 64 bits. The series have been calculated with the Intel processor

Number of decimal digits	Mean	Max	Min
1	37.801	844	7
2	14.434	984	1
3	4.436	935	1
4	2.235	902	1
5	1.124	234	1

Table 3. Mean, maximum, and minimum numbers of equal values obtained with two logistic maps using 32 and 64 bits precision with the IBM Cell Broadband Engine

Number of decimal digits	Mean	Max	Min
1	37.456	801	7
2	32.527	984	7
3	26.834	990	2
4	21.460	885	2
5	13.549	267	2

Table 2 is represented the maximum, mean, and minimum of the number of identical values in both series, when several realizations of the process are executed. Due to the internal rounding, we may get different output values as soon as the first iteration; therefore, when implementing a chaotic cryptosystem, a general requirement is to use identical calculation engines. A similar result is obtained for the IBM Cell Broadband Engine microprocessor (see Table 3) because of the difference in their rounding algorithms; the mean number of a value is one order of magnitude higher when a high precision is required. Nevertheless, the minimum number is still too low for any cryptographic purpose.

Key-space Determination

The fundamental tenet of any cryptographic algorithm lies in its secret key(s). As previously underlined according to Kerckhoffs' principle [44], the security of an algorithm must depend only on the key, never on its own secrecy. Therefore, it is of the upmost importance to decide which keys are suitable and secure, and the number of keys available for a user.

In standard cryptosystems, all values in a given interval are suitable as secret keys, for instance, in the 128-bits AES standard, any integer number of 128 bits can be used, i.e. within the range $[0, 2^{128} - 1]$. In contrast, when choosing the secret key to modify the behavior of a chaotic map, the designer of the algorithm has to take into account the existence of periodic windows in chaotic regions and make sure that no parameter value in

Table 4. Number of periodic windows for a Intel ^{TM}processor, following IEEE standard, in *float* (32 bits) and *double* (64 bits) representation

Precision	Number of digits	Number of parameters	$L = 10$	$L = 30$	$L = 100$
32	5	43000	2434	4161	5283
	6	430000	24518	41472	52768
	7	4300000	245882	414972	526967
	8	43000000	2459030	4149830	5270743
64	5	43000	2296	3453	3600
	6	430000	23047	34459	36056
	7	4300000	230173	344561	360495
	8	43000000	2301677	3446857	3605303

Table 5. Key-space dimension for a 64 bits representation, excluding the periodic windows of length $L \leq 100$ multiplied by a security factor of 1.5

Number of digits	Key-space (bits, Intel)	Key-space (bits, CBE)
5	15.198	15.198
6	18.520	18.520
7	21.842	21.841
8	25.164	25.163

the key set will result in a predictable behavior of the system. If the reader goes back to the bifurcation diagram of the logistic map in Figure 2, he/she may recognize the ranges, where only a few points are painted in black for some values of the parameter r. Although these windows have been found analytically for many years, it is very important, in the context of the encryption process, to localize them, because of the limited precision of the numbers used in calculations, they strongly will depend on the standard used for handling floating-point representations.

Table 4 shows the number of periodic windows for the logistic map when r is between 3.57 and 4, for 32 and 64 bits number representation, and with values x_n rounded at a different decimal digit. Moreover, the results are shown for different lengths of the periodic windows; depending on the application at hand, a little periodicity may be tolerated, e.g. when the logistic map is used to generate a small set of parameters. It is interesting to note how the number of periodic windows grows higher when a 32-bits representation is used, due to its low resolution.

When implementing a chaotic map in an encryption scheme, it is essential to know exactly its key-space dimension, because the resistance of the algorithm against brute force attacks depends only on it. Furthermore, we insist that not all parameter values are of use, due to the presence of periodic windows.

In Table 5 the key space is measured in bits, according to the Shannon seminal formula for information content assessment [95, 96]:

$$D_{ks} = \log_2 \left(N_v - 1.5 N_{pw} \right), \tag{30}$$

where N_v is the number of values the parameter can assume, and N_{pw} is the number of periodic windows according to Table 4. The number of periodic windows is multiplied by a security factor of 1.5, in order to exclude parameters that may lead to time series with periodic windows of length greater than 100; therefore, key space dimensions calculated this way are to be considered as a conservative lower bound of the real value. Note, that when the periodic windows are excluded, the original 64-bits space dimension is reduced to a 25-bits key, that is too small to ensure any security. So, each algorithm has to specify a sub-algorithm to help the user build a larger secret key more suitable for encryption.

Conclusions and Future Trends

In this chapter a broad selection of cryptographic algorithms based on chaotic maps was presented; their latest successes as well as their many drawbacks were analyzed and perspectives were conjured up. In spite of some limitations, this new branch of cryptography is indeed growing up very fast. New secure and fast chaotic algorithms are being created endlessly. Even though it is really impossible to predict beforehand how well these systems will stand up to a real attack because no matter the algorithm used, there will always be an experienced attacker attempting to break it, we consider that chaotic cryptography will be the solution for more complex applications as soon as the computer technology catches up.

Chaos-based cryptography has several advantages over the traditional one. (i) It provides a great assortment of chaotic functions and parameters to be used, thus diversifying the ways the message can be encoded and increasing the key size as well. In contrast, traditional cryptosystems employ algorithms where diffusion and confusion are linear functions of the number of iterations and key lengths. (ii) As stated in many papers, chaotic mapping functions are random-like without losing their deterministic properties, so that a well-designed encryption algorithm prevents any statistical analysis from revealing the spectral characteristics of an encrypted signal. (iii) Last but not least, chaos cryptography can be directly implemented in hardware without having to resort to digital-to-analogue conversion, as traditionally done. Since any form of conversion implies a loss of precision and slows down the encryption process, the build in of a continuous chaotic function (e.g., Chua, Lorenz, Rössler) or a discrete iterative map as part of a hardware circuit, increases its efficiency. This process is not limited by current computer technology and allows working at full speed on a continuous analogue signal without major difficulties. Summarizing, the principal advantages of chaos encryption are resistance to known typical attacks, diversity of possible algorithms, impossibility of frequency spectrum analysis, and suitability for implementation in analog systems.

When designing any cryptosystem, one seeks both security and velocity. Future trends in cryptography have to be directed to the search of new ways to fulfill the requirements of a growing communication technology guaranteeing both. We believe that faster and more powerful computers capable to encrypt a huge amount of data in real time will prove to be an asset for chaotic cryptography. To enhance security, new encryption algorithms will probably use families of chaotic multimodal maps, combine discrete and continuous chaotic systems, implement complex dynamical networks as secret keys, and utilize chaos synchronization. A high performance of new cryptosystems will most likely be achieved by bringing together traditional and chaotic cryptographic approaches, as well as applying some elements of quantum cryptography to send secret keys. Although quantum cryptography is the most secure, it is very slow, so that it will have to be used in combination with fast chaotic algorithms to make it practical.

We acknowledge CONACYT (Mexico) for the financial support through the project No. 100429.

References

[1] Schneier, B., *Applied Cryptography - Protocols, Algorithms, and Source Code*, second ed., C. John Wiley & Sons, Inc., New York, 1996.

[2] Daemen, J.; Sand, B.; Rijmen, V. *The Design of Rijndael: AES - The Advanced Encryption Standard*, Springer-Verlag, Berlin, 2002.

[3] Shanon, C. E. *Bell. Syst. Tech. J.* 1949, 28, 656–715.

[4] Matthews, R. *Cryptologia* 1989, XIII, 29–42.

[5] Pecora, L. M.; Carroll, T. L. *Physical Review Letters*, 1990, 64, 821–824.

[6] Kocarev, L.; Halle, K. S.; Eckert, K.; Chua, L. O.; Parlitz, U. *Int. J. Bifurcation and Chaos* 1992, 2, 709–713.

[7] Habutsu, T.; Nishio, Y.; Sasase, I.; Mori, S., *Advances in Cryptology - EuroCrypt'91, Lecture Notes in Computer Science* 0547, pp. 127-140, Spinger-Verlag, Berlin, 1991.

[8] Baptista, M. S. *Phys. Lett. A* 1998, 240, 50–54.

[9] Fridrich, J. *Int. J. Bifurcation and Chaos* 1998, 8, 1259–1284.

[10] Álvarez, E.; Fernández, A.; García, P.; Jiménez, J.; Marcano, A. *Physics Letters A* 1999, 263, 373–375.

[11] Ashwin, P. *Nature* 2003, 422, 384–385.

[12] Argyris, A.; Syvridis, D.; Larger, L.; Annovazzi-Lodi, V.; Colet, P.; Fischer, I.; García-Ojalvo, J.; Mirasso, C. R.; Pesquera, L.; Shore, K. A. *Nature*, 2005, 438, 343–346.

[13] Tang, S.; Chen, H.-F.; Liu, J.-M., *Digital Communications Using Chaos and Nonlinear Dynamics, Series: Institute for Nonlinear Science*, L. E. Larson, J.-M. Liu, and L. S. Tsimring, Eds. New York: Springer, 2006, 341–378.

[14] Shore, K. A.; Spencer, P. S.; Pierce, I., *Recent Advances in Laser Dynamics: Control and Synchronization*, A. N. Pisarchik, Ed. Kerala: Research Singpost, 2008, 79–104.

[15] Pisarchik, A. N.; Ruiz-Oliveras, F. R. *IEEE J. Quant. Electron.* 2010, 46, 279–284.

[16] Wheeler, D. D. *Cryptologia* 1989, XIII, 243–250.

[17] Wheeler, D. D.; Matthews, R. *Cryptologia* 1991, XV, 140–151.

[18] Biham, E., Advances in Cryptology - EuroCrypt'91, *Lecture Notes in Computer Science* 0547, 532–534, Spinger-Verlag, Berlin, 1991.

[19] Zhou, H.; Ling, X.-T. *IEEE Trans. Circuits and Systems I* 1997, 44, 268–271.

[20] Alvarez, G.; Montoya, F.; Romera, M.; Pastor, G. *Physics Letters A* 2000, 276, 191–196.

[21] Hayes, S.; Grebogi, C.; Ott, E.; Mark, A. *Phys. Rev. Lett.* 1994, 73, 1781–1784.

[22] Short, K. M. *Int. J. Bifurcation and Chaos* 1997, 7, 1579–1597.

[23] Ogorzatek, M. J.; Dedieu, H. Proc. *IEEE Int. Symposium Circuits and Systems* 1998, 4, 522–525.

[24] Ekert, A. K. *Phys. Rev. Lett.* 1991, 67, 661–663.

[25] Lian, S. G.; Sun, J.; Wang, Z. *Physica A* 2005, 351, 645–661.

[26] Pareek, N. K.; Patidar, V.; Sud, K. K. *Phys. Lett. A* 2003, 309, 75–82.

[27] Huang, F.; Guan, Z. H. *Chaos Solitons Fractals*, 2005, 23, 851–855.

[28] Wei, J.; Liao, X.; Wong, K. W.; Xiang, T. *Chaos Solitons Fractals*, 2006, 30, 143–152.

[29] Kocarev, L.; Parlitz, U. *Phys. Rev. Lett.* 1995, 74, 5028.

[30] Parlitz, U.; Kocarev, L.; Stojanovski, T.; Preckel, H. *Phys. Rev. E* 1996, 53, 4351.

[31] Kocarev, L.; Parlitz, U.; Stojanovski, T. *Phys. Lett. A* 1996, 217, 280.

[32] Scharinger, J. *J. Electronic Eng* 1998, 7, 318–325.

[33] Klein, E.; Mislovaty, R.; Kanter, I.; Kinzel, W. *Phys. Rev.* E 2005, 72, 016214.

[34] Chien, T.-I.; Liao, T.-L. *Chaos, Solitons and Fractals* 2005, 24, 241–255.

[35] Guan, Z. H.; Huang, F. J.; Guan, W. *J. Phys. Lett. A* 2005, 346, 153–157.

[36] Gao, T.; Chen, Z. *Chaos, Solitons & Fractals* 2007, 38, 213–220.

[37] Gao, T.; Chen, Z. *Physics Letters A* 2008, 372, 394–400.

[38] Xiao, D.; Liao, X.; Wei, P. *Chaos, Solitons and Fractals* 2009, 40, 2191–2199.

[39] Kelber, K.; Schwarz, W. *NOLTA* 2005, Bruges.

[40] Verhulst, P.-F. *Nouv. mém. de l'Academie Royale des Sci. et Belles-Lettres de Brux-elles* 1845, 18, 1–41.

[41] Verhulst, P.-F. *Mém. de l'Academie Royale des Sci. des Lettres et des Beaux-Arts de Belgique* 1847, 20, 1–32.

[42] Wong, W.-K., Lee, L.-P., Wong, K.-W. *Computer physics communications* 2001, 138, 234–236.

[43] Jakimoski, G., Kocarev, L. *Phys. Lett. A* 2001, 291, 381–384.

[44] Kerckhoffs, A. *Journal des sciences militaires* 1883, IX, 161–191.

[45] Wong, K.-W. *Phys. Lett. A* 2002, 298, 238–242.

[46] Palacios, A., Juarez, H. *Phys. Lett. A* 2002, 303, 345–351.

[47] Wong, K.-W. *Phys. Lett. A* 2003, 307, 292–298.

[48] Wong, K.-W., Ho, S. W., Yung, C. K. *Phys. Lett. A* 2003, 310, 67–73.

[49] Alvarez, G., Montoya, F., Romera, M., Pastor, G. *Phys. Lett. A* 2004, 326, 211-218.

[50] Bianco, M. E., Reed, D. A., Encryption System Based on Chaos theory, US Patent No. 5048086, Sept. 10.A, 1991.

[51] Bianco, M. E., Mayhew, G. L., High Speed Encryption System and Method, US Patent No. 5365588, Nov.15, 1994.

[52] Phatak, S. C., Rao, S. S. *Phys. Rev. E* 1995, 51.

[53] Lee, P. H., Pei, S.-C., Chen, Y.-Y. *Chinese Journal of Physics* 2003, 41.

[54] Li, P., Li, Z., Halang, W. A., Chen, G. A. *Chaos, Solitons & Fractals* 2007, 32, 1867–1876.

[55] Rhouma, R., Belghith, S. *Chaos, Solitons & Fractals* 2009, 41, 171–1722.

[56] Alvarez, G., Montoya, F., Romera, M., Pastor G. *Phys. Lett. A* 2003, 319, 334–339.

[57] Pareek, N. K., Patidar, V., Sud, K. K. *Communications in Nonlinear Science and Numerical Simulation* 2005, 10, 715–723.

[58] Wei, J., Liao, X., Wong, K.-W., Zhou, T. *Communications in Nonlinear Science and Numerical Simulation* 2007, 12, 814–822.

[59] Li, C., Li, S., Álvarez, G., Chen, G., Lo, K. T. *Chaos, Solitons & Fractals* 2008, 37, 299–307.

[60] Kanter, I., Kinzel, W., Kanter, E. *Europhys. Lett.* 2002, 57.

[61] Mislovaty, R., Klein, E., Kanter, I., Kinzel, W. *Phys. Rev. Lett.* 2003, 91.

[62] Shacham, L. N., Klein, E., Mislovaty, R., Kanter, I., Kinzel, W. *Phys. Rev. E.* 2004, 69.

[63] Kocarev, L., Sterjev, M., Fekete, A., Vattay, G. *Chaos* 2004, 14.

[64] Bergamo, P., Arco, P., De Santis, A. *IEEE Transactions on Circuits and Systems* 2005, 52, 1382–1393.

[65] Wang, X., Gong, X., Zhan, M., Lai, C. H. *Chaos* 2005, 15.

[66] Merkle, R. C. *Commun. ACM* 1978, 21.

[67] Fridrich, J. *IEEE International Conference on Systems, Man, and Cybernetics,* 1997.

[68] Pichler, F.; Scharinger, J. In: Contributions to General Algebra, *Proc. of the Linz-Conference,* June 2-5, 1994.

[69] Pichler, F.; Scharinger, J. *Proceedings of the 20th Workshop of the Austrian Association for Pattern Recognition (OAGM/AAPR) on Pattern Recognition* 1996.

[70] Salleh, M.; Ibrahim, S.; Isnin, I. F. *Jurnal Teknologi* 2003, 39, 1–12.

[71] Wong, K.-W.; Kwok, B. S.-H.; Law, W.-S. *Phys. Lett. A* 2008, 372, 2645–652.

[72] Mao, Y.; Chen, G.; Lian, S. *Intern Journal of Bifurcation and Chaos* 2004, 14, 3613–3624.

[73] Chen, G.; Mao, Y.; Chui, C. K. *Chaos, Solitons and Fractals* 2004, 21, 749–761.

[74] Wang, K.; Pei, W. *J. Phys. Lett. A* 2005, 343, 432–439.

[75] Pareek, N. K., Patidar, V., Sud, K. K. *Image and Vision Computing* 2006, 24, 926–934.

[76] Li, S.; Zheng, X.; Mou, X.; Cai, Y. *Proc. SPIE* 2002, 4666, 149–160.

[77] Pisarchik, A. N.; Flores-Carmona, N. J.; Carpio-Valadez, M. *Chaos* 2006, 16, 033118.

[78] Arroyo, D.; Rhouma, R.; Alvarez, G.; Li, S.; Fernandez, V. *Chaos* 2008, 18, 033112.

[79] Pisarchik, A. N.; Zanin, M. *Physica D* 2008, 237, 2638–2648.

[80] Zhang, L.; Liao, X.; Wang, X. *Chaos, Solitons and Fractals* 2005, 24, 759–765.

[81] Gao, H.; Zhang, Y.; Liang, S.; Li, D. *Chaos, Solitons and Fractals* 2009, 29, 393–399.

[82] Xiao, Y-L.; Xia, L-M. *Chaos, Commun. Theor. Phys.* 2009, 52, 876–880.

[83] Alvarez, G.; Li, S. *Communications in Nonlinear Science and Numerical Simulation* 2009, 14, 3743–3749.

[84] Sun, F.; Liu, S.; Li, Z.; Lü, Z. *Chaos Solitons Fractals*, 2008, 38, 631–640.

[85] Zanin, M.; Pisarchik, A. N. *Information Sciences*, in press, 2010.

[86] Savage, C. *SIAM Review*, 1997, 39, 605–629.

[87] Patidar, V.; Pareek, N.K.; Sud, K. K. *Communications in Nonlinear Science and Numerical Simulation* 2009, 14, 3056–3075.

[88] Huang, C. K.; Nien, H. H. *Optics Communications* 2009, 282, 2123-2127.

[89] Mazloom, S.; Eftekhari-Moghadam, A. M. *Chaos, Solitons & Fractals* 2009, 42, 1745-1754.

[90] Lian, S. Chaos, *Solitons & Fractals* 2009, 42, 2509–2519.

[91] Intel Corporation, Intel® 64 and IA-32 *Architectures Optimization Reference Manual*, 2009.

[92] ANSI/IEEE Std 754-1985, "IEEE Standard for Binary Floating-Point Arithmetic", *Standards Committee of the IEEE Computer Society*, 1985.

[93] IBM, *"Cell Broadband Engine: Programming Handbook"*, Version 1.1, (2007).

[94] IBM, *"SIMD Math Library Specification for Cell Broadband Engine Architecture"*, Version 1.1, (2007).

[95] Shannon, C. E. *The Bell System Technical Journal* 1981, 27, 379–423.

[96] Cover, T. M.; Thomas, J. A. *"Elements of Information Theory"*, 2006, Wiley Interscience.

[97] Tsueike, M.; Ueta, T.; Nishio, Y., "An application of two-dimensional chaos cryptosystem", *Technical Report of IEICE*, NLP96-19, May 1996.

[98] Tong, X.; Cui, M. *Signal Processing* 2009, 89, 480–491.

[99] Tsekeridou, S.; Solachidis, V.; Nikolaidis, N.; Nikolaidis, A.; Tefas, A.; Pitas, I., *Proceedings of IEEE international conference on acoustics, speech and signal processing*, 2001, 1989–1992.

[100] Nikolaidis, A.; Pitas, I., *Proceedings of IEEE international symposium on circuits and systems*, Geneva, 2002, 509–512.

[101] Tefas, A.; Nikolaidis, A.; Nikolaidis, N.; Solachidis, V.; Tsekeridou, S.; Pitas, I., *Proceedings of chaos, solitons and fractals*, vol. 17, 2003, 567–73.

[102] Escribano, F. J.; López, L.; Sanjuán, M. A. F. *Chaos* 2006, 16, 013103.

[103] Hongjuna, L.; Xingyuan, W. *Computers and Mathematics with Applications* 2010, 59, 3320–3327.

[104] Khan, M. K.; Xie, L.; Zhang, J. *Digital Signal Processing* 2010, 20, 179–190.

[105] Chee, C. Y.; Xu, D. *Physics Letters A* 2006, 348, 284–292.

[106] Singh, N.; Sinha, A. *Optics & Laser Technology* 2010, 42, 724–731.

[107] Zhou, J.; Pei, W.; Wang, K.; Huang, J.; He, Z. *Physics Letters A* 2006, 358, 283–288.

[108] Matthews, R. *Cryptologia* 2984, VIII, 29–41.

[109] Masuda, N.; Aihara, K. *IEEE Trans. Circ. Syst-I* 2002, 49, 28–40.

[110] Sang, T.; Wang, R.; Yan, Y. *Acta Eletronica Sinica* 1999, 27, 47–50.

[111] Behnia, S.; Akhshani, A.; Ahadpour, S.; Mahmodi, H.; Akhavan, A. *Phys. Lett. A* 2007, 366, 391–396.

[112] Akhavan, A.; Mahmodi, H.; Akhshani, A. *Lect. Notes Comput.* Sci. 2006, 4263, 963–971.

[113] Kwok, H. S.; Tang, W. K. S. Chaos, *Solitons and Fractals* 2007, 32, 1518–1529.

[114] Wong, K.-W.; Kwok, B. S.-H.; Law, W.-S. *Physics Letters A* 2008, 372, 2645–2652.

[115] Behnia, S.; Akhshani, A.; Mahmodi, H. *Int. J. of Bifurcation and Chaos* 2008, 18, 251–261.

INDEX

I

J

L